MAKING A MONSTER

MAKING A MONSTER

JESSE POMEROY, THE BOY MURDERER OF 1870S BOSTON

Dawn Keetley

University of Massachusetts Press

Amherst and Boston

Copyright © 2017 by University of Massachusetts Press
All rights reserved
Printed in the United States of America

ISBN 978-1-62534-273-7 (paper); 272-0 (hardcover)

Designed by Jack Harrison
Set in Adobe Garamond Prod with Wausau display
Printed and bound by The Maple-Vail Book Manufacturing Group

Cover design by Jack Harrison
Cover art based upon a contemporary newspaper illustration
of Jessie Pomeroy at age fourteen.

Library of Congress Cataloging-in-Publication Data
A catalog record for this book is available from the Library of Congress.

British Library Cataloguing-in-Publication Data
A catalog record for this book is available from the British Library.

To Kurt, without whom . . .

Contents

Preface

I have long been fascinated by inexplicable violence and by the larger questions of determinism and free will in which it is inevitably embroiled. When I cast around for the beginnings of this fascination, I always come back to the novel that did more than any other, when I was child, to change my view of the world. When I was twelve or thirteen, I read William Golding's *Lord of the Flies* and was utterly gripped by the story of a group of children—my peers, essentially—who abandoned everything they knew (or should have known), everything that was good, and ruthlessly attacked and killed the weakest among them. Why? It's a question I continually return to in my research and teaching—and while it has many answers, they are all partial, and none of them is ever entirely satisfactory.

Jesse Pomeroy was about the same age as the boys in *Lord of the Flies* when he started preying on smaller, weaker children. And he confronts us with all the same questions about the roots of violence. He tortured young boys remorselessly when he was twelve and then savagely murdered two children when he was fourteen. He was the first killer to galvanize not only the local Boston papers but the national press. He was America's first serial torturer, and, if he hadn't been caught, he would no doubt have become America's first serial killer. He was the youngest person in the Commonwealth of Massachusetts to face the death penalty. And, in the end, he spent more time in solitary confinement than anyone else ever has: he went into jail when he was fourteen, in 1874, and he died in jail in 1932. For almost all of that time, he was alone. Amidst all these sensational details, however, it is Jesse Pomeroy's enigmatic words, repeated in countless newspaper accounts, that have haunted me and that prompted me to write this book. When asked why he tortured and killed children who were utter strangers to him, and against whom he had no animus, Pomeroy could only say that he didn't know, that something made him. How could Jesse Pomeroy have done the things he did without even knowing why?

It is this question that I set out to explore in *Making a Monster,* and, in doing so, I began by taking seriously the superficially improbable explanations that so convinced Pomeroy's nineteenth-century contemporaries. Along the way, I found some surprising connections between those explanations and twenty-first-century ways of understanding crime, and I discovered that perhaps Pomeroy wasn't so inexplicable after all. In the end, his case, which has had a striking propensity to generate wild and unfounded speculation, has much to teach us about being wary of the things we think we know. Those assumptions can lead us down some perilous paths. The case also teaches us to avoid casting others as absolute monsters, casting them outside the human community. When you scratch the surface, the bonds between "us" and "them" are strong. We are all driven much more than we think by our mute bodies, I argue, by an immanent human nature shaped by millennia of evolution. There's certainly no denying that Jesse Pomeroy was exceptional, but he was not beyond the pale, as claims of his monstrousness insisted. Rather, he was near the end of a continuum of living beings that contains us all, including those nonhuman animals upon which we like to found our human distinctiveness.

I must first acknowledge one person who, in the wilderness of rumor and fabrication that surrounds Jesse Pomeroy, *has* told the truth about him and who was kind enough, near the beginning of this project, to share his unpublished paper with me: Alexander W. Pisciotta, professor emeritus of criminal justice at Kutztown University. His paper "Jesse Pomeroy: Historical Reflections on Serial Murder and the Social Construction of Punishment and Criminal Justice" is a model of responsible scholarship. I have also benefited from the equally responsible and always illuminating scholarship and conversation of Daniel A. Cohen, whose groundbreaking book, *Pillars of Salt, Monuments of Grace: New England Crime Literature and the Origins of American Popular Culture, 1674–1860* (1993), was a touchstone and an inspiration for me as I began to work on the literature of nineteenth-century American crime. Dan has generously served on conference panels when I've asked him, shared his work with me, and offered stunningly helpful comments on my work over the years, including on this project.

I thank the staff of the Massachusetts Archives in Boston, especially the incredibly helpful Autumn Haag and Caitlin Jones. Numerous archival documents about the Pomeroy family and Jesse Pomeroy's life are cited here courtesy of the Massachusetts Archives. Part of chapter 4 was previously published as "The Injuries of Reading: Jesse Pomeroy and the Dire Effects of Dime Novels," in the *Journal of American Studies* 47.3 (August 2013): 673–97. I thank the editors of the *Journal of American Studies* and Cambridge University Press for allowing me to reprint material from this article.

This book would have been vastly more difficult to write were it not for the financial support I received in the form of research leaves and travel grants from Lehigh University. I have benefited, moreover, from the unflagging support of many generous colleagues and mentors in the English Department at Lehigh, including Barbara Traister, Barry Kroll, and, especially, Scott Gordon and Seth Moglen. Seth in particular (and even his mother on one notable occasion) has heard way more than I'm sure he ever wanted to about Jesse Pomeroy.

I owe a huge debt of gratitude to Clark Dougan, former senior editor (now retired) at the University of Massachusetts Press. Clark saw something promising in this project when it was in a very nascent form and he offered his unflagging support for years. Thanks also go to Brian Halley, who took over the project, and who has made it much better with his insightful suggestions for revision. And Mary Bellino did an exceptional job editing the manuscript, identifying all my annoying stylistic propensities.

I would never have conceived of writing a book if it weren't for my parents, Reginald and Carol Keetley, who sustained and supported me through so many more years of school than they ever got and who always made me feel like it was worth it. I couldn't have gotten to this place without them, and every year that passes only makes that clearer to me.

And finally, speaking of people who have heard far too much about Jesse Pomeroy, I owe everything to Kurt Douglass, who allowed a certain nineteenth-century murderer to become a household name and who never once complained about the thousands of hours I've spent trying to telling his story. Kurt did vastly more than anyone else to make me believe I could finish this project and that it was worth finishing—despite (or because of?) his propensity to ask difficult questions, forcing me, always, to rethink what I think I know. I couldn't have done this without him.

Chronology

September 12, 1857   Thomas J. Pomeroy and Ruth Ann Snowman marry

November 6, 1858   Charles J. Pomeroy born

November 29, 1859   Jesse Harding Pomeroy born

December 1871   Robert Maies assaulted in Chelsea

February 1872   Tracy Hayden assaulted in Chelsea

July 22, 1872   John Balch assaulted in Chelsea

August 1872   Ruth, Charles, and Jesse Pomeroy move to South Boston

August 17, 1872   George Pratt assaulted in South Boston

September 5, 1872   Harry Austin assaulted in South Boston

September 11, 1872   Joseph Kennedy assaulted in South Boston

September 17, 1872   Charles A. Gould assaulted in South Boston

September 19, 1872   Pomeroy arrested for torturing several boys

September 20, 1872   Pomeroy examined by Judge William J. Forsaith

September 21, 1872   Pomeroy committed to the State Reform School at Westborough for the remainder of his minority

February 6, 1874   Pomeroy released (early) from the State Reform School

March 18, 1874   Ten-year-old Katie Curran disappears after setting off to buy supplies from the Pomeroy store

April 22, 1874   Horace Millen's mutilated body discovered on the Dorchester Bay marsh; Jesse Pomeroy arrested

April 24, 1874   Coroner's inquest into the death of Horace Millen convenes

April 28, 1874	Millen inquest closes; Pomeroy declared the probable murderer
May 1, 1874	Pomeroy arraigned for the murder of Millen
July 18, 1874	Katie Curran's body found in the cellar of the Pomeroys' former store at 327 Broadway
July 20, 1874	Coroner's inquest into the death of Curran begins
July 29, 1874	Coroner's jury delivers their verdict: Curran came to her death by the hands of Jesse Pomeroy
November 3, 1874	Democrat William Gaston is elected governor of Massachusetts
December 8, 1874	Pomeroy's trial for the murder of Horace Millen begins at the state's Supreme Judicial Court in Boston
December 10, 1874	The jury pronounces Pomeroy guilty of first-degree murder
January 7, 1875	Governor William Gaston takes office
February 1, 1875	Pomeroy's lawyers argue the two exceptions to his trial before the Supreme Judicial Court
February 12, 1875	The court overrules the exceptions argued by Pomeroy's lawyers
February 20, 1875	Pomeroy is sentenced to death by Chief Justice Horace Gray
April 13, 1875	Hearing about the commutation of Pomeroy's sentence held before the governor and his council in the State House
July 2, 1875	The governor's executive council votes to uphold Pomeroy's death sentence
July 18 and 25, 1875	The *Boston Sunday Times* prints Pomeroy's "Autobiography" in two installments
July 20, 1875	Pomeroy caught planning an escape from the Charles Street Jail
August 21, 1875	Pomeroy caught making tools to effect his escape
November 2, 1875	Republican Alexander H. Rice wins the gubernatorial election, defeating incumbent William Gaston
November 9, 1875	Pomeroy caught making tools to dig bricks from his cell wall at the Charles Street Jail

January 6, 1876	Republican Governor Alexander H. Rice takes office
May 23, 1876	The Supreme Judicial Court of Massachusetts tells the governor's executive council that the recommendation of mercy offered by the jurors in Pomeroy's murder trial is not a matter of law and thus not in its purview
May 26, 1876	Execution of Thomas Piper in the Charles Street Jail
July 18, 1876	The executive council holds a hearing about the Pomeroy case
August 1, 1876	The executive council holds a second hearing about the case
August 31, 1876	Pomeroy's sentence commuted to life imprisonment in solitary confinement by the governor and a majority of his council
September 7, 1876	Pomeroy transferred from the Charles Street Jail in Boston to the Massachusetts State Prison in Charlestown
November 2, 1876	Governor Rice elected to a second term
January 10, 1915	Ruth Pomeroy dies of pneumonia
January 25, 1917	Pomeroy's sentence commuted from solitary confinement for life to imprisonment at hard labor for life
January 5, 1928	Pomeroy's libel suit against Alice Stone Blackwell heard in the Superior Court in Boston
August 1, 1929	Pomeroy transferred to the State Farm at Bridgewater
September 29, 1932	Jesse Pomeroy dies

MAKING A MONSTER

INTRODUCTION

Becoming Monstrous

In Chelsea and South Boston in late 1871 and early 1872, twelve-year-old Jesse Harding Pomeroy tortured seven small boys: he stripped them, whipped them, beat them with boards, stuck them with pins, and finally progressed to slashing with knives. He was finally caught and spent sixteen months in reform school, but within weeks of his early release (for good behavior), he brutally murdered a ten-year-old girl and a four-year-old boy. After a highly public trial, in which his lawyers argued unsuccessfully that Pomeroy was insane, he became the youngest person in Massachusetts to be sentenced to death. In the wake of over a year of heated debate, he was finally sent to the Charlestown State Prison to serve a life sentence in solitary confinement.

Perhaps the most striking aspect of accounts of Pomeroy, and the main impetus for this book, was his refusal (perhaps inability) ever to answer the question of *why* he did what he did, a refusal that persisted to his death (still in jail) in 1932. All he ever said was "I don't know," "I couldn't help it," and "Something made me do it." Sometimes he declared, "I didn't do it," and, later in his life, he would claim, "I remember nothing from that time." Where there should have been an account of almost unthinkable brutality, there was only absence, a perplexing blankness. An editorial in the Boston *Index* from 1875 pointed out that it was precisely his "unparalleled disposition to cruelty," which was "apparently without cause," that made Pomeroy's case "one of the most remarkable ever known in the history of crime," entirely sufficient to warrant the "extraordinary interest which so generally has been manifested in it from the beginning." Pomeroy was an enigma demanding solution, a mystery begging for illumination, but his

1

inscrutability rebuffed all efforts at understanding. A letter to the editor of the *Boston Daily Advertiser* put it most aptly: Pomeroy is "a mystery to himself, as he is to others; he stands in darkness; he can neither see nor be seen."[1] Undaunted, Pomeroy's contemporaries nonetheless flung themselves into the void, offering proliferating, contradictory, and sometimes wildly improbable explanations for the boy's unprecedented violence—almost all of which turned him into a "monster."

"Monster," indeed, vied with "fiend" as one of the most common epithets attached to Pomeroy's name in the 1870s press: articles abounded with headlines and phrases like "A Youthful Monster," "A Young Monster," "Boy Monster," "moral monstrosity," and "moral monster."[2] Monsters are, at the most basic level, something unnatural, which is precisely how most of his contemporaries viewed the boy.[3] The well-known writer Gail Hamilton (the pen name of Mary Abigail Dodge) declared in an 1874 editorial in the New York–based magazine *The Independent* that the "young monster" Pomeroy should be executed not least because he was a perversion of nature: "Nature has put out a bad piece of work, and we send it back on her hands." Pomeroy and children like him, imbued in cruelty, are "defective, distorted, monstrous, fatal," she wrote. Monsters are not only unnatural but nonhuman: in a sermon he delivered about Jesse Pomeroy in 1875, the Reverend Dr. Cyrus Augustus Bartol of Boston called him "a destructive machine against others," urging that "it" should thus "cease to act, and if incorrigible, to exist." "It," Bartol continues (and the pronoun he uses is telling), "is a monster to be killed on the spot, if only so it can be kept from killing or defiling."[4]

As much as nineteenth-century Americans described Pomeroy as a monster, though, casting him beyond the pale of the human, the act of making monsters is always at the same time about the act of making humans. As Marina Levina and Diem-My T. Bui point out, "What is at stake in the representational analysis of monster images is the definition of humanness." In this book I will return to the interconnection, to the continual reciprocal making, of monster and human. Indeed, the monster *is* the human and *not* its defining antithesis: we just cannot (yet) see its humanness—or we refuse to see it. Jacques Derrida has said of the monster that it is "that which appears for the first time and, consequently, is not yet recognized."[5] The monster is indeed what is "not yet recognized." It horrifies because it defies what is already known; the "monster" is thus all those vast swaths of the human which we fail *as yet* to see. The monster is the anomaly that is not yet understood, the aberration that is not yet explained.

Pomeroy as Animal

Perhaps the definitive characteristic of "monsters" is their impurity. As the philosopher Noël Carroll has argued, monsters manifest a "categorical contradictoriness," encompassing in one body "disjoint or conflicting categories." Jeffrey Jerome Cohen has similarly described the "ontological liminality" of the monster, its refusal of "easy categorization." The monster is, Cohen writes, the "harbinger of category crisis."[6] Nineteenth-century Americans' sense of Jesse Pomeroy's monstrous impurity was expressed particularly in routine descriptions of his threatening mixture of human and animal. He is "a cruel and murderous animal in human form," declared the *Boston Daily Advertiser,* a "wildcat in human form," insisted the Worcester *Aegis and Gazette.* Another article in the *Aegis* editorialized that Pomeroy's cruelty rendered him "a tiger, and nothing better." In the end, the boy was more an "animal than a human being."[7] In his hybrid animality, Pomeroy existed beyond what his contemporaries marked off as properly human, which was only intensified by the thoroughgoing inexplicability of his actions. In his transgression of what should have been the fixed boundaries of the "human," and in his inhabiting of the shadowland beyond scientific and medical knowledge, Pomeroy indeed ushered in what Cohen calls a "category crisis."

More particularly, Pomeroy put the very category of the "human" in crisis, for across all theories about the cause of his acts of torture and murder, Pomeroy was repeatedly described as ontologically interwoven with animals. As the *Boston Daily Globe* reported in a widely reprinted description, he has "the face of an animal, intelligent to a certain extent, but still stamped with brutality and sensuality."[8] Although humans are, of course, animals, the properly "civilized" human has long disavowed its animal origins. As Pramod K. Nayar writes, "the human defines itself as such by denying the illegitimate animal within itself, by seeking an expulsion of the animal inside, as the presence of the animal makes the human monstrous."[9] It is no doubt precisely because of the terrifying actual proximity of human and animal that the animal-in-the-human has been cast as monstrous: we sense the closeness of the "animal," our heart of darkness, and so try to purge it. Certainly Pomeroy, to his contemporaries, exhibited an inhuman, polluting animality that served as both sign and cause of his monstrosity. Pomeroy's case occurred, moreover, at a time when "animal" was creeping dangerously close to the "human": in 1871, Charles Darwin had published *The Descent of Man,* a groundbreaking book dedicated to tracing the lineage and traits that humans shared with nonhuman animals.

The oft-asserted "animality" of Jesse Pomeroy crucially indicates the significance of his case: it shows how close the "monstrous," specifically an impure intertwined human and animal, actually is to the human. As Brian Massumi writes, "The human body is an animal body, and animality is immanent to human life." We are on a continuum with (not distinctly different from) other nonhuman animals; we are inevitably hybrids of a narrowly construed "human" *and* of the (animal) that has been suppressed in that "human." Indeed, Pomeroy's animality can more broadly be thought of as a kind of "nonhuman" that resides recalcitrantly at the heart of the human. Cary Wolfe claims that "*we*—whoever 'we' are—are in a profound sense constituted as human subjects within and atop a nonhuman otherness that postmodern theory has worked hard to release from the bad-faith repressions and disavowals of humanism." It was the paradigm shifts effected by Darwin and Freud, harbingers of posthumanism, Rosi Braidotti points out, which "opened up a profound nonhumanness at the heart of the subject."[10] This "nonhuman otherness" or "profound nonhumanness" is precisely what Pomeroy's contemporaries were inchoately grasping when they called him "monster" or analogized him to animals, all in their efforts to explain his inexplicable violence.

I will argue throughout, then, that our worst "monsters" have always been those that materialize parts of the human long described as before, below, or profoundly other, but that are nevertheless actually human. Describing humans' "primitive" instincts for violence, for instance, William James famously wrote, "Our ferocity is blind, and can only be explained from *below*," a claim that articulates the "nonhuman" life that, in its "blindness," underlies and precedes personal and conscious subjectivity.[11] We are either entirely ignorant of these parts of the human or we deny them, a denial upon which the entire edifice of the "human" as rational individual (which we all like to believe we are) is predicated. Each explanation of Pomeroy in some way disclosed that, as much as we disclaim the humanity of some of us, as much as we make "monsters" of those who enact the unthinkable and who contain the unrecognizable "animal" or the "nonhuman" traits of those we deem "monsters," they are in the end central to the human, not separate from it. The ultimate cause of what Jesse Pomeroy was and did (as with all of those of whom we "make monsters") is finally part of human nature itself, a human nature that will always contain anomalous eruptions of what look like "monstrosity" in that they exceed the limits of rational explanation and surpass our ability to explain them. Pomeroy's reiterated words—"I don't know," "I couldn't help it," and "Something made me do it"—are profoundly resonant. As little as they seem to explain, they explain everything. The "something" that made Pomeroy do what he did was indwelling, and neither he nor anyone else knew exactly what it was.

Pomeroy's Animals

Among the many widely circulated but false stories about Jesse Pomeroy that helped shape him as "monster," one was especially bound up with animals and animality. It was a story about Pomeroy's torture of a helpless kitten in his jail cell after he was sentenced to a lifetime of solitary confinement, and it gained so much traction not least because it made Pomeroy's cruelty dramatically manifest, even to the extent of suggesting that cruelty was cause as well as symptom: he was simply a natural-born sadist. But while the kitten in this story was on the one hand a helpless victim of an unequivocal and congenital sadist, it is an unstable signifier, and, perhaps at a more unconscious level, it also served as a mirror of Pomeroy's sadism. After all, in his widely publicized 1875 sermon about "monsters," the Reverend Bartol had not only called Pomeroy a "destructive machine" but had also likened him to a cat. "A cat playing with a mouse she intends to kill," he declared, "and Jesse Pomeroy sticking pins and knives into his fellows seems of the same temper."[12] The cat in this story, then, was both *victim* and *double* of its cellmate's cruel, purposeless violence, suggesting the multiple ways in which animals become intertwined in shaping stories about (monstrous) human nature.

At his trial, witnesses had testified to Pomeroy's having both stabbed a kitten when he was three years old and mutilated a snake in "great delight" while he was at the Westborough reform school.[13] Both of these stories seem more credible than the story that really took hold of the public imagination, though—a story that circulated for at least fifty years in newspapers across the country. This story was, like the stories about the kitten and the snake, driven by the entrenched belief that animal cruelty (especially at a young age) indicates an innately sadistic personality. While cruelty to animals supposedly comes first, however, predicting later violent criminal behavior, Pomeroy's case also demonstrates how a prior conviction that a person is a "monster" can generate and sustain enduring stories of animal cruelty that are completely unfounded. "Facts," in other words, are fabricated to support a preexisting belief, a dynamic that has been profoundly and persistently operative in narratives about Jesse Pomeroy.

In late 1878, after Pomeroy had been in the Massachusetts State Prison in Charlestown for about two years, the warden apparently gave him a kitten, perhaps moved by sympathy for the boy who was condemned for the length of his life to live alone in his prison cell. Upon receiving the kitten, the story went, Pomeroy "flayed it alive with a knife and fork provided for his meals."[14] This tale was repeated in newspapers across the country in October 1878, and some retellings emphasized Pomeroy's proximity to animals in this brutal "flaying" by prefacing the story with a note that the boy "paces his cell like a caged lion."[15] As Bartol did, the writer here compares Pomeroy to a cat, evoking that animal's associations with violence and even torture, while trying also to keep those meanings distinct from the helpless kitten-as-victim.

As this story of Pomeroy's perverse persecution of his pet kitten resurfaced over the years (and it mostly appeared, tellingly, in papers far from Boston—in Cleveland, New Orleans, Salt Lake City), it became ever more elaborate. The *Milwaukee Sentinel* reported in 1880 that, after the warden made the mistake of allowing Pomeroy to have a cat, it was discovered that the "young devil to whose tender companionship it had been intrusted [*sic*] had made a rude knife out of a spoon that he had, and with this weapon had partially flayed the cat alive." The cat was reduced, apparently, to a "pitiable state."[16] The story had clearly taken such hold in the later part of the century that Charles D. Sawin, in an 1890 pamphlet about his five-year experience as a physician at the Massachusetts State Prison, felt compelled to assert that the "various stories circulated about [Pomeroy's] 'torturing a cat,' [and] 'cutting up mice and rats,' are absolutely without foundation."[17] The story nonetheless resurfaced again in 1894, ostensibly based on a report in the *Boston Globe*. Hoping to offer Pomeroy a "companion that would help to shorten and brighten the long hours," the warden of the state prison gave him a kitten, a Michigan paper reported, but, just one short week later, "the guard found that Pomeroy had skinned the little animal alive."[18] Books published in both 1906 and 1915 repeated the story, and even as late as 1935, after Pomeroy's death, some variant of the story lingered: an article in a medical journal pointed out the persistent accusations that Pomeroy had continued "catching rats and skinning them alive" while in jail, adding, however, that such charges "were never substantiated by the prison officials."[19]

Appearing time and again over the decades, the apocryphal stories about Jesse Pomeroy's kitten-flaying proclivities came to a boiling point in the years 1925–1928, after Pomeroy had reached his fiftieth year behind bars. As calls for the governor to pardon him were renewed, so were stories about his irremediable bloodthirstiness. And in March 1925, the well-known Boston feminist and activist Alice Stone Blackwell (daughter of Henry Browne Blackwell and Lucy Stone) entered the fray. She wrote a letter to the *Boston Herald* arguing that Pomeroy should never be released, that he was still and would always be a danger to society. In making her case, Blackwell relied heavily on the story of the flayed kitten: "It is reported," she wrote, "that after he had been for some years in prison he was allowed the companionship of a kitten in his cell. He skinned the kitten alive." Demonstrating the perennial tendency of stories about Pomeroy to become untethered from the truth, Blackwell's letter also charged that he had "deliberately tortured several children to death."[20]

Blackwell had clearly long been fascinated with Jesse Pomeroy. A series of typed cards about the case is preserved in her papers, and they include another story about kittens, describing how Pomeroy supposedly lured the young Katie Curran down to the basement "to see some kittens" (yet another apocryphal animal story for which there is no evidence).[21] Alice's interest, particularly in the victimized kitten, was also shared by her family. An undated letter written by Alice instructs an unknown recipient to "tell Aunt B. [most likely Elizabeth Blackwell] that the Chaplain of the Charlestown State Prison has never answered my letter of inquiry about Jesse Pomeroy." She adds, "Aunt Emily [Blackwell] tells me that within a year or two he skinned alive a little kitten which he had unwisely been allowed to have with him in his cell as a pet; so he has evidently undergone no change of heart." As Blackwell emphatically declared to the readers of the *Herald,* "it is better that a man of these dangerous tendencies should remain in confinement."[22]

After he read Blackwell's letter in the *Herald,* Pomeroy immediately retained a lawyer, incensed at her rehearsal of the false story and fearing it would harm his chances of winning a pardon from the state's governor, a process he had already initiated when Blackwell's letter appeared. From prison, Pomeroy filed a $5,000 libel suit against Blackwell, and it seemed as if they were destined to meet until Pomeroy was denied permission to leave the state prison to attend the trial.[23] Pomeroy's lawyer, Ira Dudley Farquhar, of Beacon Street, went on the offensive, penning his own letter to the *Herald* accusing Blackwell of "many misstatements" and of contributing to the "vicious and unfounded propaganda about Pomeroy." At the center of this "propaganda" was "that ancient wheeze that Pomeroy while in prison skinned a kitten alive." Farquhar emphatically added that this accusation had "no foundation in fact or record." He went on to make the stakes of repeating this rumor clear by inviting Blackwell to appear before the governor (presumably to admit the groundlessness of her claim) when he considered Pomeroy's petition for a pardon.[24] And, indeed, Pomeroy and Farquhar may have been correct in anticipating the damaging effects of the rumors about kitten-flaying that Blackwell helped propagate: in early May 1925 (the same month Pomeroy brought the libel suit), the *Herald* reported that Governor Alvan Fuller had refused to consider Pomeroy's pardon.[25]

Pomeroy was persistent in his libel suit, however, making it clear that, pardon or not, he wanted to refute the story that he had ever tormented kittens in his cell. His suit against Blackwell held that as a consequence of her letter, "he has been held up to disgrace, odium, infamy and public contempt." The case came to trial in the afternoon of January 5, 1928, before Judge Harold Williams of the Superior Court in Boston—and Alice Stone Blackwell (no doubt reluctantly) came to testify. John F. Daly joined Ira Farquhar in representing Pomeroy, and he "asserted with emphasis that Pomeroy never skinned a kitten, but on the contrary animals were his companions in his solitary cell at state prison for many years." Blackwell was called as the first witness, and she testified to reading about Pomeroy in the newspapers during and after his trial and to listening to "general discussion" about him. When asked about the substance of her letter, she confessed that she "didn't remember having read anything about Pomeroy skinning a cat and she said she was unable to recall when she heard the story." She also admitted that she did not contact prison authorities to "ascertain the truth or falsity of the story." When her own lawyer asked her why she wrote the letter, she said she did so out of a sense of "public duty," believing wholeheartedly in accounts of Pomeroy's reputation as "bad—for cruelty."[26]

In the end, Blackwell's claim was revealed as what it was, no more than rumor: the warden of the state prison testified on Pomeroy's behalf, admitting in rather tepid fashion that Pomeroy's "reputation as to cruelty was 'as good as any other prisoner.' "[27] When the judge gave his charge to the jury, he explicitly instructed them that "there was no evidence to show that the statement of Miss Blackwell was true or made as fair comment in the public interest," and so, not surprisingly, Pomeroy won his suit. It was, however, something of a pyrrhic victory, since the jury awarded him a mere $1 in damages, perhaps thinking he had little reputation to harm. Pomeroy was apparently happy with the verdict, however, telling his lawyer that it "spikes a lie that has been in circulation for years."[28] In an interesting twist to Pomeroy's complicated relationship with animals, Buster the prison cat featured prominently in the foiling of one of his many attempts at escape. Having managed to saw through the bars of his cell late in December 1912, Pomeroy was apprehended by a guard whose suspicions were aroused by Buster fleeing along the prison corridor.[29]

The perennial importance attributed to stories of Jesse Pomeroy's cruelty to animals makes it clear that by the 1870s, animal torture served to mark an intractable human depravity. Indeed, the a priori conviction that the torture of animals symptomized sadism was undoubtedly behind the fact that the story of Pomeroy's flaying of kittens continued to spread even as it became increasingly unloosed from reality. It was also, no doubt, behind other stories of Pomeroy's cruelty to animals, all of which seem equally baseless. As early as April 1875, for instance, at the first public hearing on whether to commute Pomeroy's sentence, extraneous, lurid details were added to the single witness claim that the boy tortured a kitten when he was three years old. The *Boston Daily Advertiser* reported Pomeroy's lawyer as saying that not only had Pomeroy mutilated a kitten when he was small, but "on another occasion was known to become highly excited while torturing a rat." In a discussion of Pomeroy's insanity published in *The Lancet* in 1878, a British physician, John Charles Bucknill (who actually visited Pomeroy in jail in 1875 and should have known better), astonishingly claimed that the boy had originally been sent to the juvenile reformatory "for torturing animals." In a newspaper tidbit from 1912, Professor William Barnes, principal of the Bigelow School in South Boston, which Pomeroy briefly attended before his arrest, professed to recall "having remonstrated with Pomeroy for sticking pins in a cat; and other instances that pointed to a cruel nature." And in a 1926 story about Pomeroy's exploits, another newspaper included as a crucial part of his biography that, before he was in his teens, he "was cruel to pet dogs and cats and would laugh hysterically when they were tortured or in pain."[30]

Such stories accrued power not least because they confirmed what everyone already believed about the link between harming animals and subsequent violent behavior, a link that has widespread support even now. As Robert Hare puts it in his comprehensive profile of the psychopathic personality, "Early cruelty to animals is usually a sign of serious emotional or behavioral problems."[31] It is not surprising, then, that as late as 1987 a historian who devotes just one short paragraph to Jesse Pomeroy nonetheless gives prominent place to the assertion that the boy "had a proclivity for dismembering small animals."[32] From the 1870s to the present, it seems that stories involving Jesse Pomeroy's torture of animals are destined to garner instant credibility: they affirm what we (think we) already know.

It is worth taking a step back, though, to acknowledge that there is some reason to question the link between early animal torture and the criminal psychopath. Indeed, at Pomeroy's murder trial, the prosecutor claimed that torturing animals was in fact a fairly common boyhood pastime. (He was obviously trying to deflect the defense's claim that Pomeroy was so cruel as to be "morally insane" and thus not responsible for what he did.) He declared that Pomeroy's alleged stabbing of the kitten when he was young was "in no respect different from acts committed by all boys."[33] From the very beginning, then, we see a tension between those (Pomeroy's lawyers) who thought Pomeroy's cruelty to animals was indicative of homicidal insanity and those who thought it was fairly mundane boyish behavior. We see a tension, in other words, between those who thought Jesse's torture of a kitten was utterly aberrant and those who thought it was quite banally ordinary. What is "monstrous," in short, may actually be merely human.

The prosecutor's rather casual remark at Pomeroy's murder trial that torturing animals was common boyish behavior has actually received support in recent years. Describing a 2009 survey of all available studies on the link between violent crime and animal cruelty, the noted psychologist and anthrozoologist Hal Herzog concludes that "childhood animal abuse is surprisingly common in the general population."[34] Indeed, the survey he described found that while 36 percent of violent male offenders had abused an animal, so had 37 percent of "'normal' or nonviolent males." The authors of the survey conclude by calling for "methods of discussing" the *multiple* causes of violence, including but certainly not limited to prior animal cruelty, in ways that "depend less heavily on dichotomizing the virtuous from the violent."[35] When we recognize what Herzog calls in his title the "sadism of everyday life," and when we refuse binaries of good and evil, Pomeroy becomes less "monstrous" and more human. There is no doubt that Pomeroy displayed a horrifying propensity for violence and a virtually complete lack of empathy, precisely what prompted the Reverend Bartol to liken him to the supposedly sadistic "cat playing with a mouse she intends to kill." In the end, though, Pomeroy was less like a cat or a nonhuman "monster" whose sadism was *opposed* to the "human" than he was a human whose capacity for sadism was *on a continuum with* that of the variegated world of nonhuman animals.

Despite persistent claims, then, that Pomeroy was nonhuman, an animal, and a monster, he was actually nothing more or less than a human, though few wanted to admit their shared humanity. Noël Carroll has argued that even though humans "belong to our everyday world," they can still be turned easily into monsters. Their "presentation in the fictions they inhabit turn [*sic*] them effectively into fantastical beings," he claims, and these fictions are what endow mere humans with "powers and attributes above and beyond what one would be willing to believe of living creatures."[36] In order to become the "monster" that his contemporaries wanted and needed him to be, Pomeroy was turned into a "fantastical being," an impure monstrous hybrid, something other than human. And he was made into such a creature through the "fictions" he was made to "inhabit," all of which, however, disavowed their own fictionality and pretended they were "fact." In short, Jesse Pomeroy was, from the beginning, made into a "fantastical being," his humanity foreclosed in an effort to preserve the "human" as something else, something other than the "monstrous."

The first two chapters of *Making a Monster* describe Jesse Pomeroy's crimes, his trial, and the frenzied debate over sentencing that elicited opinions from seemingly everyone in Boston (and, by some accounts, destroyed the careers of two governors). I then turn, in chapters 3 and 4, to the two principal theories by which nineteenth-century Americans tried to understand the "moral monster" in their midst: that he was stamped in utero with an instinct for blood because his pregnant mother took intense delight in visiting the slaughterhouse; and that he imitated the savage cruelty of the Indians and white renegades who populated the pages of frontier dime novels, novels that Pomeroy read voraciously from the time he was nine years old. While these theories are, in one case, flatly untrue (Ruth

Pomeroy did not visit a slaughterhouse when she was pregnant) and, in both cases, far-fetched (from the perspective of the twentieth-first century, at least), they illustrate how Jesse Pomeroy was made into a "monster": both theories presumed that the boy's body determined his actions and that he was dangerously proximate to the animal. Along the way, though, advocates of each theory disclose how *human* subjectivity, not just that of "monsters" like Pomeroy, inevitably contains residues of "impersonal" forces that are before, around, within, and after the "person" as narrowly conceived. These theories thus proffer general truths about human nature even in the midst of their more improbable assertions.

Chapters 5 and 6 offer my explanation of Jesse Pomeroy: that he was what we now call a psychopath and that something happened to him in early infancy that made him such. In chapter 5 I argue that what nineteenth-century doctors called Pomeroy's "moral insanity" anticipated twentieth-century psychopathy, a condition defined by a catastrophic "lack" of all those traits we consider properly "human," among them empathy, conscience, guilt, fear, and remorse. From the nineteenth century to the present, the morally insane individual and the psychopath have posed an acute problem for theories of responsibility and punishment: how can someone who lacks those traits that make us human be judged *as* a (responsible) human? The philosopher Jeffrie Murphy has argued that because the psychopath cannot help what he does, cannot help what he is, he may well be considered an "animal rather than a person."[37] Indeed, Pomeroy's psychopathic "lack" pushed him into shadowy terrain beyond the boundaries of the human, thus rendering him theoretically not responsible for his crimes, and yet at the same time it led many of his contemporaries to deem him culpable and to demand his immediate execution. But Murphy's claim about the psychopath's status as "animal," as well as descriptions of the psychopath and Pomeroy himself as some sort of brute natural force, just bring us back to the fact that, as "animal," the psychopath is merely a limit case of the human, not intractably other.

While chapter 5 presents a "diagnosis" of Pomeroy, in chapter 6 I propose a possible cause of Pomeroy's psychopathy, uncovering an explanation that was not widely circulated in the nineteenth century but that was the only theory offered by Jesse's mother, although it got lost in the tide of enthusiasm for the theory she explicitly refuted (that Pomeroy was a victim of her own visits to the slaughterhouse when she was pregnant). Pomeroy may well have incurred permanent damage, I suggest, as the result of a debilitating reaction to a smallpox vaccination. His suffering—by all accounts severe—over a five-month period when he was an infant potentially created the extreme emotional deficits that made him into a monster in the eyes of many. In fact, though, those deficits only marked him as one of those tragic anomalies to which a plastic human nature is always capable of turning.

In the epilogue, I take up what I think is an erroneous theory of Pomeroy's violence, one that was not offered by any of his contemporaries; it is a theory, though, that has held an almost unshakeable grip on thinking about the origins of crime since about the middle of the twentieth century—hence its application to Pomeroy. Every twenty-first-century account has claimed that Jesse Pomeroy was abused by his father when he was a child and that he then repeated his abuse on the bodies of his victims. The story that Pomeroy was abused as a child, which has no evidentiary grounding, has nonetheless formed the central assertion of both of the books written about Pomeroy since 2000: Harold Schechter's *Fiend: The Shocking True Story of America's Youngest Serial Killer* (2000) and Roseanne Montillo's *The Wilderness of Ruin: A Tale of Madness, Fire, and the Hunt for America's Youngest Serial Killer* (2015).[38] These books, which distort and fabricate evidence, epitomize what has defined the case of Jesse Pomeroy from the beginning: they demonstrate the power that culturally dominant stories have over the facts, how the "truths" of which we are *already* convinced can blind us to other more unexpected truths. In this book, I hope to look past the familiar and the fabricated to offer not only the truth (or as close as we can get to it) about Jesse Pomeroy, but also those more unexpected truths about human nature and the origins of unthinkable violence.

1

Crimes

Who was Jesse Harding Pomeroy in those fourteen short years before he entered the prison system in which he would die? He himself describes wandering down to the Navy Yard in Charlestown where his father worked, an idyllic summer of fishing and playing ball with relatives in Maine, and delivering newspapers in downtown Boston for his brother.[1] Someone who claimed to know him in those days, however, described a sullen, taciturn boy who was always engrossed in dime novels and, while others played games, would ferociously stab the ground with a knife. His mother insisted until her death in 1915 that he was a good boy, incapable of committing the brutal crime of which a jury convicted him. And police reports describe a predator who lured a four-year-old boy to the marshes of Dorchester Bay and stabbed him countless times and who enticed a ten-year-old girl into a cellar in order to slit her throat. For the newspaper reporters who avidly covered his case, he was a "child monster" and a "boy fiend," prototype and exemplar of the many boy fiends who would follow in his footsteps, although none quite as spectacularly bad as the original. The real Jesse Pomeroy, if there is such a thing, slips into and between these versions—ever elusive, just out of reach.

First and foremost, like all notorious criminals, Jesse Pomeroy was defined by the ferocious acts that emblazoned his name on the front page of newspapers across the nation. Whoever he was before his crimes lurks largely in the shadows. He became the crimes he committed, his identity defined by his love of torture, of murder, of blood. His name, in fact, became a veritable catchword for inexplicable youthful cruelty. In the end, everything but his brutality vanishes.

Early Days

Many of Jesse Pomeroy's immediate forebears moved to Charlestown (which would later become part of Boston) from Maine, traveling the path from rural to urban world that characterized the lives of so many Americans in the mid-nineteenth century. Jesse's mother, Ruth, who would stand steadfastly by her vilified son until her death at the age of seventy-two from bronchial pneumonia, was born on February 17, 1842, in the coastal Maine town of Camden in Knox County. Her parents, John Snowman and Susan McFadden Snowman, were born just one county over, in Sagadahoc County.[2] In the summer of 1871, Jesse and his older brother, Charles, took a memorable trip to Maine to stay with their mother's family—a proliferation of aunts and uncles, as Pomeroy recalled four years later in an autobiography written for the *Boston Sunday Times*. Pomeroy described that summer as an all too brief period of happiness that was preceded by a bout of pneumonia that rendered him "crazy for nearly a week" and that would be followed by his early experiments in torture—what he ambiguously called his "troubles."[3]

Like many in his mother's family, Jesse's paternal grandfather, Thomas J. Pomeroy (who went by Jesse), also hailed from Maine, where he was born in the town of Hampden around 1807. He most likely moved to Hingham, Massachusetts, in his early twenties, where he met the significantly younger Ruth T. Penny, a native of Massachusetts born either in nearby Scituate or Hingham in 1817. A *Boston Daily Globe* article would later report that Jesse's grandfather was working in Hingham and renting a room in the home of Ruth's father, which is likely where he met her. Jesse Sr. and Ruth were married on November 17, 1833, and at some point after their marriage relocated from Hingham to Charlestown.[4] Jesse's father, also Thomas J. Pomeroy, was born in Massachusetts (in either Hingham or Charlestown) in 1834 or 1835.[5] The Charlestown census of 1850 identifies forty-three-year-old Jesse Sr. as a ship carpenter and his wife, Ruth, as thirty-three. Their oldest son, Thomas, was fifteen or sixteen, and his younger brother, Uriah, was eight; a twenty-year-old girl born in Ireland, Mary O'Brien, also lived with them. It appears the family lived by the Navy Yard since their neighbors included two sailors and a sea captain, as well as a laborer, a carpenter, two painters, and a beef packer. It was clearly a working-class community, and the twelve families, who hailed mostly from New England, Ireland, and Sweden, lived in a stretch of eight dwellings.[6]

The Pomeroy family underwent an upheaval two years later, on November 3, 1852, when Thomas's mother, Ruth, died of consumption. She was thirty-five and her son was about seventeen.[7] Shortly afterward, Thomas found himself living in a very different kind of family. The 1855 census reveals that the household was now headed by Thomas's sixty-four-year-old maternal grandmother, Temperance C. Penny, who was caring for her grandsons Thomas, now twenty and working as a laborer, and Uriah, thirteen.[8] Thomas's father must have left his family at some point between 1850 and 1855; whether he left before or after his wife died is unclear—but he does appear to have abandoned his two sons, leaving them with his wife's mother.

If there is any trouble to be found in Jesse Pomeroy's extended family before his own career of torture and murder, it is to be found with his paternal grandfather, a man whose name he shared. According to an account of (the younger) Jesse's antecedents published in the *Boston Globe* as he awaited trial, the union of his paternal grandfather and grandmother had never been a "happy one," and the fault, reportedly, "was with the man." The *Globe* noted that in "some subsequent divorce proceedings it appeared that Pomeroy ill-treated his wife in various harsh ways. The woman afterwards died and he married again in New York, this time a woman who is said to be equal to the emergency and maintains her position as mistress of the situation."[9] While Jesse Sr.'s alleged abuse of his wife and the ensuing divorce proceedings seem a matter of speculation, it is clear that he left his family, including two teenage sons, in order to begin a new life in New York.

Thomas must have met his future wife, Jesse's mother, not too long after his own mother died and his father left: he and Ruth Ann Snowman were married in Charlestown on September 12, 1857. Thomas, a "laborer," was listed on the marriage record as twenty-two and living in Charlestown at the time. Ruth lived in Boston, and her age on the marriage certificate was given as seventeen. If she was indeed born in February 1842, however, as her death record showed, she may have lied about her age and been only fifteen on the day she married Thomas. It seems, though, that neither Ruth nor Thomas was entirely sure about when they were born; the birthdates and ages they offered when asked by officials vacillated within a roughly two-year range. And in census records, the birth dates each of them gives is typically preceded with an "abt.," indicating their inability to name the precise date.[10]

Thomas and Ruth's first child, Charles J. Pomeroy, was born in Charlestown on November 6, 1858. The small family then lived at 4 Tremont Street, and Thomas was now apparently working as a fireman, rather than (or as well as) a laborer.[11] The couple's ill-fated second son, Jesse Harding Pomeroy, was born in Charlestown just over a year later, on November 29, 1859, and Thomas was still listed on the birth record as a fireman.[12] He may, however, have held more than one job, since Ruth would later recall that from four years before Jesse was born until six years after (from about 1855 to 1865 or 1866), her husband worked in the Navy Yard at Charlestown.[13]

There is scant information about the Pomeroy family between Jesse's birth and the publicity that swirled around his torture and murder of small boys twelve years later. In the 1860 census, the year after Jesse was born, life seemed much as it was the year before, except Thomas's occupation was no longer fireman but just "laborer," no doubt indicating the job at the Navy Yard that his wife recalled him holding. The Pomeroy family lived in a dwelling with at least one other family, a machinist/journeyman in his forties, his wife, and their eleven-year-old daughter, as well as a twenty-one-year-old schoolteacher from Maine. Of their neighbors—some twelve families living in five separate dwellings—eleven out of forty came from Ireland and the rest were native born.[14]

Thomas's work at the Navy Yard was interrupted in 1862 by the Civil War, an event Jesse does not mention in his autobiography—not surprising since he would have been only around three years old when his father left to serve in the Union army. Thomas was a private with Company H of the Fifth Massachusetts Volunteer Infantry, and his headstone would be provided by an organization recognizing deceased Civil War veterans who fought for the Union.[15] Thomas served for nine months with Company H, from September 1862 to July 1863, and he almost certainly volunteered, since the draft was not instituted until July 1863, right after Company H returned to Boston. Thomas Pomeroy may not have enlisted for entirely noble reasons, however. As Alfred S. Roe points out in his history of the Fifth Regiment Massachusetts Volunteer Infantry, late 1862 saw "the opening days of bounty giving," since "while many men were willing to go, there were as many, or more, quite content to stay at home." The initial war fervor had worn off, and the $13 per month the government paid was not much incentive to confront hardship, disease, and death. So during the period when Thomas joined up, towns were offering "bounties" to lure volunteers, anything from $100 to $200, surely an enticing amount to a man who worked as a laborer his entire life.[16]

Filled mostly with men from Charlestown, Company H was sworn in on September 16, 1862, and went to training camp at Wenham, Massachusetts. About a month later they set off for Newburn, North Carolina, and most of the company's nine months of service were spent in North Carolina, with at least one foray to Washington, DC. Soon after getting back to Boston, in July 1863, Company H was called on to police a violent draft riot erupting in Boston's North End; one wonders if Thomas Pomeroy answered the call, or if he had had his fill of the army by then.[17]

By 1865, Thomas was again working as a "fireman," according to census records, and the family lived in Charlestown's second ward. The Pomeroys were still living with another family: Samuel Robins, a mason, along with his wife, Abby, and their five children, who ranged in age from five months to nine years.[18] In his autobiography Jesse recalled that when he was six years old (around 1865), he was sent to the public primary school on Bunker Hill Street. He would have attended the red brick school, built in 1805, at the time (between 1866 and 1867) it was being expanded from its original size of 35 by 25 feet to about 60 by 90 feet.[19] Jesse remembered his father working at the Navy Yard during this period, and, according to his son, Thomas Pomeroy would pump water from the dry dock and tend the engine. At the time, Jesse noted, his family lived on Lexington Street, near the Mystic River.[20]

Around 1868 or 1869, when Jesse was ten, he and his brother were "promoted" to the Winthrop Grammar School, which he attended continuously until 1872. He also wrote that his father left the Navy Yard and began working in Boston, driving a horse and wagon for a Mr. Hayden. Jesse reported that the family had moved, in 1868 or 1869, from Lexington Street to 78 Bunker Hill Street, and that in 1870 they moved again, to the house next door, which was "a better house than we had ever lived in before."[21] Indeed, the 1870 census shows that, for what appears to be the first time, the Pomeroys were not sharing a house with another family. Of the families around them, nine lived in eight dwellings, and their occupations seemed more upwardly mobile than the uniformly manual occupations of the Pomeroys' neighbors before 1870; they included a salesman, coffee dealer, school teacher, clerk, grocer, dressmaker, traveling agent, carpenter, and cabinet maker. These neighbors were all from New England, with only one Irish immigrant identified, a domestic servant working in the carpenter's household.[22]

The 1870 census lists Ruth as "keeping house," even though by at least 1871 (much earlier, by Ruth's account) she was supporting herself and her sons by sewing, her success at which may have accounted for the family's slight upward mobility. The 1870 census also confirms that Thomas's job had changed: it was now listed as "porter," which accords with Jesse's memory of his father's driving a wagon and Ruth's claim that her husband became a porter in Quincy Market in Boston—a job he would still be doing when Jesse was arrested for torturing boys in September 1872 (when he was listed as a "meat porter at Quincy Market") and when Jesse murdered Horace Millen in April 1874.[23] Jesse claimed, in fact, that he was looking for his father at the market when he was actually brutally stabbing Millen to death.[24]

Shortly after 1870, and despite the seeming improvement in the family's living conditions, the marriage between Ruth and Thomas clearly became untenable and they separated. It took several years, though, for Ruth to file for a divorce, which she did in 1878, on the grounds of her husband's drunkenness. The divorce papers were served to Thomas on March 11, 1878, and the case was heard in the May 1878 term of the Supreme Judicial Court, well after Jesse had been sentenced to jail for the rest of his life.

The divorce petition, filed in March 1878 by Ruth's attorney, claimed that Thomas "contracted gross and confirmed habits of intoxication" after his marriage to Ruth in 1857, and that he "grossly, wantonly and cruelly neglected to pay suitable maintenance for her, he being of sufficient ability to do so." As a result, Ruth "deserted" her husband on the first day of August 1871, "and such desertion has continued to the present time." Ruth claimed that from the day she left Thomas, "as well as for a long time before," she had "wholly supported herself by her own labor."[25] A notice in the *New York Times* in May 1878 described the divorce petition, noting the details that Ruth lived with Thomas until August 1871, and that in the last year she lived with him, he "contributed nothing toward the support of either herself or her two children." Even though she was forced to provide for herself and their children (and even pay some of his bills) with what she could make by sewing, she finally left him not because of his unwillingness to provide for her, but "on account of his habits of intemperance." The court "did not consider that the allegations had been sustained," however, and dismissed Ruth's petition.[26] She remained married to Thomas until his death in 1898 and is described as a "widow" on her death certificate, but there is no evidence that after 1871 they ever lived together again.

Although in her divorce petition Ruth claimed that she and Thomas separated in August 1871, it is not entirely clear how accurate this date is and whether she moved, or he did, or both. It is clear that as of August 1871, Thomas had already been working in South Boston for at least a year or two, even though his family remained in Charlestown. It is also clear that around August 1872, Ruth moved herself and her two boys from Charlestown to South Boston, where she established a business as a dressmaker at 327 Broadway; there is no indication that Thomas was living with them. Ruth's eldest son, Charles, set up a periodical business in the same building as his mother's dressmaking business. And Jesse was still going to school: in early September 1872, when he was arrested, he claimed he had just begun attending the Bigelow School at the corner of E and Fourth Streets in South Boston.[27]

If Ruth and Thomas did indeed stop living together as of August 1871, the upheaval in the household might well have had some effect on Jesse's career of torture, which he had embarked on by at least December 1871, when his first victim was reported in the local newspaper. (Since the severity of his crimes consistently escalated, though, it is very likely he assaulted several boys before December, when he came to the attention of the police and the press.) But there is no unequivocal evidence that Ruth and Thomas were separated until Ruth and her sons (without Thomas) moved to Boston a year later, in August 1872. As of this date, Jesse's victims no longer lived in Chelsea, which is just north of Charlestown, but in South Boston: he abducted his last known victim in Chelsea in the previous month, July 1872, and his first victim in South Boston on August 17.

"Outrages"

With little apparent reason besides his parents' troubled marriage and his father's departure from the household (although not from his life)— neither of which seem sufficient to explain what followed—from around the time he turned twelve, Jesse Pomeroy began assaulting small boys. He did not at first seem particularly unique, as his early assaults were reported as part of a wave of youthful crime: he was just another delinquent boy. In May 1872, after Pomeroy had started torturing boys but before he had been identified by name in a newspaper (although the suspicions of the local police may already have turned in his direction), the *Globe* printed what turned out to be a prescient editorial decrying the recent nationwide upsurge of youth "running amuck." After giving some examples of shoot-ings and stabbings by hooligan boys, the editorial went on to declare that "these sudden and almost simultaneous outbursts of bloodthirstiness on the part of our youth through the length and breadth of the land" seem "unaccountable." Yet they are not so "unaccountable" that the editor of the *Globe* didn't finally identify the problem as excessive freedom—the solution being more discipline, a prescription the *Globe* would later assert about Pomeroy himself after his conviction for murder.[28]

Just two months later, on the evening of Monday, July 22, 1872, the Boston area experienced its own "outburst of bloodthirstiness on the part of our youth" when eight-year-old John Balch suffered a "brutal assault" in Chelsea. He had been enticed by two or three other boys, the *Globe* claimed, to a building in the rear of Powder Horn Hill, "where he was stripped, his hands tied, swung from a cross-timber, and then beat with a rope from head to foot till black and blue welts covered his entire body." It was supposed that the "young scamps" who assaulted him were the same as those "who similarly maltreated the Hayden boy, several weeks ago." The public, the report concluded, was "considerably excited."[29] Boston, it turned out, was not immune to the national epidemic of "young scamps," although as yet the multiple boys who were presumed to be responsible were cast by the *Globe* as more mischievous than malicious.

The beating of John Balch was taken a bit more seriously by those who actually lived in Chelsea. Only three days after the assault, a note appeared in the paper averring that the Chelsea police "are unremitting in their efforts to detect the party who cruelly beat the Balch boy." By the end of July, a reward had been posted for any information leading to the arrest of the assailant. An account of the session of the Chelsea Board of Aldermen on the night of July 29 notes that the "order offering $500 for the detection and conviction of the party who beat the Balch boy was passed in a new form, so as to benefit police officers, if such evidence should convict." And on August 15, the *Advertiser* printed a short notice declaring the story "that the perpetrator of the outrage on the Balch boy has been discovered" to be "without foundation."[30] Rumors had apparently been running rampant. Indeed, the attack on Johnny Balch was soon recognized as one of a series of "outrages" perpetrated on small boys in Chelsea, and by August concern was so high within the community that authorities had raised the reward to $1,000 for anyone who helped convict whoever was responsible.[31]

Balch was not the first victim of the as yet unknown assailant. It seems the first documented attack took place seven months earlier, in December 1871, around Christmas.[32] Robert Maies was taken by a bigger boy up to Powder Horn Hill in Chelsea, where the attacker stripped him of his clothes, bound, gagged, and whipped him, all the while running around him jumping, laughing, and dancing "in a strange manner." The boy apparently then drew Maies home on a sled.[33] The second documented attack, of Tracy Hayden, took place two months later, in February 1872, and, as before, a larger boy enticed the smaller Hayden to Powder Horn Hill. Again, the larger boy stripped, bound, and gagged his victim and then beat him. According to the *Boston Post,* Hayden was beaten five times "with a rod as large around as his thumb"; the *Herald* included the detail that, this time, the boy's "privates" were "injured." And, again, the assailant took the boy home, "nearly to his house."[34]

The case of seven- or eight-year-old John Balch received the most atten- tion, perhaps because it was the most vicious attack—and perhaps also because, by the time he was assaulted, it was becoming clear the attacks were not isolated incidents. On July 22, 1872, Balch had been enticed by the promise of money to go with an older boy—later determined to be Pomeroy—to Powder Horn Hill. Once there, he was stripped, tied up, swung from a beam, and then beaten with a rope "till black and blue welts covered his entire body." He was so badly hurt that a physician had to be summoned to treat him.[35] Pomeroy had told Balch that there was "a man" who wanted Balch to run an errand for him, for which he would pay him a quarter. As Pomeroy was flogging the bound and gagged Balch, the boy asked "why he did so" and Pomeroy apparently replied "the man told me to do it." In this uncanny moment, Pomeroy seems to express the dissociation that characterized his crimes, his sense that some force beyond him (here described as "a man") compelled him to do what he did.[36] Omi- nously, Pomeroy did not return Balch to his home as he had done with his first two victims.

After the assault on John Balch in July 1872, the "outrages" on boys in Chelsea suddenly and inexplicably ended. Beginning in August, though, boys began to be assaulted in South Boston, and the attacks were even more ferocious than those in Chelsea. As we've seen, this shift in the locale of the attacks was clearly prompted by the removal of Ruth and her two sons from Charlestown to South Boston in early August 1872. While Ruth's decision to move may have been connected to her failing marriage, she in fact moved closer to where her husband was working (he had been working in Boston for a while). One of her principal problems with her husband, moreover, seemed to be that he was not supporting her and their children, so there is a chance she moved to Boston to keep the connection with Thomas stronger, in hopes of obtaining more economic support.[37] What she was moving *away from,* however, may have been a stronger motivator. It is possible that Ruth relocated because of the outcry over the assaults in Chelsea. Perhaps, despite all her later denials, Ruth had her own suspicions about who was victimizing small boys and had hopes of a fresh start.[38] Certainly by the end of July 1872 public outrage in Chelsea about the attacks was running very high, and the reward that was offered for any information about the assailant would no doubt have made Ruth nervous, if she had any inkling of her son's involvement. If she did, she would take her misgivings to her grave; her public support for her son would be unwavering and uncompromising.

The first of Pomeroy's South Boston victims was seven-year-old George Pratt, who was assaulted on August 17, 1872. He recounted that Pomeroy offered him money to go to the beach and boat house at City Point in South Boston, forced him to take off his clothes, tied him to the seat of a yacht and then "tortured him by sticking pins into his flesh."[39] The *Daily News* reported in lurid detail how Pratt's body was "completely punctured by the instruments of torture," adding that "after torturing the boy till his whole body ran blood," Pomeroy apparently danced "in savage glee at seeing the red blood flow." The unfortunate Pratt was "in an insensible condition" until he was rescued by a girl who happened by.[40] After Pomeroy's trial, the newspapers delivered still more detail about Pratt's ordeal, drawing on the account given by Pomeroy's lawyer. According to these later reports, Pomeroy beat Pratt's "naked limbs with a strap," bit him, and stuck pins into him, including into his "private parts." The *Herald* reported that Pomeroy told Pratt he "had told him three lies, and now he was going to give him three lickings for it." The *Herald* also recounted (as had the *Daily News*) that Pomeroy, "the young savage," danced "in great glee at seeing the blood flow."[41]

Only nineteen days later, on September 5, Pomeroy met six-year-old Harry Austin on a street in South Boston and lured him under a railroad bridge with the promise of money. Testimony before a juvenile court judge later that month would disclose that once Pomeroy had coaxed Austin to the isolated spot, he stripped him of all his clothing and "stabbed him several times between the shoulder blades, under each arm, and in other

places." The doctor who saw Austin on the day of the assault confirmed
that he suffered stabs "made by some sharp instrument" between the
shoulders and under each arm, "and the penis nearly half cut off."[42] The
most complete newspaper account of the assault, published in the *Daily
News*, agreed with the details in the State Reform School's case history,
describing how Pomeroy "with a large, many-bladed knife . . . slashed away
at [Austin's] neck, back and legs, and finally concluded his tortures by horribly mutilating and gashing parts of the little boy." Like Pratt, Austin was
left "in an insensible condition from the loss of blood and mutilation" and
was rescued by a passer-by. The *Herald*'s account agrees with these reports,
and is, indeed, a little more restrained, noting that Austin "received one
cut in the groin and three in the back with a knife."[43]

A mere six days after the attack on Austin, on September 11, 1872, Joseph
Kennedy was assaulted in a strikingly similar fashion. In fact, the *Globe*'s
account of Kennedy's testimony at Pomeroy's murder trial noted that it
was "nearly the same as that detailed by the previous victims," although
poor Kennedy took "nearly an hour in describing the manner in which
Pomeroy had punished him." Pomeroy had by this point clearly developed
a distinct pattern—a fantasy (however unconscious) that he was driven to
enact with each victim. The *Herald* gave more specifics about the assault
on Kennedy, reporting that it took place at Shepard's boat house and that
Pomeroy hit the boy in the head, washed his wounds with salt water, cut
him three times, and also compelled him to repeat the Lord's Prayer on his
knees, under threat of being killed.[44]

Pomeroy's next victim, only six days later, was Charles A. Gould, who
was reported as being somewhere between and five and seven years old at
the time of the attack on September 17. Gould later testified that he was
standing on Broadway when Pomeroy asked him "to come and see the
soldiers." Gould described how they walked down to the Boston, Hartford & Erie railroad track, where Pomeroy stripped him and tied him to a
telegraph pole. He then "drew out a big knife and a small one and cut me
five times on the head and once back of each ear; one cut was made with
the big knife." Gould described how he was saved from still worse torture
because a man came along and Pomeroy "was frightened away."[45]

Charles Gould was Pomeroy's last torture victim—for now. On the
afternoon of Thursday, September 19, 1872, Pomeroy was arrested in his
home at 312 Broadway in South Boston. Apparently the police had been
"working up" the case for four weeks, since the first South Boston assault.[46]

Newspaper accounts do not indicate what led to his arrest. Pomeroy himself, in his autobiography (which differed from the newspaper account), described how he happened to be walking up Broadway toward his home when he stopped and glanced into the Sixth Police Station. Moments later, an officer with a small boy in tow dashed out, grabbed Pomeroy by the arm, and told him he needed to come into the station. Pomeroy was then identified by several of his victims.[47] However he ended up in custody, Pomeroy was charged first with the assault on Charles Gould, who may have been the first to identify him as the assault took place only two days before Pomeroy's arrest. Officers were then apparently dispatched to bring Harry Austin to the police station, and he too "immediately identified Pomeroy." When he heard of Pomeroy's arrest, Chelsea's city marshal, W. P. Drury, traveled to the city with at least two boys, including John Balch, to see if they could identify Pomeroy as well. They did. Indeed, Balch apparently recognized his assailant immediately, exclaiming "That's the boy who cut me!" and appearing "to be overjoyed at his discovery."[48]

The next afternoon, September 20, 1872, Pomeroy was examined by Judge William J. Forsaith, recently appointed under a new law directing how juvenile offenders were to be tried.[49] Pomeroy was charged with the assaults not only on the four boys in South Boston, but also on two boys from Chelsea. Jesse confessed to the attacks before Judge Forsaith, who interrogated him about each boy, asking whether he had done what he was charged with. Jesse said " 'yes' to all." Forsaith asked Pomeroy the reason for his crimes, and the boy "replied that 'he did not know.' "[50] Newspaper accounts reported that he said he was "very sorry for what he had done," although he added that he "could not tell what prompted him to do it."[51] As another newspaper account summarized the boy's explanation of his "singular conduct," he said "he could not help it."[52] Forsaith sentenced Pomeroy to the State Reform School at Westborough, just outside Boston, for the remainder of his minority, and he was committed the next day.

Some of the first words we hear Jesse Pomeroy say, uttered at this examination in 1872, are words he would repeat over and over: he did not know why he did what he did, and he couldn't help it. From the beginning, the question of motive was a profound puzzle, and its central absence produced the multiple, often contradictory versions of who Pomeroy was. Writing about the "child-monster's" inability to explain his acts of torture, for instance, the *Congregationalist* declared that "no motive can be assigned

for this fiendishly cruel pastime. It would seem to be a clear case of mania."
The *New York Times* similarly noted that "it is very generally conceded that
he is mentally deficient." The *Boston Daily Advertiser,* however, described
Pomeroy's "good reputation as a quiet and peaceable boy" and added that
he "appears perfectly rational, and has not the least indication of insanity." The *Boston Daily Globe* agreed, reporting that "it is claimed that he
shows no evidences of insanity."[53] On the one hand, then, two periodicals
promptly declared that Pomeroy was a maniac, mentally deficient at best,
while on the other hand, two others asserted that there was "not the least
indication of insanity." Two opposed judgments—and neither did much
to explain what led to the crimes.

While Pomeroy was charged and sentenced for assaults on only six boys,
the account of his examination by Judge Forsaith notes that there were
"several other similar assaults committed by defendant upon other small
boys" in Chelsea.[54] Newspapers also reported on rumors circulating in
the local community about Pomeroy's other victims. While Pomeroy was
awaiting his sentence for murder, for instance, around two years later, a
letter to the *Globe* noted that "it is well known" that Pomeroy targeted
"several" boys in 1872 who turned out to be too "plucky and strong" for
him, and so he had to let them go, even after he had stripped them, because
they caused him too much trouble.[55]

It is impossible to know exactly how many boys Pomeroy victimized,
since so many of the events involving him have been so consistently exaggerated. An article in the *Register* in nearby Salem reported that "between
twenty and thirty boys from four to ten years of age, were supposed to have
suffered from his ungovernable and horrible propensity." An article in the
Boston Post, which recounted Pomeroy's arrest for murder and the discov-
eries made in its wake, similarly declared that "some thirty boys had been
attacked in Chelsea and Charlestown" before the Pomeroy family moved
from Charlestown to South Boston.[56] While both of these articles are accurate in other details, twenty to thirty victims seems a little high—the first
of many instances in which the number of Pomeroy's victims would be
overstated.[57] It is hard to know, though, whether the *Salem Register* and
the *Post* were simply engaged in hyperbolic reporting or whether twenty
or thirty victims had indeed come forward. The hysteria after Pomeroy's
arrest for murder in 1874 was so intense that presumably every actual and
imagined assault on a boy within recent memory was attributed to him
by his horrified contemporaries. While the charge of thirty assaults strains

credulity, it does seem likely that Pomeroy committed more crimes than the six with which he was charged before Judge Forsaith and the six who testified against him during his murder trial (a number that included one boy who had not appeared before Forsaith).

One reason why some of the attacks in Chelsea might not have been officially reported, and thus Pomeroy never charged with them, was that at least some of them might have been relatively minor. Pomeroy showed a clear pattern of escalation in his crimes that, it turned out, would be undeterred by his nearly sixteen months in reform school. The severest of the assaults with which he was charged were the last ones, those of the four boys in South Boston. They all occurred within one month, between mid-August and mid-September 1872, and the final three especially brutal crimes were each a mere six days apart. Although he was stopped before he could earn the title of America's first, Pomeroy fits the profile of what only later became identified as a serial killer.[58] His crimes were highly repetitive: all the boys were taken to an isolated place, stripped, tied up, gagged, beaten and, later, cut. What differed from one case to the next was mostly an increase in the brutality, an experimentation with more violent forms of torture, as Pomeroy moved from ropes and sticks to pins and then knives. His victims, while chosen seemingly at random, also fit a pattern: they were unknown to him and they were younger and smaller than he was. All of his torture victims were male. Accounts of Pomeroy dancing and laughing during the torture indicate his pleasure, and he displayed a frightening preoccupation with the genitals (cutting at least two boys in the "private parts") that was somewhat obscured by newspaper editors' obvious concern for the sensibilities of their readers. The increasing frequency and ferocity of Pomeroy's attacks suggest that whatever compulsion drove him, he was finding it increasingly difficult to keep it under control.

During the process of Pomeroy's examination and remand to Westborough, no official appears to have tried to understand his motives for committing "outrages" on small boys—or to have grasped how serious his crimes were. There is no evidence of such awareness, for instance, in the state reform school's case history of the boy, which was taken when he was admitted. The shared assumption, perhaps because he was so young, was that he was still malleable, and that the discipline of the reform school would mold his still unformed character away from such proclivities and toward the habits of a normal industrious young man. Pomeroy's pathology also seemed to be genuinely unprecedented—and he was sent away to live with boys who engaged in mundane theft and street brawls. No one, in 1872, seemed to heed the warning of the boy's repetitive, seemingly unmotivated, and escalating drives.

There is some evidence that Pomeroy's urges might have been rooted in part in his own bodily experience. Although press coverage of Pomeroy's initial arrest and examination was relatively sparse (especially compared to coverage of his murders, trial, and sentencing), several articles offer a very significant detail that had disappeared from accounts of the tortures by 1874, after Pomeroy's arrest for murder. One article describes all the "favorite methods" of torture that were detailed in other reports but adds that Pomeroy would puncture "small holes under the eyes," and another article similarly recounts that "in a number of instances he has cut small holes under each of the eyes of several boys' faces, which leave them disfigured for life."[59] One description of the wounds of Pomeroy's first murder victim, Horace Millen, included the detail that the boy's left eye was "partially removed from its socket by a deep cut close to the bridge of the nose."[60] This is all significant because Pomeroy himself had a notoriously damaged eye—what his contemporaries called an "evil eye," an eye with a "white veil"—that was undoubtedly a source of humiliation for him, perhaps a source of taunts and bullying. He could very well have been visiting his own injury and humiliation on other, smaller boys—marking their bodies with his own loathed disfigurement.[61]

In his autobiography, Pomeroy explained the damage to his eye as the result of a boyish accident, claiming that a fishing hook got lodged there. In reality, though, as his mother reported, his eye was damaged when he was an infant, the residual effect of abscesses that covered his body after an adverse reaction to a smallpox vaccination. That Pomeroy recast his injury in the way he did suggests an effort to normalize it, making it part of a prosaic boyhood rather than a mysterious deformity beyond his knowledge and control.

Despite all the indications that Jesse Pomeroy would not stop committing brutal crimes, that whatever drove him would not easily be reformed, he was dispatched to the nation's first state reform school, unaccompanied by any real effort to understand him. He was to test the hopes of the school's founders that discipline, productive work, and a "family" environment would reform recalcitrant young boys.[62] And he would prove those hopes to be catastrophically misguided.

At Reform School

Pomeroy was admitted to the Massachusetts State Reform School for Boys at Westborough on September 21, 1872. The commitment register reads that he was twelve at the time, and that he was committed by Judge William J. Forsaith for assault with a knife.[63] There were between 250 and 300 boys in the reform school at any given moment in the early 1870s. In the annual report for 1872, the superintendent reported that there were 254 boys in the school on September 30 of that year, just after Pomeroy was admitted. Pomeroy was an anomaly principally in terms of the offense for which he was committed, which was far more violent than the norm. In 1872, for instance, out of a total of ninety admitted boys, he was one of only two convicted of assault with a knife. The vast majority found themselves at Westborough for larceny (forty-five), breaking and entering (fifteen) and stubbornness and disobedience (fourteen).[64] The report for 1873 discloses a similar picture. Of 140 boys admitted, only seven had committed some form of battery (none with a knife), while seventy-one were admitted for larceny, thirteen for breaking and entering and twenty-six for stubbornness and disobedience.[65]

The questions that structured the history of each boy, which was taken on admission, suggest certain reigning beliefs about the causes of delinquency, notably the malign influence of a failing family life, poverty, and bad habits such as drinking alcohol and using tobacco. The authorities at the school wanted to know about the boys' parents—whether they were still alive, whether they were living together, and whether they were "intemperate." In an attempt to determine social class, each was asked the occupation of his father, the number of towns and tenements his family had lived in over the past year, and the amount of rent paid. The boys were also asked about their own prior arrests (and those of family members), whether or not they used tobacco and "ardent spirits," and whether they attended school, church, and Sunday school.[66] From his answers, Pomeroy seemed like an exemplary child: no use of spirits or tobacco, no arrests, regular attendance at school, church, and Sunday school. He was not especially rootless, having lived in only two towns and two tenements in the preceding year. The largest number of boys (twenty-two out of ninety) had lived in four tenements over the past year.[67] The history does record, twice, though, that his parents were separated: "his father not at home" and "His parents do not live together."[68] Pomeroy would also have found himself in the minority in terms of ethnicity, since both his parents were American-born. In 1872, out of ninety boys admitted, only nineteen had parents born in the United States. And of the seventy-one boys whose parents were foreign-born, fifty-six of them had parents from Ireland. The overwhelming predominance of children born of Irish immigrants held true in 1873 also. Pomeroy would have been surrounded by Irish American boys.

When it opened in 1846, the state-run reform school at Westborough was the first of its kind in the nation, as well as the first form of compulsory public education in Massachusetts. But it was more than a "school." The reformers of the mid-nineteenth century aspired to provide a substitute for what they believed must be lacking in the life of any boy who resorted to criminal behavior: a stable family, which seemed to be disappearing as the nineteenth century wore on and as waves of immigrants (especially Irish) poured into Boston. As the historian Peter Holloran puts it, the school "was seized upon as the best way to shore up the imperiled American family," another way of saying, perhaps, that the school system (especially the reform school) was what Holloran later calls an "instrument of social control." Indeed, with its new system of compulsory, even carceral, education and discipline, the state was solidifying its role, Michael Katz claims, as "the actual parent of the boy."[69] Ideally, the school aspired to provide "kindly parental discipline" and a "family system"; thus many of the boys lived in separate "houses," and the school made a point of hiring female teachers to ensure the presence of a maternal influence. The boys were also to be engaged in constant, invigorating manual labor (as well as school-work), and the hope of the school was to involve as many boys as possible in the school farm, since farming was "the best possible occupation."[70]

The reality was far from the ideal, however. A fire set by an unhappy young inmate at Westborough as early as 1859 revealed, as Steven Mintz puts it, "the bleak underside of reform-school life." Inmates who had been accused of assault, arson, and attempted escape were found "manacled to the floor in dark, poorly ventilated cells and fed bread and water."[71]

Conditions only worsened through the 1860s. Annual reports from the early 1870s disclose an embattled school administration. The report for 1873 (after Pomeroy had been in the school for a year) began by declaring that the institution was "losing its character as a reform school for boys," becoming instead "a place of confinement for criminals." More boys between the ages of fourteen to sixteen were being admitted to an institution designed to reform much younger boys (seven to fourteen). The trustees remarked that while the public demanded that "the discipline should be parental," the conduct of the boys "was not filial," and thus discipline was—of necessity, they claimed—becoming more severe. The authors worried about the dire effects of keeping "the comparably virtuous" surrounded by the influence of the "vicious," and lamented the loss of the school's ability to give boys trades: "They know only how to seat chairs." Not only could the majority of boys not be trusted on the farm, but local farmers were positively fearful of them and "will not employ them." Running away became a persistent problem; on May 5, 1873, for instance, almost a hundred boys escaped, an increase over the fifty-three who had "eloped" the year before.[72] Pomeroy writes of this mass escape in his autobiography, noting that he didn't join the others only because he was sick and confined to the hospital. Ironically, given his clear indication that he would have joined in the exodus from the school—"if I had been down there I would have gone, too"—his *not* doing so was taken as a marker of the good behavior that would lead to his early release.[73]

Since even the school's own annual reports hinted at trouble, it was not surprising when, three years after Pomeroy was released from Westborough, scandal again erupted at the institution.[74] A committee of the Massachusetts legislature heard testimony in April 1877 from trustees of the school, former and present superintendents, teachers, and the boys themselves about the forms of punishment used at the school—and the details were shocking.[75] Boys were regularly locked in a sweat-box about seven feet high, ten inches deep, and between fourteen and seventeen inches wide—in one case for a whole week from early morning until night. Boys reported vomiting while inside and fainting upon release. They were also put in straitjackets and gagged, their hands bound behind their back—again, often for days at a time with release only at night. And there were chilling accounts of flogging, including reports that boys were regularly ordered to remove their clothes. One boy testified that the assistant superintendent of the school at the time, William Phillips, made him take off his jacket and pants and bend over. When the boy finally got to his knees, "He put his hand on my throat. I could not speak, but made a motion for him to take his hand off my throat. He whipped me until the blood ran down my legs." The boy continued: "My pants were off as far as they would go. Every time I got down on my knees he gave it to me over my head."[76] Small wonder that outrage ran high after the release of such details.

Indeed, given that Pomeroy was remanded to Westborough for torturing boys, it is perversely ironic that those who ran the school seemed themselves to provide dangerous models of such practices. A *New York Times* article about the revelations in the 1877 hearing declared unequivocally that what was happening at Westborough was in fact "torture." It was inconsistent with any notion of reform, the article claimed, "that boys are to be made better by bodily torture and degrading punishment." In fact, the writer claimed he could not dwell any more on such "sickening details," for to describe "some of the more repulsive features of the torture would only disgust, without edifying, the reader."[77] If Westborough was supposed to provide troubled boys with a "family," then the family that awaited those boys seemed a very dysfunctional one indeed, teeming with abusive, even sadistic fathers.

The inhumane practices at Westborough preceded the scandalous exposé of 1877, making it clear that what the *Times* called "torture" occurred during Pomeroy's tenure there. As early as 1860, a *Boston Daily Advertiser* article about abuses at Westborough had expressed worry about the routine sadistic punishments at the school and what they might "implant" in the boys who suffered them—and one wonders in particular what they might have "implanted" in a boy like Pomeroy, impressionable and already delighting in tying up and whipping other boys.[78]

Pomeroy himself does not appear to have suffered from the "system of torture" at Westborough, though he must have heard of the horrors around him. He was released early, after about sixteen months, for exemplary behavior, and in his autobiography he claims, "I never was punished while there in any way, shape, or manner; a thing few of the boys can say." Indeed, Pomeroy describes his promotion to duties of increasing responsibility, from chair-making (the staple employment) to working in the "hall" (taking care of the rooms where the boys slept), where he was eventually put in charge, and then to the kitchen, where he helped prepare food. A note at his discharge confirms his own account: "The boy's conduct since coming here has been excellent."[79]

Pomeroy's unblemished record at Westborough suggests that he adapted with alacrity to institutional structures. Peter Holloran has described what he calls the "rituals of depersonalization" that boys underwent as they entered the Westborough Reform School: "bath, haircut, delousing, physical examination, loss of personal possessions, uniforms, numbering, marching, regimentation, strict military-style discipline, involuntary confinement, asceticism, and enforced celibacy."[80] For Pomeroy, whose "person" seems to have been attenuated at best, such rituals may not so much have stripped away an already existing interiority as provided a compensatory substitute for its absence. As he describes his life at Westborough in his autobiography, for instance, Pomeroy launches a detailed exposition of "the daily life of boys"—the schedule by which their days were regulated—as well as a list of what they ate each day. He also uses the positions he held at the school, and the promotions he earned, as evidence that he "was a good behaved boy."[81] He uses external events, in other words, to describe who he is, thus marking a lack of interiority.

Pomeroy was discharged from Westborough on February 6, 1874, and the discharge notes reveal that he was "released to mother to work in [a] periodical store," the business his older brother ran out of a store the family owned.[82] In a little over two months, however, Pomeroy would be arrested for the brutal murder of young Horace Millen. Inevitably, questions arose about his early release, which, it turned out, had not been uncontested. The *Globe* reported that the assistant visiting agent of the State Board of Charities (which oversaw the reform school) had opposed Pomeroy's release because of his "inhuman treatment" of so many boys. One of the school's trustees, however, John Ayres, "actively pressed" the pardon Pomeroy's mother had requested.[83] The *Boston Medical and Surgical Journal* cryptically reported, in the wake of Pomeroy's murder trial, that the boy had been released "through the efforts of one of our 'philanthropists,' whose name has been very carefully hidden from public execration."[84]

Questions persisted in the months that followed. On July 23, 1874, the *New York Times* reported that since the question of Pomeroy's early release has "exercised the public mind," Gardiner Tufts, agent of the Board of Charities, had issued a statement explaining the decision, citing the boy's "exceedingly good" conduct and the lack of any evidence of a "cruel disposition." His mother, moreover, who had been deserted by her husband, "was a worthy woman" whom her son could "materially assist." He had been released, in short, "in accordance with the best judgment of careful and honorable men with the facts before them."[85] While Tufts articulated the official version, lurking beneath it is the sense of virtual desperation felt by those who ran the school—the trustees, the superintendent, and the teachers. The school was overcrowded and had severe discipline problems; thus anyone who seemed "exemplary" on the surface (and the surface was clearly all they saw of Pomeroy) seemed to have a better chance outside of an institution that was broken, that had even become a positive danger to the boys it was trying to reform.

The bottom line, though, was that Jesse Pomeroy was an anomaly—and no one could be faulted too severely for not knowing what to do with him. His crimes were vastly different from those for which others boys were admitted to Westborough, and officials were unable to recognize this difference. Pomeroy's criminal career was repeatedly proclaimed by everyone to be unprecedented. As early as 1872, after his string of tortures came to light, the *New York Times* called his conduct "singular" and declared his case "one of the most remarkable on record." Two years later, the *Globe* editorialized that Pomeroy's career was "one of the most remarkable in the annals of crime." And the *Advertiser* summed up the defense attorney's words at trial: Pomeroy's "diabolical" crimes were "without a parallel in our criminal records."[86] Pomeroy's crimes created a category that simply did not exist before him.

"Horrible" Murder

After Jesse Pomeroy was released from Westborough, it was not long—just over two months—before he loomed into the spotlight again. His name appeared on Thursday, April 23, 1874, as a possible suspect in the case of a "horrible" local murder.[87] The body of four-year-old Horace Millen, who had been missing since late morning on Wednesday, was found, brutally lacerated, at around 5 p.m. that same day on a marshy section of beach in Dorchester Bay, in the southern part of Boston Harbor.[88] The *Herald* suggested that Millen's first wound was probably to the right eye, followed by about eighteen shallow cuts to the chest. The throat was slashed twice, and the scrotum was also sliced, most likely after death. The many cuts on the boy's hands suggested he had tried desperately to shield himself from his attacker.[89]

It did not take long for the local police to remember Jesse Pomeroy (strangely identified by the press, that first night, as Willie Pomeroy). James R. Wood, the police officer who would draw an initial confession from Pomeroy, recalled that he and several other policemen were sitting in the office of the chief of police, Edward H. Savage, discussing Millen's murder, when Savage said, "There's a strange resemblance about this thing to the work of a young scoundrel we've got in the Reformatory. He used to have a mania for taking little boys, slashing them about the face with a knife, and then tying them to a railroad track. . . . If that fellow wasn't in the reformatory, I should say this was the work of young Pomeroy."

One of the officers promptly interjected that not only had Pomeroy left the reformatory, but he was living with his mother in South Boston. Savage immediately telegraphed the Sixth Station, in Pomeroy's district (indeed, on Broadway itself, the street on which the Pomeroys lived), and asked them to send an officer to Pomeroy's home and bring him in to the station. Wood and two other officers headed over to South Boston, arriving shortly after 10 p.m., just as Pomeroy was coming in the door.[90] Pomeroy was arrested and spent the night at the Charles Street Jail (formally known as the Suffolk County Jail).[91]

The coroner's inquest into Horace Millen's death took place at the Ninth Police Station on Friday, April 24, presided over by Dr. Ira Allen. But it is the events of Thursday, the day after Pomeroy's late-night arrest, that seem crucial. Officer Wood interviewed Pomeroy during the late morning, asking him, "What made you cut those little boys, before?" Jesse replied that "he did not know what made him." Wood continued, "I don't suppose you knew what you were doing, did you?" Pomeroy replied, "I don't think I did. I don't know." Wood pushed still further: "Might not you have killed that little boy yesterday and not known it?" Pomeroy admitted, "I don't know, I might. I guess I did."[92]

Wood and two other policemen, including Officer Adams, then drove Pomeroy to the undertaker's where Millen's body was laid out. They testified that he did not want to go. On the way there, he apparently admitted that he did know Millen; Wood then suggested, "If you know him, you killed him, did not you Jesse?" Pomeroy again said, "I guess I did, if I did I am sorry and I don't want my mother to know it." When they got to the undertaker's, Pomeroy repeated that he didn't want to go in—that he could see Millen through the glass, and that he knew him. Wood, though, "took his right arm and partially pulled him in." Jesse was trembling and shaking "like a leaf," and when he got to the little boy, he turned his head away. Remorselessly, Wood turned him back, and Jesse finally looked at Horace Millen: "Tears came in his eyes and he was much affected." Wood said to him, "Jesse, do you know him?" Jesse replied, "Yes." Wood tried to make him look at Millen again, but Jesse protested, "No, I have seen him enough." As they stepped out of the room where Millen's body lay, Wood asked Jesse again, "Jesse, did you kill him?" Again the reply was, "Yes." And then, once more, this time in front of Officer Adams, Wood asked, "You say you know him and you killed him?" Pomeroy said he did. In the carriage ride back to the Sixth Station, Wood took Pomeroy's knife from

Adams, opened both of its blades, and asked, "You cut his throat with this blade, Jesse, didn't you?" When Pomeroy said nothing, Wood asked the boy how he got the blood off, whether he washed the blood off the knife. "No, I stuck it in the marsh, in the mud," he replied. Wood also asked Pomeroy if he washed the blood from his hands, and Pomeroy said, "No, I did not get any on my hands."[93]

These confessions to Wood were the first time Pomeroy conceded his guilt. He would later deny having said any of it, and so began a pattern by which he would admit guilt when pressed and then, later, unequivocally deny both his guilt and his confession.[94]

The boy's confession to Wood was made under the kind of coercive pressure that would be unimaginable in our current judicial system. Indeed, the *Boston Herald* published an editorial titled "Innocent until Proved Guilty" questioning some of the practices of the police, notably their having kept Pomeroy in jail overnight and then taken him to see the murdered boy's body without informing him "of the charge against him," as well as questioning him, while he was with the corpse, "with the view of getting him to confess the murder," all before the boy saw a lawyer.[95] Wood in particular was relentless in his interrogation: he grasped Pomeroy by the head and forced him to look at the body, and later confronted him with his knife. Wood made the crime palpably real, and under those conditions— physically confronted with his crime, with the murdered body, with the knife he used—Pomeroy admitted to the crime, perhaps unable, momentarily, to imagine any alternative to the scenario Wood conjured up so compellingly. Before too long, though, Jesse would have a crucial conversation with a man who did open up for him another possibility—and he happily slipped into that alternative narrative of events.

After Wood returned with Pomeroy to Station Six, he and two other detectives went to lunch, giving strict instructions to the captain of the station, Henry T. Dyer, to let no one see Pomeroy while they were gone. When they returned thirty minutes later, they went to Pomeroy's cell to get his earlier confession in writing. However, as Wood later put it, "Judge of our surprise when he absolutely refused to tell us anything, recanted his previous confession, and denied that he had committed the murder."[96]

Dyer, it turned out, had let someone in to see the boy after all, despite Wood's clear instructions, and Jesse now told a different story. "I don't want to answer any more questions," he declared. "I know what you came here for . . . and I was told, if anyone asked me any more questions to say, if you please, don't ask me any more questions." When Wood asked who told him so, Jesse replied that Stephen G. Deblois, one of the directors of the reform school, had told him so—and that "he is my friend and he says the whole seven directors will be my friends." Deblois even offered to be Jesse's lawyer, telling the boy that he did not believe in Pomeroy's guilt and that there was nothing against him but circumstantial evidence. Pomeroy then not only refused to talk about Millen but also denied that he had had anything to do with the six boys who were tortured in Chelsea and South Boston. He even offered up the name of the boy whom he claimed committed those crimes, declaring he'd never given this information to anyone before. Pomeroy added that this boy was dead—another comment, like the one about the "man" who commanded him to beat John Balch, that seems to articulate Pomeroy's profound dissociation from his acts of violence.[97]

As one of the trustees of the Westborough State Reform School, Deblois had undoubtedly hastened to the police station because he foresaw the outrage that would erupt over the school's early release of Pomeroy. He provided the impressionable boy with an alternative story to the one forced from him by the proximity of Horace Millen's mutilated body. And Jesse seized on it: he would provide the story Deblois offered him when he testified at the inquest the next day.

Pomeroy's own testimony at the inquest, then, belied everything he had reportedly said the day before to Wood and Adams and others. He stated that he had "made no admission as to my complicity in the crime to any body [*sic*]." He said that he had seen Millen's body at the undertaker's but that he "made no remarks then to the officers." Pomeroy also recanted his comments about Deblois, acknowledging that he talked to him but saying that "the nature of the conversation was inquiry" and that "he gave me no advice as to what to do."[98] Pomeroy instead offered a detailed account of his movements on the day Millen was killed. According to Pomeroy, he saw no one from around 11:30 a.m. until around 2 p.m. He claimed he was simply walking around Boston: "went down Broadway, over Federal street bridge along Federal street to the new Post Office, up Milk street to Washington, up Bromfield to Tremont, and thence to the Common; walked over the Common to the Public Garden; sat down on the benches there to rest; went up Beacon Street to the Common and thence to Presbo's dining rooms on Congress street."[99] There is a disturbing absence of inner life here, its possible presence displaced onto the streets of Boston, named with precision as if they mattered. This evidence of an interior lack, which was so often apparent in what Jesse Pomeroy said and did, is all the more chilling given the almost certain truth of what Pomeroy was in fact doing during this time.

The inquest into Horace Millen's death began on Friday, April 24. Further hearing of the case, and the necessity of Pomeroy's answering to the charge, was postponed, however, until the detectives had completed their task of gathering evidence and Pomeroy had consulted further with his lawyers.[100] Meanwhile, Pomeroy remained in the Charles Street Jail as the city recovered from the worst April snowstorm in fifty years, which dumped up to eighteen inches of snow, uprooting trees and destroying buildings.[101]

The inquest continued in "secret," though the press seemed to ferret out most of the details, as witnesses for both sides were amassed.[102] On Tuesday, April 28, in the evening, the coroner's inquest finally closed: Horace Millen was declared the victim of murder and Pomeroy pronounced the probable perpetrator. Pomeroy was arraigned before a municipal court judge on Friday, May 1, and was in short order indicted by the grand jury. Apparently, however, there was a mistake in his indictment, as the words "malice aforethought" were omitted; the grand jury would have to indict him again and he would not be tried until later in the year.[103] The press noted, however, that the case against him was convincing.[104] Pomeroy would remain in the Charles Street Jail for the next eight months while both prosecution and defense prepared their cases.

Although the trial did not begin until late December 1874, Pomeroy's name was once again splashed across the newspapers in July when the body of ten-year-old Catharine (Katie) Curran was discovered. Katie had been missing since March of that year, and her parents had been frantic in their search for her ever since. She had been heading toward the Pomeroys' shop intending to buy some papers, or a book, when she vanished on the morning of March 18.[105] Although suspicion had certainly fallen on Jesse Pomeroy, rumors had also circulated that her disappearance had something to do with the differing religious affiliations of her parents (one was Catholic and the other Protestant); at least one witness claimed to have seen her disappear into a carriage, and some believed she had been abducted by friends and "was concealed in some institution."[106]

Katie Curran's disappearance had nonetheless caused quite a stir in the South Boston community, so much so that the mayor offered a reward of $500 to anyone who could provide information leading to the conviction of her abductor. In the minutes for the meeting of the alderman's board on March 30, Alderman James Power, who proposed the measure, told the board that Katie's parents "are poor and have not money to prosecute the matter" of their daughter's disappearance, and he asked the board to direct the mayor to appropriate $500 for the reward. He noted that there was no need to tell the board the details of the abduction because the facts had become known through newspaper reports. The board agreed without debate to the appropriation, and posters were disseminated in South Boston.[107]

Despite the rumors about her feuding parents, it undoubtedly came as no surprise to many in the South Boston community when Katie Curran's body was found in the cellar of what used to be the Pomeroy family store on 327 Broadway. Indeed, the police (Officer Adams, on orders from the chief of police, Edward Savage) had searched the premises for Katie at least once after Jesse Pomeroy was arrested for Horace Millen's murder.[108] Ruth Pomeroy and her oldest son, Charles, had moved out of the store not too long after Jesse's arrest and after their business had fallen off dramatically. Crowds of people had started flocking to the store, but they were interested only in looking, not buying, so Ruth and Charles retrenched and moved their businesses to their place of residence at 312 Broadway, nearly opposite the shop.[109] A man who already owned property at 342 Broadway purchased 327 and in short order sent workmen down into the cellar to begin excavating and remodeling the building.[110] It was these unlucky men who discovered the skeletal remains of Katie Curran on Saturday, July 18. Not only had Katie's body been found in the Pomeroy family store, but it turned out that Jesse had "several times asked of the attendants [in the jail] what reward was offered for the whereabouts of the Curran girl, and what would be given him if he should reveal her hiding place."[111]

Although Jesse was already locked up in the Charles Street Jail, the police went to work immediately (probably abashed at their inability to find Katie's body earlier) and arrested his mother and brother. Gossip was rampant that it was inconceivable the body could have lain for so long in their cellar without Ruth and Charles having some knowledge of it.[112] The *Herald* reported that Ruth Pomeroy was "loth to go" with the police, "but her arguments were useless and she was locked up . . . on suspicion of being connected with a felony."[113] In fact, the arrests seem mostly to have been for Ruth and Charles's protection. As news of the discovery of Katie's body spread like wildfire through the streets of South Boston, an angry crowd amassed outside 327 Broadway and people started pelting Ruth Pomeroy's store sign across the street. For some time, the *Boston Post* reported, "it seemed as if the excited mass of humanity would wreak its vengeance on all of the Pomeroy family found in that house." Another paper reported quite explicitly that Ruth and Charles were taken in by the police because it was feared they would be "lynched."[114]

The ire of the public was directed in particular at Jesse's mother. Indeed, according to the *Boston Herald,* when the verdict of the inquest into Horace Millen's death was announced months earlier, Ruth Pomeroy had received numerous threatening letters. The *Herald* published one of those letters, which told her to leave Boston: "You stay at your Pearl [peril] *Oh you Devil in human shape* you are the cause of that poor Boys Death."[115] While Ruth was released soon after her arrest, Charles seems to have been held in jail, as a material witness, until the end of August. Newspapers did not report until September 1 that he had finally been released, on the grounds that his confinement was an unnecessary financial hardship for his mother.[116]

The discovery of Katie Curran's body whipped to new heights the frenzy that had surrounded Jesse Pomeroy since April. Just as reports emerged after Pomeroy was sent to reform school of twenty or thirty other alleged victims, so too, after his arrest for Horace Millen's murder and the discovery of Katie Curran's body, stories swirled about still more victims. A paper in the western part of the state, the *Springfield Republican,* reported that, since Pomeroy's arrest, "several cases of cruelty to children, inflicted by a 'big boy,' have come to light in Boston, and the general feeling is that Pomeroy was caught none too soon."[117] In October 1874, several newspapers reported that a girl named Margaret Lauk had been missing since around the time Katie Curran disappeared. And she had worked for none other than Ruth Pomeroy—had been, in fact, one of the girls who sewed in her shop. Lauk was from Canada, and her father had just arrived in Boston to search for her. One article ended forebodingly: "It is certainly very remarkable that Margaret should disappear so suddenly and so mysteriously just at the time she did."[118] After these reports, however, Lauk vanished from the news as completely as she seemed to have vanished from Boston. We cannot know, then, if she was another of Pomeroy's victims.

Excitement about the Pomeroy case remained at fever pitch as the inquest into Katie Curran's murder began at the Sixth Police Station before a Suffolk County coroner on the afternoon of Monday, July 20; it lasted over a week, not concluding until late in the day on Wednesday, July 29. The most compelling testimony was that of Police Chief Edward Savage, the first witness, who had talked to Pomeroy before the inquest began. Savage had elicited a detailed confession from Pomeroy, a confession he would later deny in a repetition of what happened with Officer James Wood in the case of Horace Millen. Pomeroy had even, apparently, drawn a diagram of his house and cellar for Savage and explained what happened "by means of this diagram." He said that Katie Curran came to the store early on the morning of March 18, asking if she could buy some papers. "I told her," he was reported as saying to Savage, "there was a store down cellar." Pomeroy later amended "cellar" to "stairs," reportedly saying, "If I had said down cellar she would not have gone." As Katie walked to the middle of the cellar, Pomeroy followed her "and put my left arm about her neck, my hand over her mouth, and with my knife cut her throat, holding my knife in my right hand. I then dragged her to behind the water-closet, laying her head furthermost up the place, and put some stones and some ashes on the body."[119]

Pomeroy told Savage, "I do not know why I did it; I couldn't help doing it."[120] Another account notes that after Savage read Pomeroy's confession aloud at the inquest, one of the coroner's jurors asked him if the boy gave any explanation of why he did it. Savage replied, " 'Well,' he said, 'I could not help it.' " The account continued, chillingly, that "to another question of the same nature [Pomeroy] replied that he 'wanted to see how she would act.' "[121] Pomeroy also added in his confession that he "awoke that morning with a pain in his head and a dizziness about his eyes. He could not resist the demand upon him and did the deed."[122]

Pomeroy confessed the same grim details about Katie Curran's murder to his lawyer, Joseph Cotton, and when asked why he did it, Pomeroy told Cotton, " 'I do not know; I couldn't help it; it is here,' accompanying the word 'here' with a gesture indicating it was in his head." He continued that he wished his parents had sent him to sea—because then he would never have come back. He also believed that when he became a man, he would be able to "resist the temptation to do such bloody deeds, but at present the temptation was too strong for him."[123] In the autobiography he was apparently preparing for his lawyers while he sat in jail, Pomeroy wrote that he was swayed into his crimes by "a power not to be shaken off." And that while he recognized that he might go to jail for a few years, he wanted to go to sea after his release, and then "I shall be a man and strong enough to overcome this desire that seizes me."[124] Cotton also apparently told a *Boston Journal* reporter that after Pomeroy had told him the "most blood thrilling story" about Katie Curran's murder, he "calmly asked that his mother send him a clean shirt and a pair of socks, and said 'What do you think of Jesse H. Pomeroy?' "[125]

When the crowd outside the police station heard of Pomeroy's confession, they "seemed almost crazy with excitement, and rushed about, spreading the news rapidly."[126] Indeed, public outrage had continued to run high after Katie Curran's body was discovered on Saturday afternoon. In the days since, there had been what some described as a near riot outside of Station Six: according to the *Advertiser,* "the station house was besieged by an infuriated crowd of six or eight thousand persons."[127] Perhaps inevitably, someone had to be sacrificed to the fury of the mob, and Boston's mayor, Samuel C. Cobb, turned on the officer who had been captain of the Sixth Station for the last fifteen years, Henry Dyer. Captain Dyer was accused of a variety of offenses: being "too intimate" with Ruth Pomeroy and helping to procure the release of her son from the state reform school, allowing the school's trustee Stephen Deblois to see Pomeroy in his jail cell when the officers had charged him not to let anyone in, egregious incompetence in the matter of searching for Katie's body (Dyer had apparently been content with his officers' claims that they found nothing in the Pomeroys' store), and abdication of duty on Saturday night, after Katie's body was finally found. Indeed, when violence seemed imminent that night, Dyer said he was "nervous" and had to go home. He was, as he put it, "completely prostrated" by the discovery of Katie Curran's body and by the realization that their efforts to find the girl had been such a "horrible failure." He went on to tell a *Boston Post* reporter that he was "nearly unmanned" and "unfit for further duty." The mayor agreed and demanded Dyer resign, no doubt hoping that he would thus deflect public anger from himself.[128]

Certainly someone had been remiss in the search for Katie Curran. As the *Springfield Republican* caustically noted, "There was no possible excuse for the failure to discover the girl's body till nearly four months after she disappeared."[129] Her mother had told the police that Katie had gone to the Pomeroys' shop on the morning she disappeared; Pomeroy had been convicted of torturing children and in just over a month would be arrested for murdering another; neighbors had complained of the stench coming from the cellar of 327 Broadway; and the search of the cellar was apparently done by flickering candlelight as an officer prodded halfheartedly around with a cane. The *Herald* summed up its scathing critique of the police in its efforts to find Katie Curran: the public needed to know "that when incompetent officials are discovered they will be unflinchingly rooted out."[130]

Meanwhile the coroner's inquest continued, and new and disturbing information came from the doctor who performed the autopsy and whose report was printed in its entirety in the *Globe*. Although much of Katie Curran's body had decomposed, the coroner found clear evidence of multiple stab wounds in her groin and abdominal area, around her genitals in particular. The wounds occurred, moreover, after her clothes had been ripped or cut apart.[131] Pomeroy's "confession" that he merely cut her throat and then dragged her behind the water closet and buried her was clearly incomplete at best.

Testimony from the Pomeroys' neighbor, with whom the family shared the cellar, spoke of discord in the Pomeroy family. Jesse and his brother, Charles, apparently quarreled a lot, and on one occasion Charles reported to the neighbor that they had fought because Jesse wanted to lock the store early and sleep there. Charles also remarked to the neighbor, in baffled frustration, that Jesse seemed to waste a great deal of time lingering around the water closet in the cellar.[132]

Despite pervasive unofficial reports of Pomeroy's confession to Katie Curran's murder, he refused to testify at the coroner's inquest.[133] Nonetheless, the coroner's jury took only fifteen minutes, after the testimony was concluded, to reach a verdict: they found that Katie Curran had come to her death at the hands of Jesse H. Pomeroy. "He has acknowledged the crime," the jury declared, "and the evidence obtained corroborates his statement."[134] The jury also found that either before or after death, Katie's body had been mutilated with a knife.[135] Since Pomeroy was never tried for Curran's murder, this verdict was all the legal justice she and her family ever received.

Close on the heels of Pomeroy's admission of Curran's murder, and while the inquest into her death was still ongoing, the newspapers started buzzing with reports that he had also confessed (again) to the murder of Horace Millen (which he had denied at the inquest into Millen's death). Rumor had it that Pomeroy told both his lawyer, Joseph Cotton, and "Uncle Cooke" (Rufus R. Cooke, the chaplain at the jail) that he killed Millen. As reported in the *Globe*, which claimed to have been the first to acquire Pomeroy's confession, the boy stated that on the fateful morning of April 22 he had been at his mother's store until about 11:30 a.m., when he left to go to the city. He went up Dorchester Avenue to Eighth Street, where he encountered Horace Millen. Immediately, Pomeroy claimed, "his evil genius got possession of him, and he determined to torture him, if not kill him."[136] As the *Post* put it, "he was at once seized with a desire to torture him," or, as the less restrained *Herald* reported, the sight of Millen "excited in him an unconquerable desire to gratify his fiendish propensity to shed human blood."[137] Pomeroy asked the boy if he would like to see "the steamer" and the two boys set off toward the marshes of Dorchester Bay. Arriving at an isolated spot, Pomeroy asked Horace to lie down. When he did so, Pomeroy leaped on him, put his left hand over the boy's mouth, and cut his throat. As Horace continued to struggle, Pomeroy "stabbed him repeatedly in the bowels and chest." He then cleaned his knife and took a streetcar to central Boston, spending some time in Boston Common before returning home.[138]

When asked why he killed Millen, Pomeroy reportedly said "that he did not know, but supposed he could not help it." He continued that he had no intention of hurting anyone until he actually saw the boy, and that then "the feeling that he must do it took possession of him and overcame a thought he had while on the way to the marshes that he had better not." In a comment that anticipated his defense at Pomeroy's murder trial, Joseph Cotton said that he wouldn't contravene reports of Pomeroy's confession but, in "extenuation" he would say that the boy "has a mania for butchering people which he cannot overcome."[139] Cotton's statement, however, yoked two utterly incompatible concepts—"mania" and "butchery"— suggesting at the same time that his client was insane *and* depraved. These two opposed labels, with the abyss that lay in between, would define (and thwart) all attempts to explain Jesse Pomeroy, both at his murder trial and in the much more extended and colorful trial that ensued in the press.

2

On Trial

Throughout 1874, in the lead-up to Jesse Pomeroy's murder trial, commentators speculated wildly about what was wrong with the boy. Some leaned toward his being pure evil; others argued he was possessed by demonic spirits; still others proclaimed that his nature had been fatally twisted before he was even born. His defense lawyers, however, as they were duty-bound to do, labored against all the odds (and most of the facts) to prepare a seamless story of innocence. It was a story shaped and supported by contemporary medicine, as Pomeroy's lawyers claimed that the boy suffered from "moral insanity." They focused on three elements of the crime: that it manifested his longstanding propensity toward cruelty, that it was utterly without motive, and that it was the irresistible result of a compulsion he could not control. These three claims formed the scaffold of the defense argument that Pomeroy was not guilty: Jesse Pomeroy was simply not responsible for killing four-year-old Horace Millen.

Murder in the First Degree

When the doors of the Supreme Judicial Court in Boston were thrown open at 9 a.m. on Tuesday, December 8, 1874, the *Globe* reported that there was "a large crowd in the corridors eager to gain admittance." Curious onlookers surged into a courtroom presided over by the chief justice of the state's Supreme Court, Horace Gray (who had been appointed just the year before), and associate justice Marcus Morton Jr. Representing the commonwealth were the state's attorney general himself, Charles R. Train, and the Suffolk County district attorney, John W. May. Pomeroy was defended by Charles Robinson Jr. and Joseph Cotton.[1]

45

To the horror of onlookers, and supporting his lawyers' defense of moral insanity, when the brutal crimes with which Pomeroy was charged were read aloud in the packed courtroom, he "frequently found it difficult to restrain his laughter, and his face throughout gave evidence of a secret pleasure."[2] A jury of Boston men was soon assembled, and they took their seats in front of a large map of the areas of South Boston that were to feature in the narrative about the murder.[3] In short order, the prosecution opened its case, arguing quite simply that Pomeroy was depraved. Their straightforward case was certainly aided by the fact that Pomeroy's lawyers never contested that Pomeroy had killed Horace Millen. The question became solely one of assessing his state of mind and thus his culpability: Was he sane or insane? The prosecution argued that the very facts of the crime formed a prima facie case of intent and thus guilt. And so District Attorney May, in his opening statement, declared that what the jury had before them was a case of murder in the first degree, with clear evidence of "premeditation and malice aforethought."[4]

The prosecution then went on to demonstrate what everyone already seemed to take for granted: that Pomeroy brutally killed Millen. Particularly compelling pieces of evidence were plaster casts of boot prints taken at the scene, which police testified matched the boots taken from Pomeroy "exactly." Dr. Ira Allen, the coroner at the inquest into Millen's death, testified that the pocket knife Pomeroy had acknowledged as his own was stained with something that "very strongly resembled blood." (Another doctor was called later to testify that he had also examined the knife, and he too "was of the opinion" that it was indeed stained with blood.) Other witnesses came forward, of varying reliability. A neighbor of the Millens, Mrs. Eleanor Fosdick, testified to looking from her window at around eleven on the morning Horace Millen was murdered and seeing Pomeroy waiting around, looking "nervous and excited," and then following the small boy around the corner. A couple of other witnesses claimed to have seen Pomeroy and Millen together that morning; the most direct and compelling evidence was that of fifteen-year-old Robert Benson, who said he saw Pomeroy lift Millen over a creek on the marsh, close to where Millen's body was later found. Indeed, Benson's had been the most persuasive testimony at the inquest into Millen's death several months earlier, when he recounted that he "saw Pomeroy and Millen together within ten minutes' walk of the scene of the murder, and described quite minutely how they were dressed and what they were doing." Benson identified Pomeroy by the "white spot on his right eye."[5] A police officer then testified to a long scratch on Pomeroy's face, as well as "other marks of violence on different portions of the face, all evidently new and fresh," statements that confirmed the coroner's conclusion that little Horace Millen had struggled with his attacker.

Most damningly, the prosecution produced Pomeroy's own confession, written in July of that year, shortly after Katie Curran's body was discovered in the Pomeroys' cellar. The chaplain of the jail, Rufus R. Cooke, testified that the confession was written by Pomeroy "of his own free will while in his cell, and given up without any reluctance, the only condition being that he [Cooke] would keep it from the papers." (Not surprisingly, Cooke seems to have immediately sent it to the *Globe* where it was, in short order, reproduced.) As much as Pomeroy's confession appeared to make his guilt indisputable, it should have raised doubts about the prosecution's claim that the boy displayed "premeditation and forethought." Pomeroy wrote that he had no intention of hurting or killing anyone until the *very moment* he saw Millen in the street, that "the nefarious plan entered his head on the instant he beheld the boy." He also said that something prompted him to turn back, but that something else "seemed to draw him on and 'he had to go'"—not exactly unambiguous evidence of careful planning.[6] There is no indication, however, that the prosecutors addressed this apparent inconsistency in their narrative about the murder. With the reading of Pomeroy's confession, the prosecutors rested their case at some point in the late afternoon of the first day, apparently satisfied their case was airtight.

As the day waned, the defense offered its opening statement. Charles Robinson began by "virtually admitting the truth of the indictment" but immediately adducing extenuating circumstances. He began with Pomeroy's age, noting that while children younger than seven are considered incapable of committing crime, the years between seven and fourteen are murky in terms of legal responsibility. They are "the debatable period, and no definite conclusion has as yet been reached." Pomeroy was, though, fourteen years and five months old when he killed Horace Millen, beyond even the outer edge of the "debatable period," and so, perhaps wisely, Robinson dropped the defense of Pomeroy's age right after he raised it.[7]

The principal thrust of Robinson's argument concerned Pomeroy's state of mind: the boy appeared completely bereft of the normal human emotions, felt no empathy, pity, or remorse, and reveled in brutality. Since his "infant years," Robinson argued, Pomeroy "had always shown peculiar tendencies toward blood and cruelty." Robinson then detailed precisely the events of Jesse's life that one would think any defense attorney would try desperately to hide. He laid out a chilling history, beginning at age five (age three in one account) when Jesse "was caught in the act of torturing a cat by stabbing and cutting it," adding that at school Jesse was "unmanageable," continuing through the litany of Pomeroy's acts of torture and the ensuing remand to reform school, and ending with the horrific mutilation and murder of Katie Curran and Horace Millen. "Taking all these facts into account," Robinson declared himself convinced that "only an insane person could be capable of doing the deeds which [have] been narrated."[8] Robinson's statement marks not the first but perhaps the most explicit and public linking of "insanity" with behavior that any "normal" person would find inexplicable. "Insanity" is manifestly conflated here with all that lies beyond the recognizably human; it is tantamount to a core of mystifying nonhumanity.

Robinson called numerous witnesses to bolster his story of Jesse's long-standing and unnatural propensity for cruelty. Ruth Pomeroy's testimony was central to this story, clearly designed to provide a physiological origin for Pomeroy's "insanity"—to ensure, in other words, that it conformed to the prevailing "disease" model of mental illness; after all, if the symptoms Jesse displayed were not the product of "disease," they were merely the manifestations of a bad character. No doubt alluding to her son's serious and prolonged reaction to a smallpox vaccination when he was a baby, Ruth testified that when Jesse was very young he had suffered "a violent attack of sickness, which almost reduced him to a skeleton." She added that much later, in April 1871 (the year he seemed to have begun torturing small boys), he had again been seriously ill—had been "out of his head" for two or three days and subject, ever since, to severe headaches, pains in his eyes, dizziness, and vivid, disturbing dreams.[9] Another account of Ruth's testimony is more specific, reporting that she claimed her son had been very sick with pneumonia (in August, not April, 1871), and that ever since "he has acted strangely and seemed to delight in human suffering." Ruth continued that her son "often imagined the most foolish things and would persist that they were true." He would talk to her of "imaginary things," which she called dreams.[10] In September 1872, Ruth had testified to the same pattern of symptoms before Judge Forsaith—saying that, just over a year before, her son had had a sickness with fever, had been "deranged" part of the time, and "was not so well and bright since this illness, as before," suffering from repeated headaches.[11]

If Ruth's testimony was accurate, Pomeroy's illness in the summer of 1871 did indeed predate by a few months his first documented act of torture. Her accounts of his dreams, or "imaginary things," moreover, which he appeared often to believe were real, formed something of a pattern with his crimes, which he often claimed were not real. For Pomeroy, the boundaries between the real and the imaginary were tenuous at best. One of the defense's medical experts testified, "He also said it seemed to him sometimes as if he did it, and sometimes as if he did not do it," adding, "There was a cloudiness about it in his mind."[12] Ruth Pomeroy's testimony, then, helped both to demonstrate her son's rather attenuated connection to reality and to give it a physiological basis.

Shortly after Ruth Pomeroy's testimony, the judge adjourned until the next day. At 9 a.m. on Wednesday, even more people tried to push into the crowded courtroom. It was the day on which the most important evidence on behalf of Pomeroy was offered.[13] Jurors and onlookers were positively regaled with instances of Jesse Pomeroy's depravity, all, paradoxically, offered with the intent of *exonerating* him of the charges against him. One former neighbor recalled Jesse's unspecified "violent actions," and another, Lucy Ann Kelly, recounted the infamous torture of the kitten: "When he was three years old, she caught him one day in the yard behind a pump, with a small kitten in his hands, which he had cut and stabbed in the throat and other parts of the body."[14] Another newspaper reported that Kelly testified to the kitten's having been cut in three places and recalled that Jesse had said to her that "he was playing with it, and that it was his little baby." Another neighbor described how, when Jesse was older, after his illness in the spring or summer of 1871, he had seemed "very wild" and wanted her to let her young son go out of town with him. Abbie M. Clark, who taught Jesse at the Winthrop School in Charlestown from 1870 to 1872 (during the time he engaged in serial torture), said that he had "a very peculiar and seemingly unaccountable proclivity for 'making faces,' also a tendency to annoy the other children." When she spoke to him about it, he always claimed "he couldn't help it." She punished him for the faces and other infractions, but he never seemed "penitent or sorrowful," always insisting that he was being "punished wrongfully."

Adding to the evidence of Pomeroy's longstanding proclivities and compulsions, not only did Robinson read the record of Pomeroy's examination before Judge Forsaith as a juvenile offender, but he called six of Pomeroy's torture victims to testify about their suffering at his hands (only Harry Austin did not appear at the trial). The boys must have made quite an impression. As the reporter for the *Globe* described the testimony of ten-year-old John Balch, "The little fellow gave his evidence with a clear, ringing voice, and on two or three occasions was almost choked with tears." Another boy, Joseph Kennedy, "occupied nearly an hour in describing the manner in which Pomeroy had punished him." This brutal testimony was, it is worth repeating, evidence for *the defense*.

Pomeroy's lawyers also unearthed the lone person who defied the reigning story that Jesse had behaved in an exemplary manner while at reform school. One of the teachers at Westborough, Laura Clark, told the court that on two occasions Jesse seemed "wild and excited," threatening those around him.[15] According to the *Herald's* account of her testimony, the first occasion was only two or three days after Pomeroy arrived. Clark came into the shop where Pomeroy was working and found a boy crying about something Pomeroy had done to him. When Clark confronted him, Pomeroy seized a knife and "appeared very much excited and crazy, and remarked that he was not afraid of anybody." The other occasion on which Pomeroy acted strangely, according to Clark, was when he killed a snake in the garden, something that seemed to give him "great delight"—and "he insisted upon stamping and beating it long after it was dead." The *Globe's* account of Clark's testimony described how Pomeroy "jumped upon [the snake] and mangled it in a fearful manner, all the time showing symptoms of a strange desire to shed blood." Robinson also tried, unsuccessfully, to introduce the testimony of an officer at the Charles Street Jail, where Jesse was being held, who was prepared to describe the boy's "indifference and want of feeling." After "a long debate between the lawyers," the judge ruled, however, that such after-the-fact evidence was irrelevant to Pomeroy's state of mind when he committed the murder.[16]

The second day of trial also saw medical experts take the stand. The two physicians who spoke in Pomeroy's defense, Dr. John E. Tyler and Dr. Clement Walker, helped to frame the disturbing details of Jesse's life within a legitimating narrative of disease.[17] Tyler, who had worked at the nearby McLean Asylum for thirteen years and who had visited Pomeroy in jail at least twice (in September and October), and perhaps as many as four or five times, claimed that insanity was clearly indicated in Jesse's case by the boy's headaches, "the extraordinariness of the acts," his "desire for blood and other strange proclivities," and by the "utter insensibility of the accused to the consequences of his acts." Walker, who had headed the Boston Lunatic Hospital for twenty-three years, likewise claimed that he believed Pomeroy was insane because of "the extraordinary number and nature of the crimes with which he was charged," as well as his utter moral insensibility: he "showed not a particle of pity or remorse" and "he had no visible sign of any such thing as moral responsibility, and seemed dead to all the finer emotions which are met in sane persons." Both Tyler and Walker initially suggested that Pomeroy might have been suffering from epilepsy; aside from his frequent headaches, the boy told Tyler that before he committed his "terrible deeds," he usually felt "a pressure on his head, which started about the region of his chest, and passed over or through his brain."[18]

Tyler and Walker stressed the possibility of epilepsy significantly less than the striking fact of Pomeroy's affect, however. It was the boy's complete insensibility, his absence of all emotions such as empathy, remorse, and guilt, and his reiterated claims that he was compelled to do what he did, that garnered their interest. (Indeed, Tyler later rejected his initial diagnosis of epilepsy.) In focusing on Pomeroy's strange lack of affect, both physicians put front and center the defendant's "moral insanity."

By 1874, the designation "moral insanity" had a lengthy genealogy and carried increasing weight in the medical and legal professions in both Europe and the United States. The disorder was first described in the work of a French physician, Philippe Pinel, in the early 1800s and was subsequently developed by Jean-Étienne Esquirol in France, James Cowles Prichard in England, and Isaac Ray in the United States—all of whom were reading, and were profoundly influenced by, each other's work. In his groundbreaking *Treatise on Insanity* (1835), the English physician James Prichard was the first to transform "moral insanity" from a marginal to an accepted (albeit perennially contested) psychiatric term, and he formulated its authoritative definition. Moral insanity, Prichard wrote, was "madness consisting in a morbid perversion of the natural feelings, affections, inclinations, temper, habits, moral dispositions, and natural impulses, without any remarkable disorder of the intellect or knowing or reasoning faculties, and particularly without any insane illusion or hallucination."[19] The key parts of this definition were the perverted "natural feelings" and the lack of any derangement of the reasoning powers—in particular, the absence of delusion or hallucination: a person could appear sane, in other words, could reason correctly, and could even apprehend the difference between right and wrong, and yet still be "insane." Prichard pointed out, moreover, the tendency of the morally insane toward motiveless violence, arguing that their malignity could make them appear as if "possessed by the demon of evil."[20] Prichard's influential description of the morally insane certainly seemed tailor-made to Jesse Pomeroy's compulsion toward blood and cruelty and his apparently complete inability to feel empathy, remorse, or pity.

The defense no doubt realized, though, the dangers of equating "moral insanity" and "moral perversion"—a strategy that could easily be viewed as denying evil, turning it into excusable insanity. An editorial published in the *Boston Daily Advertiser* the summer before the trial voiced what was undoubtedly the opinion of many when it protested "the morbid and dangerous sentiment that the horrible nature of his crimes must itself be taken as a proof of insanity."[21] Pomeroy's lawyers therefore tried not to rely exclusively on the symptoms of "moral perversion" as they made the case that Pomeroy was insane. They also emphasized the boy's *lack of motive* and the corollary inexplicable *compulsion* that, by his own account, drove him. In other words, they stressed what was called by doctors and lawyers an "irresistible impulse"—a symptom of moral insanity that was particularly associated with the work of the American physician Isaac Ray. In his influential *Treatise on the Medical Jurisprudence of Insanity* (1838), Ray described what he called "moral mania"—identical to Prichard's moral insanity.[22] Like Prichard, Ray insisted that moral insanity could drive its sufferers to commit violent acts against the dictates of reason and will.[23] For Ray, "irresistible impulse" was central to moral mania: he described the "simplest form of homicidal insanity" as that in which "the desire to destroy life is prompted by no motive whatever, but solely by an irresistible impulse, without any appreciable disorder of mind or body." Cases of homicidal mania, he wrote, "all possess one feature in common, the irresistible motiveless impulse to destroy life."[24] Even more, perhaps, than Prichard's perversion of the "natural feelings," Ray's "irresistible motiveless impulse" described Jesse Pomeroy's crimes.

Dr. Tyler crucially testified for the defense that when he asked Pomeroy about why he tortured and killed, Pomeroy said " 'I had to,' 'I had to,' as if there was an influence which he could not resist bearing upon his mind."[25] From these inarticulate phrases emerged a complex defense of insanity involving both the absence of an understandable motive and the claim that Pomeroy was *compelled* to crime. That Pomeroy was driven by an irresistible and unknowable impulse had shadowed every instance in which he was asked to explain himself. As we've seen, in his examination of Pomeroy in September 1872, Judge Forsaith directly asked him why he had beaten and mutilated his victims, and Pomeroy replied only that "he did not know," and again at the inquest into the death of Katie Curran in July 1874, Police Chief Savage testified that when asked why he killed Katie, Pomeroy said only, "I do not know why I did it; I couldn't help doing it."[26] We've seen too that Jesse told the same story to his lawyer Joseph Cotton, who testified about the interview at the inquest: "On being asked why he did the deed," Cotton said, Pomeroy replied, "'I do not know; I couldn't help it; it is here,' accompanying the word 'here' with a gesture indicating it was in his head." Jesse was "of the opinion," Cotton continued, "that, when he grew to be a man, he could resist the temptation to do such bloody deeds, but at present the temptation was too strong for him."[27] The next day, the *Globe* reported that Pomeroy had also, finally, confessed to killing Horace Millen, and that the "young murderer gives the same reason for committing this deed as he did for killing Katie Curran, 'that he could not help it.'"[28]

At Pomeroy's murder trial, the defense used these baffling statements as evidence that the boy was not responsible for his actions, convinced, as Isaac Ray had articulated it, that both the lack of a motive and the presence of an irresistible impulse were strong indications of insanity. Dr. Tyler testified that Pomeroy had "none of the ordinary motives that exist as inducements to crime" and that the boy said "I had to do it," and thus "there seemed to be 'an impulse'" Dr. Walker likewise noted "the apparent want of ordinary motive for the commission of [Pomeroy's acts of cruelty]" and further stated that "the apparent want of any purpose . . . would, in my mind, raise a suggestion of insanity."[29]

In his closing argument, on the third and last day of the trial, Pomeroy's lawyer relied on the expert testimony of Tyler and Walker when he claimed that the "pivot" on which the defense of insanity hinged "was the want of motive to impel the boy to the commission of his deeds of atrocity." He repeated part of Pomeroy's confession about killing Horace Millen (the part that should have been a sticking point in the prosecution's charge of premeditation): that while he was walking along with Millen, he felt he should turn back, "but was again impelled by some unaccountable and irresistible impulse to go on and commit the murder."[30] Robinson's defense narrative stressed that Pomeroy "cannot control himself," reiterating that there is "not a power in him by which he can control his actions, or control those impulses, when those impulses come over him." When taken with the fact that there was no motive at all for what Jesse Pomeroy did,

Robinson insisted that there could be no alternative but to conclude that "he is not a being responsible. In other words, it comes within the language of the statute that he is an insane person."[31]

Medical opinion about Pomeroy was by no means undivided, however, and after the two physicians testified in Pomeroy's defense on the second day of the trial, an equally reputable physician testified for the prosecution. Dr. George Choate, superintendent of the Massachusetts State Lunatic Asylum for seventeen years and in private practice in New York at the time of the trial, testified that his two interviews with Pomeroy in October had convinced him that the killing of Horace Millen was "not the result of insanity, at least of the ordinary kind." Choate focused on Pomeroy's intellectual capacity, saying he was "apt to learn and to retain knowledge," including knowledge of his own legal situation. Pomeroy apparently told Choate that he knew he had done wrong but that the authorities of Massachusetts would not hang him "as he was too young."[32] Choate also reported that Pomeroy had told him he wished he could get a particular lawyer (whom he had read about) for his defense, since he was "the best counsel in such a case, and had been very successful recently in other trials."[33] As others had discovered before him, Choate also found that Pomeroy completely changed his story from one interview to the next. At first the boy admitted his guilt to Choate, but, at the second interview, he denied his earlier confession "and made other contradictory assertions which," Choate believed, "were evidently the result of education on the subject." Choate declared he was not at all convinced that the boy suffered from "irresistible impulse," and that he would need to see "more palpable signs and evidence of mental disease." Like many experts and lay people alike, Choate believed that without tangible signs of disease, Pomeroy's "condition" seemed more akin to depravity than insanity.[34] With these damning words, the witness testimony ended and the court adjourned for the day.

The third and last day of the trial began with closing arguments. Pomeroy's lawyer highlighted, not surprisingly, the defendant's lack of motive, his compulsion, and his consequent insanity. Indeed, Robinson seems quite clearly to argue that Pomeroy *must be* insane because nobody could be so vicious as to brutalize a little boy intentionally: insanity became the mark of the unthinkable and the inhuman. Robinson even argued that the Commonwealth of Massachusetts, in particular, could never birth a "boy fiend" who would *willingly* enact such violence.[35] Robinson asked the jury, in short, to contemplate the "unseen and inexplicable power" that drove Jesse Pomeroy to brutal violence and to call it insanity, *not* a consciously embraced and purposeful cruelty bred in an unexceptional Boston family. By framing Pomeroy's crimes as the product of disease, Robinson cordoned them off from the healthy and rational body (both human and political), decreeing the boy an utter aberration from the "norm."[36]

As Train took up the closing for the prosecution, he quickly moved to explain away the principal weakness of their case, one that had loomed from the beginning: the difficulty of proving Pomeroy's forethought. Train declared that the "premeditation" with which Pomeroy was charged did not mean that the murder must have been "determined upon for any great length of time, but only that the will of the perpetrator be under his control, and that he was a free agent." He as good as conflated premeditation with both intent and responsibility, three concepts that should have retained a measure of autonomy. Train claimed not only that as long as an intent was willfully formed, no matter how fleetingly, then premeditation was present, but also that as long as the defendant was sane (a "free agent"), as presumed by law, then premeditation was present. There was no room in this definition for an actor to be "sane" and *not* to have predetermined his act. Train thus compelled the jury to presume premeditation if they ascertained Pomeroy to be "sane."

Train then spent some time interpreting Pomeroy's words and acts as evidence of "shrewdness"—a word he used more than once and which was obviously designed to combat the defense's language of compulsion. In fact, he declared that Pomeroy's actions and utterances "clearly established mental capacities of more than ordinary force: and shrewdness which is not often met in boys of his age and education." Train interpreted the many contradictions and reversals Pomeroy engaged in as evidence of his command of his legal situation and of his ability to manipulate others to further his own interests. Train tackled the defense's expert witnesses last, questioning their interpretation of the boy's actions and pointing out that under cross-examination both Tyler and Walker had admitted that what Pomeroy did was also consistent with a "theory of sanity." Tyler and Walker simply took "a series of sane acts," Train concluded, and "constructed therefrom a proof of insanity." Train did not attack the two physicians, who were inarguably reputable men, but he did shift their testimony from the realm of fact to the realm of interpretation, thus permitting, even encouraging, the jury to make their own assessment.

After the lawyers rested their cases, Chief Justice Gray delivered his charge to the jury. It is very hard not to read this charge as sympathetic to the prosecution, and the defense lawyers must have been in quiet agony as it was being imparted.[37] Gray first instructed the jury on the charge of first-degree murder, which, he said, was indeed defined by *any* amount of premeditation, no matter how fleeting. He stated that the law did not prescribe any time limit to premeditation, did not specify how much time was necessary for a defendant to have "premeditated." He said only that a crime must have been "thought upon long enough" so that "it can be said, reasonably, to have been purposed." This definition didn't absolutely conflate premeditation and intention, as Train's had, but it came close— suggesting that the defendant might have anticipated a crime and framed a purpose in a matter of only seconds before its commission. Gray went on to make it clear, though, that under Massachusetts law it was not necessary to show premeditation in order to convict Jesse Pomeroy of first-degree murder. The jurors could render a verdict of first-degree murder if they only ascertained that the murder of Millen involved "circumstances of extreme atrocity and cruelty." And what "extreme atrocity and cruelty" meant was up to the jury to decide. Gray thus effectively swept the question of premeditation (which the prosecution had struggled to prove) off the table: the jury could convict Pomeroy for first-degree murder if they decided the act was "atrocious" and "cruel"—regardless of whether he planned the crime or not.

As far as Pomeroy's capacity went, Gray quickly dismissed the suggestion that Pomeroy's youth was relevant. A boy of fourteen, he said, was responsible "to the same degree as an adult person." The principal issue, Gray pointed out, was whether Pomeroy was "of sufficient mental capacity to be held criminally responsible for his acts." As he addressed this question, he undercut the defense's position in two principal ways. He warned the jury away from total reliance on the expert testimony of the physicians, as Train had done, declaring that while they certainly may see "symptoms which an ordinary observer would not notice," they can also "get into the way of looking too much for evidence to support their own theories." Of course the physicians involved in the case were not the only ones who were potentially biased by their own professional preconceptions, their "own theories," when they confronted Jesse Pomeroy. Chief Justice Gray himself (who had been practicing law for over twenty years) demonstrated a great deal of skepticism about the medical complexities of Pomeroy's alleged insanity and was clearly influenced by a longstanding (and very narrow) *legal* tradition of conceptualizing guilt and excuse.

While Pomeroy's defense lawyers (and their supporting physicians) had placed roughly equal emphasis on Pomeroy's "irresistible impulse" and on his consistent moral perversion as evidence of his disease, Gray's summation of the defense's argument in his charge to the jury generally ignored the "moral perversion" argument and addressed only the "irresistible impulse" that allegedly overcame the boy. "It is said that the defendant was under an irresistible impulse," Gray intoned, continuing that Pomeroy's defense, "as we understand it, is based upon this position: that the prisoner was capable of understanding the difference between right and wrong; that he knew that his acts were wrong at the time when he did them, but that, to use his own expression, he had to do those things,—he could not help it; there was something, there was an overpowering insane impulse that drove him to do these things." Gray quoted his predecessor Chief Justice Lemuel Shaw (in the landmark case of Abner Rogers, heard before the Supreme Court of Massachusetts in 1844) on the point that "irresistible and uncontrollable impulse" excuses to the extent that it is able to demonstrate that the mind was "in a diseased and unsound state." Gray's sympathies for this defense did not extend very far, however, as he also pointed out that " 'I had to do it' is a very old defence of wrongdoers," akin to "The devil tempted me." Gray's reading of "irresistible impulse" opens it up to diametrically opposed meanings: the overpowering impulse could be the symptom of disease, but it could also be the sign of sin and thus guilt. With that, Gray left it up to the jury to decide whether Jesse Pomeroy's overwhelming, inexplicable impulse to torture and kill was the mark of disease or the devil.

The case went to the jury at 5:50 p.m. on Thursday, December 10. While some of the spectators initially dispersed, they began amassing again at around 7:30, clearly expecting a relatively short deliberation.[38] There was a "general buzz" about the possible verdict. Every movement in the corridors "created a corresponding sensation in the court room," and there were a few false alarms that inflamed the already "excitable feelings" of the audience. At 8:20 a representative of the jury did emerge, but only to ask for clarification on two points. First, he asked whether the killing was premeditated if Pomeroy had taken Millen to the marshes with the intent only to torture him, but then had "concluded at the last moment to kill him." He also asked whether the jury could convict of first-degree murder if they determined the crime was indeed "atrocious and cruel," but not premeditated. Judge Gray told them, in response to the first question, that, as he had stressed in his closing, premeditated action could be "almost momentary"—that is, it took only a moment to form a premeditated intention to kill. The second question, Gray responded, was clearly covered by statute: a homicide need only be *either* premeditated *or* atrocious and cruel to be considered first-degree murder. Both of the foreman's questions suggest that the jurors had been debating the question of premeditation, but then had come to wonder if such a discussion was even relevant given the quite clearly "atrocious and cruel" circumstances of the murder.

The jurors went back to deliberating, armed with Gray's responses, and it is clear that they were taking their role seriously, struggling to understand both Pomeroy's state of mind when he killed Millen and the requirements of the law. After four hours and twenty minutes, at 10:10 p.m., they emerged. In a "clear, firm voice," while looking directly at Pomeroy, the foreman announced that their verdict was "murder in the first degree." At the reading of the verdict, "an involuntary exclamation of surprise and horror ran through the crowd," although it was "quickly suppressed." Pomeroy sat down with "stolid indifference." One reporter noted that he seemed so "careless and indifferent" that it was difficult to tell if he actually understood the verdict. "He made not the slightest motion, showing either absolute stupidity or a hardness and stubbornness that was aggravating to witness." The boy's mother, however, who sat a few benches away, was rendered "almost insensible." Her "stifled heart-broken sobs mingled painfully with the buzz of excitement that came from the crowd."[39]

The jury then gave the judge two documents, one of which was signed by the foreman explaining that their verdict of first-degree murder was based on the "acts of atrocity" that accompanied the murder and, significantly, was "apart from premeditated malice aforethought." The second document, signed by all the jurors, requested that the punishment of death be commuted to life imprisonment "on account of [Pomeroy's] youth."[40] The judge said that he would submit the second document to the governor and his council. Significantly, Massachusetts at this time did not allow the courts alone to determine death penalty cases. The death warrant, which necessarily followed on a first-degree murder conviction, had to be signed by the governor, guided by the advice of his council. While the trial was over, then, the most important decision—whether to execute Jesse Pomeroy—now lay in the hands of Democratic governor William Gaston, who would take office on January 7 of the coming year. Gaston's political career was, by most accounts, about to be ruined by Jesse Pomeroy, whose case would soon be dubbed "the most dreaded issue in Massachusetts politics."[41]

To Hang or Not?

Everyone in Boston, it seemed, had an opinion about whether or not Jesse Pomeroy should hang. Editorials sprang up by the hundreds. Regular people furiously penned letters to newspapers, signed petitions, and formed committees to meet with the governor. As the *Boston Daily Advertiser* editorialized, "It is a long time since the fate of a criminal has caused such profound feeling in this community as has been excited by the case of the young felon, Jesse Pomeroy." Opinions on the commutation question were divided and passionate, and there was no middle ground. As the *New York Times* aptly declared in 1875, the Pomeroy case "presented the singular spectacle of a great community divided into two parts, the one urging and the other deprecating the execution of a duly-convicted murderer."[42] The battle over Pomeroy's punishment was not only virulent but long: in the end, it would be waged for almost two years.

Famous Bostonians were not slow to weigh in. Francis Parkman, the well-known historian and author of *The Oregon Trail,* signed a petition unconditionally demanding the boy's execution.[43] A petition from mothers urging that Pomeroy be hanged featured the names of what one letter dubbed the "most refined and cultivated ladies of our city": Mrs. Charles Sumner, Mrs. S. Parkman, Mrs. R. H. Dana, Jr., Mrs. George Lowell, Mrs. Edward B. Everett, Mrs. George Ticknor, and Mrs. Augustus Lowell.[44] The popular writer Mary Abigail Dodge (under her pen name, Gail Hamilton) argued fiercely for Pomeroy's execution. Henry James Sr., father of the novelist, was one of the few to remain neutral, but argued that if Pomeroy were to be put to death, it should be by chloroform, not barbarous hanging.[45] Wendell Phillips, the famous Boston lawyer and former staunch abolitionist (who had been indicted in 1854 for trying to free the fugitive slave Anthony Burns from his jail cell), visited Governor Gaston to plead for Pomeroy's life. And the physician, professor, and writer Oliver Wendell Holmes Sr. signed a petition urging that the boy be imprisoned for life, not hanged.[46]

"Hang him!"

In what had to be one of the most spectacularly inaccurate predictions swirling around Pomeroy, the editors of the *Springfield Republican* wrote in early 1874, in the immediate aftermath of Horace Millen's murder, "We cannot suppose that any voices will answer, 'Hang him!'" in response to the question, "What shall be done with him?"[47] As it turned out, very many voices answered exactly that—and loudly.

The most vociferous of those who cried "Hang him!" were mothers, many of them claiming that they had been prompted, sometimes unwillingly, to enter the public realm for the first time out of an inescapable sense of duty.[48] They were all motivated, as they repeatedly put it, by the urge to protect their homes and children. As early as March 12, 1875, reports circulated that at least three hundred South Boston women had petitioned Governor Gaston not to commute Pomeroy's sentence.[49] As the *Globe* reported, the "women who petitioned for this young criminal's execution were for the most part mothers," prompted to take action because Pomeroy had made "helpless and unprotected children" his victims. The *Advertiser* wrote that the mothers of South Boston saw Pomeroy as a "test case," feeling that, until now, "great criminals, who prey upon innocent children and upon the peace and happiness of families, have not been pursued and punished as they deserve."[50] The execution of Pomeroy, these women felt, was, "the only assurance [mothers] can have of the protection of their own children, and the security of their own homes."[51] The draft of one petition from "mothers" offered a heartfelt plea: "If murderers are to escape the penalty due their crimes, what mother knows what sight may greet her eyes in her own cellar, on her next return home?"[52] Jesse Pomeroy was a malign and predatory threat to the home, and while the occasional mother might urge the governor to mercy, most were set against it.

Gaston must certainly have felt besieged by the mothers of Boston. On March 19, 1875, about twenty-five ladies of Chelsea and South Boston visited the governor and "urged upon him the necessity for Jesse Pomeroy's execution."[53] Gaston wasn't alone; over a year later, in May 1876, after Gaston had been voted out (in part because of his inaction in the Pomeroy case) and Alexander Rice had been in office for four months, the *Globe* announced ominously that a "committee" of mothers was "planning a campaign" to influence Rice.[54] Wives and mothers sent a multitude of petitions to both governors demanding execution of the law. A petition from "the ladies of Chelsea" opposing commutation of the death sentence was signed by 153 people, and it makes a point of noting Pomeroy's "career of unparalled [*sic*] cruelty." A second petition from the "Ladies and citizens of Chelsea" had 114 signatures, a third from the "ladies and parents of

Chelsea" had 127 signatures, and a petition from the "wives, mothers and daughters of East Boston," protesting any effort at commutation, had 219 signatures.[55] The *Advertiser* reported on and even reprinted other petitions, including two from "mothers," noting that the governor has received "a large number of petitions," and that if the sentence were to be commuted, it would be in the face of "one of the most powerful protests that was ever sent to the executive council."[56]

The watchword for the mothers of Boston was "protection"—and they thus participated in shaping what was, in the words of the historian Larry Sullivan, the "primary aim of punishment" in the 1870s.[57] And Boston's mothers were by no means the only people making this particular argument. While most physicians who entered the fray urged that Pomeroy's life be spared, the leading medical journal in Boston consistently argued for the boy's execution on the grounds that the community needed to be safeguarded from his depredations: "It is necessary to protect the public against this monster," wrote Dr. J. Collins Warren and Dr. Thomas Dwight, the editors of the *Boston Medical and Surgical Journal,* adding that there "is no place but the grave from which silly and reckless sentimentalists will be unable to free him."[58] Indeed, throughout the execution controversy, the editors of the *BMSJ* never missed a chance to denounce the "philanthropist," the "sentimental philanthropist," and the "sentimentalist" who would undoubtedly agitate to get Pomeroy's sentence commuted the moment he was spared execution.[59] After all, Pomeroy had been let loose on the community once before by such sentimentalists—and those who advocated execution in order to protect the community warned frequently of the hordes of misguided philanthropists in New England, all ready to loose "the monster" once again on the helpless community.[60]

The claim that only Pomeroy's hanging would fully safeguard society overlapped with the second principal argument for the boy's execution: deterrence. Commentators disagreed, as they do today, about the deterrent power of execution; some asserted that the death penalty discouraged crime, while others insisted that not only did it not deter crime, but that it may well increase its prevalence with its potentially contagious brutality.[61] In the Pomeroy case, most of those who joined the debate argued that hanging did deter crime—and many of those opinions were no doubt inflamed by what ended up being some of Pomeroy's most notorious words. At the murder trial, the medical expert for the prosecution, Dr. George Choate, had testified to Pomeroy's confident assertion that the commonwealth would never hang a boy of fourteen. These words were paraphrased, quoted, and misquoted in countless letters and editorials during the furor surrounding Pomeroy's punishment, and almost all of them asserted the deterrent power of hanging. Because Pomeroy knew his youth was a "protection," wrote the *Globe*, he "persisted in the commission of these atrocious acts." A letter to the same newspaper claimed that Pomeroy "looked upon the result of his crimes with composure, because 'they never hang boys in Massachusetts.'" And another letter began with Pomeroy's words that "they would not hang a boy like him," before arguing that if the commonwealth *did* hang every boy "of his stamp," his crimes would "never be repeated."[62]

Pomeroy's complacency spurred calls not only for a punishment that was immediate and inexorable, but also one equivalent to the harshness of the crime itself. The *Globe* editorialized that it was precisely the "ignominy and suffering" of hanging that allowed it to work "more powerfully as a deterrent." Hanging, the editors of the *Advertiser* agreed, has as its principle "the only motive, that of fear, which has ever been found sufficiently powerful to restrain selfishness and cruelty." We punish through "the motive of corporeal fear," they declared. It was no doubt in the spirit of inducing "corporeal fear" that the *Globe* reported in detail on the grisly hanging of a murderer named Samuel J. Frost in Worcester, who was executed on the same day (May 26, 1876) that Pomeroy's fellow prisoner Thomas Piper was hanged in the Charles Street Jail. As Frost dropped from the platform with the noose around his neck, his body was ripped almost entirely away from his head. From "the fearful rent in the throat," reported the *Globe*, "the life blood gushed and spurted in jets with each pulsation of the heart," spraying "as if from a fountain," flowing "over the body," and pouring "into a large pool beneath the feet."[63] Since hangings were no longer public spectacles, and were barred to all but a select few, newspapers took it upon themselves to instill, through their florid descriptions, the salutary "corporeal fear" of the state execution.[64] Of course, it was precisely such portrayals that served as fodder to those who argued that the death penalty actually incited violence.[65]

While such bloody descriptions may arguably have deterred potential criminals, they without a doubt supported arguments that the death penalty was not only unnecessarily cruel but also a residual form of an obsolescent barbaric and despotic rule of law. Such arguments had flourished in America since the late eighteenth century, and by the 1870s proponents of hanging were under increasing pressure to make the case that execution served a salutary function that compensated for its brutality. Thus, as the historian David Garland writes, in mid-nineteenth-century America, "for the first time the death penalty came to be represented as a humanitarian institution." Garland writes that the "executioner took lives in order to save lives," and that what had once been "the savage will of the sovereign" had become "a means of social welfare." To equate death with social welfare was, to say the least, counterintuitive—although all those who argued for Pomeroy's hanging as a means to protect the community clearly embraced (or ignored) this paradox. Nonetheless, as Garland points out, the death penalty was becoming increasingly "surrounded by anxiety and embarrassment."[66] The frequent bloodthirstiness of many of those who agitated for Pomeroy's hanging (one letter claimed that he should be "fastened to an iron ring and four horses would pull off his arms and limbs while a fifth would run away with the head") only intensified this anxiety.[67]

In truth, unease over the brutality of execution in a "civilized" commonwealth may well have been one of the forces behind the shaping of Jesse Pomeroy as a "monster." As Garland aptly notes, "To see hanged men or women as human was to create a friction between capital punishment and modern liberal culture. Rendering them monstrous served to reduce dissonance and lubricate the machinery of death."[68] Since upstanding citizens of Massachusetts did not (unlike vicious criminals) kill other humans, when those same upstanding citizens actually needed to engage in (state-sanctioned) murder, those they killed, the argument went, must not be properly human. Indeed, the ethicist Judith Kay has argued that one of the principal myths propping up the death penalty even today is that which designates certain people "monsters"—freaks, deformities of nature: "This goes beyond the fact that some people act abominably," she writes, "to the claim that they are abominable by nature."[69] There were certainly many people of the opinion that Pomeroy was a monster by nature, and the step to demands for his execution was then a short one. "We doubt whether there is any hope of reforming such a moral monster," one editorial declared, asserting that Pomeroy should never have been born and that it is "better now if he were put forever beyond the power of crime." Another editorial concluded that while it may appear "dreadful" to advocate for the execution of "such a monster" as Pomeroy, there are, nonetheless, "monsters so wild they ought not to live." And one of Boston's notable ministers, the Reverend Cyrus Bartol, proclaimed from the pulpit that Pomeroy was "a monster to be killed on the spot, if only so it can be kept from killing or defiling."[70] The boy's status as nonhuman legitimated his destruction as not only a *humane* act but also as a means to protect what was properly *human*.

Unease over the barbarism of the death penalty was also allayed when proponents of Pomeroy's execution represented him as an animal, which was, like the monstrous, beyond the pale of the human. An editorial in the *New York World* declared that the "responsibility of putting [Pomeroy] to death is neither more nor less than putting a mad dog out of the way."[71] The influential New York physician Dr. William Hammond was quoted approvingly in his declaration that "where a human being is so insane as to be dangerous as a wild beast, he should be treated as a wild beast." His "extirpation," Hammond argued, "like that of all noxious pests, is demanded by the law of common safety."[72] One Bostonian who was slated to testify in favor of hanging at a hearing before the governor and his council in April 1875 wrote to the *Globe* that Pomeroy was akin to a "wolf" lying in ambush, or to any other "dangerous animal." He must be promptly dispatched, not pondered over.[73] Within the debate over his punishment, then, commentators deployed the idea of Jesse Pomeroy as some kind of monster or animal—all in an effort to justify the persistence of hanging within a liberal, humanitarian state. Such a state only hangs humans when they are *not* "human," the logic went, when they are, as the *Advertiser* wrote of Pomeroy, a "cruel and murderous animal in human form."[74] While a civilized state might demur at hanging a "human," it could have no compunction about exterminating an animal.

A "fault which is his fate"

There was, of course, at least one stark logical flaw in the pro-execution argument. Advocates of hanging frequently argued that Jesse Pomeroy was both entirely culpable for his crimes *and* an inhuman monster or animal. To be held responsible for one's actions, however, one must be a rational human. One Boston physician, Dr. Theodore Fisher, who interviewed Pomeroy in jail and staunchly opposed his execution, astutely pointed out this contradiction. Responsibility, Fisher pointed out, necessarily indicated free will and was thus incompatible with the status of "monster" or "animal": "The press speaks of the actor [Pomeroy] as a fiend, a brute, a moral monster rather than a human being," he wrote, "but inconsistently term the acts of such an actor crimes."[75] If Pomeroy was in fact not human, as many argued, then he should not be punished *as* a human. If he were a "brute," his acts would by definition not be "crimes," which demanded "human" qualities such as intention, consciousness, and volition.

It was not surprising, then, that the loudest voices opposed to Pomeroy's hanging came from those who insisted he was not responsible for his crimes; they did not deem him an "animal," however, but a victim of insanity.[76] Certainly the majority of physicians who pronounced on the case believed that Pomeroy's mind was diseased. A letter to the *Advertiser* claimed that of the twenty-one men who had passed judgment "officially" on the question of Pomeroy's punishment, only five had argued that he should hang; the other sixteen thought he should be imprisoned for life.[77] At the hearing before Governor Gaston and his council in April 1875, four physicians spoke in favor of commuting Pomeroy's sentence, while none advocated his execution. All four of those physicians—John Tyler, Clement Walker (both of whom also testified at Pomeroy's murder trial), Theodore Fisher, and Norton Folsom—argued that Pomeroy was suffering from some sort of moral, impulsive, or emotional insanity at the time he killed Katie Curran and Horace Millen.[78] Such opinions traveled from experts into the wider population, and Pomeroy's insanity (often broadly termed "monomania") also featured in the arguments of numerous lay people. A local attorney named Max Fischacher, for instance, wrote an impassioned letter to the *Globe* arguing that there was something "exceedingly abnormal" about Pomeroy and that all evidence tended to support his diagnosis as a "monomaniac." Fischacher quoted from Isaac Ray's *Medical Jurisprudence of Insanity* to support his claim that what appeared as Jesse Pomeroy's "cunning" was actually a common symptom of madness. To hang Pomeroy, Fischacher concluded, would be to ignore the truths of science and accede to distracting emotional appeals about imperiled children.[79]

To say that Pomeroy was insane was to argue that he had little to no control over his actions. While advocates of hanging typically emphasized a very intentional evil, then, proponents of commuting Pomeroy's sentence argued for his lack of choice over what he did and even who he was. He should not be punished, the *Springfield Republican* argued, for "a fault which is his fate." Pomeroy "is not so by choice," claimed a letter to the *Advertiser*.[80] Most believed that Pomeroy's "fate" was inherited. It is clear, asserted one letter-writer, that the boy "inherits the infirmities of one or more of his ancestors. Is he accountable for that? Most surely not."[81] A physician far removed from Boston, Mrs. Laura A. Leonora Hooker from Decatur, Michigan, felt compelled to write directly to Governor Gaston in a letter dated April 22, 1875, expressly to make the case that no child should suffer death "for that which has been forced upon them in antenatal life." A letter to the *Globe* several months later made the same argument: we are all, the writer argued, shaped by influences that are "ante-natal as well as post-natal," and there is no doubt that "we inherit from our progenitors certain aptitudes and tendencies" that "make us what we are."[82] Such arguments drew on prevailing late nineteenth-century beliefs about the crucial role of inherited characteristics in shaping personality, but when extended too far they began to threaten those reigning institutions that adjudicated and punished crime: they could, after all, lead to the claim that *no one* was responsible for what he or she did.[83]

Despite their greater compassion for Pomeroy's unchosen "fate," however, many of those opposed to the boy's hanging offered the same pronouncements about his monstrosity and animality as those who wanted him dead. One of Boston's leading newspapers claimed that Pomeroy suffered "a mania that takes him out of the pale of humanity" and that he demanded a "forbearing and gentle regard," even while the writer called him a "torturing wild beast."[84] One of Pomeroy's staunchest defenders, former Massachusetts Supreme Court judge Dwight Foster, who argued that the boy's life be spared at the hearing before Governor Gaston and his council, nevertheless claimed that Pomeroy was "born a moral monster."[85] And the *Springfield Republican* argued both that Pomeroy was morally irresponsible, deserving of the "profoundest pity," and that it was "unsafe" to leave such a "wild beast at liberty."[86] While David Garland is correct, then, to point out that the new languages of "medicine, abnormal psychology, and positive criminology" all functioned to provide "a new language of monstrosity," that language did not always, as he claims, provide "a positive source of scientific legitimacy for the institution" of the death penalty.[87] While the "language of monstrosity" always spoke of difference, sometimes it spoke for compassion.

There were few, even among those opposed to Pomeroy's execution, who argued that Pomeroy was *not* an unnatural anomaly. Hardly any commentators made the case that would become dominant in the second half of the twentieth century—that environment (family and social conditions) made Jesse Pomeroy what he was. At trial, Pomeroy's lawyer Charles Robinson suggested this explanation, but did not develop it. Pomeroy was not "a monster born under barbarous influences," Robinson urged; rather "he was a product of Massachusetts—an outgrowth of her civilization for the last fifteen years."[88] Pomeroy's moral state, Robinson insisted, was integrally bound to the community that created him. An article in the Philadelphia *Bulletin* (adducing Pomeroy as an example) explicitly argued against casting youthful criminals as "new and strange animals," since that view involved a willful ignorance of the social conditions that in fact created them; the article continued by describing how such children were often neglected and given no education, care, or protection.[89] Certainly in the minority, such opinions insisted that crime was a result of *conditions* that could be ameliorated rather than the inevitable result of the (often biological) *condition* of the criminal, which was fixed at birth.

Some of those opposed to Pomeroy's execution simply believed that, no matter what made the boy what he was, capital punishment flatly contravened the tenets of Christianity. One person who penned a letter to the *Globe* declaimed the "infamy of strangling another image of God."[90] Countering those who argued that "Nature" or God rejected an abomination such as Pomeroy, Judge Dwight Foster argued that even though Pomeroy was indeed "born a moral monster," he was nonetheless part of God's creation, insisting that "when God permitted such beings to be born, he did not think the law ought to take their lives."[91] As Angela Smith has pointed out, religious figures in the late nineteenth and early twentieth centuries, in general, fiercely opposed eugenic arguments with their underpinning of "hereditary and biological determinism." Instead, they strove to "inculcate morality in the criminal" and to offer charity to all. They tried, in other words, to bring everyone within the borders of a human community that was ultimately determined by God alone, resisting the efforts of those who would cast some out as irreparably broken and deformed.[92]

Exemplary of the inclusive Christian argument against hanging Pomeroy was a letter Mrs. M. S. Wetmore sent to the *Globe* in March 1875. If mothers epitomized the argument for executing Pomeroy, with their demands that the domestic sphere be protected, Mrs. Wetmore embodied a countering "maternal" plea to spare the boy's life. A dedicated philanthropist who worked tirelessly with condemned prisoners, Mrs. Wetmore wrote a lengthy missive (to the *Globe,* but addressed to Pomeroy himself), expressing disbelief that any mother could desire Pomeroy's death: "It cannot be possible that any lady asking for your execution could have been a Mother, or, *ever* have known a mother's love," she wrote. Wetmore believed that the "unfortunate" Pomeroy, sent into the world "with inherited traits," needed only love—and that the gallows should be torn down and replaced by "*Homes of Love*."[93] Expressing a distinctly minority view, Mrs. Wetmore's letter was received with derision by the *Globe*'s readers, some of whom challenged her to accept Pomeroy into *her* home if she believed so strongly in the power of loving homes. Someone called their bluff, though, writing to the *Globe* to say that both he and another man (now a well-known Bostonian) had in fact been received into Mrs. Wetmore's home when they were down-on-their-luck ex-convicts and that she *had* transformed their lives.[94] Mrs. Wetmore embodied the ideal of society as a loving home, embracing a family from which *no one* would be excluded.

"Thwarting the action of the judiciary"

Given the strong and polarized public opinions about Jesse Pomeroy's punishment, it's not surprising that the governor and his council, responsible for signing the death warrant, were paralyzed. For twenty-two months from the time Pomeroy was convicted of first-degree murder (December 10, 1874) and eighteen months from the time the court overruled his lawyers' two objections (February 12, 1875) and officially sentenced Pomeroy to death (February 20, 1875), two governors and their respective councils sat on the fence.[95] Their inaction was no doubt due in part to the inevitable desire of elected officials not to alienate a significant portion of the voting public, particularly in a state with yearly gubernatorial elections. Since the voting public remained divided, the executive dithered—and, as long as the executive delayed, the public became still more divided. Despite hearings, despite a majority vote from his council upholding the death sentence, despite urgings from thousands of Bostonians, Democratic governor William Gaston ended his term in office after only one year, still refusing to sign the death warrant. Gaston's Republican successor, Alexander H. Rice, took office in January 1876, and if those who helped throw Gaston out of office and elect Rice had hoped, finally, for justice to be served, they were disappointed. Rice also balked at signing the death warrant.[96] Through it all, Jesse Pomeroy remained in jail, by all accounts relatively unaffected by the storm swirling around him. He continued to believe that they wouldn't hang a boy in Massachusetts.

Thus as the citizens of Boston angrily voiced their opinions about Pomeroy's fate, they increasingly did so against a backdrop of political events that also began to draw their ire. At first, though, the public's anger was directed only at Pomeroy and their opponents in the debate over his execution. Governor Gaston *seemed* to be doing his job. Three months after the Supreme Judicial Court ruled against the two objections of Pomeroy's lawyers, on April 13, 1875, Gaston and his council held a hearing on the question of punishment. Numerous witnesses testified that the boy's sentence should be commuted to life imprisonment, notably his lawyer Charles Robinson, who rehearsed the argument he made at the murder trial. Four physicians testified that Pomeroy was insane. Former Supreme Court justices argued for mercy, emphasizing the plea for commutation made by the jurors (on account of the boy's youth), and pointing out that, historically, similar recommendations by the jury had been honored. Others argued against the efficacy of capital punishment more generally or marshaled statistics to demonstrate the unlikelihood of Pomeroy's ever being pardoned, strengthening the case for life imprisonment.

There were fewer advocates at the hearing making the case that Pomeroy should suffer the fate the law demanded. A Mr. S. H. Dudley presented a petition signed by two hundred of the "leading citizens of Cambridge" asking for the death sentence.[97] Colonel Henry Wilson, a former state representative for South Boston, proclaimed Pomeroy "the most atrocious criminal which the State has produced" and argued that what he did was a malevolent act warranting punishment, not a "disease to be restrained." The principal spokesperson for the "remonstrants," those determined to see Pomeroy hang, was a lawyer named Paul West. He mapped out the two principal claims of the pro-execution argument: first, Pomeroy's execution was the only sure way to protect the community from the boy's depredations, and, second, his execution would provide a salutary example for anyone inclined to imitate his crimes. Like Henry Wilson, West dwelled on the cruelty of the crimes, adding that Pomeroy had assiduously cultivated his urges, not least by indulging in reading "yellow-covered literature." The day-long hearing ended without any action on the part of the council—an occurrence that would become all too common in the months ahead.[98]

By July 1875, as the hearing on the matter of punishment was receding into the distant past, the citizens of Boston began expressing frustration about the delay in deciding Pomeroy's fate—especially since, on July 2, William Gaston's executive council had finally voted *not* to commute the sentence. The deliberations prior to the vote were closed to the public and lasted about four hours; apparently the vote was six in favor of executing the sentence, three in favor of commuting it.[99] The way forward now seemed clear. Pomeroy's execution seemed so certain, in fact, that the *Boston Traveler* ended its story on the hearing by declaring, "It is thought that the day for his execution will be decided by Governor Gaston early next week."[100] Gaston, however, wasn't listening to the *Traveler*, to the people of Boston, or to his council, which he was constitutionally bound to do. "Who shall say how many of the numerous murders which since then have occurred in this vicinity have been derived from the encouragement to violence and crime afforded by the conduct of the Executive in this case?" wrote one outraged citizen to the *Globe*, expressing the burgeoning doubt that Pomeroy would ever be hung at all.[101]

Commentators started leveling at Gaston the charge that he was not merely engaging in the kind of delay one might expect from a politician skirting a controversial issue, but that he was usurping power not rightly his. A letter to the *Globe* angrily demanded the meaning "of the first delay of execution; then of the extraordinary proceeding of an advertised public hearing before a committee of the Council, followed by an unpublished report; another period of silent delay; a refusal by a majority of the Council to commute, and then another suspense and more silence?" The writer answered his own question and declared that Gaston was engaging in a "usurpation" of the office of the governor, imposing his own personal views where they manifestly did not belong. A letter to the *Advertiser* argued that Gaston's illegitimate inaction meant that the citizens of Massachusetts were living "not under a government of law, but under the despotic rule of one man." The writer accused Gaston of engaging in a "gross usurpation" by taking it upon himself to assume the "functions of the jury, the court and the executive council." He has no more right than a mob to stay the execution, the letter concluded.[102] That Gaston's delay in executing Pomeroy was fundamentally undemocratic, that he was arrogating for himself the power of the court, the jury, and the executive council, that he was even exerting a "despotic rule," interestingly turned on its head one of the longstanding post-Revolutionary arguments *against* the death penalty—that it was a relic of a tyrannical monarchy.[103] In this case, it was not the death penalty itself but a governor's increasingly active *prevention* of an execution, his interference in the "government of law," that became the truly "despotic" act.

Adding fuel to the fire, in its report of the closed session on July 2 when the council voted not to commute Pomeroy's sentence, the *Globe* noted that, prior to the vote, Gaston spoke "with great earnestness in favor of commuting the sentence of Jesse Pomeroy." Clearly Gaston was seeking to interpose his own views where they did not belong, attempting to sway the members of his council and then ignoring them when they produced a vote he did not like.[104] Indeed, there were references in several letters to the fact that Gaston was on principle opposed to the death penalty, lending substance to the claim that he was being guided by personal conviction rather than the constitutional requirements of the office he held (not least that he be directed by his council, which had, after all, recently voted not to commute the sentence).[105] As the *Congregationalist* put it, while it pitied Gaston for having to put his name to an execution he "does not think ought to take place," his signing is "purely ministerial," not "personal."[106]

As the November gubernatorial election drew closer, it seemed clear that Gaston's inaction would cost him. In the summer, the Boston correspondent for Connecticut's *Hartford Courant* had predicted that Gaston's failure to sign the death warrant "would affect his vote in a considerable degree; for the people of the state feel touchy upon the subject, and among the middling class the large majority would resent any action on the part of the executive that appeared to favor this offender."[107] There were reports in the papers on October 29, 1875, on the eve of the November 2 election, that a committee of "ladies" had called on Gaston's opponent, Alexander Rice, to ascertain his views on the Pomeroy case. In an obvious effort to distinguish himself from Gaston and to conciliate his visitors without actually committing himself to anything, Rice apparently said that, while he would not pledge himself to any course of action, he did not think that Pomeroy was "different from other criminals, or should receive exceptional treatment," and he did not view the veto power over judicial verdicts as "a weapon in the hands of the executive for the protection of individual scruples." The last comment was clearly a thrust at his political adversary, encapsulating as it did the charge that Gaston was arrogating the power of his office to promote his individual beliefs. The interview was apparently "satisfactory" to the committee.[108] Indeed, the *Springfield Republican* subsequently reported that the Jesse Pomeroy case was the only real issue that divided Gaston and Rice: "Rice says, hang; Gaston, no hang."[109] Unfortunately, however, for those who may have been instrumental in putting Rice in Governor's Gaston's place, Rice took office on January 6, 1876, and did . . . nothing.

In late May 1876, cries protesting the governor's continued inertia intensified from all sides, not least because another notorious Boston murderer,
Thomas Piper, whose cell was in the same corridor as Pomeroy's and who
had also received a death sentence, was hanged in the Charles Street Jail.
And he had killed his victim and been arrested *after* Pomeroy, highlighting
the unconscionable delay in the latter case.[110] In an effort to at least seem
as if he were moving forward, Governor Rice invited the Supreme Judicial
Court back into the Pomeroy case. He and his council asked the court to
rule on whether the recommendation of mercy added to the verdict by all
twelve jurors at Pomeroy's murder trial was in any way binding. The SJC
responded that the recommendation was not in fact a part of the judicial
proceedings, and that the question of what consideration the governor
and his council were to give to it "appears to the Justices not to depend
on any question of the law."[111] The SJC thus passed the question back to
the unlucky governor, supporting the case made by the anti-commutation
forces that the recommendation appended to the verdict was merely, as
one letter put it, "an appeal from the twelve citizens who formed the jury,"
thus carrying no more or less weight than a similar appeal from any other
group of citizens.[112]

Meanwhile Jesse Pomeroy was not entirely miserable in the Charles
Street Jail, where he enjoyed conversations with the many people who
came to see him, including his mother, and where he took up the study
of languages and history. "He has grown quite stout and has not appeared
to be greatly concerned regarding his fate"—remaining convinced, apparently, that he would not be hanged.[113] He did spend some time in the
summer of 1875 penning his autobiography, published in two installments
in the *Boston Sunday Times* on July 18 and 25. The scrawled pages of this
document were apparently smuggled out of jail in soiled laundry by Jesse's
"friends," although Ruth Pomeroy ended up bearing the responsibility and
was barred from seeing her son for some months, until October 21, according to news reports.[114] Jesse apparently did not want for company, however,
even after his mother's banishment.[115] Ruth's publicized unhappiness about
her exile included the accusation that Jesse had been "exhibited" to an
agent for Barnum's Hippodrome, who had asked him if he "would like to
go around with a circus and show himself to the public."[116] The *Globe* published a qualification of this charge, reporting that Pomeroy had not been
"exhibited" but that the Barnum's agent and a visiting Masonic group, the
"Richmond Sir Knights," had been allowed to see him and that they all
enjoyed conversing together.[117]

Pomeroy was also caught making plans to escape at least three times, all of them after July 2, 1875, when the executive council voted to go ahead with his execution. Each time he attempted to escape—on July 20, August 21, and November 9—he was punished with between three and four days of solitary confinement.[118] The first attempt reached the ears of reporters, and the published details of his matter-of-fact plan to "lay out" any guards who stopped him and flee to Canada must not have helped his case very much. Indeed, the *Traveler* reported that "upon being detected, Pomeroy is stated to have become very indignant, and to have said that had he had a knife he would have knifed the man who frustrated his efforts."[119] Fodder, certainly, for the pro-hanging cause.

Pomeroy continued to receive visitors despite his apparent willingness to stab anyone who thwarted his effort to escape. On April 7, 1876, the state legislature's Joint Standing Committee on Prisons visited the Charles Street Jail and its members conversed with Pomeroy. He told them the jail had become a "second home to him" and that he spent his days reading books from the prison library and brought to him by his friends.[120] He also devoted some time to learning Latin and Greek.[121] A *Globe* editorial claimed that Pomeroy was actually enjoying himself in confinement, reading with interest about the case of Thomas Piper, "his brother in crime," and consoling himself "with the thought, as he has expressed it, that 'they don't hang boys in Massachusetts.'"[122] They did, though, hang adults, and while Pomeroy was in jail both Piper and George Pemberton (the latter in October 1875) were executed. Even as Pomeroy heard the "thud made by Pemberton's fall," he remained "in excellent spirits," although two other condemned criminals in the Charles Street Jail were "entirely unmanned."[123] As in all the moments in which his life became public, then, accounts of Pomeroy's time in jail are bifurcated: on the one hand, his behavior is called exemplary; he's reading and studying, calling the place a second home. On the other hand, he plans to escape and is prepared to kill any guard who gets in his way.

While in jail, Pomeroy continued to withhold any explanation of his crimes. To his lawyer Charles Robinson—who, along with Ruth Pomeroy, was one of his most frequent visitors and staunch advocates—he persistently claimed that "he did not know" why he committed the murders and "that the whole affair seemed like a dream to him." As Pomeroy told Robinson, the murder seemed to pass "before me in a mist," and "I could not help doing what I did."[124] A year later, to the members of the Joint Standing Committee on Prisons, he "freely acknowledge[d] his guilt" for the deaths of Horace Millen and Katie Curran but could "give no reason for committing such barbarous deeds, other than a sudden impulse which came over him." He told the committee he preferred to spend the remainder of his days in prison and didn't think it was "safe" to let him out.[125] Needless to say, this statement was somewhat at odds with his attempts to escape.

In July 1876 there was another closed hearing in front of the governor and his council. The only person who testified was Charles Robinson, Pomeroy's lawyer; representatives of the pro-execution forces weren't even notified of the hearing. Their counsel, Paul West, wrote a letter to the *Globe* expressing his displeasure at the glaring one-sidedness of the hearing. His protest, though, was surprisingly tepid, a fact explained, perhaps, by his confidence that the arguments for Pomeroy's execution were unassailable and held by the "majority of the people of the State and of the country at large," as well as by the majority of the governor's council.[126] After the July 18 hearing, though, the council adjourned for two weeks without making a decision. In the meantime, as the next gubernatorial election loomed, Rice must have been feeling the pressure to do something. Jesse Pomeroy is "the most dreaded issue in Massachusetts politics," the *Globe* editorialized in late July, adding that Governor Gaston "found his chief element of unpopularity in his inability to condemn the miserable boy to the gallows," and the "same faction . . . is now abusing Governor Rice for a similar exhibition of weakness."[127] The governor's executive council convened yet again in early August and yet again discussed the Pomeroy case. No vote was taken, but the discussion apparently indicated (to those who weren't there) that Pomeroy would soon face execution and that Governor Rice in particular was in favor of that outcome, believing that "justice and the safety of the community alike demand that the boy shall suffer the full penalty of the law."[128] Other newspapers reported with equal assurance, however, that Governor Rice was in favor of commuting Pomeroy's sentence.[129]

The wrath of the citizens of Boston seemed most definitely to be turning on its elected officials as the summer of 1876 moved inexorably onward. In nearby Lowell, the *Daily Citizen* entered the fray, insisting that "humanity as well as justice demands an early decision," though it seemed a little too late for "early" decisions. Two days later, the paper added that since it appeared the executive council was thoroughly "divided in opinion," Governor Rice must make the decision himself.[130] Others objected to this position. The *Globe* published a sharp editorial decrying the power given to the governor "to intervene between the court and the execution of its judgment." The governor had been allowed an undue power that permitted him to "thwart the action of the judiciary" and to decide Pomeroy's sentence and punishment to all intents and purposes himself, ignoring the verdict of the jury and the mandate of the law.[131] The response to the *Globe*'s editorial was yet another meeting of the executive council four days later, on August 14, in which, once again, no action was taken.

But September 1876 dawned with a decision. Jesse Pomeroy had been right all along: they would not hang a boy in Massachusetts. On the first of the month, the Boston newspapers reported that the council had voted to commute Pomeroy's sentence to life imprisonment, sending him to the state prison where he would be "compelled to labor for his own support." Governor Rice had approved the commutation. The official pronouncement of Pomeroy's reprieve was printed in most of the city's papers, and it claimed as crucial factors in the council's and governor's decision the unanimous recommendation of mercy by the jury and the influential testimony of members (and former members) of the Suffolk bar—Judges George Taylor Bigelow, Benjamin F. Thomas, and Dwight Foster—all of whom had testified in favor of commutation at the first hearing in April 1875.[132]

The people of Boston were not happy. The *Globe* declared that "the general expression of opinion seemed to be decidedly adverse to the judgment of the Executive and his advisers," quoting an unnamed "gentleman" as proclaiming, "Well, . . . the Pomeroy business killed Gaston last year, and it will send Mr. Rice to private life."[133] The *Congregationalist* editorialized that there would have been greater contentment with the verdict if the citizens of Boston could be sure that the boy would actually be confined for life—but "alas! as pardons go in the State of meddlesome philanthropists and soft-hearted governors, there is no such certainty whatever." There was "properly only one course to be taken," the editors concluded, "to execute the law." The *Aegis and Gazette* of Worcester agreed, writing that Pomeroy should have been hanged "because the safety of the community demanded it." The governor and the council had opened the possibility that Pomeroy would be pardoned, or would kill guards at the state penitentiary in a desperate bid to escape, all "to gratify a morbid sentimentality, of the kind to risk the terrible death of a whole village full of children rather than kill a mad dog." The *Boston Medical and Surgical Journal* wrote flatly that the "sentimentalists have won the day" and that "the pleas of parents that their infants should be protected from torture and mutilation have been set aside." Statistics show that a life sentence lasts about seven years, the editorial continued, and undoubtedly, one day, "Mr. Jesse Pomeroy will be a free man."[134] All fears about the future aside, though, for now at least, the case was finally over—and all of Boston could agree to be relieved about that.

Jesse Pomeroy had spent two years and four months in the Charles Street Jail, unsure of his future, or whether he even had a future. As with everything surrounding Pomeroy, reports of his response to the dispensation of his fate were contradictory. One account stated that he "brightened up for a moment and then his face resumed its usual stolid expression." The same article noted that his jailers claimed he had been consistently "well-behaved."[135] Another story, however, reported that he rubbed his hands enthusiastically and said "Ain't that nice; oh, ain't that good!" and that the officers at the jail professed their heartfelt happiness at his impending departure since he had made several attempts to escape.[136]

On the afternoon of September 7, 1876, Pomeroy was transferred to the Massachusetts State Prison in Charlestown, where he would remain mostly in solitary confinement until just three years before his death in 1932. Pomeroy was led to his room in the upper arch of the west wing, a room that was nine feet long, eight feet wide, and seven feet high, lighted by two "crevices" that were two feet long and six inches wide. His room contained only a wooden bedstead, bed clothing, and a stool. He was shut in by an iron door fastened with a heavy padlock. Three times a day, Jesse's solitude would be broken by officers bringing food, "but no conversation will be allowed between him and any person, except the chaplain." He would be permitted reading material from the prison library, along with religious papers. When he saw the room that was to be his world for the foreseeable future, about which he had not surprisingly "manifested a good deal of curiosity," its appearance "did not suit him apparently, although he expressed no disappointment."[137] Another report claimed that, as he was taken to his new cell, he "was looking pale and jaded, but simply asked if he was to stay there always, saying he would 'be a good boy and make no trouble.' "[138] By the end of September, he was employed making brushes.[139] While his sentence of solitary confinement would eventually be commuted, in 1917, Pomeroy spent forty-one years almost completely alone—by all accounts the longest anyone has ever spent in solitary confinement.

Jesse Pomeroy had been spared hanging, but he faced an utterly isolated life that was its own kind of death. Some, indeed, had argued that life imprisonment was a more brutal kind of punishment than execution. "The certainty of imprisonment for life," one writer had declared in a letter to the *Globe,* "would be a far greater terror to evil-doers than the uncertainty of being hanged."[140] Pomeroy now confronted the undoubtedly existentially terrifying prospect of confinement, and solitude, for the rest of his life.

Pomeroy's "social death" within the walls of the state penitentiary was in the end a fitting conclusion to the debate over his punishment. No one, after all, with the seemingly solitary exception of Mrs. Wetmore (and, of course, his mother), wanted him ever to return to the community. Whether they were for or against the death penalty, the majority of those who wrote impassioned letters and editorials about him wanted him gone from Boston, gone from the "civilized" modern state. For the most part, the logic of everyone's explanations and assessments cast him beyond the pale of humanity. Whether they wanted him executed or sent to permanent solitary confinement, virtually all of those who entered the fray over Pomeroy's punishment wanted him "dead to the rest of society."[141] Reform was never an option. The fact of his monstrosity, of his irredeemably diseased, deformed, or simply evil nature—the fact of his fundamentally *nonhuman* nature, in other words—hung more heavily in the words of his contemporaries than did any efforts to think of him as human.

"The Mark of the Meat Market"

Unmoored from the constraints of the law and the either/or exigency of the death-penalty debate, some of Jesse Pomeroy's contemporaries did explore the causes of his unthinkable crimes, filling in the gaping hole left by own inability to explain his acts of torture and murder. Many accepted (to some degree, at least) the boy's own enigmatic words that he "could not help" what he had done, that something "made him" do it. They described Pomeroy as driven by forces over which he had no control, formed by conditions not of his own making or choosing. This chapter explores the most widely held and persistent theory about why Pomeroy tortured and killed children: that his mother watched his father butchering cattle, sheep, and pigs while she was pregnant, thus stamping him in utero with what one account colorfully called "the mark of the meat market."[1] According to this view, the desire for blood was indelibly impressed on Pomeroy before he was born; this theory thus construed him as profoundly determined by events that took place before his birth, his flesh etched with a past that was not his own. "That time is surely out of joint which can produce boys like Jesse Pomeroy, the child-killer of Boston," one newspaper pronounced.[2] By all accounts, for Jesse Pomeroy time was indeed "out of joint," as he was possessed not only by the past but by something ineffably strange and impersonal that came from that past, something out of his control that was rooted in his unwilled encounter, in the womb, with slaughtered animals.

Arguing that the course of Pomeroy's life was shaped before his birth, commentators attributed determining power first and foremost to the activities of his father and mother while he was in utero, especially the "perverse" desires of his pregnant mother. But some also maintained that

Thomas and Ruth Pomeroy were themselves victims of a barbaric meat-eating society, the dire consequences of which were evident in their son's bloody acts. These claims of causality—all rooted in the killing of animals, in the butchering and eating of meat—suggest not only a particular familial history but also an inherent human nature, beyond the damaging encounters of individual pregnant mothers. Pomeroy was shaped not only by a particular shocking encounter in his prenatal past, but by flesh all humans share, flesh that has its own indelible qualities and is always subject to the vagaries of chance. In other words, Jesse Pomeroy, and humans in general, are *already* traversed by an internal *nature* that is shaped by a long evolutionary history inimical to the rational, autonomous, and volitional "human." The various permutations of the "butcher theory" all urged the underlying truth that the body, our inevitably corporeal nature, forms an intractably mechanical presence at the heart of the human. Pomeroy's uncomprehending violence was a particularly exaggerated form of a common human condition, making it clear how much our bodies possess us, even as we struggle to possess them.

The Butcher Theory

The "butcher theory," widely reported in the press both at the time and for decades afterward, broke while Jesse was awaiting trial for the murder of Horace Millen. The *Boston Herald* recounted how, directly after Pomeroy's interrogation by Judge Forsaith in 1872, which led to his remand to the juvenile reform school at Westborough,

> a party of three well-known physicians, who were anxious to learn all that they could about the boy, called upon his mother and had a very pleasant and candid interview with her. They told her their errand, and she kindly gave them all the information in her power. Among other things, she said that her husband was a butcher, and that during the period of her pregnancy she went daily to the slaughter-house to witness the killing of the animals, and that somehow she took a particular delight in seeing her husband butcher the sheep, the calves and the cattle, and not unfrequently [*sic*] she assisted him in this bloody work. She also said that after Jesse was born, and became old enough to have a knife in his hands, he was all the time, when opportunity offered, jabbing a knife into pieces of meat, and, when still older and about his father's market, he did the same thing. These facts certainly explain in a measure why Jesse could not help doing these things, as he told the court. He was simply *marked* by his mother, as other children have been, only in a different way.[3]

The *Boston Globe* reprinted the *Herald*'s story the next day (on July 21), but then immediately retracted it (on July 22), relating a subsequent interview with Ruth Pomeroy in which she flatly denied the story. The *Globe* went on to editorialize that, after all, the butcher theory seemed a "fabrication, invented evidently for the purpose of deepening the mystery that involves the case." According to the *Globe,* the version of the story sanctioned by Ruth herself was quite different:

> Before going into the butcher business, my husband worked in the Navy Yard at Charlestown, where he was employed for a period of ten years. He was at work there four years before Jesse was born, and remained there until he was nearly six years of age. It was after this he went into the butcher business. He did not kill cattle, but carried the carcasses about the market. *I never saw an animal of any kind slaughtered.* I do not believe in the theory of persons being marked. *The statement regarding the visit of the three physicians is false.* . . . *The story of Jesse sticking knives into raw flesh is also false.*

The *Globe* writer added that Ruth Pomeroy's story "refutes one pet theory and gives the lie to a greatly credited story," which suggests how much sway the butcher theory had gained in a very short time.[4]

The story that Jesse was "marked," however, marched inexorably onward despite the few published refutations. Claims that the story was baseless were thrown to the wind, engulfed by the sensational theory of Jesse's blood-soaked prenatal origins, a theory that struck such a chord with his contemporaries that its truthfulness did not seem to matter. The force of the story is evident when, more than a year later, in August 1875, Ruth Pomeroy had to debunk it again:

> To my knowledge Jessie [*sic*] has no birth-mark whatever. His father never was a butcher, and therefore I could not have watched him kill beasts. At the time Jessie was born, his father was working at the Navy Yard. The only thing he ever had to do with meat in his life was carrying beef from wagons on his shoulder into Faneuil Hall Market. I don't believe he ever killed an animal in his life. During the period of my pregnancy with Jesse I was, I think, more secluded than two-thirds of the women of Boston. There were times when I did not go out of my house for two months. The whole story about pre-natal influences on Jesse was a malicious slander.[5]

Verifying Ruth's claim, the historical record gives no indication that Thomas was ever a butcher. As we saw in chapter 1, in the 1870 federal census he was listed as a porter, and all available evidence attests that he worked at Quincy Market. As Ruth said, he may have carried meat while he worked there, but he almost certainly did not slaughter animals. Even this tangentially related job, though, he held well after Jesse was born in November 1859. In the 1855 and 1860 censuses Thomas was working as a laborer (at the Charlestown Navy Yard, as Ruth stated), and in 1862 (in enlistment papers) and 1865 (in the state census), he gave his occupation as fireman. The falseness of the "butcher" story, however, bore no relation whatsoever to its wild proliferation—and it was told and retold with greater and lesser degrees of adherence to the original throughout the remainder of the nineteenth century and into the first two decades of the twentieth century.

The belief that Jesse Pomeroy was stamped before his birth with the love of blood seems to have carried significant weight within the legal proceedings that embroiled him—again, despite Ruth's quite convincing refutation. In an 1893 interview reported in the *Boston Daily Advertiser*, a former member of Governor Gaston's council, Edward H. Dunn, claimed he voted for commuting Pomeroy's death sentence because it "was urged that the prisoner might through heredity have acquired a desire for blood-letting as his father was a butcher accustomed to killing various sorts of animals."[6] Dunn was not alone in having been influenced in the contentious debate over Pomeroy's sentencing by the theory that the boy was "marked" in utero by his mother. In a short biographical sketch written in 1896, the social reformer Julia Schlesinger credits Addie Lucia Ballou with having singlehandedly influenced Governor Gaston and eventually won Pomeroy's commutation. Ballou apparently worked as tirelessly as she did on the boy's behalf because she believed that he had been subject to damaging prenatal conditions: "Being well versed in the laws of pre-natal conditions," Schlesinger writes, Ballou "was shocked by the monstrous laws which by a legal murder are [sic] supposed to atone for a murder perpetrated by a boy whose mother had frequently assisted her husband in butchering cattle while the unborn baby was beneath her bosom."[7]

While the established community of physicians (including those who rendered their official pronouncements at Pomeroy's trial) remained for the most part committed to Pomeroy's moral insanity as an explanation for his crimes, the world beyond that rather narrow community seemed convinced by the butcher theory. The only explanation that even came close to vying with this theory was one I discuss in chapter 4: the similarly widespread belief that Pomeroy assimilated his love of torture from the dime novels he read so voraciously.

Divided Parental Inheritance

The story that Jesse Pomeroy was impressed in his mother's womb with a love of blood was repeated in newspapers, journals, and books throughout the decades, as he wore away his life in the state prison. In its many iterations, the story retained the general contours of the original report in the *Herald:* Thomas supposedly worked at a slaughterhouse in 1859 when Ruth was pregnant with Jesse, and she would routinely come to visit him as he worked. Some accounts stressed that Ruth merely witnessed the slaughter; others insisted that she took "a particular delight" in it, as the *Herald* had put it in 1874.[8] For most of those who rehearsed it, the butcher theory exonerated Jesse, laying the responsibility for his crimes instead at the feet of his parents. In 1881, the spiritualist Edwin Dwight Babbitt wrote that because of the force of prenatal conditions, "when Jesse Pomeroy and similar children came into the world with the spirit of hatred and murder in the very web-work of their constitution, their parents are more culpable than they."[9] As blame was transferred to Jesse's parents, however, it was not apportioned equally.

Thomas Pomeroy came in for very little censure. Indeed, only a small minority of those who touted the butcher theory as an explanation of Pomeroy's crimes turned their attention toward Thomas at all. He was invoked more fleetingly and described with significantly less florid detail than his wife; when commentators did mention him, moreover, they tended to argue that it was the (neutrally considered) habitual routine of his occupation as butcher, rather than any wayward urges, that ended up being transmitted to his son. A newspaper account from 1887 is typical. Arguing that Pomeroy's "morbid impulse" was inherited, the writer added, "His father was a butcher, and before Jesse was born his mother, otherwise of quiet and gentle extincts [*sic*], took a morbid delight in visiting the shambles to enjoy the death agonies of animals." And a letter to the editor in 1902 parsed the responsibilities of the parents similarly: "His father was a butcher and his mother before his birth loved to witness the animals die and took the greatest delight if they suffered."[10] Both accounts referred matter-of-factly, in a single terse clause, to Thomas's *work* as butcher, while lavishly elaborating on Ruth's perverse *desires*. He had to be there; she wanted to be there—a difference worth pointing out even though it is, of course, explained by the gendered division of labor in the nineteenth century.

The few accounts that expended more effort discussing Thomas's part in creating his son generally hewed to the (supposed) fact that it was his job to slaughter cattle, and so, while he may have been partly *responsible* for his son, he was not to *blame*. Theories that considered Thomas Pomeroy stressed the importance of habit rather than desire in the transmission of characteristics to offspring. Indeed, popular beliefs about the hereditary nature of acquired characteristics stressed that the habits of one generation could be transmitted to the next specifically as *instinct:* in their transmission, traits and behaviors moved from the conscious to the unconscious. In 1875 Francis Fairfield published an account of his "personal examination" of the Pomeroy case, and while he was one of the few "inclined to credit" Ruth Pomeroy's claim that she had never gone to the slaughterhouse, he did appear to believe that Thomas was a butcher by trade, writing that he "contracted" a "habit of mutilation" in the slaughterhouse, which, "like all habits, primarily impressed the nervous system and was recorded in the nervous organism as a transmissible bias." According to Fairfield, Thomas's business of butchery, "impressed" on his own body, was transferred to his son as a "monomania." Fairfield concludes that the Pomeroy case demonstrates more generally how "mere customary action on the part of a progenitor" returns in the case of the child as a "morbid nervous phenomena" or a "perversion of nervous function."[11] Demonstrating the persistence of this view, in 1904 Maud Lord Drake similarly suggested that the "father's business" created "the form and quality of brain through which the spirit of the child was ever after forced to operate with no consciousness of moral wrong."[12] While stressing the influence of Jesse's father, both of these commentators are nonjudgmental, noting only the hereditary influence of his "business." Far from blaming Thomas, they position him as a victim of his necessary occupation, unwittingly transmitted to his son.

When attention turned to Ruth, however, the discussion of her role in transmitting baleful characteristics to her son became much more freighted with moral judgment. While Thomas was engaged in the butcher trade (as the story went) out of necessity, his wife's presence at the scene of slaughter was entirely voluntary and seemingly purposeless. The imputation of deviant desire rushed to fill this vacuum of purpose. In a guide to family happiness published in 1915, Elizabeth Jones Towne presented an account of the

Pomeroys (who in her version lived in Chicago) that exemplifies the different motives attributed to husband (necessity) and wife (perverse volition). Towne writes that Jesse's father "skinned sheep stolidly and drew his wages every Saturday night," while his wife was "fascinated by his deft killing and skinning."[13] This account perfectly illustrates what was, by then, the well-established split under industrial capitalism by which emotions were delegated to women within the private sphere, while work in the public sphere was men's part.[14] Indeed, Ruth Pomeroy undoubtedly became a galvanizing figure precisely because she (supposedly) left the home and entered the space of labor—of butchery, no less. Not surprisingly, then, part of her refutation of the butcher theory was that she was, as she told a reporter in August 1875, "more secluded than two-thirds of the women of Boston," and at times "did not go out of my house for two months." But Ruth could not stem the stories about her repeated departures from the domestic sphere and her transgressive penetration of the slaughterhouse.

The focus on Ruth Pomeroy by proponents of the butcher theory is also explained by the fact that mothers were obviously much more implicated than fathers in the transmission of characteristics (including mutations) to their offspring.[15] After describing how Ruth Pomeroy visited "the shambles" when she was pregnant and passed on the habit of shedding blood to her son, Hartland and Herbert Edward Law, in a handbook of hygiene published in 1915, insisted that "mothers have much more to do with the transmitted qualities of children than fathers have." This fact is due, they add, to gestation and to her physical nourishment of her unborn child, but also to the fact that the child is "subject to all the nervous conditions that affect her" during pregnancy.[16] In his *Maternal Impressions* (1897), Charles Bayer went much further, arguing that maternal impressions produce compulsive crime and irresistible homicidal mania.[17] For Bayer, crime is "the result of an abnormal brain action, or unbalanced brain structure with which the mother has, through ignorance, endowed the individual, thus creating a desire which that person is unable to resist." The mother, he repeats, "shapes the brain structure for good or evil." It is interesting that while Bayer seems inevitably to be blaming mothers for just about everything that ails society, from congenital blindness and epilepsy to the "tramp problem" and homicidal insanity, he nonetheless claims to have grounded his book in interviews with women. The paradox stems from the fact that his castigation of women correlates to the immense power he gives them, the power literally to shape a person.[18] This sense of the power women have, along with its corollary anxiety, are central to the ways in which Ruth Pomeroy featured in the most influential story of her son's origins.

Highly influential in the nineteenth century, the theory of "maternal impressions" held that unusual and alarming events could etch themselves so deeply on a pregnant woman, specifically on her nervous system (though some thought the influence was carried by blood), that her unborn child was stamped with that event.[19] Instances of maternal impressions fell into two broad categories, aptly described by a physician at a meeting of the St. Louis Medical Society in 1882. Impressions are transmitted, he claimed, "either from the emotions beginning subjectively, or from impressions excited objectively."[20] While accounts of the Pomeroy case mostly pursued the effect of "emotions beginning subjectively," some commentators did see Jesse Pomeroy as the product of his mother's unwilling and unwitting witnessing of the sight of slaughter. As Judge Warren W. Foster put it in 1909, "It was commonly reported and believed that the blood-thirsty impulses of the boy were the direct result of prenatal influences." When pregnant, Ruth Pomeroy was "much about the shambles," watching her husband butcher animals, "and the *sight* of blood" was "thus worked out in the child."[21] The editor of the *Journal of Heredity* similarly recounts: "Before the birth of Jesse, his mother went daily to the shop to carry a luncheon to her husband, and her eyes naturally fell upon the bloody carcases [*sic*] hung about the walls. Inevitably the sight of such things would produce bloody thoughts in the mind of the child!"[22]

In both of these versions of the story, Ruth is acting in a benign and socially appropriate way (carrying her husband lunch, for instance), and the external world assaults her, striking her with *sights* that appall—shocking her nervous system to such a degree that the unborn child inside her is somehow (the process is always vague) formed in the image of that sight. As Mary Teats wrote in 1906, after having described how Ruth Pomeroy would "watch" her husband slaughter animals, "Children have been rendered vicious by evil effects *produced upon* the minds of their mothers."[23] Women don't necessarily act in this model, then, beyond stumbling into a shocking scene. Instead, they are passive receptors, the sensory impressions of the external world transformed, through the medium of their bodies, into baleful effects on their offspring.

In the second category of maternal impressions, however, the pregnant woman was more active, branding her unborn infant with her often wayward desires.[24] As Marie-Hélène Huet writes in her study of this obsolete scientific belief, rather than "reproducing the father's image, as nature commands, the monstrous child bore witness to the violent desires that moved the mother at the time of pregnancy or during pregnancy." The infant "carried the marks of [the mother's] whims and fancy rather than the recognizable features off its legitimate genitor."[25] The formative role of the mother's will and imagination in producing monsters (moral or physical) inevitably ended up drawing censure to the mother—or, as Rachel Adams puts it, laying "the blame squarely on the inappropriate and perverse maternal imagination."[26] While Ruth Pomeroy was described as both the victim of the shocking sight and the agent of transgressive desire, the latter theory, no doubt because of its more sensational nature, was by far the more pervasive.[27] Indeed, most commentators asserted that Ruth wasn't merely confronted with the horrifying spectacle of butchery; they claimed instead that she repeatedly sought it out. Shifting slightly from the explanation that Ruth was struck by the sight of slaughter, for instance, one newspaper article chose words that rendered her more active: "Jesse's father had worked in an abattoir and his mother, before his birth, was in the habit of *going to see* him kill animals marked for slaughter—cattle, sheep, and hogs."[28] Most commentators, however, pushed past going and seeing to desiring.

While the original story in the *Boston Herald* in 1874 had noted that Ruth took a "particular delight in seeing her husband butcher the sheep, the calves and the cattle," an editorial in *Scientific American* later that year was the first to develop at length the idea that Ruth's own transgressive urges had injured her unborn child. Jesse Pomeroy's crimes constituted a clear case of "moral warping by vicious influences, systematically brought to bear on the child *in utero* as well as in infancy," the writer declared, adding that "had the mother's desire been to breed a monster of bloodthirstiness, her course could not have been more surely adapted to accomplish that end." The "mother's morbid pleasure at the sight of blood," moreover, "was not only inherited but cultivated by the child, who was a butcher by instinct, taking up his father's trade almost as soon as he could walk."[29] Ruth's "desire" and her "morbid pleasure" would both be emphasized in subsequent discussions of how her alleged visits to the slaughterhouse, and the emotions that drove her there, shaped her child. A year later, for instance, a physician named John Ruttley, in *Nature's Secrets and the Secrets of Woman Revealed*, offered the case of Jesse Pomeroy to establish "the fact beyond question that the child may be affected by the emotions of the mother during pregnancy." Ruth Pomeroy, he wrote, "experienced a morbid pleasure in witnessing the flowing of blood," and thus her son "experienced an unconquerable desire to see the flowing of blood." The Pomeroy boy, he repeated, "was impressed by his mother to delight in the sight of blood."[30] For Ruttley, the fatal "impression" was explicitly *generated*, not merely received, by Jesse's mother.

Many writers followed Ruttley's example, interpreting Ruth as driven to the bloody slaughterhouse by an indwelling morbid desire. In an 1889 article on diseases of the fetus, for example, another medical doctor, Barton Cooke Hirst, claimed that the "mother of Jesse Pomeroy took delight, while carrying this child in utero, in watching her husband, a butcher, ply his trade," and that "the boy's irresistible inclination to torture and slay may well have had its origin in his mother's perverted taste during pregnancy." In his 1897 compendium of cases of maternal impressions, Bayer argued that Jesse Pomeroy's otherwise inexplicable crimes were precipitated by the fact that "before his birth [Ruth] loved to go to the slaughter house to see them kill the cattle—delighted to see the blood flow." "There is no doubt," he concluded, "but that maternal impression was the main factor in his case." A physician writing in an 1899 issue of *Physician and Surgeon*, closely following Hirst's lead, argued that Jesse's "irresistible inclination to torture and slay could have had its origin in his mother's perverted taste at that time"—in her "delight" in watching her husband butcher cattle. The theory is repeated even as late as 1915, when Elizabeth Jones Towne attributed Pomeroy's crimes to his mother's emotions when she watched her husband work: "But the mother hated and at the same time was fascinated by his deft killing and skinning. It took hold of her imagination and thought, which at that time were busy creating a baby. And Jesse Pomeroy got it all."[31]

In all of these explanations, instead of the external world working through the passive medium of the maternal body to stamp itself on the malleable clay of the unborn child, the mother's own mental state is reproduced in her monstrous child. The mother *herself* constitutes the threatening environment for her unborn child. Her "perverted taste," her "delight" in slaughter, her "morbid pleasure at the sight of blood," her "fascination" with killing, all shape her son in their likeness. Those who promoted this theory all employed active verbs, writing of Ruth "watching," "witnessing," and "seeing"—not of her being simply struck with the "sight" of something.

Writers emphasized the way that Jesse embodied Ruth's wayward "taste" and "desires" by using the same language to describe both of them, a

repetition that heightens the mirroring of the mother by the son. As Ruttley put it, just as the mother took pleasure in the "flowing of blood," so
the son desired to see the "flowing of blood." Indeed, the interest of many
commentators in emphasizing the son's literal replication of his mother
may explain some of the more unusual variants of the butcher theory:
in what is no doubt an unconscious inversion of the causal trajectory of
maternal impressions (in which the son mirrored the mother), Ruth's
actions (about which much less was known than her son's) were imagined
in a way that made them conform to what Jesse was known to have done.
In a couple of versions, for instance, Ruth did more than just enjoy the
sight of her husband butchering animals. An article in the *Vegetarian Magazine* in 1902 claimed that she would visit the meat market where her husband worked and "would sit down on the meat block and amuse herself by
stabbing a large loin of beef with a large butcher's knife. This grew to be her
habit, and a passion for stabbing the cold meat was developed." In a 1911
sermon, a Michigan preacher, Edwin Whitney Bishop, after asserting that
Pomeroy lived in Missouri and killed nine "little playmates before he was
eleven years old," declared that both Jesse's "father and mother worked in a
slaughter house," the "mother as well as the father being an adept in cutting
hogs' throats." "As is the mother, so is her child," he added, paraphrasing
the Book of Ezekiel to drive the point home.[32] Jesse's propensity to jab with
knives and cut throats is in these instances rather blatantly displaced back
onto his mother, as commentators shaped their stories to make her the
undisputed origin of his crimes.

In explaining Pomeroy as the inevitable result of his mother's transgressive emotions, commentators inevitably condemned Ruth for the
perverse desires that helped to shape a monster. In remarking on the
nineteenth-century theory of maternal impressions, the historian Martin
Pernick argues that it "provided a purely natural explanation" for defective
births, an alternative to viewing "monstrous" births as divine punishment;
mothers were still held responsible for such defects, "but their fault was
negligence not sin"[33] To the extent that physicians focused their attention
on the mother's emotions, however, the fact of her "sin" was often as fully
insinuated as it had been when monstrosities were considered the work
of God's displeasure.[34] It is difficult, it seems, to proffer a "purely natural
explanation" that is entirely disentangled from the human propensity to
make meaning and thereby assign blame.

The enormous influence that the theory of maternal impressions gave women explains much about the hyperbolic nature of stories describing Ruth Pomeroy's delight in butchering, stories that stray far from any grounding in reality and that thus betray the fact that they are to some degree at least driven by a *fear* of women, specifically of the pregnant woman's unpredictable and uncontrollable desires and of her inherent lack of boundedness, her openness to the world.

Anthropologists and feminist theorists have long argued that the liminal status of the pregnant woman endows her with power and consequently shapes her as a figure of dread. In her classic anthropological study *Purity and Danger,* Mary Douglas asserts that both power *and* danger inhere "in the margins of the human body." In exploring why this should be so, she argues that "all margins are dangerous. If they are pulled this way or that the shape of fundamental experience is altered. Any structure of ideas is vulnerable at its margins." For Douglas, the potential permeability of the margin, and the fear of that permeability, explains the pervasive, cross-cultural disgust with bodily refuse—with spittle, blood, milk, urine, and feces. By the very fact that they issue forth, they "have traversed the boundary of the body," thus illustrating the dangerous vulnerability of that body, its susceptibility to crossings from inside out and outside in.[35] Pregnancy, of course, inherently involves many bodily transgressions—and is itself a thoroughly marginal experience, as the borders between human beings, between what should above all else be kept separate, are profoundly destabilized. Ruth Pomeroy was inextricably bound to her unborn child, who received, the story went, the impress of both her experiences with the external world and her wayward desires. Nineteenth-century beliefs about maternal impressions—the dangerous ways in which the outside world went inside, and in which the inside (of the mother) seeped into her child—all literalized lurking fears about the permeability of women's bodies.

Recognizing the (frequently irrational) dread induced by women's power, desires, and bodily permeability must go hand in hand, however, with the fact that pregnant women do indeed shape their unborn children. While science has put to rest the theory of maternal impressions, including the belief that mothers can "stamp" their unborn children with particular emotions, research has confirmed that a pregnant woman's ingestion of drugs and alcohol, and even severe prenatal stress, can detrimentally affect the fetus's brain. While we no longer believe, in other words, that an expectant mother shocked by the sight of blood will have a child who revels in blood, many if not most people in the scientific community do believe that "harmful agents or maternal experiences can have a huge impact" during the crucial months of gestation, perhaps even shaping a psychopathic brain, one bereft of the ability to acquire empathy and other caring emotions.[36] Alcohol consumption in particular, as well as severe stress during pregnancy, can have "dire effects"—and the former has been unambiguously linked to the "physical and neurological conditions that predispose American babies to aggressive and violent behavior."[37]

The dire effects of drinking alcohol during pregnancy were not known in the late 1850s, when Ruth was pregnant, and so she may have consumed beer or liquor without worry, although there is no evidence that she (unlike her husband) drank to excess. But she may certainly have been suffering from stress when she was pregnant with Jesse. She already had one small child (Charles was just over one year old when his younger brother was born); she would (much later) seek a divorce from a husband who, she claimed, had for years been intemperate and refused to support herself and their children; her family lived in poverty (in a house with at least one other family), a fact that, while coming with its own form of stress, would also have meant her access to healthcare was limited; and Boston was in the midst of its worst smallpox epidemic of the century—indeed, the scourge was at its height between November 1859 and February 1860, precisely when Jesse was born (in late November).[38]

Intriguingly, scientists have recently identified what are called "minor physical anomalies" (MPAs): "external physical signs that correlate highly with central nervous damage during gestation."[39] MPAs appear to be caused by both genetic and antenatal environmental factors such as anoxia (lack of oxygen), bleeding, infection, malnutrition, and maternal stress. Researchers believe that the same damage that causes MPAs also harms the nervous system and results in a predisposition toward impulsive behavior and violence, especially for those with other risk factors (including unstable homes). Adrian Raine, one of the researchers at the forefront of work in the neuroscience of violent behavior, concludes that "prospective biosocial findings generally implicate disruption in neural development during gestation in adult violent offending," and, more specifically, that MPAs—indicative of what Raine calls "fetal neural maldevelopment"— have been "linked to peer aggression as early as age three."[40] Perhaps not coincidentally, Jesse Pomeroy might well have displayed the most common kind of MPA: small, low-seated ears. A correspondent for the *Brooklyn*

Eagle, who gave a detailed description of Pomeroy's appearance, noted that his "ears, small and clean cut, were low down." Descriptions of Pomeroy provide a provocative yet elusive suggestion that while Ruth's imagined haunting of slaughterhouses did not injure her child, some trauma in her pregnancy—alcohol consumption, malnutrition, stress, or an unnoticed infection—might well have.[41]

There are certainly, though, absolutely no grounds for the intense censure heaped on Ruth Pomeroy for decades after her son's crimes came to light. Instead, Ruth's purported urges for blood and butchery were far more indicative of the anxiety evoked by women's role in the reproduction of the species, a by-product of which, so many seemed to think, was the reproduction of women's destructive desires.[42] "Female desire is so powerful," the critic Cristina Mazzoni writes, "as to be deforming to the next generation; as a consequence, it needs to be observed, disciplined, even cured."[43] While Jesse himself was exonerated in these theories of Ruth's culpable proclivities, public opprobrium, looking for somewhere to go, shifted instead to an inoffensive hard-working woman. For by all accounts Ruth was mild-mannered, vocal only in her unswerving loyalty to and defense of her son. She spent her life trying to get him released from prison, unfailingly visiting every month (when she was allowed) and sending him the single monthly letter he was permitted to receive.

In 1914, the year before she died, Ruth was interviewed by a reporter for the *Boston Globe,* who declared that she "appears to live absorbed in the great sorrow of her life." Yet she "appears never to give up the hope and expectation that her son will yet be restored to her," the reporter continued. "And her firm conviction that the 'boy,' as she still calls him, is the victim of misunderstanding and injustice remains unshaken. . . . She never wavers in her belief that her son was wrongfully convicted. 'And I need him to take care of me!' is the pathetic plea which she urged upon the present writer during a recent visit."[44] A year later, in January 1915, when Ruth's death was reported in the *Globe,* her life is defined only by her son. "For more than 40 years she has been known as the mother of Jesse Pomeroy." Indeed, the article offers scant detail about her life apart from her monthly visits to him and her yearly presentation to the governor of a petition for his pardon.[45] In other versions, then, versions that are much closer to reality, Ruth Pomeroy was a "good" mother—hard-working, selfless, devoted to her family, and to a large extent utterly powerless (she never did get her son pardoned). But for a fleeting moment, when she was pregnant with her infamous son, she accrued enormous power, elicited intense anxiety, and unleashed a storm of blame.

The Injuries of Meat Eating

It was not only Jesse Pomeroy's mother, however, who was condemned in the theories that he was "marked" by the meat market. Most of the blame, it is true, devolved to Ruth—or, more precisely, to the fictional "Ruth Pomeroy" that subsumed the real Ruth Pomeroy. But still larger forces than women's dangerous impressibility and perverse desires were situated in the chain of causality that began in a slaughterhouse and ended with Jesse Pomeroy's mutilation and murder of small children. In a strange turn (certainly one I never anticipated), Pomeroy's crimes ended up becoming fodder for the fledgling vegetarian movement in the United States. While most commentators conceived of Pomeroy's birth as the *unnatural* product of either a shock experienced by his mother or perverse and abnormal maternal desires, a smaller contingent saw him as the quite *natural* outcome of a society that wallowed in the senseless and callous slaughter of innocent animals. The by-all-accounts cruel methods of transporting and killing animals for food in late nineteenth-century America, and meat-eating itself, were all implicated in a mass brutalizing of humanity. At best, such practices hardened Americans' moral sensibility; at worst, they produced murderers.

The conviction that cruelty to animals brutalized both animals *and* humans crystallized into a social movement in the early nineteenth century, first in England (where the Society for the Prevention of Cruelty to Animals was established in 1824) and, about forty years later, in the United States, where the first animal rights organization (New York's ASPCA) was founded in 1866.[46] The arguments that supported the animal advocacy movement, though, were being made as early as the 1750s (in England, at least), and while the primary impetus of the fledgling movement was to prevent pervasive cruelty to animals, one means by which reformers, from the beginning, attempted to convert people was to talk about how the mistreatment of animals *also* brutalized those humans who engaged in it.[47] An oration delivered in 1782 by the influential Philadelphia physician Benjamin Rush, for instance, articulated a belief that would become a commonplace of animal activism throughout the nineteenth century: "Cruelty to brute animals," he asserted, "is another means of destroying sensibility."

Rush then invokes William Hogarth's famous engravings *The Four Stages of Cruelty* (1751), arguing that they demonstrated the link that would later underwrite so many theories about Jesse Pomeroy, "the connection between cruelty to brute animals in youth, and murder in manhood."[48] By the nineteenth century, arguments that tied the moral well-being of humans to animals were pervasive, and they only became more so as the meat industry grew by leaps and bounds in the latter half of the century, providing countless hair-raising examples both of mass cruelty to animals and the concomitant corrupting of humans.[49]

While most writers targeted the meat industry itself, one of the more famous commentators on the Pomeroy case used the link between brutalizing animals and brutalized humans to illustrate the "moral danger," even "moral crime," of medical vivisection. Best known as the first female physician in the United States (earning her medical degree in 1849), Elizabeth Blackwell was also an ardent anti-vivisectionist, and she used Pomeroy as an example of how killing animals hardened the moral sensibility, warning mothers in particular about transmitting imperviousness to suffering to their offspring.[50] In an 1891 address to the Alumnae Association of the Woman's Medical College of the New York Infirmary, Blackwell spoke out about the pernicious effects of medical experimentation on animals. She argued that watching "the slow process of lingering death" both pandered to the worst aspects of human nature—the instinct of morbid curiosity, the craving for excitement, and cruelty—and served "to blunt the moral sense and injure that intelligent sympathy with suffering." Even though it had been seventeen years since Jesse Pomeroy's trial, Blackwell used his case as evidence, invoking the story of Ruth Pomeroy's visits to the slaughterhouse as her single compelling example of how witnessing butchery causes a "slow deterioration in the moral nature." Jesse Pomeroy's crimes are "a terrible example of the evil effect which the mind can exercise, in deteriorating individual character and in extending its evil influence to others."[51] In Ruth's alleged "vicious parental tendencies," in the persistent and morbid delight she took in watching the slaughter of animals, and in the consequent "atrocities" of her son, Blackwell claimed, we see that the inurement of one individual's moral sense can become manifest, exponentially multiplied, in the next generation.

It was the meat industry, however, that was most persistently attacked as the origin of Jesse Pomeroy's murderous proclivities. For many reformers, it was the simple fact of what Thomas Pomeroy did for a living that produced the boy fiend of Boston. As one vegetarian activist, Curtis Atherton, was quoted as declaring in the *Vegetarian Magazine* (published by the Chicago Vegetarian Society), the nature of the "terrible trade" of butcher makes all who participate in it "sink lower and lower in the scale of humanity." Everyone should abstain from meat-eating on the sole ground of "justice to animals and justice to one's fellow men," for those "fellow men" employed in the meat industry, Atherton proclaims, are necessarily "degraded." Upton Sinclair's enormously influential 1906 novel, *The Jungle*, offers hundreds of pages detailing brutality to animals and the corollary dehumanizing of workers in Chicago's meat-packing factories. Sinclair's claim that "there seemed to be something about the work of slaughtering that tended to ruthlessness and ferocity" was a relatively mild indictment compared to his graphic accounts of life after life being destroyed by Chicago's Beef Trust, "the Great Butcher," and his sustained portrait of a man, Jurgis Rudkus, who comes very close to losing his soul by working there. For Sinclair, the meat industry was quite simply "a monster devouring with a thousand mouths, trampling with a thousand hoofs."[52]

It is in one of the many scathing late nineteenth-century indictments of the butcher business that Jesse Pomeroy makes his first appearance in the literature of vegetarianism. In a letter to the Vegetarian Society of Manchester, England, dated July 21, 1874 (the very day after the butcher theory first appeared in the *Boston Herald*), Dr. M. L. Holbrook of New York began by recounting the details of Pomeroy's crimes, erroneously giving his age as eighteen and noting that the crime for which he was confined to jail was killing a girl of ten. Holbrook repeated Pomeroy's claim that "he could not help it," and then went on to elaborate what is manifestly the purpose of the letter:

> Now comes the point. Why could he not help it? On asking his mother relative to his case, she states that while pregnant with this child, she worked in a butchering establishment, assisting in the various duties there. The boy, born soon after, she declares has ever had a fondness for sticking knives and forks into flesh; has often bound his playmates and stuck pins into them, and treated them as a butcher would do. He was not sensual, but *loved to kill*. The mother had marked him in the blood. He had killed two children before being caught at it. Does not this boy's confession that he "could not help it," and his mother's statement that she was a butcher when the child was being formed in her womb, give us a hint? How many murderers may have received a similar taint, not, perhaps, from the mother, but from the father?[53]

Holbrook deviated rather improbably from the account in the *Boston Herald* by making Ruth herself a butcher, a version of the story that would be picked up by later commentators and that seems to have had its inception in Holbrook's expressly vegetarian agenda. It is important for Holbrook (hence his either making it up or credulously falling for a rumor) that Ruth herself "worked in a butchering establishment," since he is not interested in indicting her "perverse" desire to see blood flow; rather his target is the trade of butchering. Whether those who slaughtered animals were themselves hardened to butchery, or whether they passed that "taint" on to their offspring, Dr. Holbrook insists that killing animals for food breeds murderers.

Even a few commentators who were not explicitly allied with the vegetarian and animal rights movements offered some criticism of the meat business for its role in producing the boy fiend of Boston. They, somewhat tepidly, claimed that butchery "inured" Thomas and Ruth to bloodshed, an indifference presumably either "caught" or inherited by their son.[54] An article in the *Scientific American* in 1875, for instance, claims that what Thomas did (his "calling as a butcher and slaughterer") and what the young Jesse supposedly saw (butchery) is indeed a "moral danger," as both father and son became habituated "to scenes of violent death," leading to Jesse's "murderous propensities." The writer claims that the "wanton torture, killing and mutilation of brutes," as well as the public execution of criminals, are twinned sources of veritable "moral contagion."[55] Two health reformers (not opposed to meat-eating) wrote in 1905 that both Ruth and Thomas were so "inured to the taking of lower lives and the shedding of blood" that this "habit" was "translated" into a "homicidal tendency" in their child.[56] Other writers suggested that the problem was less the slaughterhouse per se than its accessibility, focusing on Ruth's proximity to the butchering site. The solution, they suggested, was to move slaughterhouses to remote locations, "so far out of the city limits, that butchers' wives could not spare the time to call on their husbands" when pregnant. The article in *Scientific American* agreed that "measures would be needed tending to the isolation of slaughterhouses and the prevention of public access thereto."[57]

The argument that slaughterhouses should be moved out of the line of vision is uncannily close to the almost unanimous calls to remove Jesse Pomeroy himself, monstrous product of the slaughterhouse, butcher and animal, out of sight—either by executing him or confining him for life. Society removes what troubles it. This logic has dictated the now virtually complete isolation of slaughterhouses from public view, a fact that the political scientist Timothy Pachirat targets in his book describing his many months working undercover in a slaughterhouse. His countering narrative, which he knows will evoke "disgust" in his readers, makes visible the "repugnant" reality of the inside of the slaughterhouse. Pachirat argues that power operates precisely "through the creation of distance and concealment and that our understandings of 'progress' and 'civilization' are inseparable from, and perhaps even synonymous with, the concealment (but not elimination) of what is increasingly rendered physically and morally repugnant."[58] The similar desires to "hide" both Jesse Pomeroy and the bloody "shambles" that many believed produced him in the first place are, then, fundamentally about the deeper societal need to repress monstrous eruptions of flesh and blood that belie the smooth ascent toward increasing civilization.

Some radical commentators within the vegetarian and animal rights movements, however, debunked the ploy of merely removing from sight what offends and pretending that society thus becomes more humane. They insisted that it was the mass of meat-eaters themselves who drove the industry of butchery and who mandated the presence of the blood-drenched slaughterhouse. The problem was not confined to the discrete site of slaughter, in short, but existed everywhere outside it. Jesse Pomeroy was not an anomaly because meat-eaters brought the scene of butchery into every single home, imperiling every child. For instance, an article in the *Journal of Zoöphily*, a Philadelphia anti-vivisection publication, begins with a rather standard account of a visit to the Kansas City slaughterhouses, an account that graphically described the brutalizing work of both adult and child laborers and pointed out that the "bloody contagion" is extended still further by the fact that a platform has been erected to allow spectators to oversee the horror. Apparently female visitors in particular often became so "fascinated" that they were "with difficulty driven from the spot." The writer's solution, though, is not to take down the platform and hide the slaughterhouse. Instead, she indicts "each and every one who uses flesh as part of his diet." There is, she continues "a perennial supply of brutality and murder and the production of beings more or less resembling Jesse Pomeroy." And everyone who eats meat is responsible.[59]

Other commentaries also indicted those who consumed animals, refusing to mask the brutality of the butcher industry and arguing that Jesse Pomeroy remained exemplary of the inevitable spread of that brutality.

We've seen that even as late as 1902, an article quoted earlier in this chapter from the *Vegetarian Magazine* claimed that Ruth's alleged visits to her husband at the meat market, and the passion she supposedly developed there for "stabbing the cold meat," led to Jesse's fondness for slashing with knives. But the real problem, according to this article, was in actuality neither the slaughterhouse nor Jesse's parents but the practice of meat-eating itself. Pomeroy's crimes were rooted not only in the shambles but in the kitchen, in "the extensive practice of handling and cutting up flesh meat, meat with the blood oozing from the veins and arteries." This practice, the writer insisted, necessarily produced children "with a desire for shedding blood." The article concluded with a ringing declaration: "We never see a woman handling or cutting up meat without a feeling of horror at its possible effect on succeeding generations."[60] The writer tellingly refused to evade "the blood oozing from the veins and arteries," a rhetorical strategy designed to urge everyone who eats meat to recognize—to *see*—their own butchery, their own culpability.

Several writers drew the line of causality directly and unambiguously from meat-eaters to Jesse Pomeroy himself. A paper read before the Vegetarian Society of New York in 1896, which again placed the Pomeroys in Chicago, described Jesse as being jailed there for the murder of "several children ere he was twelve years old" and stated that he could not be trusted around any living creature, whether "a kitten or a dog," because, before his birth, his mother would stand for hours watching her husband "as he plied his bloody work" in the city's stockyards. If Jesse's parents did damage to their son, however, it was only because "every flesh-eater . . . compels a class of the human race to an avocation" that brutalizes human nature.[61] In yet another iteration of the butcher theory ten years later, Daniel Hull, a vegetarian physician, recounted that when Thomas Pomeroy was out of the grocer shop in which he worked, his wife had to attend to the customers—and "One of her duties would be to cut off steaks for those requiring them. Under these conditions the boy was born, and that psychological mark, for which all meat-eating customers of Mr. Pomeroy were innocently responsible, was placed upon him, and the state of Massachusetts is now punishing him for what the gastronomic habits of the people have made him."[62] For many, then, Jesse Pomeroy was shaped by his mother only after she herself had been shaped by a population willing to wallow in bloodshed (though not willing to look at it) just so they could continue to eat meat.

In sum, there were various versions of the butcher theory: that Thomas Pomeroy habitually slaughtered animals, that his wife was perversely fascinated by the bloodshed, and that consumers continued to eat animals, to devour, as the *Vegetarian Magazine* put it, "blood oozing from the veins and arteries." What they all shared, though, was their locating the root cause of Jesse Pomeroy's crimes in the scene of predatory slaughter, a scene that revealed humans not only as needing to eat animals but as themselves animals. In his 1891 *Principles of Psychology*, William James insisted that if "evolution and the survival of the fittest be true at all, the destruction of prey and of human rivals *must* have been among the most important of man's primitive functions."[63] The butcher theory suggested that Pomeroy embodied not only an immediate and particular prenatal past (the scene of slaughter in which his parents were embroiled) but also a collective and distinctly predatory evolutionary past.

An article about Pomeroy written by the editors of the *Vegetarian* (a New York publication) in 1895, shortly after *The Principles of Psychology* was published, agreed with James's claim about the centrality of the predator–prey relationship in human evolutionary history. Beginning by locating violence toward animals at the center of its theory of (degraded) civilization, the editorial recited the familiar tale of Thomas Pomeroy's work of butchery and his wife's witnessing of that work. It went on to identify butchers and the equally culpable "flesh-eaters who hire them to do their bloody work" as the cause of Jesse Pomeroy's brutal murders of "several" children before he turned twelve—adding for good measure the apocryphal story of Pomeroy's having skinned a kitten alive in jail, another depravity to be traced back to "flesh-eaters." The writer asserted an ethical mandate to overcome what James had called those predatory "primitive functions"—not least by eschewing meat-eating, a practice which kept humans in thrall to their savage past. "Civilization is but a very thin veneer to the man who lives on the flesh of animals," the editorial declared, adding that brutality and murder are "universal with all who live on a flesh diet."[64]

Killing and eating meat, in this account, marks the primitive heritage of humans (as James had argued), although it insists that the recurrence of this primitive past in the present world is not inevitable. Our residual savagery can be overcome by adopting vegetarianism, by refusing the barbaric encounter with animals at the heart of meat-eating. Indeed, the editorial implies that such encounters are not only about confronting real animals (cattle, sheep, pigs) but also about animating the "animal" within the human—the vestige of the savage we used to be and the animal we continue to be. Meat-eating brings the animal dangerously close; indeed, the ingestion of animal flesh serves as a metaphor for precisely that "animal" inside that is vivified by meat-eating.

Animal Nature

It was not just a dread of women's reproductive power and a burgeoning vegetarian activism, then, that motivated stories about the effect of "the meat market" on the body and mind of Jesse Pomeroy. In the end, what lay at the heart of the butcher theory of Pomeroy's origins was the inextricable connection of the human to the nonhuman animal. Pomeroy's story, like the vast majority of purported cases of maternal impressions described in the late nineteenth century, centrally involved encounters with animals that terrified pregnant women, deforming the unborn child by imprinting it with the external natural world, by mixing it (the inviolable human) with the nonhuman.

Such cases abounded in medical journals. A mother was taking a walk while pregnant, for instance, and, to her horror, "caught upon her left foot and ankle a common striped snake." She subsequently gave birth to a child with "a mark which quite closely resembles the common striped snake." A sleeping pregnant woman was awakened by a braying jackass, and she delivered a still-born child with "the head and complete ears of a jackass." Another pregnant woman saw a "two-headed nightingale" and, sure enough, she delivered a "twin monstrosity, the two children being connected from neck to umbilicus." A mother "frightened by a rabbit" gave birth to a "child born with hare-lip." And another expectant mother, who was "frightened by a pet squirrel attempting to bite her," gave birth to a baby "born with compact mass of hair extending from eyebrows over head and back, and closely resembling a squirrel"; the infant also sported "two well-developed incisor teeth."[65] All of these cases represented the dangerous merging of the mother's body with an unpredictable external nature. In fact, it seems to be precisely the *unpredictability* of nature against which the theory of maternal impressions, with its tight causality, was designed to defend. The troubling lack of control that humans experience in reproduction (the unwilled birth of "monstrosities") was displaced onto animals' capricious comings and goings.[66] But then the mechanistic cause-and-effect implicit in the theory of maternal impressions exerted an order, a logic, explaining the fickleness of a nature (including an internal nature) that always risked escaping human control.

The infant that embodied these encounters—that was part human, part animal—was "monstrous" because it transgressed what should have been one of the most inviolable of borders. In *Purity and Danger,* Mary Douglas offers the "monstrous birth" as exemplar of the polluting event, one that confuses cherished classifications: part child, part animal, "monstrous births" menaced the "defining lines between humans and animals."[67] Jesse Pomeroy may not have had the ears of a jackass, the incisors of a squirrel, or even a hare-lip, but he nevertheless inhabited the border between rational being and irrational animal. Contemplating Pomeroy in 1895, the spiritualist John Reynolds Francis explains the "juvenile monstrosity" as a literal mixing of human and animal "molecules." He writes that witnessing "the horrid butchery of oxen, hogs, etc." when she was pregnant aroused Ruth's "animal nature (animals in her nature), and the result was, she formed around the spirit of the embryonic Jesse an organism composed of cruel, savage molecular brutes, and they actuated him to commit murder." What Francis called "molecular brutes" possess, he writes, "the seeds of crime" and "incite acts of cruelty."[68] In this rather singular theory, Francis argues that watching animals being slaughtered formed animalistic molecules that shaped the embryo Ruth was carrying, creating a human–animal hybrid who became a brutish murderer. While some infants have their bodies stamped with the traces of animals that horrified and fascinated their pregnant mothers, Francis believed that Pomeroy's *soul* was similarly stamped.[69]

The best-known Bostonian to become embroiled in the butcher theory of Jesse Pomeroy's crimes was the physician, Harvard professor, and writer Oliver Wendell Holmes Sr., and his contributions elucidate the way in which this theory was, at bottom, about an ungovernable human nature. At first, Holmes entered the debate despite himself, as others rushed to point out the relevance of his most famous novel to the murder case that was convulsing Boston. In 1861, when Jesse Pomeroy was only two years old, Holmes had published his first novel, *Elsie Venner,* whose protagonist is the reptilian result of her mother's having been bitten by a rattlesnake when she was pregnant. Elsie is driven by compulsions she doesn't understand and cannot control—and Holmes clearly lays the roots of her nature in the human past, in human flesh, which the snake encounter serves to allegorize.

After the story that Jesse Pomeroy was "marked by the meat market" emerged in July 1874, commentators immediately noted the parallel to Holmes's novel. Indeed, the first such link was made on July 21, 1874, just one day after the butcher theory first appeared in the *Boston Herald.* The New York *Evening Post* repeated the *Herald's* story of Pomeroy's prenatal impression, writing that Jesse's mother "daily went to the slaughter-house with her husband, where she not only watched with pleasure the process of killing the cattle, but sometimes took part in it herself." Her son then "manifested the same unnatural taste for blood," loving nothing more than to plunge his knife into pieces of meat. He was born "with the desire implanted in his nature to hurt something." The writer then compared Pomeroy's origins to the "powerful and entertaining story of 'Elsie Venner,'" in which Dr. Holmes "has treated this subject very fully," selecting the case "of a child endowed with the instincts of a rattlesnake through the fright given to the mother by one of these reptiles."[70]

On the next day, July 22, the same day that the *Globe* (fruitlessly) refuted the butcher theory, a writer for the *Springfield Republican* referred to *Elsie Venner* in an article that explained Pomeroy by means of maternal impressions. It has been "familiarly known since far back in the ages," the writer declared, that "the child in the womb may receive the compelling influences that shall shape its character and life." After giving several "real" examples, the writer continues: "Nor will anyone forget that remarkable picture of a congenital curse, drawn by Dr. Holmes in the story of 'Elsie Venner.' Such a curse, only more terrible and mischievous, rests upon the luckless Jesse Pomeroy. He knows not why he feels that lust for torture, for blood, for life; how, in the unconscious dawn of his existence, his mother's abnormal whim was warping him into a monster so exceptional that his fellows must put him out of the way, like a noxious reptile."[71] Evidently influenced by the plot of the novel he was describing, the writer for the *Republican* not only compared Pomeroy to Elsie in their both having been deformed before birth, but he also described Pomeroy, like Elsie, as snake-like in his hybrid and monstrous origin.[72]

Eventually, Holmes entered the Pomeroy controversy himself, standing on the side of mercy and signing a petition to Governor Gaston urging him to commute Pomeroy's sentence to life imprisonment.[73] Holmes's subsequent references to Pomeroy explain why he would have leaned toward commuting the boy's sentence: for Holmes, free will (and thus culpability) was deeply qualified by the determining power of the past. In his 1892 study of Ralph Waldo Emerson, Holmes expressed skepticism about the Romantic belief in a child's instinctual grasp of what is true. He pointed out that a child's instinct is not unvarying, that it depends on the "set of moulds" that shape his or her particular brain: "If the mind comes into consciousness with a good set of moulds . . . from good ancestry, it may be all very well to give the counsel to the youth to plant himself on his instincts." But some infants are born with flawed "moulds" and "dangerous" instincts, also inherited from their forebears. Holmes concluded that what might be "a safe guide for Emerson might not work well with Lacenaire or Jesse Pomeroy."[74] Holmes's desire to see Pomeroy's sentence commuted must have come in large part, then, from his belief that Jesse was a product of his ancestry and thus not entirely culpable for what he did.

Determinism structures Holmes's novel of thirty years earlier. Elsie's transmitted antenatal "injury" is above all a source of *uncontrollable and unconscious* action, what Holmes variously called an "automatic action" or a "reflex action."[75] Elsie is thus framed as not responsible for what she does, even when she is fatally violent. The narrator, Bernard Langdon, contemplates Elsie's "alien impulse," which "swayed her will," and concludes that it "came from some impression that reached far back into the past," and that she had "brought her ruling tendency, whatever it was, into the world with her."[76] Another character, the Reverend Doctor Honeywood, ruminates, "If by the visitation of God a person receives an injury which impairs the intellect or the moral perception, is it not monstrous to judge such a person by our common working standards of right and wrong?" People readily accept that a blow to the head might cause insanity, Honeywood thinks, but "how long will it be before we shall learn that for every wound which betrays itself to the sight by a scar, there are a thousand unseen mutilations that cripple, each of them, some one or more of our highest faculties?"[77] Holmes makes it clear by his language—*injury, wound, mutilation*—that Elsie was traumatized before her birth, and that whatever physical scar she may have (and she does have a "faint birth-mark" on her neck), the *visible* wound pales in comparison to the *invisible* mental and moral wound she suffered. This wound, not her will, directs what she unknowingly does and also absolves her.[78] It is telling that Honeywood does not call Elsie herself a monster, but rather calls "monstrous" those who would judge and condemn her.

The prenatal injury that shaped Elsie implanted within her a kind of memory that was unavailable to consciousness, one which she would never be able to access and never understand. Strikingly akin to Jesse Pomeroy, Elsie is unable to put into words the emotions that wash through her or explain the impulsive actions she is driven to commit. Indeed, like Pomeroy, she is almost completely inarticulate. As the narrator ruminates: "Poor Elsie! She never sang nor played. She never shaped her inner life in words: such utterance was as much denied to her nature as common articulate speech to the deaf mute."[79] Without knowledge (of herself), Elsie just strikes at others as the rattlesnake struck at her mother, and she keeps returning to the terrain inhabited by the snakes—repeating her mother's wounding, which is, indeed, her own wounding. She repeats her injury precisely because she does not *know* her injury. Elsie is thus much like Pomeroy, who mutilated and killed unthinkingly and mutely, who was compelled, as many commentators would have it, to blindly re-create the scene of butchery that scarred his mother and wounded him before he ever attained consciousness.

Although he did not mention him by name, Holmes actually took up the case of Jesse Pomeroy earlier than his fleeting reference in 1892. In an essay titled "Crime and Automatism," published in the *Atlantic Monthly* in 1875, Holmes expounds more fully than in *Elsie Venner* his views on the fundamentally hereditary nature of crime. And he begins with Pomeroy, the conundrum that all those who think about crime must strive to explain. His is a "moral nature very unlike that of ordinary human beings," Holmes wrote, evoking the enigmatic character he did not have to name for his readers to recognize.[80] He went on to argue that what many construe as evil in this young criminal was in fact the product of "hereditary instincts." Pomeroy, like all of us, was driven by "organic tendencies, inborn idiosyncrasies, which, so far as they go, are *purely mechanical.*" These tendencies are "the best excuse that can be pleaded for a human being, exempting him from all moral responsibility when they reach a certain extreme degree, and exculpating him just so far as they are *uncontrollable.*" Violent actions are the inevitable product not only of an individual's past but of an "organic" cause: they are "reflex movements, automatic consequences of practically irresistible causes existing in the inherited organization and in preceding conditions." "Monsters of crime," Holmes concluded, "do not come into the world by accident; they are the product of antecedent conditions."[81] According to Holmes, then, Pomeroy had nothing of what we call free will, for the will obeys the laws of heredity and of "organic tendencies." Every individual becomes what his ancestors necessitated he should become.

While Holmes's *Elsie Venner* dramatized the heritability of nature as a result of the seemingly random bite of the snake, "Crime and Automatism," fourteen years later and in the wake of the Pomeroy case, extended the inevitability of one's inborn nature to everyone: a natural law, not a singular accident. Holmes argued that *all* humans are traversed by a substratum of automaticity that prompts them to act mechanically, without reason or choice. After all, everyone inherits "reflex movements, automatic consequences" from those who come before. *Elsie Venner* represents the particular violent incursion into the human body and mind of a rattlesnake bite, and Jesse Pomeroy embodied the intrusion of the scene of violent slaughter, but Holmes argued that all of us contain the automaticity of our own "alien" nature, an internal nature perhaps even more inimical to the rational and volitional "human" than an external predatory environment.

What Holmes described in *Elsie Venner* and "Crime and Automatism" was the intractable fact of humans' possession by their nature—by their body and flesh. The notion of Pomeroy's actual "possession" came up here and there in the 1870s, enough to prompt an editorial in *Scientific American* in October 1874 debunking the idea—the same editorial that blamed Jesse's troubles on his pregnant mother's transgressive desires. "The devil dies hard," the piece began, citing an article from the *Christian Observer* (reprinted in the *New York Observer*) that suggested Pomeroy was possessed by the devil. The *Observer* had described Pomeroy's crimes and then asked: "Do they not look as if the devil had more power over human nature than he is ordinarily credited with? In view of them, can we say that demoniacal possessions are impossible?" Contemptuously dismissing such a theory, *Scientific American* insisted that Pomeroy was explicable "without the devil's assistance" and, as we've seen, invoked the butcher theory to argue that he had been morally warped by "vicious influences"—Ruth's "morbid pleasure at the sight of blood"—which he inevitably "inherited."[82]

What the author of this editorial, like all proponents of the butcher theory, and in tandem with Holmes, posited was "possession" of another kind than the demonic. In the end, Pomeroy was possessed by his own body, a body formed (and deformed) by his pregnant mother and, through her, by the slaughterhouse and the flesh-eaters of the "civilized" world—even, still more remotely, by the animal and predatory instincts and what Holmes called the "organic tendencies" of the entire species, by the flesh to which all humans are heir. While the theory of maternal impressions has gone the way of demonic possession and has long been debunked, it nonetheless served as an apt way to describe the shaping power that a perennially mysterious body wields over conscious, intentional selfhood. The philosopher Dylan Trigg has articulated this power as a struggle between "the body as *possessed* by the subject"—that is, the body we think we "own," control, and direct—and the "body as *possessor* of the subject," which is a body that dispossesses us, that always and everywhere exceeds our grasp. It is this body, this flesh, that Jesse Pomeroy made so strikingly manifest. And we all have a body that we struggle to possess but that also possesses us. Something "more enigmatic than the lived body," Trigg writes, "protrudes into the life of personal existence, a fossil that bears the trace of an origin still resounding in the hollows of bodily being."[83] It is this idea of the body as potentially legible "fossil," bearing the traces of a life inaccessible to consciousness, that those who espoused the butcher theory provocatively attempted to describe.

4

"Dime Novel Pomeroy"

Only one theory of Jesse Pomeroy's origins vied in popularity with the theory that he was "marked by the meat market." It was the claim that his crimes were imitations of the violent scenes in dime novel westerns. One newspaper article, tellingly titled "Dime Novel Pomeroy," pointed out that ever since Ruth Pomeroy refuted the theory that her son was "pre-natally cursed," there was nothing to ground an explanation of the boy's unthinkable acts except for the persistent rumor that he had been an avid reader of dime novels. This rumor was confirmed when a well-known Boston publisher, James T. Fields, interviewed Pomeroy in his jail cell in 1875. Fields emerged from that interview to pronounce that Pomeroy had indeed been "an inveterate reader of dime novels and other stories of violence." The word spread, and soon hundreds of Americans believed what the writer of "Dime Novel Pomeroy" had suggested: Pomeroy's damaging reading habits were "sufficient explanation of his murderous inclinations." With Fields's dissemination of his conversation with Jesse Pomeroy, the case promptly got swept up in the late nineteenth-century hysteria about the dire effects of dime novels.[1]

When late twentieth- and early twenty-first-century critics have cast a glance toward this theory of crime's origins, they have been uniformly skeptical. This chapter takes seriously, however, his contemporaries' claims about the powerful effect sensational literature may have had on Pomeroy. For one thing, his acts of torture and murder do seem to adhere uncannily closely to those he might have been reading between around 1868 and early 1874. Indeed, the ways in which torture was represented in western dime novels may have contributed not only to Pomeroy's fantasy life—a defining feature of the serial killer—but also to the "nonfulfilled experiences" that drive the repetitiveness of serial killers' crimes.[2] Most importantly, though, the ways in which late nineteenth-century Americans conceived of the connection between literature and its effects resonate with what we are increasingly learning about humans' fundamental imitative propensities and about the contagious power of media images.

Like the "butcher theory," the dime novel explanation suggested that Pomeroy was not entirely responsible for what he did—that he was, in this case, under the sway of what he read. As one of the many advocates of the theory put it, "It is difficult for us to realize how completely we are made up of our images from the external world."[3] If the butcher theory at bottom claimed Pomeroy was possessed by his own body, the dime novel theory asserted he was possessed by the fiction he read, by its powerful, inciting images. But the dime novel theory also comes back to the body. Like the shocking impressions and wayward maternal desires that were stamped on the unborn child, the scenes of fiction made their impress on a body that is only ever partially under our control.

The Injuries of Reading

Only two days after Horace Millen's mutilated body was found on the marshes of Dorchester Bay, the *Boston Daily Globe* stated that, according to Pomeroy, "he had not read any murder stories or dime novels, but had only read his school books." Four days later, the *Globe* reversed its own reporting: "Contrary to the previous statements, there is plenty of evidence to show that the reading of dime novels and narratives of bloody tragedies among the Indians and others constituted a good share of the boy's mental nourishment."[4] Jesse's reading of dime novels came up at his trial, when Dr. George Choate (the physician who testified for the prosecution) described his conversation with Jesse about his motive for killing Millen: "He once told me that he had an uncontrollable desire to commit torture on boys, which he thought might have come from reading cheap novels, which he had done a great many times; he took great delight in reading Indian tales where cruelties were described."[5] After the verdict was returned, the *Globe* editorialized about the causes of Jesse's crimes, offering one of the very few denunciations of Thomas and Ruth Pomeroy outside of the baseless butcher theory: "Can there be a question that instead of allowing him to gloat over the recital of Indian atrocities, which stimulated the worst tendencies of his nature, the best parental care would have ascertained and corrected these bloodthirsty characteristics?"[6] The alacrity with which the press attributed Pomeroy's crimes to his reading habits certainly suggests a predilection for that explanation on the part of his contemporaries; then, as now, popular culture was seen as a powerful influence on young people, and parents were excoriated for not moderating that influence.

It was not until Fields's interview with Pomeroy in April 1875, though, that knee-jerk assumptions about the dire effects of mass culture seemed vindicated; after that interview, public outcry over the boy's reading habits and his purportedly dangerously imitative reading practices really gained momentum. The notes Fields made before and after his handwritten transcript of the interview suggest that he planned to write a lecture on the perils of cheap fiction—and, indeed, reports confirm that, despite his failing health, he did adduce Pomeroy as a negative instance on several occasions.[7] Fields described his interview with Pomeroy at some length in lectures he gave at, for example, a church in Manhattan in December 1875, in Worcester, Massachusetts, in January 1879, and at the Brooklyn Atheneum in late February 1879. He was spreading the word about the dangers of cheap fiction, with Pomeroy as his leading object lesson, for at least four years.[8] After Fields's death in 1881, an extended portion of the interview with Pomeroy, along with his commentary on that interview, was published in a collection of biographical notes and personal sketches assembled by his wife, Annie, who was also interested in social reform.[9] Fields's lectures, the press accounts of those lectures, and his wife's posthumous publication of the interview, all meant that the information Fields elicited from Pomeroy received wide circulation. Indeed, once the interview was published, in 1881, writers who took up the question of Jesse Pomeroy and the dangers of cheap fiction invariably referred to it.[10]

Fields's interview with Pomeroy was unprecedented, according to his wife, who wrote that it was "altogether out of his usual plan to do anything of the kind, believing it to be a mistake to gaze upon misery or wrong which you can do nothing to alleviate." Her husband had a "definite end in view," however. According to his notes (and his wife's account), he was motivated by a long-standing conviction that "if the influence of good literature was beneficent, the opposite was also true,—the effect of bad literature must be deteriorating."[11] Fields had clearly been drawn to the case by newspaper accounts: the file at the Massachusetts Historical Society that contains his handwritten account of and notes on the interview also includes an article clipped from the *Boston Globe* about the case.[12] Fields sought out Pomeroy in his jail cell, then, with the particular intent, as his notes explain, of "conversing with the boy with reference to what books he had been brought up upon."[13] What Jesse said to Fields in this interview is the most reliable and detailed account of his reading habits.[14] As Fields recorded it:

> I then asked him if he was fond of reading. He said "Very, I read everything I can get."
> "When did you first begin to be fond of reading?" I asked him.
> "I guess about nine years of age."
> "What kind of books did you first begin to read?"
> "O, blood and thunder stories!"
> "Were the books small ones?"
> "Yes, most Beadle's dime novels."
> "How many of Beadle's dime novels do you think you read from nine years old upward?"
> "Well, I can't remember exactly, but should think sixty."
> "Do you remember the titles of most of them?"
> "No, sir, but 'Buffalo Bill' was one of the best."
> "What were the books about?"
> "Killing and scalping injuns and so forth, and running away with women; a good many of the scenes were out on the plains."
> "Were there any pictures in the books?"
> "Yes sir, plenty of them, blood and thunder pictures, tomahawking, and scalping."
> "Did your parents know you were reading those books all through those years?"
> "No, I kept it away from them."
> "Do you think you read more of those books than any of the boys who lived near you?"
> "Yes, sir, a great many more. I had a kind of passion for 'em."
> "Do you think those books were an injury to you, and excited you to commit the acts you have done?"
> "Yes, sir, I have thought it all over and it seems to me now they did. I can't say certainly, of course, and perhaps if I should think it over again, I should say it was something else."
> "What else?"
> "Well, sir, really I can't say."[15]

Adding evidentiary heft to the speculations that had been circulating prior to 1875, Pomeroy told Fields that he read around sixty of Beadle's dime novels; he identified the plot elements ("killing and scalping injuns and so forth") that presumably were so pernicious; and he even seemed to agree with Fields that the books were an "injury" and "excited" him to commit acts of torture and murder. Not surprisingly, Fields was convinced by this interview that reading dime novels precipitated the boy's descent into violent crime. In his notes after his transcript of their conversation, Fields wrote, "I came away from the young murderer's cell with the conviction more deeply impressed on my mind than ever that the chief curse of youth in our day is that wide spread degrading, unwatched literature, called 'cheap,' which if unchecked by law is destined to sap the morals of our land and render crime a thing of daily and hourly occurrence."[16] While Fields clearly went to see Pomeroy already convinced that cheap literature was a curse (it was a conviction only "*more* deeply impressed" on his mind during the course of the interview), Pomeroy seemed living proof that he was right.

Plenty of late nineteenth-century Americans shared Fields's view, and from late 1875 on the revelations elicited by his interview circulated widely in the press and in literary culture more generally. One of the first instances, from December 1875 (eight months after the interview), is exemplary in what it cites from the interview as Fields was recounting it in his lectures, laying out phrases that formed a kind of iterable trope. Summarizing the talk Fields delivered in Manhattan, an article in the *Boston Journal* reports that Pomeroy told Fields "he had always been a great reader of blood and thunder stories, having read probably sixty novels, all treating of scalping and deeds of violence. The boy said that he had no doubt that the reading of those books had a great deal to do with his course, and he would advise all boys to leave them alone." Accounts of this lecture—and these words— spread from Portland, Maine, to Cincinnati, Ohio, and Quincy, Illinois.[17]

Fields's interview with Pomeroy added fuel to a swelling moral panic about the flood of cheap fiction washing over the nation. The surge of anxiety about dime novel reading in the 1870s was undoubtedly attributable to several causes. Notably, publishers were newly targeting boys as well as working-class readers generally, and the middle-class arbiters of culture (represented not least by the publication Fields edited for years, the *Atlantic Monthly*) were afraid they were losing their ability to shape the tastes and values of the lower classes.[18] But the fact that Fields's interview with Pomeroy so explicitly linked his horrendous crimes to sensational literature, confirming the gossip that had been flying since Jesse's arrest and trial, must surely have contributed to the panic.

It is primarily as the most notorious reader of late nineteenth-century dime novels that Jesse Pomeroy has made his several fleeting appearances in late twentieth- and early twenty-first-century scholarship. His supposed enacting of violent cheap literature is repeated in histories of juvenile delinquency, late nineteenth-century literary culture, and media effects. In a 1971 study of nineteenth-century juvenile delinquency, for instance, Joseph Hawes begins his chapter on children's literature with Pomeroy's confession that he devoured dime novels and that they had most likely been, as Fields put it, an "injury" to him. Jon Savage's more recent study of the creation of youth culture describes how, in struggling to understand the boy's vicious crimes, Pomeroy's contemporaries found one possible solution in his "avid consumption of dime novels" and in his reveling in fictional "descriptions of torture and murder." Edmund Pearson's ground-breaking 1929 study of dime novels mentions the widespread belief that "Pomeroy might have been prompted to his offences by cheap 'literature of the dime novel type.'" And sixty years later, in his equally influential work on dime novels, Michael Denning invokes Jesse Pomeroy as part of the class-inflected debate over the deleterious consequences of cheap fiction.[19] Pomeroy has also appeared in recent studies of the effects of the mass media. Demonstrating the persistent influence of Fields's interview, in his contribution to a collection titled *Ill Effects: The Media/Violence Debate*, Graham Murdock cites Pomeroy's admission to Fields that he read many "blood and thunder tales," and that they most likely injured him. Murdock claims that Pomeroy's crimes precipitated the first major wave of hysteria about the dire influence of the mass media on youth. Indeed, in a survey of modern media law, Roger Sadler even posits the Pomeroy case as America's "first media copycat claim," the originary instance in which the media seemed to have *directly* incited dangerous behavior and created an "undue risk of harm."[20]

None of these writers actually takes seriously, though, the late nineteenth-century conviction that dime novels contributed to Pomeroy's proclivity to torture and murder. Some dismiss it out of hand: "It is rather unlikely that dime novels or sensational literature actually caused any of these problems," Joel Shrock writes in a study of popular culture in the Gilded Age. Others argue that the Pomeroy case simply provided fodder for the "vice ideologues" of the 1870s and 1880s in their ongoing class struggle.[21] Historians of the dime novel have been especially defensive, arguing that the genre became one of a succession of easy scapegoats for crime. Pearson puts it particularly colorfully, proclaiming that dime novels served as "the most useful explanation of crime, and the easiest excuse for the offender, until its place was taken by the cigarette, and then by the moving pictures. Finally, we achieved the psychosis, the inhibition, the slave phantasy, the fixation and the pituitary gland, and at last think there are no more evil-doers." In a more sophisticated version of this argument, Savage contends that while late nineteenth-century social commentators were busy worrying about dime novels, they "barely considered" what he obviously deems the real cause of juvenile crime: harsh and impoverished urban life and, in Pomeroy's case, an abusive alcoholic father (a theory I take up in the epilogue).[22]

Treating it as a symptom of class anxiety, an illustration of the perennial need to find a ready culprit for rising crime rates, and a poor substitute for modern (and thus better) theories of crime and its causation, twentieth- and twenty-first-century scholars have routinely disdained what Pomeroy's contemporaries were so sure of: that dime novels played a critical role in shaping his violent tendencies. There are certainly compelling reasons to approach this theory with some skepticism. The rush to blame dime novels did ignore the systemic social and economic conditions that produced crime, and it did manifest escalating middle-class worries about working-class youth—their literacy, their leisure, their sheer growth in numbers in urban areas, and their potential increase in political and cultural power. But unlike the theory that Pomeroy was stamped in utero by his mother's visits to the slaughterhouse, the influence of dime novels is not so easily brushed aside. Not least, Pomeroy actually admitted that cheap fiction might have influenced him, even before James Fields came to see him armed with his earnest convictions.[23] Moreover, theories of reading, increasingly bolstered by science, continue to suggest that literature can indeed be powerfully transformative, that reader and character, reality and fiction, can become profoundly confused.

Scenes of Torture

What exactly was Pomeroy reading, though, that influenced him so powerfully, that constituted such an "injury"? We've seen that he confessed to James Fields that he started reading dime novels when he was nine (around the end of 1868) and that his preference was fiction of the frontier ("killing and scalping injuns and so forth") issued by the pioneering dime novel publisher Beadle (later Beadle & Adams). Dr. Theodore Fisher, who, like Fields, visited Pomeroy in 1875 (more than once), also reported that

Pomeroy was "fond of reading stories of savage warfare." And confirming what Fields and Fisher learned, though less reliable than their accounts, someone who claimed to have been a "schoolmate" of Jesse's wrote in the *Globe* in 1891 that Jesse was never without a "brick-colored 'Beadle' or a white-covered 'Munro' in his pocket or hand." Pomeroy's schoolmate also noted Jesse's unusual preference for western stories of Indians and renegades.[24]

Pomeroy would certainly have had ready access to Beadle's frontier stories. From at least the date of his release from reform school in early February 1874 (and perhaps even before he was sent to the school), Jesse helped his brother run a newsstand out of their store at 327 Broadway in South Boston. In fact, one of the reasons Jesse was released early was precisely so he could help his brother: the authorities were convinced that he had salutary and stable employment. Part of Jesse's job involved picking up newspapers from the New England News Company, which was one of Beadle's distribution outlets.[25] So if Pomeroy had ready access to Beadle's western dime novels from around late 1868 until he was sent to reform school in September 1872, and then from his release on February 6, 1874, until his arrest on March 18, 1874, what might he have encountered in their pages?

One thing that is immediately clear about the western dime novels Pomeroy could have been reading in the late 1860s and early 1870s is that they abounded with stories of Indian atrocities.[26] From the earliest captivity narratives published over two hundred years before, images of Indian torture, scalping, and general malignity had been continuously and widely propagated in American literature. From the mid-1860s through the 1890s, dime novels became the principal source of such images.[27] One Beadle novel, originally published in 1866 (and then reprinted at least twice, in 1869 and 1882), dramatized the stereotype that pervades them all: "ruthless savages," as the novel described them, are "actuated by an insatiable thirst for human blood," and their "savage spirits" gloried in "the writhings of the body of the doomed wretch" under "merciless torments."[28] The writers of dime novels for the most part repeated available tropes rather than innovating; as Roger Nichols writes, these authors "tended to popularize existing views of Indians," sometimes copying the characters of the influential James Fenimore Cooper. He adds that "before the end of the century nearly everything which might have been said about the Native Americans had been said, so usually the later novels repeated ideas."[29] Dime novels didn't just purvey stereotypes, then; they purveyed the *same* stereotypes over and over. Pomeroy's own repetitive acts of torture, in other words, modeled the mechanical reiterations at the heart of the fiction he read.

The plots of frontier dime novels from the late 1860s and early 1870s are typically structured around the capture of a beautiful girl by Indians and their white renegade allies—the latter often based on historical characters such as the brothers Simon, George, and James Girty, who are portrayed as even more depraved than the Indians with whom they live. The bulk of the narrative involves the heroic frontiersmen (with an occasional "noble" Indian) tracking down the girl and other prisoners who are confronted with the prospect of torture and death. (The girl is often threatened with something worse than torture—marriage, official or otherwise, with the white renegade or Indian chief.) Numerous scuffles ensue, involving shooting and scalping, until the climactic conflict and the rescue of the girl and the other imprisoned whites. While the arc of each plot is (as Beadle often defensively claimed) relentlessly moralistic (good always wins out), the novels are filled with sudden outbursts of explicit violence that are much more viscerally compelling than the tepid morality of the ending. In *The Backwoodsmen*, for example, one Indian "whipped out his scalping-knife, passed it rapidly around the unresisting head" of another and "tore the scalp loose from the bleeding skull." And in *The Wood Rangers*, the white renegade, having seized a man by the hair, "ran the keen point of the knife, in his right hand, round the crown, and with a coarse laugh, jerked the scalp from his head."[30] Good may win out, but only after numerous forays into the savage side of frontier life.

At the very heart of Beadle's westerns is the promise of sustained torture, and the elements that compose such scenes are ritualized through endless repetition. Victims are first stripped and bound to a tree or post. In *The Mink Coat*, for instance, the Indians "were rudely tearing the garments" from two white men as they prepared "their victims for the fiery sacrifice."[31] The victims are typically taunted remorselessly. In *The Wolf-Queen*, once his victim is bound, renegade Jim Girty insulted him "in every way that suggested itself to his devilish mind. He struck him with his open hand, spit in his face, and plucked out a handful of his beautiful beard!"[32]

Dancing, as well as abuse, often precedes more violent torture. In *The Mink Coat*, scouts attempting to save the prisoners see "the forms of the half-nude Indians dancing around the glade in drunken glee, screeching and yelling in diabolical tones!" In *The Black Princess,* the Indians do the "scalp dance" for at least an hour while their victim is tied to a stake, and (in a narrative interjection unusual in dime novels) the writer comments that "amid all savage nations, or nations in a primitive state of existence, dancing is a favorite amusement." Another form of extended overture involves the captors stabbing the victim with an assortment of accessible objects, a practice in which the whole tribe can participate. In *The Indian Spy,* the prisoner is bound to a stump and "surrounded by a pack of mischievous children, who were emulating the deeds of their fathers, with tiny bows and arrows, sticks, stones, and such missiles as lay to their hands." A little later we are told that the savages are "preparing splinters or instruments with which to add to the prisoner's tortures." In *The Black Princess,* an Indian "prepared splinters with which to puncture [his victim's] flesh; another sharpened a knife which was to gash his limbs; while others placed near him the faggots which were to consume his body when death had claimed his victim."[33]

Descriptions of violence then intensify even more, moving from elaborate preparation to intimations of violent cutting and burning. In *The Wolf Demon,* Simon Girty tells Harvey Winthrop in loving detail what will happen to him: "The tomahawks of the Indians will cut your flesh from your bones, even while you are a living man.'"[34] The Prophet of the Manitou, in *The Wolf-Queen,* pronounces the doom of the three prisoners: they are to be flayed alive and then burned. In the same novel, Jim Girty tells the prisoner he loathes the most that he looks forward to "sawing" off his skin and, later, that he will "skin" him alive.[35]

The parallels between these reiterated scenes and the tortures Jesse Pomeroy inflicted on his victims are striking. As we saw in chapter 1, Pomeroy stripped and bound all his victims. On the first three occasions, he mostly confined himself to beating the boys with a rope or a board. In the case of Robert Maies, his first victim, Pomeroy also "ran around him, jumped up and down and laughed," or, as another account put it, "whipped him and danced around him in a strange manner." In the case of his third victim, Johnny Balch, Pomeroy stripped him, then tied him to a beam and whipped him and then, in a distinct progression in cruelty, took the boy to a salt creek and washed off his wounds.[36] Putting salt water on a victim's wounds seems a deviation from typical accounts of Indian torture, but in one Beadle dime novel, significantly printed twice in the period that Jesse would have been reading (serialized in June and July of 1868 and then published in its entirety in late March 1869), the infamous Simon Girty does exactly that. After beating his victim with a hickory stick, Girty "went to a barrel, which stood near the door, and stooping, lifted a little of the contents in his hands and threw it on the bleeding back of the young man. Every drop scorched like a burning coal, for it was a strong brine which he had used in pickling venison." Pomeroy also washed the wounds of his penultimate torture victim, Joseph Kennedy, with salt water.[37]

After limiting himself to whipping and beating his first three victims, Pomeroy soon progressed to more vicious methods of assault, routinely stabbing, cutting, and gashing in ways that continued to emulate the acts detailed in dime novels. After enticing his fourth victim, George Pratt, onto an old boat at South Boston Point, Pomeroy began "beating his naked limbs with a strap, sticking pins in his face, limbs and private parts, biting and other methods of torture." The *Boston Herald* reported that "the young savage" was "at the same time dancing in great glee at seeing the blood flow." A fifth victim, Harry Austin, was allegedly cut on the back and the groin, and in the cases of Pratt and Austin, Pomeroy began attacking the genitals with pins and then a knife, an escalation in violence that culminated with the murdered Horace Millen, whose penis was almost entirely severed from his body.[38] (Explicitly detailing this kind of torture was certainly beyond the pale for Beadle, given the firm's aspirations for a family readership, but in at least one novel Indians are described as cutting unspecified body parts off their naked victim: "To show what human nature can endure, we must mention that his ears, fingers and other parts had been cut off.")[39] Pomeroy cut his sixth victim, Joseph Kennedy, three times with a knife and soon moved to his last victim, still further escalating his violence. As Charles A. Gould recounted at trial, Pomeroy "stripped me and tied me to a post, putting a string around my legs and body; he tied my hands and took off all my clothes; he drew out a big knife and a small one and cut me five times on the head and once back of each ear; one cut was made with the big knife."[40] Gould's testimony suggests that Pomeroy was attempting a scalping, but the boy was saved by the fact that a man passed by, frightening Pomeroy away.

While Pomeroy appears to have tried his hand at scalping, the theory that his acts of torture were influenced by his reading of dime novel westerns is weakened by one striking absence: fire. Every torture scene in these novels is meant to terminate in the immolation of the victim at the stake, yet there is no explicit mention of fire in any of the accounts of Pomeroy's crimes between 1871 and 1872. Evidence suggests, though, that he may have tried to burn Katie Curran's body, most likely after she was dead, in early 1874. At the July 1874 inquest into Curran's death, witnesses were repeatedly asked whether they had seen a pile of burnt papers in the basement of the Pomeroys' store, where Curran's body was finally discovered four months after she went missing. According to the *Boston Post,* four people testified to seeing burnt paper in the basement, both in the water closet and under the stairs. A man named Mitchell, who owned the store next door and shared the basement with the Pomeroys, testified not only that he "found a lot of paper in the vault" but also that he "found him [Jesse] at one time burning paper under the stairs."[41] That the judge at the inquest found the burnt paper significant is evidenced by the fact that he asked Jesse's mother if she had ever seen burnt paper in the basement.[42] Newspaper reports of the inquest proceedings, unfortunately, do not explain *why* the judge or the lawyers thought the burnt paper was significant. But given that his crimes were becoming increasingly violent (flaying and scalping) and much less tentative, and that they followed the arc of torture described in western dime novels, one of the things Pomeroy may well have been doing in the basement was experimenting with burning human flesh.

As much as Pomeroy's crimes seemed to repeat the scenes of torture in western dime novels, there is a further connection that is not about the details of the plots. Perhaps the most arresting element of the fictional torture scenes of Beadle's westerns is that *they never actually happen.* Or, more accurately, the torture is described only in anticipation, in its imagining by the torturer ahead of time. The prisoner must hear about it and dread it, but then he or she typically manages to escape before it is complete, or sometimes even begun. Usually around page 70 of the hundred-page novel, the protagonists are captured by the Indians and their white-renegade cohorts, and elaborate preparations begin. *The Indian Spy* is typical. On page 74, the prisoner is bound to the stake and "biting taunts and jeers" are poured on him, children assault him with their "tiny bows and arrows, sticks, stones, and such missiles as lay to their hands," and "savages" prepare "splinters or instruments with which to add to the prisoner's tortures." Then, seven pages later, he escapes.[43] Some novels are quite explicit about the role that the anticipation of torture, rather than its actuality, plays in their narrative. In *The Black Princess,* for instance, the hero's captors describe what will happen to him: "with a devilish refinement of cruelty" they "filled his mind with images of what was to come, more hideous than the truth." In perhaps the prototypical frontier romance, *Buffalo Bill* (serialized in 1869–70), which Pomeroy named as his favorite in his interview with Fields, the writer describes how the Indians "gloated in imagination over the pleasure of dancing around the stake of torture and seeing victims writhe in the death-agony," which "aroused their wild passions to a frenzy of anticipation."[44] In each instance, expectancy intensifies feelings surrounding the torture.

This dynamic of unfulfilled anticipation, dramatized in the text itself, may also be at work *beyond the text:* along with the scenes of torture themselves, it may well contribute to shaping the experience of the reader. Jesse Pomeroy undoubtedly read many novels structured around the prospect of torture, and he too may have "gloated in imagination," had his mind filled "with images of what was to come." He was potentially led by the text to a state of expectancy, but then the promised scene never materialized—no consummation and no release. There was, in the end, as the author of *Queen of the Woods* puts it, "no exquisite enjoyment of torture at the stake."[45] In short, dime novels self-consciously aroused acute emotions through powerful images and then abandoned the reader, denied him the "exquisite enjoyment of torture" and potentially—dangerously—left him to consummate his pent-up, provoked passions *outside the text.*

The fact that the torture in dime novels was rarely accomplished within its pages, that the reader was left hanging, redoubles the ways in which Jesse Pomeroy's reading may have helped shape his perverse fantasies. For the plots of dime novels doubly fed those fantasies, not only providing Pomeroy with the content he would subsequently enact (the methods of torture), but also mimicking the psychic logic of those who murder repetitively. Robert K. Ressler, a former FBI agent, who coined the term "serial killer," claims that he was drawn to this term because of his experiences viewing "serial adventures" at Saturday matinees. "Each week," he recalls, "you'd be lured back to see another episode, because at the end of each one there was a cliff-hanger. In dramatic terms, this wasn't a satisfactory ending, because it increased, not lessened the tension. The same dissatisfaction occurs in the minds of serial killers. The very act of killing leaves the murderer hanging, because it isn't as perfect as his fantasy."[46] Serial murder, according to Ressler, is fundamentally about foreclosed pleasure, about the continual repetitive failure of fantasy's culmination—and just as Ressler describes how this logic works in the cliffhangers of Saturday matinees, so it worked in dime novels, and so it worked in the fantasies those novels might have helped shape for Pomeroy. Like all serial killers, he evinced a steady escalation in his acts, first of torture, then of murder—an escalation that suggests precisely the thwarting of anticipation, the failure of perfect enactment, that Ressler articulates as the central force driving serial killers.

Integral to Ressler's claim about the importance of foreclosed pleasure is his larger argument, drawn from his extensive study of serial killers, that the single most important characteristic they share (even more than early trauma or abuse) is the propensity for fantasy. Serial killers "are obsessed with a fantasy, and they have what we must call nonfulfilled experiences that become part of the fantasy and push them on toward the next killing. That's the real meaning behind the term serial killer."[47] Pomeroy may well have imbibed the stuff of his violent fantasies in part from western dime novels, but he may also have learned the *logic of serial violence* from the cycle of anticipation and frustration at the heart of these novels' representation of torture. Dime novels implanted what Ressler calls the "nonfulfilled experiences" that pushed him on to the next act of torture and finally to murder.

Pomeroy's "Indian" Crimes

Pomeroy's contemporaries were quick to point out the parallels between his acts of torture and sensational accounts of Indian barbarity. An 1874 article in the Unitarian magazine *The Repository* claimed that the Indian, "like Jesse Pomeroy, . . . delights in torturing his victims." A letter to the editor of the *Globe* noted that Pomeroy carried "a large butcher-knife stuck in his belt, Indian fashion." And, much more floridly, a report that seems to have circulated in several western newspapers described how "many children were found in Boston with wounds in different parts of their bodies, as of pieces of flesh cut out after the manner of wild Indians of old, who tortured their prisoners before they gave them the *coup de grace* in the middle of the blazing faggots."[48] Pomeroy's weapons, how he carried himself, and the particular tortures he committed all evoked the Indian (or the fantasy of the Indian) for his contemporaries.

Pomeroy's crimes seemed, in fact, so nearly a repetition of Indian atrocities that shortly after he was arrested for Millen's murder the *Boston Herald* ran a story that he was actually possessed by the spirits of Indians.

The headline says it all: "The Dreams of a Spiritual Medium. Pomeroy the Agent of Young Indian Devils Avenging Themselves on 'the Whites.'" The medium claimed that Pomeroy had been "the tool of a bloodthirsty and cruel band of spirits" and that, because of his apparent mental and moral "weakness," he had attracted the spirits of several Indian boys who had "within a few years been massacred by the whites in the far Western plains." As evidence of the truth of his (or her) claims, the medium noted "the published fact that the boy would dance around his victims, real Indian fashion, and seemingly delight himself as he saw the blood flowing from the wounds of the tortured captives."[49] At least one other writer agreed with the diagnosis of spirit possession. In an 1874 book on spiritualism, Eugene Crowell, M.D., argued that many "unaccountable murders," Pomeroy's in particular, were "attributable to the instigation of the spirits of slain or starved Indians," who find "mediumistic persons whom they can influence to the commission of crimes, which gratify their revengeful feelings upon the pale faces." While Crowell insisted that there should be no difficulty "in placing this case as one of obsession, or possession, by a dark spirit," theories that Jesse Pomeroy was influenced by *reading* about Indians were both more widespread and more credible: they suggested that instead of the spirits of dead Indians, Pomeroy was "possessed" by reiterated *images* of Indians.[50]

There is evidence, however, that Pomeroy identified more with Indians' white renegade allies than with Indians themselves. According to the reminiscences of Pomeroy's alleged schoolmate published in the *Globe*, while the other boys clamored to be frontier heroes (Wild Bill, Buffalo Bill, Simon Kenton, and Daniel Boone), Jesse's "hero" was the man almost universally considered an infamous traitor to the white race and to the American nation: Simon Girty (1741–1818). Girty achieved infamy when he defected to the British and their Indian allies in 1778 and then, still worse, became implicated in the brutal torture and murder of an American commander, Colonel William Crawford, in 1782; Crawford was tortured for hours and then executed by Delaware Indians in retaliation for the equally notorious Gnadenhutten massacre—and many accounts had Girty playing an instrumental role.[51] Jesse's role model, then, had his own history of torture. As his purported schoolmate wrote, "Simon Girty, I remember, was his hero"; Jesse "used to think that it was a fine thing to be a renegade like Girty; to be the one white man in a great Indian tribe like the Shawnees." This claim was repeated in the notice of Pomeroy's death in the *New*

York Times in 1932: "His hero was Simon Girty, the renegade who lived with a Shawnee tribe."[52]

Girty was routinely depicted in dime novels as evil incarnate, even more savagely cruel than the Indians. Thoroughly alienated from the white race, Simon and his almost equally notorious brothers, Jim and George, lived only to destroy it. In *The Wolf-Queen,* for instance, Jim Girty leads a "destroying band" of Indians against a white family and murders all but one of them.[53] This is not a lone example, and the historian Daniel Barr has pointed out that Girty was cast as the "originator" of Indians' "determination to retaliate against white encroachment with violent force." Indeed, nineteenth-century writers often claimed, according to Barr, that "the presence of [Simon] Girty and other renegade whites among the essentially docile Indians empowered them with the ability to overcome their racially superior antagonists."[54] In identifying with those who committed torture (mostly against whites, no less), Pomeroy may not have had to cross the racial divide: at the bottom of it all was a powerful, sadistic white man. And the fact that Girty was white yet cast out from white civilization, driven by an animus against it, may well have appealed to the boy whose strange appearance and white eye, along with his even stranger proclivities (compulsively making faces at other boys, for instance), assuredly made him an outcast.[55]

One particular torture scene in *Queen of the Woods* epitomizes Girty's pitiless sadism and provides a particularly near comparison to Pomeroy's own acts of torture. Girty has taken a prisoner, Edward Harris, for whom he has contracted an irrational burning hatred. Talking to his Indian friends, he tells them that he wants to do something new, something he's heard of but never seen: "cutting off toes, ears, and fingers, and then skinnin' alive." As in other scenes of torture, Girty enjoys the anticipation: "With a fiendish delight, [he] gloated over the prospective agony of his prisoner." Ensuring that his captive must await his fate with terror, he assures him that "it will be many bloody hours before you will see the end," adding, "Oh, when I hear ye howl, when the red hot tire-brands are stuck into yer flesh, won't I laugh" (echoing the "glee" Pomeroy, by all accounts, demonstrated). And then, just as Pomeroy did to his victims, Girty proceeds to whip Harris's back until it is "crimsoned with the flowing tide." He also douses his back in brine (as Pomeroy did to two of the boys he tortured) and then threatens him with the culminating act, skinning him with hot knives. Under Girty's prompting, his Indian accomplice "made an incision in the shoulder of the young hunter, at the base of the neck; the muscles shrunk, and the flesh seemed to shrivel up, under the infliction." Pomeroy similarly progressed to cutting his victims in the same place (shoulder, neck), and he may have been, like Girty, attempting to skin or scalp them.[56]

In the fictional account, Harris is (as was typical) rescued at the last minute, thwarting Girty's enjoyment. But Girty's pitilessness suffuses the scene. At one point, Harris looks at those around him for some sign of pity and finds none: "Not a face gave a sign of sympathy. Yet the countenances of the savages were not so terrible as that of Simon Girty."[57] Instead of pity, there is only pleasure.

"There is a good deal of monkey in a bad boy"

When his contemporaries traced clear connections between the "boy fiend" and the supposedly cruel Indians and sadistic white renegades of western dime novels, they might have merely been explaining Pomeroy by analogy: his crimes were *like* the scenes of torture detailed in the pages of cheap literature; he himself was *like* their depraved antagonists—both statements that beg the question of causality. Many of Pomeroy's contemporaries, though, did go on to offer causal explanations, hypothesizing *how* he might have been impelled to torture and murder by the novels he read. The crucial mechanism, all agreed, was imitation.

Some commentators believed that Pomeroy's savage imitations only heightened his culpability, presuming that he was intentionally imitating what he read. One wrote of "the young mind striving to imitate the example set by [crimes in novels]." Another argued that "getting insane on the weak concoction of dime novels" should be as much of an extenuation as committing a crime "under the influence of strong drink," which was no extenuation at all. And the lawyer for those urging that Pomeroy should be executed, Paul West, wrote in an 1876 letter to the *Boston Globe* that "as [Pomeroy] read, the eye grew to know the look of murder, and the brain to gloat on it, and the arm was nerved to strike."[58] The language of intent ("striving," "know") and a consequent culpability pervades these comments, rendering Pomeroy a volitional imitator.

Most commentators, however, saw Pomeroy's imitativeness as much more involuntary, as a force that diminished his responsibility. Rather than exerting the powers of reason and will that were supposed to be the domain of the "civilized" human, Pomeroy blindly repeated what he read. He thus slid into a state of savagery, even animality. According to a view current in the late nineteenth century, both the individual and the species passed through a kind of primitive "prehistory" characterized by imitativeness. As infants grew up and as cultures advanced, however, they were supposed to free themselves from the thrall of mimesis, becoming capable of forging their own ideas and directing their own actions. As Patterson DuBois, a lecturer on child culture and religious education, writes, quoting educator Susan Elizabeth Blow, the baby is at first a wholly "imitative being," but "from imitation he rises to transforming and productive activity, and tries to stamp himself upon the little world which, through imitation, he had stamped upon himself."[59] Jesse Pomeroy seemed not to have overcome his past as a wholly "imitative being," however. In an uncanny extension of the theory of maternal impressions, which involved the external world stamping itself on the child in utero, that world, because of Pomeroy's entrenched imitativeness, continued to stamp itself upon him long after birth.

From the very first, nineteenth-century Americans identified Pomeroy's disturbing propensity for imitation as a crucial part of what was wrong with him, while at the same time noting the heightened propensity of *all* children to imitate. As was the case with the butcher theory, then, what on the one hand pathologized Pomeroy (being heir to a body beyond his control) served also, on the other hand, to link him to the state of being human. Lecturing in May 1874, shortly after Pomeroy was arrested, an influential New York physician, Dr. William Hammond, argued that the boy was a victim of "morbid impulse," which led him to commit acts "against his normal inclinations." The most "powerful cause of morbid impulse," he continued, "is *imitation.*" People are compelled to do things they would not normally do, according to Hammond, simply by seeing them done (or written about). Not everyone is equally subject to such compulsions, though; Hammond went on to say that "imitation is of more force when the intellect is less fully developed" and that "even in the normal condition we find it more strongly exercised in children and women than in adult men."[60]

Several physicians developed Hammond's insight that Pomeroy's crimes were imitative, exacerbated by both his youth and his evident mental disorder, whether it be morbid impulse, moral idiocy, or moral insanity. In a lecture on the Pomeroy case delivered in Boston in 1875, for instance, one of the physicians who visited him in jail, Dr. Charles Folsom, argued that Pomeroy might well be a moral imbecile. Pomeroy's "weak-minded" condition was manifest particularly in his tendency toward imitativeness: "Every child," Folsom maintained, "recognizes the mimetic creature of a spinal cord and cerebellum who kills a baby because he has just seen a butcher kill a calf, and without being able to see any difference between the degrees of criminality of the two acts."[61] Dr. Theodore Fisher (who as we've seen also visited Pomeroy in jail) agreed with Folsom about the boy's weak-mindedness, which for Fisher was full-blown moral insanity, as well as with its manifestation as "mimetic." Describing what Pomeroy told him about his love of "stories of savage warfare," Fisher noted that the "impressions" made by those stories "passed uncontrolled into the horrible acts of torture and murder which have startled the community." And Dr. Allan McLane Hamilton, writing in 1903, argued that Pomeroy was "absolutely" the product of "pernicious literary influences," which were "so powerful" that "by a species of auto-suggestion he identified himself with the bloodthirsty hero" and "reproduced" the books' violent episodes.[62] Imitation, mimesis, identification, and reproduction became key terms, then, to describe *how* dime novels played a role in Pomeroy's crimes.

As much as imitativeness was a symptom of mental weakness, even insanity, and thereby (often) of criminality, for late nineteenth-century Americans it was also a sign of a "stuckness" in infancy and a regression to a sort of species childhood—that is, a regression to a *shared* human prehistory of savagery and animalism. The psychologist George Dawson, in an article published in 1900, elaborated on this idea, arguing that imitativeness was one of several primitive or "feral" qualities—qualities "found among animals"—that persisted into the present. Both the idiot and the youthful criminal typically displayed this atavistic and animalistic imitativeness, Dawson wrote, and he argued that homicidal children were more often than not of a regressive "imitative disposition" and took their cues "from accounts of murders, sensational stories, etc." For Dawson, the "inhuman crimes" of Jesse Pomeroy could only be explained "on the hypothesis of an imperfectly developed human being," in whom "from some cause the psychical qualities of the animal or sub-human ancestors have persisted." Moral idiocy and crime (including, notably, imitative crime) were inseparable, then, from regression. Instead of being "eliminated" as they should, "the instincts and habits of his animal and sub-human ancestors" remained, overriding any more civilized qualities.[63]

All the connotations of primitivism and animalism that freighted late nineteenth-century accounts of imitativeness were crystallized in the description of boys as monkeys. An 1874 account of Hammond's lecture on morbid impulse (and the pivotal role imitation played in its development) succinctly encapsulated his point about the cause of Pomeroy's crimes: "Imitation large, as in monkeys." In his discussion of the dangers for young readers of dime novels, the morality crusader Anthony Comstock proclaimed, "There is a good deal of monkey in a bad boy. He delights to imitate."[64] Developing the comparison in 1892, a noted English psychologist, Daniel H. Tuke, described imitation as an "instinct" that is "common to us and the lower animals, and performed unconsciously, at all epochs and in all the conditions of material life." Imitation rules supreme in the monkey, he wrote, and it is also the driving force behind the actions of "idiots" and children: "A monkey will imitate to the extent of self-destruction, as in an instance we know in which a medical man, annoyed with the imitative actions and grimaces of a monkey, placed a razor in its hands, and then went through the dumb show of drawing another across his own throat. The monkey immediately imitated the act, and with fatal consequences."[65] Epitomizing the mind bereft of reason, the monkey (in these accounts) is directed only by the strictly reflexive instinct of imitation. To many of his contemporaries, Jesse Pomeroy embodied this essentially animalistic reflexive or automatic imitation: he reiterated actions described on the pages of dime novels, without any mediation of consciousness or will. To repeat Dr. Fisher's apt words, the "stories of savage warfare" that Pomeroy read "passed uncontrolled" into his acts of torture and murder.[66]

Psychologists have described a phenomenon called the "chameleon effect"—the human "instinct to imitate one another—to synchronize our bodies, our actions, even the way we speak to each other."[67] The chameleon effect describes Jesse Pomeroy perfectly. His imitation of dime novels aside, he had a quite distinctive tendency to agree with whomever he happened to be speaking to—becoming, when in their presence at least, the living embodiment of his interlocutors' theories, a topic I will explore more fully in the next chapter. Hence his repeated confessions and retractions, as well as his surprising eagerness to concur with James Fields that his dime novel reading was most likely an "injury." (Pomeroy's extreme suggestibility was undoubtedly why his lawyers would not let him testify at his trial.) While there is certainly a chance, then, that Pomeroy may have consciously emulated the scenarios he read about in dime novels, he was (also) potentially engaging in a completely nonconscious imitation, thus profoundly troubling the idea that he was an intentional or a culpable actor, that he *knew* or consciously *strove* to copy what he read.

The notion of humans' immanent propensity for automatic imitation is increasingly recognized, in the early twenty-first century, as a crucial part of human life—all human life, not just the infantile, the pathological, the "savage," or the "animal." Susan Hurley states the grounding tenet of a recent scholarly collection on the science of imitation: "A general tendency to imitate is fundamental to and distinctive of human nature."[68] The discovery of mirror neurons has been central to this emergent science. Located in an area of the premotor cortex, mirror neurons fire not only when we do something but when we *see someone else do something*. Marco Iacoboni describes the radical nature of this discovery: no one, he writes, "could have imagined that motor cells could fire merely at the perception of somebody else's actions, with no motor action involved at all." What this means is that, before and beyond consciousness, we are experiencing bodily what we only see. At the neuronal level, we are *imitating* what we see. Iacoboni drives his point home by asserting that "to see athletes perform is to perform ourselves."[69] Although mirror neurons were discovered during experiments on macaque monkeys, there has since been significant research verifying their presence in humans.[70]

Research uncovering how much imitating humans do, and the role of mirror neurons in particular, has revivified the media effects debate and has led to many convincing assertions that violent media do, in fact, produce more violence. It seems clear, one scholar maintains, that "children and teenagers who view greater amounts of violent television and movie portrayals are more likely to behave in an aggressive and antisocial manner."[71] Iacoboni has claimed that "mirror neurons may also be very important in imitative violence induced by media violence."[72] Violent media not only prime violent action in the short term (a somatic reflex, possibly involving mirror neurons), but they also shape cognitive schemas in which violence is acceptable. Claiming that "mere perception of violent behavior will increase the likelihood of automatically engaging in similar behavior, in ways subjects are not aware of," Susan Hurley claims that "violent stereotypes or traits" in particular will "prime unconscious automatic assimilation, mental as well as behavioral."[73] While the debate over media violence is more urgent in the era of film and television, it has only extended the late nineteenth-century controversy over dime novels, which aimed at a visceral sensationalism and a lack of complexity (repeated stereotypes) that similarly enthralled their consumers.

Such claims not only about human imitativeness but about its happening at an automatic, somatic level, outside of conscious awareness, fundamentally challenge the notion of the volitional self. It is, researchers in the field agree, one of the reasons why there is so much resistance to the accumulating weight of studies demonstrating that children *are* affected by violent media representations. Hurley puts it bluntly: "These results may threaten our conception of ourselves as autonomous."[74] Mirror neurons, in particular, Iacoboni writes, "produce automatic imitative influences of which we are often unaware and that limit our autonomy by means of powerful social influences."[75] Late nineteenth-century commentators signaled the way in which Pomeroy's compulsive imitativeness eroded his autonomy by arguing that his voracious devouring of dime novels rendered him "insane"—a medical and legal way of marking his lack of volition and consequent diminished culpability.

The Reign of Images

If one explanation of the way in which dime novels shaped Jesse Pomeroy's crimes turned inward, to the "blind" and inherent imitativeness of humans, another explanation turned outward, to the environment that was being imitated, that was *demanding to be imitated*. Another explanation, in short, turned to the image, which was, since the emergence of mass print culture in the early nineteenth century, propagating itself with ever more ferocious intensity. As Patterson DuBois wrote in 1903, "It is difficult for us to realize how completely we are made up of our images from the external world." We are, he asserted, "under an incessant rain of them."[76] While much of the recent neuroscientific work on imitation has considered face-to-face encounters, mediated experience (via film or print) is also critical, not least because so much of our experience *is* mediated. One of the first examples Iacoboni gives of how mirror neurons work, for instance, involves watching a film: "Mirror neurons in our brain re-create for us the distress we see on the screen." We know how those "fictional characters" feel, Iacoboni claims, "because we literally experience the same feelings ourselves."[77] What most shaped Pomeroy, his contemporaries argued, was not visual images but words—words in cheap sensational fiction that drew stereotypical characters engaging in simple and repetitive action, undiluted by complexity, painting stark forms that were reiterated over and over again. The words of dime novels, in other words, crystallized powerful verbal images, something Patterson DuBois aptly called "vivid word picture[s]," "word-cartoon[s]" and "concrete images," and which he argued gained a powerful and lasting influence over the reader. "Nothing is so persistent in the memory as an image," wrote DuBois and "nothing so controls ideals."[78]

DuBois specifically addressed how crime (especially youthful crime) is produced by the images in which people are immersed. As well as adducing Pomeroy as an example, DuBois described a boy who stabbed another child for no apparent reason. As he cut the child's throat, he allegedly said: "I have often read novels, and in one of them I found the description of a scene parallel to this which I have executed." According to DuBois, moreover, readers of newspapers "do not need to be told that it is a matter of almost daily occurrence for boys to be brought before the courts charged with offenses whose psychological genesis is to be traced in the literature found upon them." In summing up his discussion of how crime is generated by the popular press and cheap fiction, DuBois concluded that it "is easy to see that all the foregoing criminals had vivid mental images of criminal deeds of which they heard or read the details. Any one [sic] can see," he added, "how certain crimes become epidemic" through the detailing of them "in picture and in verbal description."[79] The sensational "verbal descriptions" and "vivid mental images" that circulated widely in the mass media became, then, the somatic, and often unconscious, motives of crime. These images certainly tapped into a human propensity for imitation (more evident in some than in others), but they were a force in themselves.

A central trope by which late nineteenth-century Americans expressed the power of the image was, as DuBois put it, the idea of the "epidemic." This key concept was crucial in shifting the mechanism driving imitative crimes from the person doing the imitating *to the image being imitated*, even, perhaps, to the image *compelling its own imitation*. Images (compressed, uncomplicated verbal scenarios) parasitized readers, spreading infection to those who got too close, to those who were exposed for too long. After his interview with Pomeroy, Dr. Fisher argued strenuously that the reports of violence pervading newspapers were contagious, literally replicating themselves: "The publication of the details of murder, rape, executions, insane homicides and suicides, and tales of assassination and crime, in the newspapers, spreads an infection which, taking root in the congenial soil of a disordered and enfeebled brain, brings forth a ghastly harvest," he wrote, adding, "The contagiousness of hysteria and suicidal impulse is well known to the profession, and this contagion of homicide is of similar character."[80]

The Reverend Francis Edward Clark moralized that the danger of such fiction is not only that a "few morbidly ferocious boys like Jesse Pomeroy" will be affected by it, but that "the mass of our boys and girls who are neither brutal, nor ferocious, nor feather-headed, will be tainted by this mass of corruption. Like the exhalation from a foul but unseen sewer," Clark continued, "it may poison the very air our children breathe before we wake up to the fact that the air is poisoned."[81] For Clark, cheap literature polluted the atmosphere and infected its readers' minds just as surely as (in the late nineteenth-century view) poisonous air spread diseases of the body like cholera, smallpox, and yellow fever. In their arguments, DuBois, Fisher, and Clark all drew on the longstanding theory of moral contagion, which, while it had its origin in the experience of bodies in close proximity, was by the late nineteenth century being translated into the realm of text.[82]

In the late twentieth century, the social scientist Paul Marsden traced a similar arc from the contagion of bodies to that of images, beginning by describing the phenomenon of contagion among people who are physically proximate, but then moving to the ways in which the *media* spreads ideas. He quotes a standard definition of social contagion as "the spread of affect or behavior from one crowd participant to another; one person serves as the stimulus for the imitative actions of another," but adds that "there is no reason for the contagion phenomenon to be restricted to the crowd scenario," and that "the mass media allows for the possibility of contagion through dispersed collectivities."[83] This crucial shift from literal crowds to what Marsden aptly calls "dispersed collectivities" interposes a nonhuman factor, perhaps even a nonhuman *agent*, into the contagious relay. The nonhuman agent (the media image), just like the other nonhuman agent to which it is often analogized (the virus), mixes with the human to form a kind of nonhuman/human hybrid, a human who is also an assemblage of images, a mixing that severely undercuts what we like to think of as "human" consciousness and volition.

Late nineteenth-century notions of moral contagion and the autonomy (and power) of the image are strikingly replicated in the late twentieth-century discourse of memetics.[84] Memes, the theory goes, parasitically inhabit (and some say actually *constitute*) human minds, striving only to copy themselves, struggling against other memes for our attention, for their *own* survival and longevity, not for ours.[85] As Susan Blackmore writes, "Instead of thinking of our ideas as our creations, and as working for us, we have to think of them as autonomous selfish memes, working only to get themselves copied." All theorists of memetics argue that to one degree or another, memes drive our thoughts and our behavior. Robert Aunger encapsulates it succinctly: "We don't have ideas; ideas have us!"[86] Memes, especially successful memes, are highly contagious, and several recent thinkers have likened them to a virus, thus marking the ways in which theories of memes have continued nineteenth-century debates over moral contagion. The idea that Jesse Pomeroy might have been impelled by the powerful and reiterated "memes" of Indian and white renegade savagery is a provocative one, and the view that he didn't have ideas but that *ideas had him* actually fits perfectly with his reiterated claims that he "had to do" what he did.

Several books about memetics, for the most part unconsciously drawing on nineteenth-century theories of moral contagion, have in fact explicitly adopted what Aunger calls "an epidemiological approach to the study of communication events."[87] The epidemiological model (like the term *meme* itself) originated with the evolutionary biologist Richard Dawkins, who quotes with approval a colleague's summary of his groundbreaking chapter on memes in *The Selfish Gene:* "When you plant a fertile meme in my mind you literally parasitize my brain, turning it into a vehicle for the meme's propagation in just the way that a virus may parasitize the genetic mechanism of a host cell." Successful memes, Dawkins adds, are those that have an "infective power." Dawkins later wrote an essay titled "Viruses of the Mind," in which he elaborated on the idea of epidemics of memes, arguing that "minds are friendly environments to parasitic, self-replicating ideas or information," and that our "minds are typically massively infected." Among the symptoms Dawkins offers of an "infected" mind is one that resonates with descriptions of Jesse Pomeroy: the "sufferer," Dawkins claims, typically "finds himself impelled by some deep inner conviction . . . : a conviction that doesn't seem to owe anything to evidence or reason, but which, nonetheless, he feels as totally compelling and convincing."[88] Pomeroy's "I had to do it" certainly partakes of this notion of mental contagion more than it does of any notion of a rational, volitional self.

Confronted with Jesse Pomeroy, late nineteenth-century Americans faced the dawning possibility that along with ideas being created *by* humans, ideas might also be *creating humans*. Thus the threat posed by "moral contagion" in the nineteenth century, like that posed by the theory of memetics today, is the dissolution it augurs of the autonomous self—a "distinctly unsettling, even appalling" prospect, as the philosopher and cognitive scientist Daniel Dennett has put it. Indeed, Dennett claims that memetics directly confronts us with the question "Who is in charge . . . we or our memes?"[89] If we are "made up of our images from the external world" (as Patterson DuBois claimed), what happens to what we like to think of as our (inherent) self, our reason and our will?[90] Like those entering the debate over memes today, writers of the late nineteenth century who raised the questions of moral contagion, the infectious power of images, and epidemics of crime took up the question "Who is in charge?" Are "we" in charge? Or are the images purveyed by mass media and cheap fiction in charge? Memeticists often use the language of possession to express this threat. As Kate Distin puts it, is a mind indeed "something that possesses, rather than being composed of, concepts"? Aunger, too, proposes that "perhaps we are literally possessed by thoughts imported from those around us." Do we, then, possess images? Or do they possess us?[91] Theories of Jesse Pomeroy's literal possession by spirits (including his possession by the wraiths of vengeful Native Americans) were one way in which late nineteenth-century Americans expressed his apparent uncanny lack of volition, or even of "self." His possession by fictional images is, of course, another way—and distinctly more likely than spirit possession.

"Jesse Pomeroy" Crimes

If media images were infectious, if powerful and iterable mental images were gaining a dangerous autonomy, Jesse Pomeroy could not be the only sufferer. And he wasn't. In 1878, newspapers reported that a thirteen-year-old boy in Richmond, Virginia, had struck a man with an axe. When asked why he did it, the boy allegedly replied that he had "no particular reason for it, but did it because he wanted to." He added "that he had heard a great deal about Jesse Pomeroy, and wanted to imitate him."[92] In 1890, the "Boy Bandit" of Lake View, Illinois, popped up—a boy who rubbed blinding red pepper into another boy's eyes after he had apparently "somewhere read of the cruel acts of Jesse Pomeroy" and determined to follow "as closely as he can in that boy desperado's footsteps."[93] What soon became apparent to horrified late nineteenth-century Americans was that Jesse Pomeroy did not only "catch" the contagion of torture and murder from cheap literature. He also spread it to other boys, becoming the nodal point, the "patient zero," of a veritable epidemic of boys impelled to crime by what they read.

It's not entirely accurate, though, to say that Pomeroy himself spread this contagion of youthful violence. It was the press. Contemporary newspapers turned Jesse Pomeroy the person into "Jesse Pomeroy" the "image" (or meme), a flattened mental image that signified seemingly unprovoked and motiveless juvenile depravity. The press then spread this image far and wide. And while newspapers repeatedly used the words "imitate" and "imitator" to tie reports of youthful crime to Pomeroy, other boys (and girls) did not seem to claim, as the boys from Richmond and Lake View did, that they were aware of emulating Pomeroy. It was the press that claimed and thereby spread the idea of a youthful brutality that was tied to Jesse Pomeroy. To the extent that children themselves enacted this motiveless brutality, it seemed largely unconscious, suggesting that media images, not a specific person, constituted the actual "patient zero" at the heart of the epidemic.

Even before Pomeroy's trial, criminals began to be identified as imitators of the nation's most notorious child killer, leading to proliferating headlines proclaiming "Parallel for the Pomeroy Case," "Another Boy Fiend," and "Rival for Jesse Pomeroy." As one Boston journal put it, "Pomeroy seed is taking root, and there is promise of a bountiful crop."[94] The "crop" flourished on the heels of widespread coverage of Pomeroy's arrest, trial, and sentencing—and reports in the *Boston Globe* referred to the "mania" of cruelty "spreading" among the "criminal classes" and constituting a "criminal epidemic."[95] After Thomas Piper was arrested and tried for the murder of a young girl in a Boston church in 1875, George F. Pentecost, the well-known minister of the church, was reported as saying that the "crime appeared to him to be one of an entirely Jesse Pomeroy character" and that "it is a well-known fact in the history of crime that after the commission of a terrible deed others of similar character frequently follow, the actors in which appear to have no other motive actuating them than that of imitation, induced by a sort of maniacal impulse. Such periods are known as criminal epidemics."[96] Pomeroy was cast as nearly as dangerous, and certainly as contagious, as the smallpox that regularly invaded the city.

Crimes "of an entirely Jesse Pomeroy character" were not confined to Boston, however. Indeed, reports of Pomeroy imitators spread across the country. An article titled "The Black Fiend. An Imitator of Jesse Pomeroy" described how, in Cumberland County, New Jersey, an eighteen-year-old boy tortured and drowned a young man for no apparent reason, offering up a case "marked by much the same features as those of the Pomeroy case in Boston."[97] In August 1875, in Newton, Massachusetts, Archibald Jackson, described as "about eighteen years of age and respectably connected," enticed his young victim into a field, stripped, bound, and whipped him; his story was dispersed across the country under the title "An Imitator of Jesse Pomeroy."[98] A "Jesse Pomeroy" popped up in San Francisco in September 1875, when a boy of ten tortured several young children, almost cutting off a three-year-old child's ear with a bone and inflicting nineteen other wounds, as well as skinning a dog alive, all with no apparent motive; report of his exploits again spread across the country under the declaration "They have an imitator of Jesse Pomeroy in San Francisco."[99] A year later, in September 1876, a twelve-year-old boy in Great Bend, New York, enticed two boys whom he didn't know into a barn, stripped and beat them, and tried to hang them; articles about him appeared from east to west proclaiming "An Imitator of Jesse Pomeroy."[100] A year after that, a paper reported that Sacramento, California, "has an apt imitator of Jesse Pomeroy" in a boy of ten who almost killed a three-year-old girl by trying to bury her. He did it because he was "impelled to do it by a sort of irresistible desire to hurt and bruise her."[101]

The stories continued throughout the decade and beyond. In a school in St. Louis in 1879, the principal's son "hit upon a plan for having fun" by running into a crowd of girls and sticking as many of them as he could with his knife. The report about the incident was titled "Youthful Depravity. Principal Tallman's Boy, Leon, Imitates Jesse Pomeroy." Another "rival of Jesse Pomeroy" appeared in California in 1885—a ten-year-old boy who slashed at least nine victims. He "said that he liked to use his knife."[102] In 1889, a ten-year-old "colored" boy "started out yesterday to imitate Jesse Pomeroy," randomly attacking and stabbing a girl. And in 1890, two boys in Manchester, New Hampshire, were charged "with acts rivaling those perpetrated by Jesse Pomeroy"; after taking another boy to an outhouse, they "stuck pins in nearly every part of his anatomy, poured boiling water upon him, burned his face with powder," and left him for dead. They were dubbed "Childish Imitators of Jesse Pomeroy."[103]

In none of these cases did the boy declared to be an "imitator" actually *claim* that he was imitating Jesse Pomeroy. Instead, these reiterated examples imply automatic, reflexive imitation, manifesting, as Dr. Theodore Fisher put it of Pomeroy himself, the way in which what is read "passed uncontrolled" into "horrible acts of torture and murder."[104] These "Jesse Pomeroy" crimes are imitations without awareness, and it is the newspapers that spread the Jesse Pomeroy "virus," which, as they reported, took over the bodies of other boys like a contagious disease and compelled acts which then must be reported, fanning the flames of the epidemic still further.

As Jesse Pomeroy imitators flourished even at the end of the century, what "Jesse Pomeroy" stood for became increasingly untethered from what Pomeroy had in fact done. When Philadelphia was beset by its own "Jesse Pomeroy," Samuel Henderson, in 1898, the *Philadelphia Inquirer* published an article titled "Many Crimes by Boy Fiends," which stated of Pomeroy, who "heads the list of American child criminals," that he "would hold the hands of a small boy or girl on the top of a hot stove," a crime of which Pomeroy was not actually guilty. That honor goes to Freddy Reilly, the "Jesse Pomeroy" of Jersey City, but the mistake demonstrates how "Jesse Pomeroy" became a catchall label, synonymous with "boy fiend," amassing under it all manner of youthful depravity.[105] The meme "Jesse Pomeroy," more and more often detached from reality, came to wield a greater power than anything that had actually happened, and it was undoubtedly one of the reasons so many inaccuracies have circulated about "Jesse Pomeroy" (the fictional construct) over the years.

In the end, the stubborn "Jesse Pomeroy" meme only confirms the power of what DuBois called the "incessant rain" of images over their readers, offering still more reason to believe that Jesse Pomeroy was "infected" in some way by the dime novels he voraciously read. He committed his crimes just as print culture experienced an explosion of growth—and crime (along with suicide) is indisputably contagious. Perhaps there is some truth to Roger Sadler's claim that Pomeroy was America's "first media copycat," and perhaps Boston's famous boy "monster" inspired imitators, with or without their conscious awareness.[106] It is certainly true, though, that late nineteenth-century newspapers did what they could to propagate the "virus"—distilling "Jesse Pomeroy" into a flat verbal image, a meme, with little to no regard for the complex details of historical accuracy.

As Pomeroy imitated what he read, and as he became a meme spread by the burgeoning national press, he was turned into and revealed to be something other than completely human; he became a hybrid of the human and nonhuman—part flesh-and-blood human, part assemblage of images. Those images, disseminated by cheap literature, lived in his brain, influenced his body, and exerted an uncanny force, inevitably eroding anything resembling a distinctly *personal* subjectivity. Pomeroy's case discloses how both mirror neurons and memes—that is, our inherent imitativeness and the shaping, even parasitizing, force of images themselves—can hijack personal subjectivity. The very iterability of Pomeroy's crimes hints at a core of the nonhuman lodged in the human: it bespeaks something mechanical, something beyond volition, beyond the grasp of the will. As the critic Christopher Peterson puts it, "Iterability complicates the juridical command to hold humans accountable for their actions insofar as it betrays an inhuman mechanicity at the origin of all 'human' responsibility."[107] To the extent, moreover, that part of what constitutes the self comes in from the outside (the nonpersonal outside, moreover, in the case of media images), something thoroughly inhuman and impersonal parasitizes the organic human, further complicating the notion of personal accountability and, indeed, the very notion of the person in which accountability is grounded.

The literary theorist Georges Poulet has written of the loss of self in the act of reading: "As soon as I replace my direct perception of reality by the words of a book, I deliver myself, bound hand and foot, to the omnipotence of fiction." He writes of being "taken over," subject to a "dispossession," by the fictional world.[108] Writing in the mid-twentieth century, Poulet strikingly anticipated the ways in which theories of reading have been animated by the discovery of mirror neurons. As William Major writes in 2014, summarizing the work of the Yale psychologist Paul Bloom: "We might posit that there is a sort of connection, perhaps even *identification*, when we lose ourselves in a literary work. We may or may not consciously see ourselves in the main characters, but mirroring presents the possibility that *we become the story*, at least at a subconscious level." Such "somatic interconnectedness," Major continues, demonstrates that at a neural level at least, we may be unable "to recognize the difference between what is real and what is fiction."[109]

Pomeroy may well have been "possessed" by the scenes of torture in the dime novels he devoured—"dispossessed" by the fictional world, as Poulet puts it. The science of mirror neurons, though, along with the theory of innate human imitativeness of which it is a part, insists that Pomeroy's "possession" by images was at the same time a "possession" by his own body and brain. The theory that Pomeroy was compelled by what he read to torture and kill is thus not unlike the theory that he was marked before birth by the scene of slaughter and, more generally, by the inheritance of his flesh. In both cases, the body that should have been his possession came instead to possess him. As with everything concerning Jesse Pomeroy, his case was extreme but not, for all that, entirely different from more mundane human experience.

5

"A Moral Monster"

Threaded through every part of the public debate over Jesse Pomeroy was the specter of his "insanity"—moral insanity specifically. It was, many said, the very reason he committed such barbarous acts of torture and murder. It was his defense at trial. It was the result, in the view of some, of his having been marked in the womb by Ruth Pomeroy's visits to the slaughterhouse. And it was either the reason he was so susceptible to the sensational torture scenes in western dime novels or it was the fatal effect of his reading those scenes. Claims of the boy's insanity proliferated, in short, either as serious and sustained medical diagnoses or as more uninformed lay opinion. But what did it mean, exactly, to say that Jesse Pomeroy was insane?

At bottom, what nineteenth-century Americans meant when they called Pomeroy morally insane was that he *lacked* certain qualities believed to be inextricable from the state of being "human." If the press was intent on casting Pomeroy as "a moral monster rather than a human being," as one Boston physician put it, it was because he was profoundly bereft of certain defining human characteristics.[1] The language of lack, or absence, was everywhere when people tried to describe Jesse Pomeroy. As an 1874 editorial in *Popular Science Monthly* summed it up, Jesse Pomeroy was "an inhuman monster, *wanting* in moral sense and *destitute* of the common attributes of humanity."[2] It was precisely this "inhuman" core of Pomeroy—this catastrophic absence of all empathy, conscience, remorse, guilt, and fear—that nineteenth-century physicians took up and diagnosed as moral insanity. It is also exactly what has been defined, since the middle of the twentieth century, as psychopathy. Indeed, nineteenth-century physicians' descriptions of Jesse Pomeroy as morally insane constitute a near-perfect portrait of what we now call the psychopath. And then, as now,

137

both conditions are characterized by a profound lack of those things that are supposed to be intrinsic to humans. Physicians who deemed Pomeroy morally insane pathologized that absence, turning it into a medical diagnosis. But laypeople also noted it as a defining characteristic of the boy, often using more florid language: he was "a moral monster."

Moral Lack

James Cowles Prichard's 1835 *Treatise on Insanity*, which helped shape moral insanity "into a standard, if disputed, psychiatric term," as the historian Nicole Rafter puts it, crucially identified moral insanity as marked by lack: by a loss of self-government, by an incapacity for "decency," and by the absence of the usual provocations to crime.[3] The "power of self-government is lost or greatly impaired," Prichard wrote, and the sufferer is rendered incapable of "conducting himself with decency and propriety in the business of life."[4] Psychopathy, too, is persistently defined in terms of lack, absence, or deficiency—notably of morality, conscience, remorse, guilt, and empathy.[5] In his foundational description of the psychopath, *The Mask of Sanity* (1941), Hervey Cleckley consistently reiterates "lack" and its synonyms: the "lack" of shame or remorse, an absolute "incapacity" for object love, a "general poverty" of affect, a "complete lack" of strong feeling, a near-total "loss of insight," with "no capacity to see himself as others see him," a "total absence" of the ability for self-appraisal, an "almost total lack of self-imposed restraint," a "persistent lack of ability" to experience life as others do, and finally, an "amply demonstrated incapacity to lead an adequate or socially acceptable life." Similarly, Robert Hare, in the groundbreaking *Without Conscience: The Disturbing World of the Psychopaths among Us*, continually returns to the psychopath's lack: his hallmark is "a stunning lack of conscience"; he demonstrates a "deeply disturbing inability to care about the pain and suffering experienced by others—in short, a complete lack of empathy"; he manifests a "smooth lack of concern" at being found out in a lie, a "lack of normal affect and emotional depth," and a "lack of the internal controls we know as conscience." The psychopath's violence "lacks normal emotional 'coloring,'" and his or her language is "two-dimensional, lacking in emotional depth." Indeed, psychopaths are often characterized as profoundly empty. Adolf Guggenbühl-Craig writes in *The Emptied Soul: On the Nature of the Psychopath* that psychopaths suffer from "*lacunae*, unoccupied rooms in the house of the psyche." These areas, "uninhabited or uninhabitable, the deserts, barren areas, or *lacunae, . . .* represent psychopathies."[6]

Some commentators on both moral insanity and psychopathy have articulated this marked lack of an ineffable humanity by analogy to more tangible missing body parts or senses. The same 1874 *Popular Science Monthly* editorial quoted earlier argued that Pomeroy was a "deficient human being," just as if he had "been born blind, deaf, or without arms." Much more recently, the legal philosopher Antony Duff writes that we should think of the psychopath as akin to those "whose limbs are partially or wholly non-functional—those who simply cannot move in the ways that human beings can ordinarily move." Cleckley writes that the psychopath is "blind" to "major affective experience," and Hare famously described the psychopath's inability to experience the full range of emotion as color blindness: "Like the color-blind person, the psychopath lacks an important element of experience—in this case, emotional experience." He sees only in gray, as it were; the full range of affective coloring is unavailable to him.[7] The psychopath's lack of affect and lack of will is so profound that it seems, then, viscerally embodied.

Those who encountered Jesse Pomeroy were struck, perhaps above all else, by precisely this profound absence: a lack of moral feeling generally, but also, more specifically, a lack of guilt or remorse, along with an apparent lack of volition. One of the physicians who visited Pomeroy and wrote extensively about his case, Theodore W. Fisher, described Pomeroy's "moral insanity"—or "moral idiocy" as he preferred to call it—in terms that emphasized the absence at the very heart of Pomeroy's self. Everyone concedes, he wrote, that "moral deficiency" and "weakness of will" are characteristics of his mind. "We observe a moral deficiency and incapability for the assimilation of moral ideas," and his cruel acts were "more or less motiveless in the ordinary sense." Pomeroy lacked moral sense, will, and motive in Fisher's account; indeed, Fisher reiterated the "congenital absence" of the moral sense in Pomeroy: the fact that he felt "no compunction" and that he had "felt no remorse since."[8] His visit to Pomeroy's jail cell in 1875 only deepened Fisher's conviction that the boy was absolutely bereft of moral feeling. Pomeroy "recounted his horrible deeds," he wrote, "without reluctance and with perfect *sang-froid.*"[9] For Fisher, moral deficiency, absence of moral sense, and lack of compunction or remorse are all bound up with Pomeroy's seemingly "motiveless" crimes. Lacking a basic moral sense, he, unsurprisingly, acted without any recognizably human motives.

A significant part of Pomeroy's defense at his murder trial was that he was bereft of moral sensibility, a defense bolstered in large part by the testimony of Dr. Clement Walker, who talked to the boy on at least five different occasions and who, like Fisher, never strayed far from "lack" and its synonyms in his descriptions of Pomeroy—both lack of "feeling" and lack of free will. According to Walker, Pomeroy "had no visible sign of any such thing as moral responsibility, and seemed dead to all the finer emotions which are met in sane persons."[10] As the *Boston Journal* put it, Walker "found the boy of no depth of mind and having not the slightest conception of his crimes," and "consequently gave no indication of sorrow or remorse." Walker apparently "tried to excite the boy to some heart emotion, but utterly failed." The *Herald* reported Walker's testimony that Pomeroy was "without the slightest sense of moral responsibility; he never, with a single exception, showed any sorrow or pity for his wrong acts . . . [and] failed to grasp the enormity of his crimes or their result or responsibility."[11] What struck everyone who met Pomeroy was less some palpable presence—no active evil smoldered in his eyes—than an equally palpable absence: he was blank, empty.

As psychiatrists have defined the psychopath since the term was coined in the early twentieth century, perhaps the most devastating affective lack is that of empathy: the psychopath seems unable to feel for others, to recognize their suffering. Cleckley writes that "the psychopath's incapacity for object love is absolute"; "he is capable of affection for another in literally no degree" and displays "absolute indifference" to the hardships he brings on others. Hare concurs: psychopaths have a "stunning lack of concern for the devastating effects their actions have on others" and suffer a "profound lack of empathy." Hare elaborates that the "feelings of other people are of no concern to psychopaths," who resemble "the emotionless androids depicted in science fiction, unable to imagine what real humans experience." They view others "as little more than objects to be used for their own gratification."[12]

Lack of empathy is arguably at the root of other psychopathic traits, most clearly the absence of a conscience. The psychologist Martha Stout has written eloquently about how conscience is less a cognitive than an affective capacity—it's about emotion, she argues: "Conscience is a sense of obligation ultimately based in an emotional attachment to another living creature" and "does not exist without an emotional bond to someone or something." It is "deeply and affectingly anchored in our ability to care about one another." Without the ability to feel love for someone or to empathize with someone else's interior life, the psychopath cannot *feel* the difference between acting rightly and wrongly. Psychopaths' lack of empathy is thus causally linked to their ability, even propensity, to harm others. R. J. Blair and his coauthors write, "The psychopath does not seem to represent the specific nature of moral transgressions, that they have victims," and is consequently "less likely to consider another's pain." The psychologist Simon Baron-Cohen has even proposed that "evil" resides in a catastrophic lack of empathy. Evil, he argues, is an imprecise and amorphous term—a "nonexplanation"—but the ability to cause extreme hurt to another person (which most people would understand to be "evil") is actually rooted in the erosion, even absence, of empathy. As he develops this argument, Baron-Cohen devotes significant time to the psychopath and to recent neuroscientific evidence demonstrating that the psychopathic brain is deficient in those areas known to produce empathy for others.[13]

Although most of the time Jesse Pomeroy either denied that he killed Horace Millen and Katie Curran or claimed he had no memory, occasionally brief and chilling accounts slip into the historical record, accounts that disclose a deep detachment and a complete inability to recognize his victims as human—characteristics that have traversed descriptions of both moral insanity and psychopathy. Pomeroy described how he killed Millen to John Charles Bucknill and Edward H. Clarke, two physicians who visited him in April 1875. As Bucknill later wrote, "He told me that he sat upon the child and stabbed him with his penknife blade until he thought he could feel no longer; then he opened the longer blade of the knife and cut his victim's throat at the angle of the jaw, because he knew that the bloodvessels [*sic*] were nearest the surface there."[14] Pomeroy recounted luring Katie Curran down into the cellar in the same calculating way he killed Millen: he explained that he carefully avoided using the word "cellar," suspecting that "she wouldn't go down the steps if he did."[15] Finally, he infamously told police chief Edward Savage that he killed Curran because "he 'wanted to see how she would act.'"[16] Pomeroy's detachment persisted long past the murders themselves. While in jail awaiting trial, before Curran's body was discovered, Pomeroy "several times asked of the attendants what reward was offered for the whereabouts of the Curran girl, and what would be given him if he should reveal her hiding place."[17] And after he detailed for his lawyer the "most bloodthirsty story" of how he killed the girl, he "calmly asked that his mother send him a clean shirt and a pair of socks."[18] What is manifestly absent from every account of (and by) Pomeroy is any indication that he ever felt sorrow, guilt, or remorse for the harm he inflicted and the lives he took.

At his trial, both of the physicians who testified in Pomeroy's defense spoke of his incapacity for empathy. Dr. John Tyler, who visited Pomeroy in September and October of 1874, told the court, "His moral sensibility is obtuse. He evinces no pity for the boys he tortured or for the victims of the homicides, and no remorse or even sorrow for the acts."[19] Clement Walker testified that when he talked to Pomeroy of the "wretchedness" he had caused the Millen family, "he said he scarcely ever thought of it."[20] As the *Boston Journal* reported his testimony, Walker said he had told Pomeroy of the "desolation" he had caused the Millen family and that Pomeroy had said, in response, " 'I hardly ever think of it,' and added, half to himself: 'it's funny, isn't it?' "[21] The *Journal* also reported the account of a "friend" who visited Pomeroy in jail and was talking to him about the murder of Katie Curran. That friend apparently reported: "It was of no use to try to soften him, for he was as far off as possible from all tender strains. In the very midst of a pathetic appeal, he remarked, 'I'll bet I had a better diagram of the shop [where he killed Curran] than the papers did and I only drew mine from memory.' " He spoke of all his barbaric acts "with *sang froid*," the friend concluded.[22]

The one seeming exception to Pomeroy's inability to feel for anyone else (or to feel at all) was his apparent affection for his mother, Ruth. John Tyler testified that "the only tenderness the boy ever exhibited was in speaking of his mother, otherwise the crimes did not seem to weigh upon his mind."[23] But while Pomeroy did indeed consistently voice concern for his mother, Ruth Pomeroy was undoubtedly very useful to her son—and her son knew it. She protested his innocence from beginning to end, and many said that she helped win his early release from reform school; she brought whatever he needed to his jail cell (he even wrote her letters asking for various tools to effect his escape); and she smuggled his self-serving autobiography out of jail. Pomeroy might well have maintained his "love" for his mother, then, because of her usefulness to him—instrumentality being the guiding if not only reason for a psychopath's relationships with others. Grant Gillett, summing up the consensual view, writes that "the psychopath sees the other as a means to his own end."[24]

In one striking moment in his autobiography that puts in doubt the otherwise seeming love of Jesse for his mother, he actually seems to hint she may have been the one who killed Katie Curran. He confessed to Katie Curran's murder, he wrote, only because his mother and brother had been arrested shortly after the discovery of Katie's body in the cellar of what had been the family's shop. He "resolved to do all I could to get them out," and he figured he might as well be "hanged" for killing two as one. Jesse then changed his mind, however, deciding to insist that in fact he *didn't* kill Curran. At that point, Dr. Tyler asked Pomeroy directly if his mother might have killed the girl (since her body was found in their basement). "No gentleman would say she would" was Pomeroy's rather stunning reply.[25] It is difficult *not* to read this comment as hinting at his mother's guilt, despite his having voiced the protestations that would be expected of a good son. The comment is also shot through with Pomeroy's desire to make himself look good: he's a "gentleman" protecting a woman, his (perhaps guilty) mother. This telling moment suggests that Pomeroy's devastating inability to care for another may well have extended even to his mother.

The psychopath's profound lack of empathy for his victims can lead him to believe that those victims and their suffering are literally not real. As Cleckley puts it, the psychopath can be so incapable of understanding what experience or emotion mean to others—can enter this realm only "so superficially"—that "his reality is thin or unsubstantial to the point of being insignificant." Hare goes further and suggests that the psychopath's sense that *others are not real* can manifest in his recalling his crimes as if they were a dream. Psychopaths often "deny that [the crime] happened at all," or they might experience (or say they experienced) "memory loss, amnesia, blackouts, multiple personality, and temporary insanity." Hare suggests that while psychopaths are often good at faking these various forms of memory loss, sometimes they themselves are not sure about what is real and what isn't. Their own sense of the line between pretense and reality wavers.[26]

Pomeroy's severely attenuated grasp not just of the reality of others but of reality itself may well explain his baffling and persistent claims that he "did not know" why he did what he did. To his lawyer Charles Robinson, Pomeroy continued to say not only that "he did not know" why he committed the murders, but also "that the whole affair seemed like a dream to him." He told Robinson, "I remember distinctly meeting [Horace Millen] and intended only to beat him, but had no thought of taking his life. It seems as if the whole affair was now passing before me in a mist, and that I could not help doing what I did."[27] Cleckley has claimed that the ability of the psychopath to grasp the affective and experiential reality of others is so diminished that he assumes "other persons are moved by and experience the [same] ghostly facsimiles of emotion or pseudoemotion known to him."[28] Such a claim perfectly describes Pomeroy, who may well have projected his own "ghostly" reality onto others, redoubling their insubstantiality to him and making it all the easier to harm them.

If the conscience is in large part formed by the capacity to empathize with others, to identify with the real suffering of real others, it is also formed by the ability to feel fear and to learn from the prospect of punishment.[29] Cleckley asserts that psychopaths are characterized by "poor judgment and failure to learn by experience" as well as an "inability to refrain," and psychologists have tied these traits to lack of fear. Hare extends this description, writing that "psychopaths lack the physiological responses normally associated with fear," and he argues that fear powerfully motivates behavior, preventing most of us from breaking either conventional or moral rules. Indeed, Hare insists, fear and anxiety are "the mainsprings of conscience." Along with Cleckley, David Lykken was one of the first theorists (in the 1950s) to associate psychopathy with reduced anxiety. He argues, in fact, that reduced fearfulness "interferes with socialization" and "gives rise to the development of psychopathy." The cognitive neuroscientist James Blair confirms this decades-old theory, offering evidence that psychopaths do not respond fearfully to stimuli and that the "callous and unemotional dimension of psychopathy" is associated with low levels of anxiety.[30]

More recent explorations of the physiology of psychopathy have even identified particular parts of the brain, notably the "behavioral inhibition system," that may be chronically underactive in psychopaths. Such findings have led to the claim that perhaps the core problem of psychopaths is that they fail to learn to fear punishment and thus fail to inhibit their own antisocial behavior. Positing that a conscience is "essentially a set of classically conditioned emotional responses," Adrian Raine cites evidence that psychopaths "lack a fully developed conscience" precisely because they show "poor fear conditioning." One important study correlated fear-conditioning data that had been gathered from a large group (1,795) of three-year-olds with recorded criminal convictions among the same subjects twenty years later (137 had such a conviction). The results demonstrated that those subject who, at three years old, had *not* shown any evidence of fear conditioning mapped significantly onto the group who had become criminals by age twenty-three. As Raine puts it, those three-year-olds who would become criminals "showed no sign of conditioning at all. They were flat-liners—as a group they did not show *any* fear conditioning." Raine sums up this 2010 study as having demonstrated, for the first time, that "an early impairment in autonomic fear conditioning acts as a predisposition to criminality in adulthood" and that a "lack of conscience" has "its origins very early in life—well before the onset of childhood conduct disorder, juvenile delinquency, and adult violence."[31] To the extent that they are incapable of feeling fear, then, psychopaths are not deterred by punishment and only imperfectly (if at all) develop anything resembling a conscience; they thus demonstrate a tendency to commit and then repeat crimes, neither learning from what they have done before nor anticipating (or dreading) the occurrence (or recurrence) of negative consequences.

The lack of fear manifested by psychopaths, which severely limits their ability to internalize moral norms and thus to develop a conscience, was certainly noted by nineteenth-century physicians. Theodore Fisher wrote, of the "morally deficient" in general and Pomeroy in particular, "No punishment or reward, no instruction or restraint of religious teaching has any effect."[32] Indeed, Pomeroy displayed a rather startling propensity to commit the same destructive acts over and over again. We saw in chapter 2 that one of his teachers, Abbie Clark, testified at his murder trial about Jesse's intransigent predilection for making faces and added that whenever she spoke to him about it, he always claimed "he couldn't help it." While she continued to punish him, he never seemed "penitent or sorrowful" but instead insisted that his punishment was unfair.[33] Pomeroy's almost immediate return to torturing children after his release from reform school is another example of a complete inability to learn from experience, and while many wondered how he was able to restrain his allegedly "irresistible impulse" during his confinement at Westborough, it is safe to assume that Pomeroy did respond to immediate, externally imposed constraints, although he was completely incapable of internalizing them. Once released from the highly disciplinary structures of reform school, he went right back to doing what he had been doing as if the previous sixteen months had not happened. He demonstrated no compunction about violating the most critical moral imperatives (don't harm others) and displayed no trepidation about the prospect of incurring (again) the consequences of his transgressions.

Even while in jail, Pomeroy seemed impervious to fear conditioning, evincing a chronic propensity to try to escape over a span of more than three decades. Theodore Fisher interpreted Pomeroy's escape attempts as less the result of "cunning" (as many believed) than as the manifestation of insanity, noting that attempts at escape are common in insane asylums: "Repeated failure, and the certainty of capture and return, does not deter them," he declared.[34] Pomeroy attempted escape three times from the Charles Street Jail while he was awaiting his sentence. His most elaborate plan, discovered in July 1875, involved an intent to "knife" any guard who got in his way, and he was outraged at being thwarted.[35] The punishment records of the State Prison at Charlestown, after Pomeroy was remanded there for life in September 1876, show a startling record of repeated escape attempts, as well as continual insolence toward the prison officers, behavior that was at its height in the 1880s, when Pomeroy was in his twenties, and tailing off as he got older. His first recorded attempt at escape was on November 9, 1877, when he tried to dig the cement from his cell wall. The trail of punishable offenses continued from there: attempt to escape (1878), cutting the bars of his cell (April 1879), insolence (1879), insolence and cutting the ironwork of his cell (November 1880), refusing to obey an order (four times in November 1886), refusing to obey an order, cutting the bars of his cell door, causing a gas explosion in his cell, and tampering with his cell door (1887), digging in his cell, cutting his cell door, and writing an abusive letter to the warden (1888), cutting his cell door (two times in 1891), cutting his cell door twice, attempting to escape (1892), digging bricks out of the wall of his cell (1894), cutting bars in his cell window and digging around his window (1895), attempting to escape, digging a hole in the floor of his cell, and defacing cell walls (1897), cutting his cell door (1898), cutting the cell door (twice in 1899), cutting ironwork in his cell (1900), digging around the water pipe in his cell (1904), cutting the bars in his cell door (1912), and, finally, refusing to obey orders, specifically the commutation of his sentence from solitary confinement (1917).[36] In 1887, the Charlestown warden declared that Pomeroy had "given the prison officials more trouble than any other prisoner now confined within the prison walls."[37] His infractions and escape attempts recurred mechanically and repetitively, and he was punished equally repetitively, sent for days to the prison's strong room and deprived of what small comforts he had in his cell. Pomeroy seemed equally oblivious, however, to his earlier failures as well as their negative consequences.

Pomeroy's life shows, in short, a chronic pattern of transgression that was immune to efforts to curb it: he made faces in school and nothing his teacher did stopped him; he tortured (and then killed) small children, and imprisonment failed to stop him; and he repeatedly, almost compulsively, over decades, attempted to escape from prison. He also consistently refused responsibility for his acts. When his teacher punished him for making faces at other boys, he insisted he was being "punished wrongfully."[38] He repeatedly denied all responsibility for his acts of torture and murder (confessing them fleetingly but then always elaborately denying his confessions). And he blamed his escape attempts on the newspapers. In 1888, Pomeroy sent a long letter to the state's lieutenant governor, which included four pages devoted to "a protest against the outrageous and inhuman treatment which he has for years received at the hands of newspaper reporters," who have done nothing but "stir up public opinion against him and to misrepresent him in every possible way." "What wonder," Pomeroy continued, "that he is driven to use saws and files and to attempt in all ways to escape." Prepared to try legal means to void his sentence, he demanded from the governor "literal transcripts" of all newspaper articles related to every aspect of his case.[39] Pomeroy was, in other words, unwavering in his belief that he was wrongfully, "inhumanly" persecuted—that he was in prison because of what *others* had done.

The Mask of Sanity

While the ability of the psychopath to "know" reality is clearly weakened by his inability to "feel" various emotions—notably empathy, compassion, guilt, remorse, and fear—he does nonetheless, in some shallow sense, "know" what is right or wrong. As Pomeroy himself put it in his autobiography: "In regard to these cases I do not feel what I am charged with. I know that. I know the crime that has been committed, but *I do not feel its awfulness;* that is what I mean. And so in regard to the other cases. I know the crime has been committed, but I do not realize that with which I am charged." In a 2010 study Gillett described this characteristic of the psychopath—his capacity for an only insubstantial knowledge of both self and others: he "at one level, knows how things affect other people and may even use that knowledge to discomfort his victims but, at another level, that knowledge is split off from or has not been incorporated into, as it would be for others, the way he evaluates and then informs his actions."[40]

Those who write about psychopaths express their subjects' fathomless lack, their "nonhumanity," through the metaphor of the mask. Cleckley puts it eloquently in *The Mask of Sanity* when he calls the psychopath a "reflex machine which can mimic the human personality perfectly," adding that this "smoothly operating psychic apparatus" is able to reproduce not only apparent human reasoning but also "simulations of normal human emotion." This "reproduction of a whole and normal man," Cleckley continues, is so perfect "that no one who examines him in a clinical setting can point out in scientific or objective terms why, or how, he is not real. And yet we know or feel we know that reality, in the sense of full, healthy experiencing of life, is not here." For Cleckley, the psychopath is a "machine," an "apparatus," that generates the facsimile of a real person but is designed to disguise the fact that there is actually nothing underneath. Hare agrees, claiming that psychopaths are like "androids" when it comes to experiencing human emotion. While they can tell "unlikely but convincing stories that cast themselves in a good light," he writes, observers often get the impression that they are "play-acting, mechanically 'reading their lines.'" Since their emotions are so shallow, it frequently appears that "little is going on below the surface."[41] Hare's point about what is (or is not) going on "below the surface," or beneath the mask, raises vexing questions about psychopaths in general and Jesse Pomeroy in particular: not only *what* is going on beneath the surface but *whether* anything is going on beneath the surface.

One way to interpret the psychopath's mask is that it is maintained by quite purposeful deceit, that it is created by an unfeeling and manipulative "self" beneath the mask. Indeed, everyone agrees that psychopaths are often inveterate liars. As Cleckley writes, the psychopath "will lie about any matter, under any circumstances, and often for no good reason." Raine agrees: psychopaths "lie left, right, and center. Sometimes for good reason, and sometimes, perplexingly, for no reason."[42] There were certainly many people willing to believe that Pomeroy was simply a chronic liar. Calling Jesse a "curious character," the *Boston Traveler* claimed that he "seems to be altogether devoid of moral principle, and, although possessing an average common school education, prefers lying to the truth."[43] Sheriff Clark, who supervised Pomeroy at the Charles Street Jail for over two years, wrote an unprecedented letter to the press, lamenting his job and complaining that Pomeroy was "desperate, daring, artful and untruthful."[44] Psychopaths will lie just for the sheer enjoyment of deceiving someone (the *Traveler* wrote, tellingly, that Pomeroy simply "prefers" lying), but they also will lie, of course, for self-serving ends. Hare has called this "impression management," at which psychopaths tend to be adept.[45]

It is debatable, however, whether someone who cannot grasp the truth of an experience or an emotion can be said to lie about it. As Cleckley writes of the psychopath, his "awareness of hypocrisy's opposite is so insubstantially theoretical that it becomes questionable if what we chiefly mean by hypocrisy should be attributed to him."[46] Lying demands a "self" beneath the mask, a self that is consciously seeking to manage the observer's impressions—and the very notion of such a "self" contradicts the numerous descriptions of the psychopath as empty. It is important to acknowledge, then, that at least some of the time, perhaps much of the time, the psychopath may not be aware of lying, which means he is not actually lying at all.

Indeed, that they may not know they are lying is just one small part of a more general absence of self-awareness on the part of psychopaths, yet another lack of what we presume are innately "human" qualities. Cleckley writes that the psychopath shows a "total absence of self-appraisal as a real and moving experience," and he concludes that when the psychopath talks about himself and blatantly lies, it might well be "less a voluntary deception than a simulation in which the simulator himself fails to realize his lack of emotional grasp or that he is simulating or *what* he is simulating." The psychopath's "clever statements" are "hardly more than verbal reflexes," and, far from representing insight, they evince only "an excellent mimicry of insight."[47] The psychopath, in other words, may not be *wearing* a mask. Often, he *is* the mask. His "persona" is a simulation that for all intents and purposes is "real"—a point that Hare highlights when he calls the psychopath a "machine" that "mimics human personality perfectly." The "machine" in some cases is simply not controlled by a "real" person underneath. The machine goes all the way down; the machine is the person, and the person is the machine.

Perhaps one of the most compelling manifestations of Jesse Pomeroy's "mask," and a crystallization of the notion of the psychopath as simulation, a string of "verbal reflexes," is his autobiography, published in two installments in the *Boston Sunday Times* in July 1875. By the time Pomeroy wrote this startling document, he had confessed to the murders of Horace Millen and Katie Curran numerous times to numerous people. Written documents recorded confessions made in his own words in the summer of 1874, after Curran's body had been discovered in his family's cellar, and his lawyers had relied on the "facts" of his torture of several boys and his murder of Millen as a crucial part of their insanity defense at his murder trial in December 1874. Astonishingly, however, Pomeroy published his autobiography with the apparent intent of convincing people that he did not torture or kill anyone, although he did hedge his bets and claim that if he had, he was surely insane. Indeed, the *Advertiser* wryly noted that the autobiography demonstrated above all that two ideas were firmly fixed in Pomeroy's mind: he did not commit the crimes and, if he did, he must be insane. As the *Globe* pointed out, Pomeroy denied killing Katie Curran without its even seeming to occur to him that his prior confession conformed rather closely to how she was killed, evincing a degree of knowledge that an innocent person would not have had. Hare has written that psychopaths are rarely "perplexed or embarrassed" at being charged with lying; "they simply change their stories or attempt to rework the facts so that they appear to be consistent with the lie." The result can be a "series of contradictory statements," sometimes "from one sentence to the next."[48] If ever there were a textbook example of the psychopath's "contradictory statements," of lie layered on lie until the truth vanishes, that example is Jesse Pomeroy's quite remarkable autobiography.

The *Globe* immediately declared the autobiography a tissue of self-interested falsehoods. Writing in particular about Pomeroy's description of his early childhood, the *Globe* declared that the "object of this account evidently is to show that he was much like other boys, and thus to negative [*sic*] the idea that he was capable of committing the atrocities of which he was found guilty."[49] Pomeroy's account of his time at reform school is certainly designed to give this impression. He writes about what a "good behaved boy he was," and, as he continues in a section excerpted in the *Globe*, "Without intending to praise myself, I can see but few things to censure. I never was punished while there in any way, shape, or manner; a thing few boys can say." As evidence of his good behavior, he reports that he was promoted from the chair shop to what was called the "hall," which had laxer regulations, even in the scant few months he was there.[50] The portrait of Pomeroy as a "good boy," whose principal childhood activities were fishing, playing baseball, and going to school (according to his autobiography), was certainly at odds with the fact that he had begun torturing small boys by at least his twelfth birthday.

Such good behavior, evidence of consummate self-control, did not conform to Pomeroy's own confessions, nor to his insanity defense at trial—specifically to the claim that he was driven by an "uncontrollable impulse." The *Salem Register* summed up a widespread feeling, in an argument for Pomeroy's execution, when it insisted that "there was too much method in his proceedings. He knew enough to commit his terrible deeds when no witnesses were likely to be around. He knew enough to behave well during the few months he was confined under his former sentence, and until he was pardoned." Similarly, the generally sympathetic *Springfield Republican* pointed out the veritable "mystery" of his conduct in reform school, "where his unnatural, and as is alleged uncontrollable passion for cruelty, was cunningly concealed, or not manifested, for several months."[51] How could such self-control, a centerpiece of the persona that Pomeroy created in his autobiography, coexist with the "irresistible impulse" that Pomeroy hoped would save him from hanging?

The "good" behavior in reform school that anchors Pomeroy's autobiography seems to fit Hare's notion of impression management better than it does his lawyers' claim that he suffered from an uncontrollable impulse. Hare writes, "Psychopaths in prison often learn to use the correctional facilities to their own advantage and to help shape a positive image of themselves for the benefit of the parole board." They are less interested in *actual* self-reform than in the *appearance* of reform.[52] In 1890, after Pomeroy had been in the Massachusetts State Prison for fourteen years, the prison physician for the last five of those years, Charles D. Sawin, wrote that Pomeroy did not seem insane to him, but rather had made the most of his chances to manipulate others for his own benefit: "Jesse Pomeroy, unlike an idiot or an imbecile, seems to me a boy who has had his wits sharpened by contact with the many people who have examined him, and who has shown a considerable degree of skill in attempts to make his case a plausible one for executive clemency."[53] Pomeroy's cool self-presentation—in his autobiography, in reform school, and in jail—is clearly, as Sawin observes, difficult to reconcile with any story of him as suffering from a lifelong "insane" compulsion to inflict cruelty on others.

In fact, the question of whether Pomeroy was actually insane or just shrewdly feigning insanity (a self-serving aspect of his "mask") is one of the most contentious questions around which the opinions of his contemporaries split—and his autobiography certainly speaks to this question. When the physicians Bucknill and Clarke visited Pomeroy in jail in April 1875, they talked to him for nearly an hour, and both emerged convinced that the boy was mostly sane and entirely culpable. Indeed, Bucknill suggested that while in jail Pomeroy extracted information from his interviews with physicians, in order to learn how to feign insanity convincingly in front of other physicians and his lawyers. He wrote that the diagnosis of certain doctors (notably Clement Walker) that Pomeroy suffered from epilepsy had "come to [Pomeroy's] knowledge," and that the boy thus described to Bucknill and Clarke a symptom that he thought would be consonant with epilepsy: "He told me that he often felt a sensation like that which would be produced by a wet feather being drawn across his forehead from one temple to the other." Both physicians, however, were convinced the boy's symptom was fabricated.[54]

In his autobiography, Pomeroy admitted what some of those who talked to him had testified to: that he had read about a defense of temporary insanity in another murder trial and had then offered those symptoms up as his own. (One is tempted to read this damning admission as evidence that Pomeroy's desire to be admired for his acumen momentarily over-whelmed his competing impulses for self-preservation and to be believed innocent.) Describing his decision to confess to the murder of Katie Cur-ran (supposedly in order to protect his mother and brother), he writes that, while he "knew well enough of the facts of [his] case" (apparently from newspapers and conversations), he also "resolved to make it appear that I did not remember all the circumstances attending the crimes" because, he writes, "as I had read something of insanity, that is some of the things that accompany it, I resolved not to remember all the circumstances of the crime. I also took my cue from [James] Dwight's trial, where he said he felt a funny (queer) pain in his head from side to side, and had a very indistinct recollection of the crime. I resolved to follow him." Pomeroy also writes of telling Dr. Tyler and Dr. Walker about pains in his head that coincided with his acts of torture and came accompanied by the feeling "that I must do something," adding: "Whether it really helped my case any I can't say, but that I have that pain without the impulse to whip a person, I will not deny. I was, perhaps, wrong in telling that story, but at that time I had thought and been talked to so much that I really did believe I did do it; that is I believed it for a while, but all at once I said to myself that I did not do it."[55] At this point, even Pomeroy seems to get confused by his own multiplying fictions: he claims that he imitated symptoms of insanity for the benefit of his lawyers, supposedly doing so while knowing that he was innocent of the crimes, but he then admits that for a while he "really did believe I did do it," until "all at once I said to myself that I did not do it."

Reality dissolves here, replaced by the stories Pomeroy is telling others— and himself.

At other moments in his autobiography, Pomeroy explicitly confesses that he is not sure what is "real" as opposed to what is feigned. He writes, for instance, of getting a letter from his mother while he was in jail awaiting his trial in which she urged him to tell the truth. "Well," he continues, "it was not the first time that I had thought of that, to tell the truth. At that time I did really think I did do it, and that I could not help doing it, but at times something would say, 'Jesse, you know you did not do these things.'" Pomeroy hesitates to say unequivocally that he did not do it, then, in part because of his professed fear that his mother and brother would be charged with Katie Curran's murder, but also because, as he puts it, of "the idea that came that I did do it." Presenting himself as unsure of what actually happened, Pomeroy does not clearly seem to be lying here, which involves being able to apprehend the truth of an experience and not its ghostly approximation. Instead, we sense, as Cleckley puts it, that "the value of truth and feeling" are simply lacking.[56]

Pomeroy's apparent inability to know a "reality" that might ground either his confession or his denial is evident at another moment in his autobiography, when he confronts whether he actually killed Horace Millen or not. Pomeroy describes conversing with Dr. George Choate (the prosecution's expert) before his trial and "deciding" to say that he did *not* murder Millen (this is after he had told his lawyers and Drs. Tyler and Walker that he did, and as they were all preparing a defense of insanity predicated on that confession). Pomeroy writes: "I don't think it is a wonder that when he [Choate] asked me or said something, in which he used the words 'I did do it,' that I said, 'No, I did not.' I was thinking of something else at the time, but I did not take the trouble or think it my duty to explain why I said so." This unthinking, even automatic, moment becomes one instance (of several) in which Pomeroy switched his story and went back again, briefly, to saying he did not murder Millen and Curran. He then shortly thereafter, however, retracted (once again) what he unthinkingly said to Dr. Choate, reassuring his lawyers and Drs. Tyler and Walker that he did kill Millen and Curran and repeating his story of "insanity" (his defense at trial).[57] This moment in his conversation with Choate, which involved what anyone would surely consider a weighty claim about whether or not he committed a brutal murder, seems instead to be an example of the "verbal reflexes" that Cleckley writes about as characteristic of the psychopath: "His clever statements have been hardly more than verbal reflexes." It raises again the question Cleckley says is central to assessing the psychopath: whether he is offering a "voluntary deception" or a "simulation in which the simulator himself fails to realize his lack of emotional grasp or that he is simulating or what he is simulating."[58] Not only does Pomeroy evince no sense of reality, but *he doesn't even seem to care:* he says he didn't kill Millen in a mindless "verbal reflex," when he was thinking about something else, and then he can't be bothered to "explain himself" or address the fact that his denial contravened wholesale the prospective defense for his murder trial.

Reading the many things Pomeroy wrote in his autobiography, and the comments he made to others, it becomes unclear if Pomeroy actually knew whether he committed torture and murder or not. He wrote about the crimes as if whoever committed them was someone else; tellingly, Pomeroy actually told Detective Wood, immediately after his arrest for Millen's murder, that it *had* been another boy who tortured the many small boys in Chelsea and Boston, a boy who was now dead.[59] Pomeroy made a similar remark to a psychiatrist, William Healy, who recalled visiting Pomeroy in his cell around 1912, after he was asked to give an opinion about how Pomeroy was being treated in the Charlestown State Prison (there was apparently a group "in a Western state" making a clamor and printing leaflets about the deleterious effects on Pomeroy of extended solitary confinement). Healy reported that Pomeroy "had much to say about himself with a little tinge, perhaps to be expected, of megalomania," and noted that "he spoke in the third person of 'that boy' who had committed those misdeeds and who would not have committed them 'if he had been properly brought up.'"[60] This remark shows Pomeroy's continued detachment from the "reality" of what he did, as well as a more mundane interest in blaming others (his parents) for his crimes. The glib manner in which Pomeroy implicates his parents suggests he is merely grasping for an easy, shallow explanation, though, not that he believes they are in fact to blame.

Pomeroy's autobiography, in short, reflects his tendency to conceive of his crimes as separate from himself, as if he were simply weighing the circumstances of some abstract case, some crime that did not concern him personally. He dispassionately assesses both narratives of his crimes (he did it; he didn't do it) in his autobiography. He compiles a list of evidence that he committed the crimes and was insane ("I am imagining myself to have did [sic] that murder") and another of evidence that he did not commit the crimes. Pomeroy writes in both cases as if he hadn't actually been there, and the lists are introduced with the words "I think that if I did these things I was insane" and "I do not think I did these things."[61] The repetition of the word "think" only highlights the utter epistemological ambiguity inherent in the very coexistence of these two irreconcilable lists.

Pomeroy's dueling accounts in his autobiography of the kitten he allegedly mutilated when he was very young are illustrative of both his impersonal stance toward the events of his own life and the profound uncertainty (even in his own mind) surrounding the truth. At one point, when he is arguing that he did not commit the crimes, he writes that the testimony about the kitten is "simply absurd" and that if he had had a carving knife at that age he would have been more likely to stick it in himself than in a cat. But several pages later Pomeroy offers the tortured kitten as evidence of his insanity, including the incident in the list identified as "I think if I did those things I was insane." Immediately afterward, however, he cuts back to his initial claim, this time including the cat in the list headed "I do not think I did those things." With no internal, *felt* experience of what is real, Pomeroy balances the different versions of his own actions as if he were indulging in an intellectual exercise.[62] The two lists he creates strikingly distill how he offers narratives of his innocence and his guilt as more or less equally credible alternatives: the reader, like Pomeroy himself, just needs to pick one.

Since Pomeroy did not grasp what was real, he was, not surprisingly, highly suggestible, and the explanations of others easily supplanted his own attenuated sense of reality. Even though, for instance, Pomeroy ostensibly wrote his autobiography to make the case that he did not kill Horace Millen and Katie Curran, he writes at one point that he finds the judgments of Dr. Tyler and Dr. Walker that he killed Millen because he was insane much more persuasive than Dr. Choate's testimony that he was sane. He was swayed to Tyler and Walker's story (even though it belied Pomeroy's stated belief that he was innocent), because Tyler and Walker "have had more experience than [Choate]." In other words, Pomeroy momentarily forgot the purported "truth" here (that he is both innocent and sane) in order to agree with a convincing (and contradictory) narrative about himself created by persuasive others (that he is guilty albeit insane). Pomeroy's proneness to agree with anything that was said about him, if it was said compellingly enough, was apparently the reason his lawyers decided not to put him on the stand to testify in his own defense. When Pomeroy asked Dr. Walker whether he would be testifying at his trial, Walker apparently laughed and said that if he were on the stand, the attorney general, as Pomeroy recounted it, "would make me say that the moon was made of cheese, and that my mother gave me a slice of it."[63] Pomeroy was not only willing to adopt any mask that suggested his innocence (obviously a self-preservation tactic) but also, more mystifyingly, any mask *that others believed in,* no matter how it made him look.

The autobiography intriguingly symptomizes its writer's insubstantial sense of self and thin grasp of experiential reality (including, notably, emotion) not only in its content but also in its form: Pomeroy fills pages with obsessively detailed descriptions of the neutral, immutable aspects of a world disconnected from his own actions. This objective world seems one that Pomeroy can rely on, unlike any reality in which his "self" is implicated. Indeed, these descriptions seem to be another indicator of Pomeroy's avoidance, or perhaps even absence, of an inner life. The story Pomeroy tells about what he was supposedly doing between about 11:30 a.m. and 2 p.m. on April 22, 1874, when he was actually luring Horace Millen to the marsh and stabbing him repeatedly, is particularly chilling; it is a bare identification, a listing, of places: "I walked along Broadway and up Federal street, over the bridge, along Federal street to Milk, up Milk on to Washington, up Bromfield on to Tremont, along Tremont on to the Common. I noticed nothing peculiar in going along the streets, but I saw as I went along Federal that working men were building a cistern or well, right in front of that new dining room at the corner of Milk and Federal."[64] He continues in this vein for at least two more very long paragraphs, and while, on the one hand, Pomeroy might well be thinking he's manufacturing a convincing alibi, there is also something profoundly unsettling about sentence upon sentence detailing the world of things (an elm tree with canvas wrapped around it, a fence, an inscription with the name of the mayor) along with the complete absence of any sign of his interior life: he pauses, stops, walks, notices, looks, rests, but he never thinks or feels. Interior life is evacuated, replaced by objects and places.

There is another, more sinister reason, perhaps, why Pomeroy describes restlessly wandering during the two to three hours he was luring away and killing Millen. Numerous commentators have noted that the violent behavior of the psychopath may well be caused in part by his low arousal, adducing the striking correlation of low resting heart rate with psychopathy and violent behavior: the psychopath needs more stimulation than others; he is simultaneously empty and restless. As Adrian Raine points out, many serial killers report "intense tension and restlessness" prior to their homicides—and so the restive movement Pomeroy describes in lieu of admitting his murder of Millen may actually have had some truth to it, may actually have been some approximation of what he *was feeling*. He *needed* to move, to fill himself up with the sensation that he chronically lacked.[65] Absent on the inside, sensation, *feeling*, had to come from the stimulants of the outside world.

Heightening the sense that Pomeroy's life was lived largely through what was external to him, his autobiography emphasizes movement between, rather than attachment to, places. Guggenbühl-Craig has written that part of the psychopath's crippling inability to experience eros is that "one has no connection, one levitates above the world, one has no roots."[66] And indeed, Pomeroy does not *describe* the places he lived: he identifies them only by number, street, and town, and he focuses on removals, on not being present somewhere. He mentions living at 78 Lexington Street when he was small, then moving to 78 Bunker Hill Street in 1868 or 1869, then moving into the house next door in 1870, then being sent to spend the summer in Maine in 1871, and finally moving to South Broadway in Boston in August 1872. He does not, however, say anything about what any of these places were like, noting only of the house next to 78 Bunker Hill Street that it was "a better house than we had ever lived in before."[67] Like much else in his autobiography, Pomeroy describes critical parts of his life (his homes) as if he were an outsider.

Reading Pomeroy's autobiography evokes the feeling that Cleckley describes when he writes about confronting the psychopath: "We know or feel we know that reality, in the sense of full, healthy experiencing of life, is not here." Pomeroy's autobiography gives us empty stories, words untethered to any deep sense of what is real, or even that anything *is* real. In talking about encountering a psychopath, Hare uncannily describes how it feels to encounter Pomeroy's autobiography: "Many observers get the impression that psychopaths sometimes are unaware that they're lying; it is as if the words take on a life of their own, unfettered by the speaker's knowledge that the observer is aware of the facts." The *Boston Advertiser* declared that the "whole attempt" of the autobiography "seems like playing a part, clumsily to be sure."[68] It is, indeed, "playing a part"—and the narrative, an invented life if ever there was one, puts front and center the question of whether Pomeroy was consciously lying, for obviously self-serving reasons, or whether the real "life" that supposedly grounded his narrative was simply not available to Pomeroy, or, even more frighteningly, was just not there.

"An egoist of a rather extreme kind"

While much description of the psychopath addresses what he lacks, both Hervey Cleckley's account in *The Mask of Sanity* and Robert Hare's checklist also illuminate what psychopaths are, chronicling in particular their disproportionate sense of self, grandiosity, and narcissism. Hare writes that psychopaths "have a narcissistic and grossly inflated view of their self-worth and importance, a truly astounding egocentricity and sense of entitlement." As Heidi Maibom succinctly puts it, the psychopath is "an egoist of a rather extreme kind."[69] While these traits may seem to be at odds with the psychopath's inner deficiencies, they are, in one important way at least, bound up with the psychopath's lack of self. When there's little felt reality, anything goes.

While Pomeroy was indifferent to the feelings of others, he *was* concerned with how others viewed him. When in jail awaiting his sentence, he was taken up with what the newspapers said about him, apparently deploring, for instance, the accounts of torture: "They hurt a young man's reputation," he said.[70] And we've seen that when he confessed the murder of Katie Curran to the chaplain of the jail, Rufus R. Cooke, in July 1875, Pomeroy gave as a condition of that confession that Cooke "would keep it from the papers," since he felt that the press routinely maligned him.[71] Indeed, one paper reported that "the only feeling of any sort shown by Jesse Pomeroy, the mangler of infants, after his arrest, was a dislike to have his name mentioned in the newspapers, and he calmly requested a reporter who called on him to suppress his name."[72] On the other hand, however, Pomeroy also seemed to enjoy the notoriety that his exploits gave him. A report of a visit by the "Richmond Sir Knights" (a Masonic group) noted that "the boy appeared to enjoy conversing with them, he apparently feeling that he is quite a hero and deserving attention."[73] And after describing how he killed Katie Curran to his lawyer, he apparently asked, "What do you think of Jesse H. Pomeroy?"[74] Pomeroy clearly wanted and enjoyed attention. While the part of him that was intent on constructing his mask of "good boy" (not least to avoid his death sentence) made him anxious about reports of his acts of torture and murder, a pride in his abilities nonetheless slips through.

Indeed, those who have studied psychopaths have remarked that their egoism, their exaggerated sense of self-importance, often overcomes cautious self-preservation. Hare has written that psychopaths often "attempt to appear familiar with sociology, psychiatry, medicine, psychology, philosophy, poetry, literature, art, or law," and that, as an integral part of their narcissism and overblown sense of self, they frequently criticize their lawyers, feeling they could have done a more effective job of defending themselves.[75] Pomeroy never went as far as proposing he defend himself in court, but he did display a persistent interest in his own defense and tried to manage its terms. A story in the *Globe* in May 1875 reported that Pomeroy conversed "intelligently" on his case and seemed to "relish the fine legal technicalities of counsel." One of the officers at the jail reportedly claimed (perhaps sardonically) that Pomeroy "would make an ornament to the Suffolk Bar." A couple of months later, the *Globe* (though conceding that Pomeroy might have had "legal assistance" in preparing his autobiography) remarked on "the way in which he anticipates the defence of insanity made at trial" and on his "remarkable aptitude for legal modes of expression," including the "lawyer like way in which [he] criticizes and dissects the testimony against him," which makes him look to have "even more acuteness and intelligence than has been usually supposed."[76]

Convinced of Pomeroy's insanity, Theodore Fisher argued that the boy's "conceit and love of notoriety" were symptomatic of his disorder, writing that these traits were "especially prominent" in his recent "foolish" autobiography: "This piece of special pleading is compounded of lies, quibbles, and slang jokes put together in a sort of mock legal manner. He is evidently tickled at his own ingenuity." Fisher declared that "the waste basket of any insane hospital would furnish similar copy in abundance," and observed in particular Pomeroy's multiple contradictions: "The only point worth noting is that while denying the commission of the crimes which he had freely confessed over and over again, for months, and to many different persons both before and after conviction, he argues with apparent sincerity that if he did commit them he must have been insane." Fisher also cited Pomeroy's repeated attempts at escape as evidence of "a morbid love for such notoriety as even failure would afford," saying that they, too, are expected "as a matter of course" in hospitals for the insane.[77] Fisher makes it clear here that neither the failure to escape, nor getting caught in contradictions and lies, deters the insane person in his craving for publicity.

Above and beyond a craving for notoriety, however, is chronically impulsive behavior, another defining characteristic of the psychopathic personality. Their heedlessness is one reason why psychopaths seek notoriety: they desire fame even when it's manifested as infamy and without regard to consequences. Certainly Pomeroy's autobiography, not to mention his constant escape attempts while in jail, demonstrates his propensity to get caught up in his fantastical sense of self no matter what the cost. But behind both Pomeroy's persistent self-aggrandizement and his efforts to break out of jail lies his impulsivity, a trait that was also behind his acts of torture and murder.

Among the "key symptoms of psychopathy," Hare lists four of the characteristics—"impulsive, poor behavior controls, need for excitement, lack of responsibility"—that clearly drove Pomeroy's crimes. His defense at trial, of course, was that he suffered from "irresistible impulse," and he claimed repeatedly, as he said to Dr. Tyler, that "I couldn't help doing what I did."[78] Most physicians identified this "irresistible impulse" as central to Pomeroy's symptomology, tantamount to "moral insanity" itself, but the line between an "irresistible" impulse (as a symptom of insanity) and a culpable impulse that could or should have been restrained is thin. When the New York physician William Hammond gave his much-publicized lecture before the Medico-Legal Society of New York in May 1874, in which he offered Jesse Pomeroy as his primary example of "morbid impulse," he also strongly disagreed that Pomeroy's impulse was in fact irresistible. To the extent that a person was "aware" of morbid impulses, Hammond argued (and he believed Pomeroy was "aware"), that person was bound to do "everything in his power" to resist it, including placing himself "under restraint."[79]

Indeed, as much as impulsivity was recognized by many as a crucial component of moral insanity (as it later became integral to psychopathy), the notion that Pomeroy's impulses were "irresistible" was highly troubling to many who wrote about the case.

As commentators like Hammond argued, whether an impulse is "irresistible" or not obviously depends on an individual's strength of will, and it is finally extremely difficult, if not impossible, to know exactly when an impulse gripping *someone else* is irresistible. In a study of the insanity defense, Lawrie Reznek cites a former Lord Chief Justice of England, Hubert Parker, on this question: "The step between 'he did not resist his impulse' and 'he could not resist his impulse' is incapable of scientific proof." Compounding the quandary is that the (seemingly irresistible) impulses of the "morally insane" (or of the psychopath) may not even be particularly strong. As Cleckley points out, "the psychopath requires impulses of scarcely more than whimlike intensity to bring about unacceptable behavior." This is because the "sort of repugnance or other inhibiting force" that would prevent most people from following certain impulses "is not a factor that can be counted on to play much part in the sociopath's decisions." While psychopaths' "passions or drives" may not be "particularly strong," then, they suffer from an "almost total lack of self-imposed restraint" (yet another *lack* in the psychopathic personality).[80] Thus those who insisted that Pomeroy could not restrain his impulses may have been right, although this inability was due more to the *absence* of many traits that serve to check impulses (empathy, conscience, fear, guilt, remorse) rather than to the actual *strength* of those impulses themselves.

The psychopath's impulsivity is also spurred by a greater need than most to seek sensation and pleasure. As Hare writes, "Impulsive acts often result from an aim that plays a central role in most of the psychopath's behavior: to achieve immediate satisfaction, pleasure, or relief." Psycho- paths, he continues, "have an ongoing and excessive need for excitement." Their impulses also manifest their rootedness "completely in the present," in which they are "unable to resist a good opportunity."[81] That Pome- roy was rooted in the present (what we might call the time frame of the impulse) goes far to explain what often appeared to be his striking failure of memory—sometimes no doubt contrived, but sometimes also quite real.[82] It was also clearly behind his succumbing to passing impulses with no thought to the past or to the future, to prior punishments or antici- pated consequences. Needing perpetual stimulation, and "blocked from fulfillment at deep levels," as Cleckley puts it, the psychopath simply gets bored and will do anything to overcome his ennui. Guggenbühl-Craig agrees that a "life with little or no eros or morality can readily turn into a dreary, monotonous affair." When "Eros absents himself altogether," Guggenbühl-Craig continues, "the vacuum is filled with meaningless or destructive activity."[83] What Pomeroy tellingly let slip about his murder of Katie Curran came strikingly close to a confession that he did it merely to relieve boredom: he notoriously claimed that he "wanted to see how she would act."[84]

Pomeroy's elevated need for stimulation was hinted at in a theory of his insanity (and thus his crimes) that was avoided by the press: his pur- portedly compulsive masturbation, an explanation that circulated only in medical discussions. Theodore Fisher initially argued that Pomeroy suffered from general "moral imbecility," but after he visited Pomeroy, he shifted his diagnosis to "mania from masturbation."[85] Fisher began his paper (delivered before the Suffolk District Medical Society in September 1875) by rehearsing his belief that Pomeroy suffered from "moral imbecility or insanity," as he had laid out in his short editorial on Pomeroy a year earlier.[86] Then, quite dramatically, Fisher goes on to describe actually meeting the boy. He says he noticed immediately that Pomeroy displayed "evidence of self-abuse," the telltale marks "plainly written on his countenance, as well as in his hands, which he kept concealed at first." Fisher asked Pomeroy whether he was correct in his inference about the boy's solitary habit, and while Pomeroy at first denied it, he then acknowledged that Fisher was right. "He also," Fisher recounted, "admitted that he had practiced the habit for years, and particularly at the periods when his crimes were committed." As Fisher then described the symptoms of "mania from masturbation," they certainly resonated with aspects of Pomeroy's behavior: the "attention and memory are weakened and the judgment impaired"; sometimes "great restlessness is observed, with a tendency to go from place to place without motive"; the "moral sense is blunted, and vicious courses new to the individual are entered upon"; the "will is weakened not only to the habit in question, but as shown in fickleness of purpose, and in sudden yielding to impulses of an erratic or dangerous character." Fisher also argued that the "conceit and love of notoriety" that are characteristic of mania from masturbation were particularly evident in Pomeroy's case.[87]

While we now know that masturbation does not cause insanity, or for that matter any of the symptoms Fisher identified, he may nonetheless have been partially correct. Pomeroy's allegedly compulsive masturbation, which he confessed he engaged in excessively "at the periods when his crimes were committed," may well have been an effect, not a cause, of his underlying psychopathy, an effect specifically of his impulsivity, his need for stimulation, and his propensity for boredom. Cleckley identifies the "familiar record of sexual promiscuity found in both male and female psychopaths," and argues that it is due less to "any particularly strong passions or drives" than to "their almost total lack of self-imposed restraint."[88] In all his supposedly compulsive acts, including masturbation, Pomeroy simply found no sufficient reason *not* to do them.

With a greater than usual need to seek excitement and relieve ennui, along with an inability to recognize hurting others as a profound moral transgression, a complete lack of empathy, and a relative immunity to fear, psychopaths have no reason not to inflict pain on others. Their often capricious wants substitute for perhaps the most striking and perplexing "lack" that defines the morally insane and the psychopathic: the lack of any recognizable motive. Pomeroy simply had no reason to torture or kill that any reasonable, moral human being would find to be an adequate one. As a contemporary newspaper put it, those who commit crimes "are supposed to act from some strong motive, or under the pressure of strong temptation, such as the hope of gain. In the absence of such impulses, crimes are perpetrated under provocation, inspiring passion or revenge." The facts of the Pomeroy case, though, "leave in mystery the impelling cause of the horror."[89] The closest Pomeroy came, perhaps, to actually elucidating this "mystery"—to giving a reason—was when he said that he killed Katie Curran because he "wanted to see how she would act." He otherwise said, repeatedly, that he "did not know," which frighteningly suggests there was no reason, only, perhaps, a whim and no reason not to.

"An animal rather than a person"

In an important essay on the psychopath, the philosopher Jeffrie Murphy has argued that to the extent that the profound and deforming *lack* of the psychopath disallows him as "human," it consigns him instead to the sphere of animality. The psychopath, according to Murphy, refuses to respect the rights of others, and thus he relinquishes any claim to have his own rights considered; he rejects, in other words, the "reciprocity" crucial to the formation of a just society. Psychopaths "do not *care* about others or their duties to them," have "no *concern* for others' rights and feelings, do not accept responsibility, and do not know what it is like to defer one's own gratifications out of *respect* for the dignity of another human being." They "feel no *guilt, regret, shame, or remorse.*" Existing beyond the pale of the "moral community," indeed, "morally dead," the psychopath is, as Murphy puts it, "more profitably pictured—from a moral point of view—as an animal." Indeed, it is "very implausible to regard [psychopaths] as persons at all." The psychopath, he stresses, is "an animal rather than a person."[90]

Murphy thus places within a philosophical framework all those contemporaries of Pomeroy who argued that he was an animal—a "torturing wild beast"—and that he was beyond "the pale of humanity."[91] And they were legion. An editorial in the *Boston Daily Advertiser* declared Pomeroy, with his "insatiable thirst for blood," to be "more dreadful at loose in the heart of a city than a panther starved for the arena." Another editorial spoke of the "survival" in Pomeroy of the "wolf and hyena instincts," while yet another described him (and killers like him) as "a reversion to the wolf, or rather the weasel type, which loves blood for its own sake."[92] George Dawson, who argued that humans' "animal or sub-human ancestors have persisted" in Pomeroy, concluded his description of the boy's crimes by asserting that it "is just as in the case of the tiger that drags to the earth an antelope, gorges itself upon its flesh, and then passes on indifferently to its lair."[93] Unlike Murphy, though, most of those who portrayed Pomeroy as an animal argued for his execution: such claims illustrate the wisdom of Murphy's qualification of his own argument. He points out at the end of his essay that "considering individuals as less than persons" comes with many dangers.[94] Indeed, when a human is defined as radically other than a "person," he may be killed with impunity—just like an animal.

In claiming that psychopaths are not "persons," in large part due to their complete disregard for the rights of others, Murphy makes it clear that what is crucially at stake in diagnosing the psychopath is what it means to be a person, since a psychopath is defined by his lack of what makes a "person." As Murphy himself puts it, "In coming to term with the concept of psychopathy, one is also forced to come to terms with the question of what it is to be a *person*." The notion of the "person," however, leaves out much of what it means to be *human;* importantly, it leaves out the body. The "person," the philosopher Roberto Esposito writes, is "separate from, or even opposed to its corporeal part." The person, in other words, is that which, "in a human being, is other than and beyond body."[95] Thus while the psychopath may lack the qualities of a "person"—empathy, conscience, fear of punishment—he is nonetheless still a "living being," still "human," which encompasses much more than the qualities that go to make up a "person." Not least, it encompasses the often unruly and mystifying body. Theorists have recently engaged in the project of describing what Cary Wolfe calls a "nonhuman otherness" and Rosi Braidotti dubs the "profound nonhumanness at the heart of the subject," an inchoate core of the human that includes humans' animal origins and their unruly and nonpersonal bodies, bodies marked by a long evolutionary past.[96]

The designations of moral insanity and psychopathy have long been repositories, I think, of exactly that "nonhuman" and nonpersonal core within the human. Supporting this proposition is the criminologist Jarkko

Jalava's point that late nineteenth-century theories of atavism—the notion that some humans, often criminals, were anomalous eruptions from a primitive past—formed a bridge between moral insanity and psychopathy. "The thesis that the degenerate manifests in his or her person an evolutionary throwback," he writes, "is frequently and more or less formally made in psychopathy research." In many respects, he adds, "psychopaths do appear strange, bestial and uncivilised."[97] Claims that Jesse Pomeroy was akin to a wild beast or "a reversion to the wolf" converged, then, with his diagnosis as morally insane (and psychopathic, as we would call it now): both were expressions of something within him that escaped what it means to be a "person."

In moving Pomeroy beyond the realm of the "person" (the "civilized" human), commentators recognized his status as a part of nature—and *the part of the human that is nature,* precisely the part that has been disavowed in our construal of persons. In both popular and scholarly discourse, the morally insane and the psychopathic are often described as some force of nature. The historian Daniel N. Robinson has written that nineteenth-century diagnoses of moral insanity cast people "not in a jural or moral light but solely as natural objects subject to the causally determinative laws that govern the whole realm of purely natural objects." And in R. Scott Bakker's fascinating science-fiction novel, *Neuropath,* which strangely echoes Murphy's philosophical argument, a character declares that what makes psychopaths so "indigestible" is that, as "*humans* who were indifferent to all things human," they "were natural disasters personified." Both writers describe here the way in which the morally insane and the psychopathic in general, and Jesse Pomeroy in particular, were displaced from the category of "person" to the realm of the "natural object."[98] The problem, though, with pushing Jesse Pomeroy as force of nature beyond the "human" community, as so many did, is that *we are all "natural objects."*

We call some people psychopaths, defining them as utterly deviant, but the bottom line is that they do seem to have been with us from the beginning, a "normative" part of our species, since by most accounts there has been a relatively consistent number of psychopaths (under various labels) across time and place. Anthony Walsh and Jonathan Bolen, for instance, point out that although the term "psychopath" is relatively recent, "those whom the term denotes have preyed on us since the dawn of time." Psychopaths are also not so easy to cast off as something entirely other—and increasingly commentators acknowledge that many if not most people have "psychopathic" moments. As Jon Ronson has claimed, while the attention of doctors, psychiatrists, and lay people go to those on the outer edge of psychopathy, many people inhabit the large "gray" middle range.[99] There is, as the title of one book puts it, a "psychopathy of everyday life."[100] And Paul Babiak and Robert Hare's 2006 book, *Snakes in Suits: When Psychopaths Go to Work*, both draws on the notion of the psychopath as animal and argues that it is a much more common condition than we would think, ubiquitous in the corporate world. Murphy himself, writing of the difficulty of diagnosing psychopathy, has claimed that "we all have our psychopathic tendencies."[101]

Although not all psychopathy is expressed as violence (much of it, as Babiak and Hare point out, is channeled into success in the corporate world), it was certainly a constitutive part of Jesse Pomeroy. But even when it comes to the remorseless violence of some psychopaths, it must be noted that human nature itself contains an intractable propensity for violence. An editorial in 1874 expressed this view, arguing that the "passion of cruelty" is "one of the attributes of human nature." It was merely "excessive" in Pomeroy. Humans do share with other animals, and with their own long-dead human forebears, a propensity for violence that has been hardwired through millennia. David Livingstone Smith argues that humans "wage war" because "it is in our nature to do so"; the allure of war comes from "tendencies inscribed in our genes over evolutionary time."[102] Recent research has debunked the notion that (other) animals kill only when necessary, for instance, or that primitive cultures are less violent than civilized ones (the idea of the "noble savage"), and both of these findings suggest the persistence of violence (even purposeless violence) within animal and human nature.[103] As Steven Pinker puts it, while humans do not "have a thirst for blood that must regularly be slaked," they do have a nature that "accommodates motives that impel us to violence, like predation, dominance, and vengeance."[104] Just as other animals do.

"Psychopathy," it seems, along with "moral insanity" before it, is just a way station in a long tradition of identifying certain people as beyond the pale of the "human" community because they lack what we like to call "human" qualities. Tony Ward, like others, has described the historical evolution of the concept of psychopathy from its roots in moral insanity, and he concludes by asserting that psychopaths, like all their forebears under different names, "lack some essential element of fully human personality."[105] Indeed, psychopathy, with its constitutive catastrophic absence of "humanity," functions to demarcate a profound core of the "inhuman" lodged within the human—an inhuman core that ends up wholly defining *some* humans. As many have argued, though, in the end it partially defines *all of us,* and it must at the very least be acknowledged as fundamental in some way to human nature, not least because of its persistence in human history. Pomeroy's status as morally insane—what we would now call psychopathic—may have been a way for many onlookers to cast him as utterly aberrant, but, like other explanations of who and what he was, it marked him only as closer to one end of a more expansive, more real, human continuum.

In the end, moreover, to call Jesse Pomeroy morally insane, or a psychopath, may not explain very much—just as the more popular nineteenth-century lay term "monster" did not explain very much. As the philosopher Stephen Asma has astutely written: "Although the term *monster* is overused and often obfuscates important complexities, the more professional semantic contenders, such as *psychopath,* are not exactly great leaps forward. Even the law is still using wonderful terms like malignant heart. We are still very much at the *descriptive* phase of the science of the criminal mind, not yet at the underlying *causation* phase."[106] Asma thus puts perfectly the overwhelmingly descriptive, not causative, emphasis of those who diagnosed Pomeroy as morally insane. Such a diagnosis came with the weight of medical terminology, but finally it was not much more illuminating of what caused Pomeroy's behavior than were the claims of those who called him a panther, a wild beast, or a moral monster. But as we will see in the next chapter, there is one hint—dropped by Ruth Pomeroy—of a possible cause of Jesse Pomeroy's psychopathy and thus of his brutal crimes. It didn't push him beyond the border of the "human"—he was as human as anyone—but it did make his "psychopathic tendencies," as Murphy calls them, much stronger than the norm.

The Scourge of Smallpox

Both of the causal theories proposed by Jesse Pomeroy's contemporaries—that he was stamped in utero by his mother's witnessing, even desiring, the scene of bloody slaughter, and that he imitated (unconsciously) the scenes of torture he read in dime novels—challenge us to consider the radical idea that Pomeroy's body acted without the consent of his mind, without his ever consciously forming intent. The diagnosis of "moral insanity" proffered by most of the physicians who met Pomeroy put this notion of the autonomous body within a legitimating medical framework, highlighting the boy's diseased brain. What the case of Jesse Pomeroy offers us, then, with its unmistakable granting of a determining power to the body, even "possession" by the body, is a way to think differently about the causes of crime. It offers us a way to think about the biological origins of crime, an idea that has been gaining ground in the late twentieth and early twenty-first centuries (recapitulating a similar interest at the end of the nineteenth century). It's an idea, moreover, that has been manifest especially in the burgeoning research on the biological origins of psychopathy.[1] The case of Jesse Pomeroy suggests that the roots of crime don't lie only in the *mens rea* or "guilty mind" presumed by law or the consciously formed "motive" that is so important to the rest of us. The roots of crime can be harbored in the body. Jesse Pomeroy makes clear that crime can emanate from what is perhaps best called the "corporeal unconscious," which escapes the grasp of mind and of reason and volition.[2]

There is one last cause by which Pomeroy's contemporaries attempted to explain his crimes. It was by no means a widely held explanation, although Ruth Pomeroy, his mother, seemed to think it was a compelling one, and it was she who offered it. It is a frustratingly brief story about something that happened to Pomeroy when he was one month old and that persisted until he was six months old—an event that may well have profoundly affected his brain and created his subsequent seemingly incontrollable urge to torture and kill. It is an event, in other words, that sheds light on how Pomeroy might have developed the catastrophic symptoms of psychopathy. As much as this cause involves the body, however, it also makes clear that bodies are imbricated in their multiple environments. Biological theories of crime are always, more accurately, "biosocial" theories of crime, as the criminologist Nicole Rafter has pointed out. She concludes that we should no longer "pit nature against nurture."[3]

Rafter is not alone in propounding a model of crime that recognizes how body and world are interconnected. The body-as-cause cannot be seen in isolation from the environment, for just as the body shapes actions in the world, so too does the world shape the body. Anthony Walsh and Jonathan Bolen argue, for instance, that despite the inability of researchers to find social explanations for psychopathy, the emerging consensus about the disorder's biological correlatives does not preclude the deep effects of environment: "At least some of the neurological signatures that identify psychopaths," they assert, "can be environmentally written." The criminal psychologist Adrian Raine, who has mapped extensively what he calls the "neuroanatomy of violence" (including the dysfunctional brains of psychopaths), argues for a "neurodevelopmental theory of crime," one that recognizes the ways in which developmental conditions shape neural pathways. Criminals, especially psychopaths, do indeed have "broken brains," and while Raine unearths the biological basis of violence, he also argues that the harms that generate "structural brain abnormalities" are often environmental, occurring especially in gestation and in early infancy.[4]

To return to the most influential nineteenth-century explanations of Jesse Pomeroy, it is important to note that both were, as Rafter puts it, "biosocial": both expressed in some way the *interaction* of biology and environment, of body and culture. The story that Pomeroy was marked before birth by his mother's visits to the slaughterhouse obviously locates the roots of the boy's crimes in his body, in a brain fatally malformed before he was born. But many who made this argument then extended it to those economic, social, and cultural factors that, they claimed, led Ruth Pomeroy to a slaughterhouse in the first place: the exigencies of paid labor for Thomas Pomeroy, Ruth's own willful transgressive desires, the animal-butchering industry, and even meat-eating itself. Conversely, theories that Jesse Pomeroy was influenced by an undisputedly environmental factor—dime novels—were often imbricated in language suggesting that the images of sensational fiction (and the sensational press) impressed themselves directly on the brains and bodies of readers, changing and shaping "nature" itself, impelling action before intent, and driving an unconscious traffic between interior and exterior. The third cause, offered by Jesse's mother, involves a similar interweaving of the biological and the environmental.

"Another theory for the doctors to think on"

When Ruth Pomeroy publicly refuted the story that Jesse was "marked" at birth by her supposed visits to the slaughterhouse, she offered a countering explanation of her son's pathology, one that was equally rooted in his body but that may in fact (unlike the theory of maternal impressions) have been crucial in his making. What Ruth recounted was the story of Jesse's devastating reaction to a smallpox vaccination at the age of only four weeks.[5] As Ruth prefaced her story, "*I think his vaccination had more effect on him than anything else.*" She went on to explain:

> He was vaccinated when he was four weeks old, and shortly after his face broke out and had the appearance of raw flesh, and some fluid issued from the wounds that burned my arm when it dropped on it, from which fact I judged the fluid was poison. This lasted until he was six months old, when his whole body was covered with large abscesses, one of which was over the eye, and occasioned the cast or fallen appearance that it wears at present. At the time, it was thought he would die, but he recovered slowly, and Dr. Lane, who attended him, stated that all the sickness was occasioned by vaccination.[6]

This glimpse of Pomeroy's past offers a "new and novel theory that may be worthy of thought," the *Boston Daily Globe* commented, adding, though, that Mrs. Pomeroy "does not give this story as a reason that might be assigned for Jesse's conduct, but simply states it as a matter of interest in his history."[7] Pomeroy's early illness did fleetingly come up at his trial, when Ruth testified for the defense. In a seeming effort to offer circumstances that might mitigate her son's crimes, she told the court that "when very young," Jesse "had a violent attack of sickness, which almost reduced him to a skeleton."[8] Others did not balk at offering the incident as "a reason that might be assigned for Jesse's conduct," and, prefacing its printing of Ruth's story, the *Boston Daily Advertiser* commented that it "gives another theory for the doctors to think on." The writer goes on to speculate both that the vaccine matter could have come from "some diseased animal" and that the "animal's tendencies" might well have been "transmitted to the boy." After all, the article concludes, Pomeroy's mother does claim that this particular illness "had more effect on him than anything else."[9]

At the very least it seems that the ill-fated smallpox vaccine had a destructive and permanent *physical* effect on Jesse Pomeroy (even while its moral effects remained up for debate). It was apparently the reason for his damaged eye, what some called his "evil eye." According to Ruth, the vaccine produced "large abscesses over his body, one of which—over the eye—occasioned the cast which it now presents."[10] Dr. John Tyler, who interviewed Pomeroy and testified both in his defense at trial and for the commutation of his sentence before the governor and his council, noted, "He has lost the use of one eye, which he says is the result of vaccination." The case history taken when Pomeroy was admitted to Westborough stated that his right eye "was partially covered by a white film."[11] In his (highly unreliable) autobiography, Jesse claimed his eye was injured by a fishing hook when he and his brother were fishing; for some reason, he wanted to evade the truth about his eye in his autobiography, which is, among other things, an attempt to write his boyhood as a conventional, happy one.[12] He chose to write out and write off the months when his body was host to a debilitating smallpox vaccine, when his infancy was assaulted and marred by pain and disfiguration. But the vaccination left its enduring mark on the exterior of Pomeroy's body, evoking dread in some, perhaps making him a target for bullies, and, in the end, leading to his identification as the boy torturer and to his remand to reform school. It might well have also left a less visible, interior mark—shaping those deadly compulsions in the face of which he seemed so helpless.

This story about the dire effects of a smallpox vaccination was another way in which Pomeroy became monstrous: not only was his "evil eye" a product of its ravages, but at least one newspaper maintained that the smallpox vaccine had transmitted "animal tendencies" to Pomeroy when he was an infant, thus molding him as an impure mixture of animal and human.[13] But the story also demonstrates the tragic way in which a child became a killer. As is the case in the other stories about Pomeroy (including claims that he was marked by the "meat market" and by scenes of torture in dime novels), the killer that he became was created by the profound interweaving of both body and brain with the environment. The external world—the smallpox vaccination and the controversy that surrounded it—literally went inside and shaped a body that in turn profoundly shaped a subject, a *corporeal subject*, one whose impulses, desires, and actions were more influenced by his body than we typically imagine them to be.

At the time that the four-week-old Jesse was vaccinated in late December 1859, his older brother, Charles, would have been about fourteen months. Ruth Pomeroy most likely took Jesse to be vaccinated because she was required by law to do so—and because she was scared. After Edwin Jenner's method of vaccination (with cowpox) was introduced at the beginning of the nineteenth century, Boston had for several decades been relatively free of the dreaded scourge. But then a certain amount of complacency about getting vaccinated, combined with increasing waves of immigrants pouring into the city, led to successive epidemics beginning in 1840. While only 52 people died from smallpox in Boston between 1811 and 1839, 1,491 died between 1839 and 1861.[14] And then in the epidemic of 1872–73, 3,722 people were afflicted and 1,026 died—all in just sixteen months.[15] Presumably as a response to the resurgence of the deadly disease, Massachusetts became the first state to enforce compulsory vaccination, passing a law in 1855 mandating that all children be vaccinated before they could attend school. By 1860, the law required that parents vaccinate their children before the age of two or face a fine of at least five dollars.[16] With her oldest son already in his second year, Ruth may well have taken both of her children to be vaccinated to comply with this law.

As dutiful as she clearly was, Ruth may not have needed the directive of the law to take her children to the local vaccination center. When Jesse was born and her first child was around one year old, Boston was in the midst of another epidemic. Smallpox epidemics had struck Boston in 1840, 1850, and 1855, but the outbreak of 1859–60 was the worst yet. This particular resurgence began in January 1859 and lasted until October 1860 and was at its height between November 1859 (when Jesse was born) and February 1860. A fact that may well have induced panic in parents was, as a local physician put it at the time, that the "mortality was most severe among infants and young children." A full 41 percent of deaths were of children under five. This could be explained, he noted, "by the well-known fatality of the disease in early life."[17]

Newspapers in late 1859 and early 1860 published continuous reports of the disease's progress and its latest fatalities, describing the "return of the smallpox with so much virulence," proclaiming that there "is no abatement of the ravages of this disease," remarking on "the prevalence of the small pox in the city and neighborhood," and, even as the epidemic finally showed signs of waning, insisting that this "loathsome disease is still prevalent in many parts of the city."[18] Newspapers also impressed readers with the importance, indeed the necessity, of vaccination. "We are glad to see," the *Boston Traveler* declared in late December 1859, "that public attention has been directed towards a vigorous system of vaccination." In early 1860, readers were relieved to learn that the disease was slowly on the decline because of "the attention paid to vaccination and revaccination."[19] Prompted by law, then, as well as no doubt driven by fear, Ruth had the four-week-old Jesse vaccinated sometime around late December 1859 or early January 1860—precisely when both the alarm about the epidemic and the push for vaccination were at their height.

Despite the city-wide proclamations about the safety of smallpox vaccination, Jesse Pomeroy clearly had a devastating reaction to it. Yet it is perhaps not surprising that in the wake of his arrest for the murder of Horace Millen, the newspapers never took up Ruth Pomeroy's claim that her son was deeply affected by his vaccination, even as they reported with alacrity on the possibility that he was "marked" in utero or that he was influenced by his reading of dime novels. For in early 1874, when Pomeroy killed Katie Curran and Horace Millen, Boston had just emerged from the grip of yet another smallpox epidemic, the most devastating since vaccination was introduced at the beginning of the nineteenth century. By all accounts, moreover, the city's response to the epidemic of 1872–73 was woefully insufficient. There was no adequate hospital facility in Boston and no way to enforce laws dictating vaccination and the segregation and hospitalization of the sick. Indeed, the Boston Board of Health was established in 1872 precisely because of the city's failure to meet the threat of the 1872–73 epidemic.[20]

The lesson (re)learned in those years, a lesson that many claimed should have been learned in 1859–60, was that the inhabitants of Boston included a dangerously large proportion of the unvaccinated. Any reminders of the potential dangers of vaccination—such as attributing Jesse Pomeroy's crimes to a bad reaction to a vaccine—would have run dramatically counter to the official push to vaccinate as many as people as possible as quickly as possible during and immediately after the devastating outbreak of 1872–73. In a 1921 article surveying the history of smallpox in Massachusetts, Dr. Jonathan Henry wrote that in the wake of that epidemic, both the State Board of Health (established in 1869) and the Boston Board of Health began to bring "pressure to bear on local boards, and the existing laws began to be enforced strictly." As a result, deaths from smallpox decreased dramatically—only sixty-one deaths between 1872 and 1900.[21] In 1874, then, no one would have wanted to jeopardize the apparently renewed willingness of Boston's citizenry to line up dutifully for their smallpox vaccinations.

The Scourge of Vaccination

Despite the undoubted benefits of vaccination (manifested quite clearly in the declining deaths from smallpox after 1873), it was by no means (as Pomeroy's case makes clear) risk free. The historian Donald Hopkins points out that during the Civil War years, "attempted vaccination was sometimes almost as dangerous as smallpox."[22] Writing about the anti-vaccination movement in both England and the United States, Nadja Durbach describes the numerous horror stories that filled the pages of anti-vaccination publications, stories that fired parents' fears about the dreadful effects of vaccination on their children: "Anti-vaccinators consistently maintained that vaccination caused indescribable pain and suffering and terribly disfigured the bodies of its victims." Indeed, they warned terrified parents that the procedure "physically and spiritually transformed" its "innocent victim" into "a deformed monster." According to Durbach, white middle-class parents wrote thousands of letters to newspapers describing how their children mutated, after being vaccinated, into "terrifying monstrosities." Many of these stories are uncannily similar to what Ruth Pomeroy had said of her younger son. One mother recounted how her child had "broken out in a 'loathsome eruption,'" which she described as a "bladdery eruption" that "covered the baby's entire body so that there was 'hardly a piece of healthy skin the size of a shilling from head to foot.'"[23] As we've seen, Ruth's account also indicated that Jesse's face had broken out shortly after the vaccination and "had the appearance of raw flesh, and some fluid issued from the wounds that burned my arm when it dropped on it." The abscesses spread over Jesse's entire body in the course of the first several months of his young life, until, at six months, "his whole body was covered with large abscesses," one of which covered his eye and caused the "cast" that never went away. For five months in his very earliest infancy, Jesse Pomeroy literally embodied the nightmare visions of deformed and monstrous children furiously penned by anti-vaccinators.

It is unclear what caused Pomeroy's severe reaction to the smallpox vaccination. There is a remote possibility that he may have contracted syphilis through what was most likely an "arm-to-arm" vaccination. Physicians had reluctantly, by the 1880s, come to acknowledge that syphilis had, perhaps in untold numbers, been transmitted to the recipients of smallpox vaccine. A New York physician, George William Winterburn, wrote about the case of three children who came under his care when they developed syphilitic sores after vaccination, sores that began "like a blister," akin, perhaps, to the "fluid" that emerged from the infant Jesse's sores. The youngest suffered the worst, having at least thirty sores that covered most of his body. As with Pomeroy, it took about four months for the infant to heal completely.[24] Pomeroy did not seem, however, to suffer from other symptoms of syphilis later in life (though physicians who knew him from the beginning certainly thought he had some sort of brain disease, hence the moral insanity diagnosis). He could also have contracted one of the other most frequent complications of smallpox vaccination, erysipelas, which is a severe skin infection introduced by bacterial contamination of the lymph. According to the historian Gareth Williams, erysipelas was a "major killer of infants" in general and, more specifically, "accounted for half of all deaths attributed to vaccination" in England between 1856 and 1882.[25]

Pomeroy could also have suffered devastating consequences from the vaccine virus itself, a syndrome called "generalized vaccinia," which Williams describes as a condition in which "the whole of the skin broke out in blisters that resembled the usual vaccination-site pustules," the result of a failure by the immune system to keep the virus from spreading past the vaccination site. This particular reaction to the vaccine carried a mortality rate of about 50 percent.[26] Williams describes one tireless American crusader, Lora Little, who culminated her turn-of-the-century campaign against smallpox vaccination (from which her own young son had died after being forcibly vaccinated) by publishing a pamphlet documenting hundreds of cases she had collected while traveling the United States of vaccinations gone horribly, sometimes fatally, wrong. Little describes many cases that sound like Jesse Pomeroy—sores, blisters, and abscesses being some of the most common symptoms. She includes, for instance, the story of a girl who developed blisters on her head and face which "soon spread over her entire body." After "four or five months," they slowly healed, "but left her eyes badly affected."[27] Exactly like Jesse Pomeroy.

Part of the reason vaccination was dangerous was that in northern cities, through at least the 1870s, much of the smallpox vaccine was supplied in the form of crusts taken from those who had already been vaccinated. While wealthier people could get their vaccinations at home from private physicians, those with fewer means (and the Pomeroys certainly had few means) had little choice but to avail themselves of the free vaccinations available at the offices of city physicians; they would also have received a different kind of vaccination than wealthier people. By midcentury, everyone agreed that to be vaccinated with pure calf lymph was the preferable method; it was arguably more effective and indisputably safer, carrying no risk of transferring disease from tainted vaccine product. At public vaccination centers, however, the less wealthy would almost certainly have received an arm-to-arm vaccination. The center would have received a small supply of calf lymph with which some infants would be vaccinated—and then those children were ordered to return so officials could take more lymph from their "vesicles," which they would then use to vaccinate others. This product was called "humanized" lymph, as opposed to the pure calf lymph, and those who were vaccinated with it received a product that had passed through many human bodies, with no one being particularly discriminating about the health of those bodies. Hopkins claims that vaccine quality in the United States was "greatly improved only after the practice of propagating the vaccine virus on cows, rather than arm to arm in people, was introduced into North America in the 1860s in a herd near Boston." Even propagation in cattle, however, "did not always guarantee safe, effective, vaccine."[28] And this major improvement, despite its happening first near Boston, was certainly too late for Jesse Pomeroy.

In December 1872, shortly after Pomeroy had been sent to reform school, and as Boston was in the throes of the 1872–73 epidemic, one of the pioneers in bringing the calf vaccine to the United States, Dr. Henry Austin Martin, wrote a letter to the *Boston Daily Globe* decrying the "entire failure of the present public vaccination" to "arrest or even modify" the "violence" of the current prevalence of smallpox. Martin claimed that this failure was due to the use of a "worthless virus" from Europe, via New York—an "old long humanized virus." Martin's own "animal vaccine, or 'cow-pox virus,'" his "*true* animal vaccine," was vastly superior, he wrote, to the "effete and exhausted virus of long humanization."²⁹ In truth, most physicians seemed to agree that while no smallpox vaccination was always effective or safe, the "animal virus" was significantly more effective and much less dangerous.³⁰

Whether the vaccine was "human" or "animal," however, it inevitably breached the borders of both body and self and was thus seen by many as a profound violation. George Winterburn declared in 1886 that it was a "monstrous tyranny" that the United States had compulsory vaccination laws. Not least, he argued, those laws were visited disproportionately on poor and working-class families (like the Pomeroys). Vaccination opened "the public school to every poor man's child," Winterburn wrote, and thus the cost of defying compulsory vaccination laws was ignorance for that child. Because of the undeniable risks of vaccination—as Winterburn put it, "no amount of care on the part of the vaccinator will obviate the possibility of danger and disaster"—he believed strenuously that people should be able to make their own choice. Vaccination, in the end, "permanently impairs the integrity of the body," and no assemblage of men "have the right to violate by force the physical integrity of another human being."³¹

Winterburn was offering an avowedly "non-partisan" view; not surprisingly, avid anti-vaccinators were significantly more hyperbolic about vaccination's breaching of what should be the inviolable body. Durbach writes that anti-vaccinators saw vaccination as a brutal transgression of the body; they argued, for instance, that the vaccinators "get inside of [the subject's] skin, and invade his veins, so that the blood in his body is not his own." In a typical anti-vaccination pamphlet written by a Massachusetts physician, C. W. Amerige, and tellingly titled *Vaccination: A Curse,* the central theme was the "purity" of the child and the "blood contamination" introduced by vaccination, which did nothing but "transplant" a "mischievous poison" into the life of an innocent child, irredeemably profaning that pure life.³² Other explanations of Jesse Pomeroy had cast his as a dangerously permeable body, penetrated by the catastrophic impressions of the slaughterhouse and, in some accounts, by his mother's blood-filled desires, both of which combined to make "the blood in his body . . . not his own." He was also seen as ravaged by the sensational images and plots of dime novels, scenes of torture implanted indelibly in his brain and body. Vaccination was just one more way, then, in which Pomeroy's body was catastrophically invaded.

The fact that the cowpox-based vaccine was derived from animals only added more weight to the threat vaccination posed to the human body.

As the anti-vaccination movement swelled in the United States from the 1880s onward, the mixing of animal and human was one of the focal points of attack, drawing on fears that had shadowed smallpox vaccination ever since Edwin Jenner's cowpox variant had been introduced at the beginning of the nineteenth century. While the "humanized virus" risked transmitting disease from person to person, and was by all accounts not as effective, the "animal virus" activated a more primal fear, menacing the boundaries of the human with that from which it should remain separate, the abject animal. The fear of animal "contamination" of the human through vaccination took two related forms. The least credible, even in the early nineteenth century, was that humans would literally take on the physical qualities of animals if infused with their blood. In 1805, William Rowley, a British physician adamantly opposed to Jenner and his theories, published what he claimed were "case histories" of "the unthinkable things that cowpox did to previously normal children." One boy started "running around on all fours, bellowing like a cow." Another "grew bumps on his forehead and his face . . . took on a bovine appearance." Such reports, according to Gareth Williams, "reawakened primitive beliefs that animals could pass on their traits to humans."[33] The "primitive" fear of what might happen if human and animal became too proximate was not, in the end, all that primitive.

A less literal but more powerful and persistent anxiety was that an infusion of animal blood into the human body would introduce animalistic *moral* qualities. Particularly after Darwin, though, the fear was less that the vaccination would *introduce* than that it would *incite* (already existing) animalistic characteristics. Durbach cites several pamphlets from the 1870s and 1880s that worried about such mental and moral effects: "Antivaccinators feared that vaccination could 'stimulate their animal propensities' and thus 'brutify' and 'lower' human nature." Durbach quotes Archdeacon Thomas Colley, who in 1882 declared that when you infuse the "human system with the 'passions of the beast,'" the person "is 'dehumanized' to the degree in which 'the animal has been implanted.'" Such fears of the "brutifying" of the human were only heightened by Darwin's tracing of humans' animal origins. Durbach cites one 1871 anti-vaccination pamphlet that explicitly makes this connection. "Even if we are 'ascended from gorillas,'" the writer proclaimed, "we nevertheless refuse to have our 'natures mixed again with the disease of beasts.'" As Durbach sums up this line of argument, "Replacing human blood with that of the beast could reverse the process of evolution, these campaigners implied, returning man to an ape-like state."[34] Darwin's theories only made more possible, it seems, what could become the uncontrolled traffic between human and animal.

Late nineteenth-century Boston was not immune to such fears. One article in the *Daily Globe* as the epidemic of 1872 was worsening hearkened back to the days of widespread resistance to Jenner's vaccination, quoting an early critic who questioned "the consequences of introducing a bestial humor into the human frame" and warned that the "human character may undergo strange mutations from quadrupedan sympathy." While the article stated that such anxieties lay in the past, its own explicit recapitulation belied its banishing of them, as it literally conjured them up for its current readers. The 1874 *Boston Advertiser* article that was one of the first to relay Ruth's story about her son's vaccination itself proved that fears about the tainting of the human with "animal tendencies" was by no means in the past.[35] Other articles followed suit. An editorial in *The Index,* also published in 1874, related the argument that Pomeroy was not a "moral agent"—that he was "pushed to the dreadful outrages he has committed by something that may well be called a demon possessing him." While the writer disagrees with this position, he rehearsed for the reader Ruth's denial of Pomeroy's having been prenatally marked by her visits to the slaughterhouse as well as the alternative story she offered—the story of his vaccination, which "infected his mental nature with a kind of animal ferocity." Another article published in 1874, evoking the vaccination theory, satirized the need to find something or someone else responsible for Pomeroy's crimes: "The butcher is thus relieved of the burden of the boy's sins," the *Daily Constitution* of Middletown, Connecticut, wrote (about Ruth's denial of the story that she visited the slaughterhouse while pregnant), but "the load" now "rests upon the cattle themselves," and it will no doubt, the writer continued, "eventually come to rest upon Edwin Jenner."[36]

Fears of possession, "brutifying," and vaccination came together in the reform work of John Murray Spear and his wife, Caroline Hinckley Spear, who had campaigned to commute Pomeroy's death sentence because they believed passionately that he was not responsible for his crimes. They were strong proponents of the spiritualist movement and believed that if Pomeroy was executed he would return and wreak havoc as a "wrathful revenant." The Spears also drafted the first report of the London Society for the Abolition of Compulsory Vaccination in the summer of 1880. Like other reformers, the historian John Benedict Buescher writes, the couple "were unconvinced of the true therapeutic effect of vaccinating humans with 'impure' blood products." Because smallpox vaccines were "manufactured from cow-pox antibodies extracted from the blood of cows," spiritualists like the Spears were afraid that "while mixing humans and spirits might elevate the race, mixing humans and animals (through the injection of blood products into people) would speed degeneration."[37] The injection of the "animal" into the human body, in other words, degraded it, dragged it from its more spiritual realm. Of course, absent in these discussions is the recognition that the human body is already an animal body—no doubt the unconscious source of much of the anxiety about human and animal mixing.

Making Jesse Pomeroy

While Jesse Pomeroy's smallpox vaccination may not have introduced "animal tendencies" into his blood, or turned him into a "terrifying monstrosity," it nonetheless clearly had a disastrous effect on him.[38] At one month old, and for months afterwards, he was covered with weeping abscesses, his body nothing but "raw flesh," and his mother claimed that he almost died. Violent behavior emerges from an interaction of multiple factors (genetic, biological, and environmental), many of which are impossible to identify after the fact, especially when the person in question was born in the middle of the nineteenth century. There are some things that can be known with certainty, though—and the reaction of Jesse Pomeroy to the smallpox vaccination, and the pain he no doubt suffered for five crucial early months, is one of them. The likely effects of this suffering, moreover, align with what has been discovered, over the last several decades, about the role of very early experience in in shaping the brain and thus shaping behavior—shaping the person we become.

It is plausible that Pomeroy's dire reaction to his smallpox vaccination, first, caused him moderate to severe pain (and thus chronic stress) at an age when he was too young to grasp consciously *why* he was suffering (hence redoubling the stress), and, second, interfered with the crucial process of attachment with his mother. Both chronic stress and failure of attachment in early infancy have been directly and repeatedly linked to the changes in the brain that can cause impulsive, violent, and even psychopathic behavior. Robin Karr-Morse and Meredith S. Wiley, for instance, describe chronic stress in infancy as a "toxin" that profoundly influences early development. Specifically, stress increases the activity of the brainstem, while neglect decreases the moderating capacity of the limbic or cortical areas, both of which "will increase an individual's aggressivity, impulsivity and capacity to display violence." Chronic stress can also destroy crucial synapses in the brain (or cause them never to be formed) which can leave an individual "without the ability to connect, to trust, and ultimately to experience empathy."[39] As an infant, Jesse must have suffered intense and prolonged stress, experiencing what would have been incomprehensible pain from weeping sores across the entirety of his face and body for five months, a pain that nobody was able to alleviate.

The pain would also have affected the bonding between mother and child. Ruth said that the discharge from the abscesses "burned" her arm; she may have been unable to hold him or comfort him for prolonged periods during those five months, and he may even have felt that the pain—the threat—came from her, his primary caretaker. At the very least, he must have been aware in some way that she could not prevent it, could not protect him. Karr-Morse and Wiley sum up the plenitude of research on the importance of secure attachment in the first year, noting that it offers "three key protective factors that mitigate against later aggression." Through attachment, the infant learns to empathize with others, to control his or her feelings (especially destructive feelings), and to develop cognitive processes. Deprivation of an early bond can lead to the dysfunction of all kinds of neurobiological processes, "one result of which can be violence." Adrian Raine has argued that a break in bonding between caretaker and infant that lasts for four months or more in the first year of life "freezes the social-interpersonal development of the infant" and that this "freezing" can result in a catastrophic failure to learn empathy—can produce, in other words, "the glacial, emotionless psychopath that we see in adulthood."[40]

Failure of the caretaker–infant bond (and thus of attachment) obviously, in and of itself, produces a secondary but equally disabling consequence: stress. This failure has featured prominently in studies that demonstrate how fundamentally, in the words of Anthony Walsh and Jonathan Bolen, attachment (and its lack) "marks the brain neurobiologically." Toxic and prolonged stress, along with interrupted bonding, are known to damage key areas of the brain, specifically the amygdala and prefrontal cortex. Both areas are crucially implicated in psychopathy, as they control aversive conditioning and emotional responsiveness. Walsh and Bolen argue that "the lack of affectionate bonding postnatally" can lead specifically to the "neurological signatures that identify psychopaths." Raine advances "a 'neurodevelopmental' theory of crime and violence," promoting the idea, he writes, "that the seeds of sin are sown very early on in life." Raine is just one of many scientists doing research that shows both that poor functioning in the prefrontal cortex, the amygdala, and the hippocampus are strongly tied to violent behavior *and* that these parts of the brain are deeply affected—are literally shaped—by early experiences.[41]

There is emerging and clear evidence that dysfunctions of the brain are implicated in psychopathy, specifically dysfunction in those parts of the brain that regulate behavioral inhibition and that process emotion— that is, the orbital frontal cortex and the amygdala. Indeed, it now seems uncontestable that the amygdala is involved in the creation of psychopaths: study after study has demonstrated that those who score high on tests for psychopathy have some form of amygdala dysfunction. James Blair, for instance, who is at the forefront of neuroscientific research into psychopathy, writes that the amygdala is at the "core" of what causes psychopathy and that amygdala dysfunction gives rise to "impairments in aversive conditioning, instrumental learning, and the processing of sad and fearful expressions," leading to the behaviors that have been pathognomonic of psychopathy for two centuries—lack of fear, impulsivity, poor behavior controls, and lack of empathy, remorse, and guilt.[42] Raine describes the core of psychopathy as inhering in demonstrably "reduced activity in the amygdala during emotional, personal moral decision-making," and notes that "while the amygdala, the neural seat of emotion, shows a bright glow in normal people when faced with emotion-provoking moral dilemmas, this emotional candle is barely flickering in highly psychopathic individuals."[43] Walsh and Bolen describe studies on the neurological underpinnings of psychopathy, and they also emphasize the role of the prefrontal cortices and the amygdala. The amygdala, they write, is "a crucial area for aversive conditioning and for making appropriate emotional responses to cues from others in our social world," and the prefrontal cortex is "critical to guiding the amygdala in these endeavors." Dysfunction in one or both produces the low fear, the inability to control impulses, and the lack of empathy at the heart of psychopathy.[44]

It is clear that all the traits of psychopathy that Hervey Cleckley and Robert Hare cataloged in the mid- to late twentieth century—lack of empathy, lack of fear and inhibition, impulsivity—are being confirmed by brain imaging.[45] Researchers are increasingly able to demonstrate, moreover, that the brains of psychopaths demonstrate differences—and while some of those differences might be inherent, others can be tied to experiences in early childhood that literally mold the brain and its neural pathways. It is important to note, though, that brain imaging does not generate opposing categories (the "normal" brain and the "pathological" brain). The traits of psychopathy, and its neurological signatures, are on a spectrum with the normative; they are not its polar opposite.

The Body's Memory

In the end, then, an unforeseeable chain of events created what we would now call Jesse Pomeroy's "psychopathy." This chain included the ravages of the smallpox epidemic in Boston and the science, politics, and economics of smallpox vaccination in the mid- to late nineteenth century; it included Ruth Pomeroy's decision (prompted by the law) to have her infant vaccinated and his devastating reaction to that vaccination; it included the five months Pomeroy suffered festering, raw abscesses over his face and body, and the permanent mark they left on his eye and, less visibly, on his brain; it included the chronic stress and pain he suffered as an infant and the consequent likely breach in his attachment to his mother. Jesse Pomeroy emerged as a boy who, by all accounts, was stunningly devoid of empathy—bereft of the ability to grasp that he had caused others pain or to feel any guilt or remorse for what he had done. A boy who was unable to control his violent impulses (as he himself said repeatedly) and who was unable to process cognitively or emotionally what he had done (vacillating between utterly denying his crimes or adopting what others said in the way of explanation). A boy who seemed chronically incapable of learning from prior experience, anticipating the consequences of his actions, or being deterred by the prospect of punishment. A boy who did what he liked, acted on mere whim, and seemed to experience no internal constraints.

While experiences in early infancy may well have catastrophically changed Jesse Pomeroy's brain, rendering him incapable of empathy, prone to violence, and unable to regulate impulses, a related hypothesis recognizes the effects not only of potentially damaged structures of the brain but also of memories harbored within it. There is evidence that memory does not start with *conscious* memory; in fact, we generally do not have conscious memories of what happened to us before the age of around two years. The limbic system in the brain, however, specifically the amygdala and the hippocampus, appears to retain early, unconscious memories: "We also have a nonverbal, essentially emotional memory" that begins even before birth, Karr-Morse and Wiley note. Emotional messages can, in other words, be processed by the amygdala "before cognition." This "primitive memory" is stored at the sensory level—and one psychologist refers to these memories as " 'cellular' because they are unconscious and preverbal and are often held and expressed in specific parts of the body." While these memories are not conscious, they can, then, form " 'burned-in' images" that persist—and studies have noted how children reenact such very early experiences (especially those that are traumatic) in later play, unaware of what they are doing.[46]

It is an intriguing possibility (and I raise this only speculatively) that in being driven to stab small children, Pomeroy was repeating the pain he experienced as an infant, pain he did not, could not, consciously remember, but that his body still harbored. He reenacted these memories not in play but in brutal acts of torture, although the line between those two things may not have been all that distinct for Pomeroy: he did, after all, laugh and dance around some of his victims, and he took his first victims home. The fact that Pomeroy often disfigured the eyes of his victims corresponds to the damage caused to his eye in particular by the abscesses that covered his body. Pomeroy repeatedly declared that he was driven to kill by a force that he described as somehow outside of or separate from himself, that he could not disobey. This force could have been what Karr-Morse and Wiley call the "ghost from the nursery," the embodied and unconscious memory of the traumatized infant. Karr-Morse and Wiley use the term "ghost" to capture how what is produced by trauma in the very early months goes unrecognized and unremembered and yet persists as a haunting presence in the flesh. It is a chapter of our lives, they say, that "is nearly always missing—the first chapter, encompassing gestation, birth, and infancy. And because it goes unseen and unacknowledged," they continue, "it repeats itself over and over." What transforms the baby is invisible, and "in that invisibility lies the power of these forces to continue to haunt us."[47] Pomeroy was quite clearly haunted, and what haunted him may very well have been primitive, nonconscious memories stored in the very cells of his body, their presence so alien to Pomeroy's conscious mind that he could only articulate their force as somehow beyond him.

Indeed, to push the implications of this speculation about embodied, cellular, and preconscious memory still further, one striking fact in the history of Jesse Pomeroy is the coincidence of his acts of torture with the first major return to Boston of smallpox since the epidemic that struck in the early months of his life (in late 1859–early 1860), the epidemic that propelled his mother to get him the devastating vaccination. Pomeroy tortured the first boy (that we know of) around the end of December 1871 and the second in February 1872. The deadliest outbreak of smallpox in nineteenth-century Boston began at exactly the same time—on January 1, 1872, according to a city physician. Ruth Pomeroy and her boys moved to South Boston in early August 1872, right after the city closed the best smallpox hospital in the city (due to complaints from those who lived around it), and the number of fatalities skyrocketed throughout the rest of the year.[48] Pomeroy's torture of boys picked up both speed and ferocity at the same time the rate of infections and deaths exploded, in August and September of 1872; during those two months, he tortured and mutilated four boys in the space of four weeks, before he was finally arrested in September. In an instance of suggestive contiguity, the *Brooklyn Daily Eagle* reported on Pomeroy's remand to reform school by Judge Forsaith directly underneath an item that read "Smallpox is reported to be on the increase all over Boston." This particular account of Pomeroy's crimes included another iteration of his being asked why he did what he did. Pomeroy replied "he didn't know, he couldn't help it."[49] In this newspaper column, then, the smallpox epidemic exists alongside the glaring evidence that Pomeroy was moved by some force he simply did not understand.

Is it possible that Jesse Pomeroy's body "knew" something his mind did not? Is it possible that in a thoroughly unconscious variant of what we now call the cycle of violence, his bodily memories of smallpox—of severe pain and disfigurement—precipitated a compulsion to enact that pain and disfigurement on someone else's body? Is it perhaps not entirely coincidental that his attacks on small boys began at the height of the next smallpox epidemic to strike Boston after the one that raged during his own birth and vaccination, along with its traumatic consequences? Smallpox had a devastating effect on his body and, inevitably and unconsciously, on his mind—all in the months before he could consciously grasp what was happening to him. Perhaps his body remembered that experience and attempted to expel it onto the bodies of others. Perhaps the smallpox epidemic triggered something corporeal of which he was completely unaware.

This is, of course, a way of understanding Pomeroy's actions that strains at what is rationally known. But to apply only what we already know to every case, however mystifying, can lead to a gross distortion, even fabrication, of the facts of the case to suit generally known theories. Virtually every account of Pomeroy by his contemporaries in some way attributed his actions to his body, to effects that bypassed his consciousness and precipitated unconscious action. The theory of maternal impressions, in particular, perhaps the most popular theory of what "caused" Pomeroy to torture and kill, explicitly articulated a cause that struck Pomeroy at a moment radically prior to consciousness, even before birth. We saw in chapter 3 that in his 1861 novel, *Elsie Venner,* in which the titular heroine is blighted before birth by a rattlesnake that struck her mother, Oliver Wendell Holmes Sr. pondered whether or not there are events that happen before birth, before consciousness, that fundamentally shape behavior, shape a self, for which the person is not responsible. What the doctor in the novel says of Elsie is strikingly true of Jesse Pomeroy, if one accepts that he might have been permanently changed, permanently stricken, by his devastating reaction to a smallpox vaccine when a very small infant: "She has lived a double being, as it were,—the consequence of the blight which fell upon her in the dim period before consciousness."[50] Perhaps Holmes (a physician himself) was onto something, although that something still lies just beyond what science knows.

That Jesse Pomeroy was "haunted" by repressed corporeal knowledge, by a memory stored in and remembered by his body, is the less likely possibility, however. More likely is that the "accident" that damaged him at one month old simply changed him from who he might have been into someone different. The philosopher Catherine Malabou has written about the devastating effects of brain trauma, "destructive plasticity" as she calls it, which she argues is an inherent part of us all, not only those stricken with a brain injury. We are all, she claims, perpetually subject to the accident that could instantaneously make us something other than we are. We are all, moreover, subject to aging, and Malabou argues that aging is less a gradual process than akin to a "lesion" that "arises all of a sudden, in an instant, like a trauma," suddenly transforming us "without warning, into an unknown subject." She calls aging a "rupture," one that "breaks being at an unlocatable point, forcing it to change direction, leading it to become other."[51] In short, then, either through an accident, through aging, or "sometimes for no reason at all," we all have to face the possibility that our "self" might split, that "a new, unprecedented persona comes to live with the former person." We must "all of us recognize," she writes, "that we might, one day," through accident or aging, "become someone else, as absolute other, someone who will never be reconciled with themselves again."[52] The vulnerability of our bodies and brains to "destructive plasticity," in other words, makes the accident, the sudden rupture, inescapably part of who we all are.

What is produced by the omnipresent possibility of destructive plasticity, according to Malabou, is a cold core of indifference. This "glacial" measure, this lack, this absence of feeling, is the profound consequence of a subjectivity that has split from what it once was: "Coldness, neutrality, absence, a 'flat' emotional state, are instances of this mode of destructive plasticity." While such "virtual coldness," Malabou claims, is not only the domain of the brain-injured and the serial killer, words connoting coldness are used repeatedly to describe the psychopath. Adrian Raine, for instance, writes about the "glacial, emotionless psychopath."[53] But Malabou claims that we *all* incipiently contain this possibility, this potential lack of "human" warmth: "Isn't it time to acknowledge the existence of an element of indifference in being itself, revealed by this instance to which philosophy usually accords not the slightest ontological value: the suffering of the brain?" The elderly and the ill, in particular, develop a "look of indifference" that is a reflection of the indifference of others to them. All of those stricken with destructive plasticity, then, which is all of us, suffer an "affective coldness and indifference," which, while different in degree, is nevertheless akin to the coldness of the psychopath. It is, moreover, a "constant virtuality" for all of us.[54] The accident that (re)made Jesse Pomeroy represents a potential for change—the possibility of becoming someone wholly "other"—that inhabits us all.

In the end, this chapter makes the case that Pomeroy suffered from a very early accident: the five-month-long affliction brought on by his smallpox vaccination. This distinctly neurological trauma changed his brain and profoundly changed him—formed him as affectively indifferent, cold, lacking in so many of the characteristics we consider "human." As Malabou makes clear, though, the "accident" waits for us all, shaping a human as well as a psychopathic subjectivity. While the brain of the psychopath might well contain something profoundly "nonhuman" at its core, current research in psychology and neuroscience is finding that there is something profoundly nonhuman at the core of *all of us*. It is significant, for instance, that while the psychiatrist J. Reid Meloy writes of the psychopath as "the stranger in our midst," the psychologist Timothy Wilson has argued that we are *all* "strangers to ourselves." Jesse Pomeroy claimed repeatedly that something "made" him do what he did. Wilson argues that we all act at the prompting of countless mental processes that occur "out of view of the people who had them." Similarly, destructive plasticity, whether it be the trauma of accident or aging, ushers in, according to Malabou, "a new form of being, a stranger to the one before."[55] We are all, then, in so many ways, strangers to ourselves. Jesse Pomeroy (again, a limit case) was compelled by forces he felt to be beyond his control, outside of himself. What he experienced as external, though, was simply a thoroughly and yet mundanely alien somatic interiority. He displayed a profound blankness and absence of emotion; he seemed unable to remember or to grasp the reality of what he had done. He was above all else a "stranger" to himself, standing as an extreme example of an ontological condition that affects us all, more or less, sooner or later.

Abused as a Child?

The telling and retelling of stories about Jesse Pomeroy—about why he did what he did—certainly did not end with the nineteenth century. And neither did the highly tenuous nature of those stories' connection to reality. The dominant story about Jesse Pomeroy now is every bit as powerful as the story that his mother visited the slaughterhouse while she was pregnant, eager to watch her husband butchering cattle. Like that story, the current one taps into prevailing beliefs about the causes of crime. Like that story, it is shaped around a powerful and violent scene. Like that story, it is of highly dubious veracity. Nonetheless, wherever you find mention of Jesse Pomeroy today, you find it. It seems to be the answer—the reason he did what he did. And yet, somehow, his own contemporaries were strikingly unable to see it.

A Tale of Repeated Abuse

The story that has defined our understandings of Jesse Pomeroy since the turn of the twenty-first century is laid out by Harold Schechter in *Fiend: The Shocking True Story of America's Youngest Serial Killer*. According to Schechter, Thomas Pomeroy beat his son. He recounts how, in the summer of 1872, Ruth had finally "gotten rid" of her husband after he and Jesse had a "savage argument" and Jesse ran away from home. Thomas "had tracked the boy down, dragged him home, then—after ordering him upstairs—stripped off all his clothes and flogged him unmercifully with a belt." This beating was not the first, and Schechter describes another, even worse, a "few years earlier," in which Thomas "horsewhipped his son in the woodshed for playing truant."[1] The explanation of why Pomeroy did what he did is inherent in these details, in the stripping and the beatings. When he got older, Jesse Pomeroy was simply repeating the abuse he suffered at the hands of his father.

Schechter makes the case directly, and early on, that the whippings Thomas Pomeroy gave his son were instrumental in the boy's developing pathology: "Though the floggings he had gotten from his father hurt worse than anything he had ever felt in his life, Jesse couldn't stop thinking about them. He kept replaying them in his mind, almost as if he took some kind of pleasure from recollecting them. He often wondered if other boys were beaten in the same way." Schechter writes of Jesse seeking out other boys during his time in reform school and asking for details of the beatings they had received. The details excited him. He would lie awake at night thinking of these accounts "and bring himself to climax over and over while picturing the torture in his mind."[2] In Schechter's representation, Pomeroy is an indisputable sexual psychopath whose pathology was learned from childhood abuse. His own early beatings became a part of his fantasy life, which he reenacted on the bodies of other boys.

This theory definitely seems plausible. But is it true? At the heart of Schechter's argument is a chapter late in his book in which he discloses a cache of Jesse's letters allegedly written in June 1875 to a boy named Willie Baxter. Baxter was, according to Schechter, also incarcerated in the Charles Street Jail while Pomeroy was awaiting the disposition of his sentence. Schechter writes that these "fading, fragile letters lay hidden in an old file box, and are reprinted here for the first time," and that they offer "absolutely direct, unvarnished expressions of the 'boy fiend's' voice." He claims that "apart from the crimes themselves," they "offer the most provocative clues we have to the nature, extent, and even ultimate source of [Pomeroy's] extreme psychopathology."[3] They certainly seem to.

The letters demonstrate perfectly, in fact, what Schechter characterizes as an "avid interest" and a "deeply prurient desire" on Jesse Pomeroy's part to hear the details of whippings inflicted on other boys: "Will you tell me as I ask you," one letter demands of Willie Baxter, "about the hardest whipping you got, if it hurt much and how it was done to you and I will tell you about the hardest one I got." In another letter, Jesse tells Willie of the two beatings he received from his father, which Schechter had described earlier in the book—and in one of those beatings, Thomas Pomeroy apparently ordered his son to "take off the whole of my close [sic]." Schechter uses this letter to affirm, again, the "major *cause* of [Jesse's] pathology," elaborating on how "a brutalized upbringing" is often a "key element" of "psychopathic lust-murder" and that, "almost without exception, serial killers have suffered extreme, often grotesque, forms of abuse—physical, emotional, sexual—during childhood." Schechter does go on to suggest that Jesse's "deeply unsettling appearance" (including his damaged eye) was a source of embarrassment and humiliation and thus may also have contributed to his crimes (not least because Jesse's father, according to Schechter, found it "repugnant" and ridiculed him for it). But it is above all the abuse he allegedly received at the hands of his father that is clearly the cornerstone of Schechter's account of Pomeroy.[4] To drive home the connection between Jesse's childhood abuse and subsequent violent behavior, Schechter reprints two more notes Pomeroy supposedly wrote to Willie Baxter in which he unambiguously confesses to having committed the string of tortures and to having killed Horace Millen and Katie Curran, about which he (quite uncharacteristically) writes that he feels "very bad." The letters render utterly transparent, then, the causal link between Jesse's abuse as a child, his consequent "prurient" interest in corporeal punishment, and his particular crimes, which he unequivocally confesses to his jail-mate.[5]

As seductive as these letters are, as much as they promise, finally, a cogent and comprehensive explanation of Pomeroy's baffling crimes, I am skeptical: Where were they found exactly? Under what circumstances? Where are they now? How do we know Jesse Pomeroy indeed wrote them? Who is Willie Baxter?[6] The beatings supposedly administered by Thomas Pomeroy, while certainly not out of the realm of possibility, are not substantiated by *any other source at all*, although there is, admittedly, scanty information on the topic of Jesse's father.[7]

In an era when the corporal punishment of children was routine and pervasive, Jesse Pomeroy mentions in his autobiography, quite matter-of-factly, that others beat him—specifically, two teachers and an uncle. He does not, though, say anything about beatings by his father, and the one time he recounts his father threatening to whip him, Thomas did not carry out the threat.[8] Pomeroy's father is almost never mentioned in reports of Pomeroy's crimes, although one account reprinted in several newspapers in 1875, written by someone who claims to have known the Pomeroys for several years, notes: "Jesse's father, up to two years ago, was a porter in a shipping house. He is a rough, big-looking man, somewhat morose, but by no means given to vice of any grade."[9] The only hint of condemnation for Jesse's father in the newspapers was the suggestion of neglect, adduced in the *Boston Daily Globe* as connected to Jesse's voracious reading of sensational dime novels.[10] A later editorial in the *Globe* did claim that Jesse's "father and mother separated in consequence of their continual quarrels," but the editorial then goes on, again, to blame the parents principally for not preventing Pomeroy from reading cheap literature.[11] There was no reason offered in the 1870s, in other words, to understand Jesse Pomeroy's violence as rooted in an abusive childhood.

There is a kind of evidence, though, to support that Thomas Pomeroy was *not* abusive (in addition to the merely negative evidence of there being no mention of it anywhere), and it's in Ruth's attempt to divorce Thomas in 1878. Ruth chose to file on the grounds of her husband's intemperance and his failure to support her and her children. Ruth would have been able, if she chose, to file for divorce on the grounds of either "extreme cruelty" or "cruel and abusive treatment," and she may have had a better chance of winning a divorce on those grounds.[12] While there is no evidence that Thomas was abusive, then, there is some evidence that he drank, although the court decided that Ruth's allegation of intemperance in her divorce petition was not sustained.[13] A tantalizingly brief notice in a Vermont newspaper, in June 1875, as Boston was furiously debating Jesse Pomeroy's sentence, reported that the "father of the Boston boy murderer, Jesse Pomeroy, has taken to drinking to drown the sorrows caused by his son's crimes, and has been before the courts for drunkenness twice during the past week."[14] More persuasively, when Thomas died at Boston's City Hospital on January 27, 1898, at the age of sixty-three, the cause of death was listed on the death certificate as cirrhosis of the liver. He also was clearly not a terribly successful earner, as he was a still a porter at the time of his death.[15]

In the end, the only evidence that Jesse Pomeroy was abused by his father is the store of letters Schechter claims to have found in which Pomeroy conveniently lays out his early abuse, expresses the pleasure he takes in telling and listening to stories about beatings, and avows his acts of torture and murder. Despite the tenuous evidence on which it rests, however, Schechter's explanation has been avidly seized upon by everyone who has written about the case since. The story is repeated, with or without attribution, just as Schechter tells it—and there has never been any additional evidence added to support it, just reiterations of the same. It has become a thoroughly self-propagating story, just like the many other self-propagating stories that have swirled around Jesse Pomeroy—that he was marked in utero by his mother's forays to the slaughterhouse and that he skinned kittens or rats while in jail.

That Schechter's book offers, finally, an explanation for Jesse Pomeroy that makes sense to early twenty-first-century scholars of crime seems to have spurred a renewal of interest in his story. Carol Anne Davis begins her 2003 book, *Children Who Kill,* with the case of Jesse Pomeroy, and her account is thoroughly informed by the idea that "victim becomes victimizer," as one of her section titles proclaims. She writes that Thomas couldn't stand the sight of his son and beat him from the time he was a toddler. Davis concludes: "When a child is constantly hurt like this, he naturally wants revenge but there was no way that Jesse could stand up to his enraged, belt-wielding father. So he turned to victims that couldn't fight back."[16] In Davis's representation, Jesse simply displaced the violence he suffered onto others. And she offers no evidence for her diagnosis of Pomeroy but Schechter's book.

In his history of the emergence of teen culture in the late nineteenth century, Jon Savage also begins with the baffling, unprecedented case of Jesse Pomeroy. But whatever light this new book might have shed on the mystery of this brutal killer is foreclosed as Savage relies only on the letters Schechter prints to illuminate the "real Jesse" and to assert parental brutality as the cause of his shocking crimes. It was "the furious beatings that he received from his father that left the deepest scar," Savage writes. "His prison letters [to Baxter] revealed an obsession with 'floggings,'" which Savage is, not surprisingly, quick to tie to Pomeroy's acts of torture and murder. The letters, "undiscovered for over a century," might well "have helped to solve the vexed question that Jesse Pomeroy posed for Gilded Age America. He had simply learned all too well from adult example."[17] Having made its way into books published by reputable presses, it's no surprise that the story of Jesse's abuse at the hands of his father is pervasive on the Internet.[18]

The most recent iteration of Schechter's story of parental abuse is offered by Roseanne Montillo in her 2015 book, *The Wilderness of Ruin: A Tale of Madness, Fire, and the Hunt for America's Youngest Serial Killer.* Montillo repeats almost exactly Schechter's account of Thomas's beatings of his son, with some added hyperbole: she changes the woodshed story, for instance, to an account of Thomas taking Jesse, "just eight years old, to an abandoned shed in the woods," where he "had become so enraged that the blows from a horsewhip had nearly killed his son." Strikingly, Montillo does not cite Schechter's *Fiend* at all (even as the source for the instances she adduces of Thomas's whippings of his son), although she does list the book in her bibliography and clearly, without acknowledgment, draws much of her information from it.[19] Montillo goes still further into the realm of fiction, however, claiming that by the early 1870s Ruth had already divorced her husband, not only on the grounds of intoxication and failure to support her and their children, but also because "he was physically abusive toward her and her sons." Montillo claims there are divorce papers that extensively detail Thomas's pattern of abuse—and that the divorce was thus "quickly granted."[20] Since (as we saw in chapter 1) Ruth did not file for divorce until 1878, her petition was denied, and she is listed as a widow on her death certificate, Montillo's account is clearly fabricated.

But reviewers of *The Wilderness of Ruin* have picked up enthusiastically on the story of Jesse Pomeroy's abusive childhood. "Was he damaged by early physical abuse at the hands of his father?" the *Boston Globe*'s reviewer asks. The *Wall Street Journal* review suggests that advocates of "nurture" as the cause of crime will see their position vindicated in the portrait of Jesse's father, "a drunk and ne'er-do-well who sadistically beat his two sons." The *Kirkus* review puts abuse even more clearly at the center of the Pomeroy case, introducing the subject of Montillo's book as a killer "whose relentlessly abusive childhood may have inspired the many beating and torturing rages against youth in the Boston area in the 1870s."[21] These reviewers seize on the explanation of Jesse Pomeroy's abusive childhood with such alacrity because it fits what we already know about crime. But what happens to what we think we know when the story of Thomas Pomeroy's "sadistic" beatings of his son is revealed to be groundless?

Black Swan

Jon Savage is right when he declares that "Pomeroy burst into the American consciousness as a horrific new type," and that there "was nothing in the existing legislation to explain his affectless savagery." Jesse Pomeroy is what Nassim Nicholas Taleb has called a "black swan," a being or event that "lies outside the realm of regular expectations, because nothing in the past can convincingly point to its possibility"—just like a black swan when everyone knows swans are white. What Taleb claims we should learn from the existence of black swans is exactly what we should learn from the case of Jesse Pomeroy—and from the hundreds of stories that have presumed to explain him, circulating exactly and only what readers of the day thought they knew. Taleb, much of whose work focuses on considerations of randomness and probability, writes: "Black Swans being unpredictable, we need to adjust to their existence (rather than naïvely try to predict them). There are so many things we can do if we focus on antiknowledge, *or what we do not know.*" Our world, he asserts, "is dominated by the extreme, the unknown, and the very improbable (improbable according to our current knowledge)—and all the while we spend our time engaged in small talk, focusing on the known, and the repeated."[22] Jesse Pomeroy was—and still is—"the extreme, the unknown, and the very improbable," and yet from the beginning we have done our best to reduce him to the "known," fitting him into the categories, the explanations, that dominate the moment. What is interesting about Jesse Pomeroy, though, is that something of the unknown and the elusive has persisted, nonetheless, through all the retellings of his story.

In the present moment, the lacunae that still haunt the narratives of Pomeroy's crimes illustrate that while a great many violent offenders have certainly suffered a childhood of chronic physical, emotional, and sexual abuse, *not all of them have.* And those who have not tend to fall outside what has been by far, beginning in the mid-twentieth century, the dominant explanatory paradigm for crime. Pomeroy raises the question, What causes tendencies toward bloodshed, at a very young age no less, when there has *not* been a background of abuse? Pomeroy and other anomalies, exceptions to the truism that violence is begotten by violence (especially when suffered in childhood), challenge us to think more, and think differently, about the causes of violent behavior. What we should decidedly *not* do is distort the anomalous case so that it fits what we already know. What we should *not* do is impose already known truths onto instances that trouble such truths. Doing so negates the power of these cases to teach us something we do not already know.

Some of Pomeroy's contemporaries really believed that he was possessed by the spirits of the dead, an explanation that not only fits him within their particular paradigms about reality but also, despite itself, contains a haunting "something else" that escapes that very paradigm. It gets at the fact that Jesse Pomeroy seemed somehow divided, alienated from himself. Most of Pomeroy's contemporaries, moreover, believed that he was in some way possessed *by his own body.* And, indeed, it is the sense that his brain and body were irreparably damaged by his environment, that he was somehow a stranger to his own consciousness and volition, which makes his case so germane to our own developing knowledge, in the early twenty-first century, about the effects of biology on crime. By his own account of his irresistible compulsion, and by the accounts of almost all of those who encountered him, Pomeroy's pathology was somatic. He evidenced a "corporeal unconscious," was driven by the "body's automatisms": tics, gestures, and actions that "remember what the conscious mind ignores."[23] This can potentially be an *explanation*—centering the importance of the body—but it can also be a way of marking how the body contains much that we *can't explain.*

There is still a resistance to biological explanations of behavior. As Adrian Raine points out, even as recently as 1994, for anyone to suggest "an interaction between biological and social factors in predisposing individuals to violence was anathema." Even as he proposed exactly such an interaction, in 2013, Raine noted that "the emerging science of neurocriminology" continues to be "bogged down" in "unproductive diatribes." Among other concerns, people fear that interrogating the neurological and more broadly biological conditions and causes of crime will lead to the "erosion of the concepts of individual accountability and free will."[24] This is, of course, exactly what Pomeroy's contemporaries worried over in their furious debates about "moral insanity," which seemed to many to erase individual responsibility and the existence of evil exactly to the extent that it explained crime as disease. The search for deep causality, especially embodied causality, inevitably evokes determinism and challenges personal responsibility. But perhaps theories of individual responsibility need to take into account those ways in which humans are shaped by the inextricable interconnections of environment, body, brain, and consciousness. Ideals of individual responsibility mean little, after all, if they are an illusion.

Jesse Pomeroy's case demands an understanding of the causes of crime that is *rooted in although never reducible to the body;* it demands an understanding of a bodily "unconscious" that escapes the rational grasp of consciousness and that is always impinged on by environment. Recognizing the powerful force of body and brain does *not* ignore environment or the social causes of crime. After all, as I have shown, at the very least, the sensational torture scenes of dime novels and smallpox vaccination (itself rooted in the politics and economics of vaccination practices in mid nineteenth-century Boston) deeply affected Pomeroy's body. Recognizing the importance of the body, moreover, does not obviate responsibility, although it should certainly shape how responsibility (and free will) are understood.

In the end, we cannot know exactly why Jesse Pomeroy began torturing small boys at twelve years of age, graduating by the age of fourteen to brutal murder. In all that Pomeroy himself said, he could only describe it as an utterly inexplicable compulsion. Speculative and often fanciful theories about the origins of this compulsion abounded, but most of Pomeroy's contemporaries believed that the boy's body had been formed, and had then acted, to some degree at least without the consent of his mind. And in these theories, I have argued, there lies a truth that early twenty-first-century psychology and science is beginning to verify. The body matters: it is a "nature" in which the "person" is embedded—a "nature" that precedes, surpasses, and persists beyond the "person."

This impersonal and anonymous body is being uncovered in recent work in cognitive psychology and neuroscience, research that demonstrates we are all much less in control than we think we are. As the editors of the tellingly titled collection *Decomposing the Will* put it, there is "an amazing wealth of findings in recent cognitive science that demonstrate the surprising ways in which our everyday behavior is controlled by automatic processes that unfold *in the complete absence of consciousness.*" The editor of another collection, *Neuroscience and Legal Responsibility,* similarly declares that "despite our convictions that we consciously control our actions," they are "in fact caused by lower level brain processes of which we have little or no awareness, and what appears in our consciousness is little more than post hoc confabulation." The psychologists John Bargh and Tanya Chartrand have summed up this emerging picture of the power of "automatic processes" to direct human behavior as "the unbearable automaticity of being"—unbearable precisely because of our "understandable desire to believe in free will and self-determination."[25] Nineteenth-century commentators on Pomeroy certainly had a sense of the "unbearable" force of automaticity in his case: one newspaper wrote that "his acts are mentally automatic," and the concept of "irresistible impulse" marks, while also pathologizing, the automaticity of his behavior.[26]

As descriptions of Pomeroy's "brute animality" made clear, he became, for late nineteenth-century Americans, the exemplar of the impersonal, automatic, and monstrous body—but while they stood in horror at what Pomeroy had done, most may not have been aware of exactly why he provoked such horror. For Pomeroy evoked horror not only because of *his* anonymous automaticity, but because we all contain that same impersonal core. Horror inheres in "an unutterable and altogether abysmal reality called *life*," the philosopher Dylan Trigg writes, a life that resides in "the intersection of the human and the nonhuman."[27] The horror of Jesse Pomeroy's case, the horror we all confront, lies in the fact that our bodies are both our own and not our own: they are "us," but they also partake of an inevitably impersonal and alien nature that is before, in, and after "us."

In the end, this book takes Jesse Pomeroy at his word: he didn't do it, but if he did do it he was insane. He did it but he didn't know why; he did it but he couldn't help it; he did it but something made him do it. His explanations partake of the logic of dreams—utter confusion and inchoate inconsistency. He did it. The evidence points that way. He said he did it. Yet he didn't do it. It wasn't *he* who did it. Jesse Pomeroy is the limit case of consciousness, of human agency. He demonstrates that we—humans—do indeed act without knowing why we act or even, sometimes, *that* we act. The forces that shaped him far before and beneath what he could consciously grasp, direct, and control were so powerful that they seemed to form a veritable second self, an unconscious personality at odds with who he otherwise was. Pomeroy knew, albeit dimly and intermittently, of this constellation of traits and the terrible acts it performed, but he did not recognize it as himself. Something within him acted but it was not "him"; it was not integrated into his sense of "self." Dimly aware of this split, this rupture, Pomeroy was, tragically, unable to control his other "self." He wanted to run away from it. He wanted to go to sea and never come back. He was convinced that when he became a "man," he "could resist the temptation to do such bloody deeds."[28]

Jesse Pomeroy struggled with the autonomy of the body, with the realm of the anonymous nonhuman, and at times it overcame him. At times he looked at it, baffled, uncomprehending, and tried to deny it, to resist it. The impersonal nonhuman within him was stronger than most people's: his is an extreme case, a threshold case, but the dynamic—the conflict—he embodies is not, for that reason, any less a human one. What we hold onto as "human" (conscious choice, agency, autonomy, reason) is a very fragile thing, perennially coexisting with forces that dispossess us. These dispossessing forces are brute and silent, and commentators have tried to drown them out with the reassuring fullness of explanation. I am one of those commentators, but I hope I have also let those brute and haunting silences of Jesse Pomeroy speak.

Notes

Introduction

1. A. W. S., "Is Boston Civilized?," *The Index*, April 8, 1875, 162; "To the editors . . . ," *Boston Daily Advertiser*, July 26, 1875.
2. "A Youthful Monster," *New York Herald*, Sept. 21, 1872; "A Young Monster," *Daily Inter-Ocean* (Chicago), May 5, 1874; "Boston Produced the Boy Monster, Jesse Pomeroy," *Philadelphia Inquirer*, May 9, 1876; "The Boy Murderer," *Boston Daily Globe*, April 24, 1874; "Horrible Infatuation," *Salem (MA) Register*, April 27, 1874.
3. Karen Halttunen has tracked the emergence of the criminal as "moral monster" in late eighteenth- and early nineteenth-century America in *Murder Most Foul: The Killer and the American Gothic Imagination* (Cambridge: Harvard University Press, 1998). Daniel A. Cohen presents a countering view, arguing that the image of the murderer as monster flourished at least as early as the first half of the seventeenth century, in "Blood Will Out: Sensationalism, Horror, and the Roots of American Crime Literature," in *Mortal Remains: Death in Early America*, ed. Nancy Isenberg and Andrew Burstein (Philadelphia: University of Pennsylvania Press, 2003), 31–55. See also, generally, Cohen's *Pillars of Salt, Monuments of Grace: New England Crime Literature and the Origins of American Popular Culture, 1674–1860* (1993; repr., Amherst: University of Massachusetts Press, 2006). The work of both of these scholars demonstrates that the creation of "monsters" has a long history.
4. Gail Hamilton, "Murderers for Fun," *The Independent* 26.1346 (Sept. 17, 1874): 5; Rev. Dr. C. A. Bartol, "Monsters. A Sermon Delivered in the Unitarian Church, Sunday, June 6th, 1875," *Cape Ann Advertiser* (Gloucester, MA), June 11, 1875.
5. Marina Levina and Diem-My T. Bui, "Introduction: Toward a Comprehensive Monster Theory in the 21st Century," in *Monster Culture in the 21st Century: A Reader*, ed. Levina and Bui (London: Bloomsbury, 2013), 5; Jacques Derrida, *Points . . . Interviews, 1974–1994*, trans. Peggy Kamuf and others (Stanford: Stanford University Press, 1995), 386.
6. Noël Carroll, *The Philosophy of Horror, or, Paradoxes of the Heart* (New York: Routledge, 1990), 32, 43; Jeffrey Jerome Cohen, "Monster Culture (Seven Theses)," in *Monster Theory: Reading Culture*, ed. Cohen (Minneapolis: University of Minnesota Press, 1996), 6.
7. "The Pomeroy Hearing," *Boston Daily Advertiser*, April 12, 1875; "A case has occurred . . . ," *Aegis and Gazette* (Worcester, MA), Aug. 14, 1875; "Shall Jesse Pomeroy Live?," *Aegis and Gazette*, April 17, 1875.

8. "The Pomeroy Boy," *Boston Daily Globe,* May 29, 1875. The story was reprinted under the same title in the *Cincinnati Daily Times,* June 1, 1875, and even traveled as far as the West Coast, reprinted as "The Boy Fiend," *San Francisco Chronicle,* June 9, 1875.

9. Pramod K. Nayar, *Posthumanism* (Malden, MA: Polity, 2014), 85.

10. Brian Massumi, *What Animals Teach Us about Politics* (Durham, NC: Duke University Press, 2014), 93; Cary Wolfe, *Animal Rites: American Culture, the Discourse of Species, and Posthumanist Theory* (Chicago: University of Chicago Press, 2003), 193; Rosi Braidotti, "Animals, Anomalies, and Inorganic Others," *PMLA* 124.2 (March 2009): 528.

11. William James, *The Principles of Psychology,* vol. 2 (1890; London: Macmillan, 1891), 414. In his introduction to *The Nonhuman Turn,* Richard Grusin identifies James as one of the earliest thinkers of the "nonhuman," describing his "radical contention" in *The Principles of Psychology* that "human thought, emotion, habit, and will were all inseparable from, and often consequent upon, nonhuman, bodily material processes." Richard Grusin, introduction to *The Nonhuman Turn,* ed. Grusin (Minneapolis: University of Minnesota Press, 2015), viii.

12. Bartol, "Monsters."

13. "The Trial of Jesse H. Pomeroy," *Boston Daily Evening Traveler,* Dec. 9, 1874; "The Boy Fiend," *Boston Herald,* Dec. 9, 1874.

14. "Jesse Pomeroy," *Portland (ME) Daily Press,* Oct. 24, 1878. The story was repeated verbatim, or almost so, in "Jesse Pomeroy, the boy murderer . . . ," *Repository* (Canton, OH), Oct. 21, 1878; "Jesse Pomeroy's confinement . . . ," *Cleveland Leader,* Oct. 26, 1878; "Jesse Pomeroy . . . ," *Salt Lake Tribune,* Oct. 26, 1878; and "Jesse Pomeroy . . . ," *Times-Picayune* (New Orleans), Nov. 2, 1878.

15. "Jesse Pomeroy's confinement . . . ," *Cleveland Leader,* Oct. 26, 1878; "Jesse Pomeroy's confinement . . . ," *St. Louis Globe-Democrat,* Oct. 27, 1878.

16. "Jesse Pomeroy's Latest Deviltry," *Milwaukee Daily Sentinel,* Dec. 31, 1880. This story was also reported under the same title in the *Cleveland Plain Dealer,* Dec. 30, 1880.

17. Charles D. Sawin, *Criminals* (Boston: n.p., 1890), 11.

18. "Jesse Pomeroy's Hopes," *Jackson (MI) Citizen Patriot,* June 23, 1894.

19. Mary Teats, *The Way of God in Marriage: A Series of Essays upon Gospel and Scientific Purity* (Spotswood, NJ: Physical Culture Publishing Company, 1906), 144; Elizabeth Jones Towne, *How to Use New Thought in Home Life* (1915; Holyoke, MA: The Elizabeth Towne Co., 1921), 121; N. S. Yawger, M.D., "Is There a 'Moral Center' in the Brain?," *American Journal of the Medical Sciences* 189.2 (Feb. 1935): 265.

20. Alice Stone Blackwell, "No Pardon for Pomeroy," *Boston Herald,* March 23, 1925.

21. Alice Stone Blackwell Papers, Blackwell Family Papers, box 49, Library of Congress, Washington, DC (hereafter cited as ASB Papers). The person who typed the cards is not identified.

22. Letter, ASB Papers, box 49; Blackwell, "No Pardon for Pomeroy."

23. "Pomeroy Kept in Prison," *New York Times,* Jan. 7, 1928.

24. Ira Dudley Farquhar, "Fact and Fiction vs. Pomeroy," *Boston Herald,* April 1, 1925.

25. "Jesse Pomeroy Brings Lawsuit," *Boston Herald,* May 9, 1925.

26. "Jesse Pomeroy Sues for Libel," *Boston Herald,* Jan. 6, 1928.

27. "Lifer Refused Outing," *Cleveland Plain Dealer,* Jan. 7, 1928.

28. "Pomeroy Happy over $1 Verdict," *Boston Herald,* Jan. 10, 1928. A letter to Alice Stone Blackwell from a Miss Marian T. Hosmer, dated Jan. 7, 1928, demonstrated, perhaps, sentiments similar to the jury's. Hosmer wrote: "We are all so overcome with the audacity of that creature saying you had injured his reputation. I remember the horror of his trial and hastily send love and regards [to] you." ASB Papers, box 49.

29. "Pomeroy Downcast," *Boston Daily Globe,* Dec. 31, 1912; "Photographs and Diagram

Dealing with Jesse Pomeroy's Latest Attempt to Escape from Charlestown State Prison," *Boston Daily Globe*, Dec. 31, 1912.

30. "The Death Penalty. Efforts to Prevent the Execution of Jesse Pomeroy," *Boston Daily Advertiser*, April 14, 1875; John Charles Bucknill, "Lumleian Lectures on Insanity in Its Legal Relations, Delivered at the Royal College of Physicians, Lecture II, Part II," *The Lancet* 111.2852 (April 27, 1878): 599; "Scrap Book for Today," *Trenton (NJ) Evening Times*, Dec. 21, 1912; W. Bob Holland, "Sidelights," *Miami Herald*, Feb. 5, 1926.

31. Robert Hare, *Without Conscience: The Disturbing World of the Psychopaths among Us* (New York: Guilford, 1993), 66. For a comprehensive survey of studies that validate the conventional link between animal cruelty and later violent aggression toward humans, see Linda Merz-Perez and Kathleen M. Heide, *Animal Cruelty: Pathway to Violence against People* (Walnut Creek, CA: AltaMira, 2004), 151–52, 16, 15.

32. David Ray Papke, *Framing the Criminal: Crime, Cultural Work, and the Loss of Critical Perspective, 1830–1900* (Hamden, CT: Archon Books, 1987), 166.

33. "Jesse Pomeroy Convicted of Murder in the First Degree," *Boston Daily Advertiser*, Dec. 11, 1874.

34. Hal Herzog, "Animal Cruelty and the Sadism of Everyday Life" (blog post), *Psychology Today* website, Sept. 23, 2013, www.psychologytoday.com.

35. Emily G. Patterson and Heather Piper, "Animal Abuse as a Sentinel for Human Violence: A Critique," *Journal of Social Issues* 65.3 (Sept. 2009): 596–97, 609.

36. Carroll, *Philosophy of Horror*, 37.

37. Jeffrie G. Murphy, "Moral Death: A Kantian Essay on Psychopathy," *Ethics* 82.4 (July 1972): 295.

38. Harold Schechter, *Fiend: The Shocking True Story of America's Youngest Serial Killer* (New York: Pocket Books, 2000); Roseanne Montillo, *The Wilderness of Ruin: A Tale of Madness, Fire, and the Hunt for America's Youngest Serial Killer* (New York: William Morrow, 2015). The sensationalism and inaccuracy of both Schechter's and Montillo's books begin with their very titles, both of which dub Pomeroy "America's Youngest Serial Killer." By any definition, a serial killer must kill at least three people; Pomeroy killed only two. He was, however, a serial torturer.

1. Crimes

1. Jesse Pomeroy, *Autobiography of Jesse H. Pomeroy, Written by Himself, while Imprisoned in the Suffolk County Jail and under Sentence of Death for the Murder of H. H. Millen* (Boston: J. A. Cummings, 1875), repr., The Making of the Modern Law: Trials, 1600–1926 (Farmington Hills, MI: Gale, 2011), 2–3.

2. Registers of Vital Records, Death of Ruth A. (Snowman) Pomeroy, 1915, vol. 87, p. 475, HS6.07 / series 1411, Massachusetts Archives, Boston (hereafter MAB).

3. Pomeroy, *Autobiography*, 3.

4. "The Pomeroy Case," *Boston Daily Globe*, April 28, 1874. Ruth Penny is listed as being born in Scituate, Massachusetts, on her son's death record. Registers of Vital Records, Death of Thomas J. Pomeroy, 1898, vol. 483, p. 50, HS6.07 / series 1411, MAB. Another source, however, identifies her place of birth as Hingham; this source also records her marriage to Thomas J. (Jesse) Pomeroy on November 17, 1833. George Lincoln, *History of the Town of Hingham, Massachusetts* (Somerworth, NH: New England History Press, 1982), 109.

5. Registers of Vital Records, Death of Thomas J. Pomeroy.

6. Jesse Pomroy [*sic*] Household, 1850 US Census, Middlesex County, Massachusetts, City of Charlestown, National Archives and Records Administration Micropublication M432, roll 322, p. 207A.

7. Registers of Vital Records, Death of Ruth T. Pomeroy, 1852, vol. 67, p. 85, HS6.07 / series 1411, MAB.
8. Register of the 1855 State Census, Pomroy [*sic*] household, Charlestown, Suffolk County, Massachusetts, SC1 / series 214X, MAB.
9. "The Pomeroy Case," *Boston Daily Globe*, April 28, 1874. I have found no evidence that either Jesse's grandmother or his grandfather ever initiated divorce proceedings. I suspect the *Globe* was, at best, reporting rumor.
10. Registers of Vital Records, Marriage of Thomas J. Pomroy [*sic*] and Ruth A. Snowman, 1857, vol. 109, p. 97, HS6.07 / series 1411, MAB.
11. Registers of Vital Records, Birth of Charles J. Pomroy [*sic*], 1858, vol. 115, p. 124, HS6.07 / series 1411, MAB.
12. Registers of Vital Records, Birth of Jesse H. Punroy [*sic*], 1859, vol. 124, p. 77, HS6.07 / series 1411, MAB. Pomeroy's birth record has been digitized under "Punroy," which is how the name was originally written in the record.
13. "Jesse Pomeroy," *Boston Daily Globe*, July 22, 1874.
14. Register of Federal Census, 1860, Pomeroy Household, Charlestown, Suffolk County, Massachusetts, SC1 / series 113X, MAB.
15. National Park Service, Civil War Soldiers and Sailors System database, www.nps.gov /civilwar. Note that the records for Thomas are under Thomas J. Pomroy (not Pomeroy).
16. Alfred S. Roe, *The Fifth Regiment Massachusetts Volunteer Infantry in Its Three Tours of Duty: 1861, 1862–63, 1864* (Boston: Fifth Regiment Veteran Association, 1911), 122.
17. Ibid., 124, 128, 134, 137–223, 253.
18. Register of the 1865 State Census, Pomerry [*sic*] household, Charlestown, Suffolk County, Massachusetts, SC1 / series 214X, MAB.
19. James F. Hunnewell, *A Century of Town Life: A History of Charlestown, Massachusetts, 1775–1887* (Boston: Little, Brown, 1888), 72.
20. Pomeroy, *Autobiography*, 1.
21. Ibid., 2.
22. Register of Federal Census, 1870, Pomeroy household, Charlestown, Suffolk County, Massachusetts, SC1 / series 113X, MAB.
23. Ibid.; Pomeroy, *Autobiography*, 2; Case Histories of Boys, Lyman School for Boys, Jesse H. Pomeroy, HS8.05 / series 629X, MAB; "Jesse Pomeroy," *Boston Daily Globe*, July 22, 1874.
24. Pomeroy, *Autobiography*, 8.
25. Ruth A. Pomeroy vs. Thomas J. Pomeroy, Libel for Divorce, March 7, 1877, Supreme Judicial Archives, Boston.
26. "Jesse Pomeroy's Mother," *New York Times*, May 13, 1878. Not surprisingly, news of the dismissal of Ruth's divorce petition was widely reprinted. See, for example, "Mrs. Ruth A. Pomeroy . . . ," *Atlanta Daily Constitution*, May 17, 1878; "Ruth A. Pomeroy . . . ," *Baltimore Sun*, May 21, 1878; "Among the recent applications for divorce . . . ," *Daily Inter Ocean* (Chicago), May 23, 1878; and "Mrs. Ruth A. Pomeroy . . . ," *Nevada State Journal*, June 6, 1878.
27. Pomeroy, *Autobiography*, 4.
28. "Precocity," *Boston Daily Globe*, May 22, 1872. For the *Globe's* claim that poor parental discipline was largely to blame for Pomeroy's crimes, see "Keep Children from Crime," *Boston Daily Globe*, Dec. 12, 1874.
29. "Brutal Assault upon a Boy," *Boston Daily Globe*, July 23, 1872.
30. "Chelsea," *Boston Daily Globe*, July 25 and July 30, 1872; "Chelsea," *Boston Daily Advertiser*, Aug. 15, 1872.
31. "A Remarkable Case," *Boston Daily Advertiser*, Sept. 21, 1872. Details about the seven documented instances of Pomeroy's torture of small boys come from a few

early newspaper accounts (from 1872) and from the case history in the records of the Lyman School for Boys at Westborough, which includes Pomeroy's examination by Judge William H. Forsaith, at which he was charged with the torture of an unnamed boy (Tracy Hayden) and John Balch from Chelsea and George Pratt, Harry Austin, Joseph W. Kennedy, and Charles A. Gould in South Boston. See Case Histories of Boys, MAB. Six of Pomeroy's victims also testified at his murder trial in December 1874, some of them at great length: Hayden, Balch, Pratt, Robert Maies, Kennedy, and Gould (who was frequently called Robert Gould in some earlier newspaper accounts). All of Boston's major newspapers carried their testimony, and this trial testimony offers the most detail about the early assaults. A reliable source about Pomeroy's crimes is an unpublished paper by Alexander W. Pisciotta, Department of Criminal Justice, Kutztown University, "Jesse Pomeroy: Historical Reflections on Serial Murder and the Social Construction of Punishment and Criminal Justice" (copy in the author's possession).

32. "The Last Dorchester Tragedy," *Boston Herald*, April 24, 1874.

33. "The Boy Fiend," *Boston Herald*, Dec. 9, 1874; "Jesse Pomeroy," *Boston Daily Globe*, Dec. 10, 1874; "Jesse H. Pomeroy," *Boston Post*, Dec. 10, 1874. In *Fiend: The Shocking True Story of America's Youngest Serial Killer* (New York: Pocket Books, 2000), 13–14, Harold Schechter identifies Pomeroy's first victim as Billy Paine and claims he was attacked on December 26, 1871. Schechter most likely got his account of this attack from a later report in the *Globe*, from 1875, when Pomeroy's first victim was identified as "the little son of Mr. Paine of Chelsea," who was enticed to Powder Horn Hill and beaten "about Christmas, 1871." "The Pomeroy Boy," *Boston Daily Globe*, May 29, 1875. All the earlier accounts of Pomeroy's victims' testimony at trial, however, identify this boy, attacked in December 1871, as Robert Maies. In a book of celebrated criminal cases published in 1910, Thomas Samuel Duke also follows the later *Globe* article and identifies the "little son of Mrs. Paine, of Chelsea," as Pomeroy's first victim, on December 22, 1871. *Celebrated Criminal Cases of America* (San Francisco: James H. Barry Co., 1919), 558. I have, however, found no mention of Paine in any of the accounts of Pomeroy's victims, besides the single *Globe* report from 1875.

34. "The Boy Fiend," *Boston Herald*, Dec. 9, 1874; "Jesse H. Pomeroy," *Boston Post*, Dec. 10, 1874; "The Last Dorchester Tragedy," *Boston Herald*, April 24, 1874.

35. "Brutal Assault upon a Boy," *Boston Daily Globe*, July 23, 1872. The account in the *Globe* is confirmed in the record of the hearing in front of Judge Forsaith, which describes John Balch's testimony that he met Pomeroy in the street and was induced by a small sum of money to go to Powder Horn Hill, where "the Deft. stripped all the clothing off from the Balch boy, tied him to a post by the hands, and beat him with a rope." Case Histories of Boys, MAB.

36. From an article titled "Unaccountable Depravity" in the *Chelsea (MA) Telegraph and Pioneer*, which E. Luscomb Haskell quotes in its entirety in *The Life of Jesse Harding Pomeroy: The Most Remarkable Case in the History of Crime or Criminal Law* (Boston: n.p., 1892), 88–90.

37. "Jesse Pomeroy's Mother," *New York Times*, May 13, 1878.

38. Warren Stearns, a professor of sociology at Tufts University in Massachusetts, claimed in a 1948 article that the Pomeroy family moved to South Boston because of Pomeroy's attacks on boys in Chelsea. "The Life and Crimes of Jesse Harding Pomeroy," *Journal of the Maine Medical Association* 39.4 (April 1948): 80.

39. Case Histories of Boys, MAB.

40. "A Youthful Torturer," *Aegis and Gazette* (Worcester, MA), Sept. 28, 1872, which reprints an article from the *Boston Daily News* of Sept. 20, 1872.

41. "The Boy Fiend," *Boston Herald*, Dec. 9, 1874; "The Last Dorchester Tragedy," *Boston Herald*, April 24, 1874. The latter article covers Pomeroy's arrest for murder; only at

that point, almost two years after the fact, were most of the details about his earlier assaults on boys detailed in the press.

42. Case Histories of Boys, MAB.

43. "A Youthful Torturer," *Aegis and Gazette* (Worcester, MA), Sept. 28, 1872; "The Last Dorchester Tragedy," *Boston Herald,* April 24, 1874. A newspaper account of Austin's wounds from 1872 repeats the information later reported in the *Herald:* he "received one cut in the groin and three on the back with a knife." "The Boy Torturer— Examination and Sentence," *Boston Daily Globe,* Sept. 21, 1872. Austin seems not to have testified at Pomeroy's murder trial, perhaps because of the severity of his wounds.

44. "Jesse Pomeroy," *Boston Daily Globe,* Dec. 10, 1874; "The Boy Fiend," *Boston Herald,* Dec. 9, 1874.

45. "The Boy Torturer—Examination and Sentence," *Boston Daily Globe,* Sept. 21, 1872; "The Boy Fiend," *Boston Herald,* Dec. 9, 1874.

46. "A Very Bad Boy," *Boston Daily Globe,* Sept. 20, 1872.

47. Pomeroy, *Autobiography,* 4.

48. "The Boy Torturer: Singular Case in Boston," *New York Times,* Sept. 22, 1872.

49. "The Boy Torturer—Examination and Sentence," *Boston Daily Globe,* Sept. 21, 1872.

50. Case Histories of Boys, MAB.

51. "A Remarkable Case," *Boston Daily Advertiser,* Sept. 21, 1872.

52. "The Boy Torturer: Singular Case in Boston," *New York Times,* Sept. 22, 1872.

53. "Juvenile Depravity," *Congregationalist,* Sept. 26, 1872; "The Boy Torturer: Singular Case in Boston," *New York Times,* Sept. 22, 1872; "A Remarkable Case," *Boston Daily Advertiser,* Sept. 21, 1872; "The Boy Torturer—Examination and Sentence," *Boston Daily Globe,* Sept. 21, 1872.

54. Case Histories of Boys, MAB.

55. "The Pomeroy Case," *Boston Daily Globe,* Nov. 2, 1875.

56. "Horrible Infatuation," *Salem (MA) Register,* April 27, 1874; "The Dorchester Tragedy," *Boston Post,* April 24, 1874.

57. In a notable example, Max Haines, a syndicated crime columnist, writes in a wildly inaccurate portrait of Jesse Pomeroy that that "the murders of 27 young girls and boys were attributed" to him. *The Collected Works of Max Haines, Volume 4: 1993–1995* (New York: Penguin, 2000), 280. This article was first published as "Teen Murderer Allowed to Go Free to Kill Again," *Ottawa Citizen,* April 21, 1984.

58. One article from 1874 compared Pomeroy to two of history's most infamous serial killers: the Marshal de Retz (actually the fifteenth-century Breton nobleman Gilles de Rais), who "enticed children to his feudal castle," and Martin Dumollard, "the wolf, as he was not inaptly called," a mid-nineteenth-century French serial killer. "The Pomeroy Verdict," *Boston Daily Globe,* Dec. 11, 1874.

59. "Juvenile Depravity," *Congregationalist,* Sept. 26, 1872; "A Remarkable Case," *Boston Daily Advertiser,* Sept. 21, 1872. The words about Pomeroy cutting small holes under several boys' eyes are repeated in "The Boy Torturer: Singular Case in Boston," *New York Times,* Sept. 22, 1872; "A Youthful Torturer," *Aegis and Gazette* (Worcester, MA), Sept. 28, 1872; and "A Monster Child with an Unaccountable Mania," *Daily Evening Bulletin* (San Francisco), Oct. 3, 1872.

60. "Horrible Infatuation," *Salem (MA) Register,* April 27, 1874.

61. An article published in the *Globe* in 1891 purporting to be a recollection of Pomeroy by someone who knew him as a boy was titled "Pomeroy's Evil Eye." *Boston Daily Globe,* Aug. 17, 1891.

62. Michael B. Katz, *The Irony of Early School Reform: Educational Innovation in Mid-Nineteenth-Century Massachusetts* (Cambridge: Harvard University Press, 1968), 166.

63. Commitment Register, Lyman School for Boys, Jesse Pomeroy, number 4126, HS8.05 / series 244X, MAB.

64. *Twenty-Sixth Annual Report of the Trustees of the State Reform School, October 1872* (Boston: Wright and Potter, State Printers, 1873), 5, 18, 29.

65. *Twenty-Seventh Annual Report of the Trustees of the State Reform School, October 1873* (Boston: Wright and Potter, State Printers, 1874), 35.

66. Ibid., 33–35; Case Histories of Boys, MAB.

67. *Twenty-Sixth Annual Report*, 28.

68. Case Histories of Boys, MAB.

69. Peter C. Holloran, *Boston's Wayward Children: Social Services for Homeless Children, 1830–1930* (Cranbury, NJ: Associated University Presses, 1989), 23, 107; Katz, *Irony of Early School Reform*, 187.

70. Katz, *Irony of Early School Reform*, 194. Donald Shoemaker similarly argues that mid-nineteenth-century reformers felt that they could turn around the lives of boys in their care "not only by separating the youngsters from the criminogenic environments" but also "by employing a family-like environment within the institutions." *Juvenile Delinquency*, 2nd ed. (Lanham, MD: Rowman and Littlefield, 2013), 19.

71. Steven Mintz, *Huck's Raft: A History of American Childhood* (Cambridge: Belknap Press of Harvard University Press, 2004), 161.

72. *Twenty-Seventh Annual Report*, 4–8; *Twenty-Sixth Annual Report*, 18.

73. Pomeroy, *Autobiography*, 6.

74. There was an investigation of reports of abuses at Westborough in 1860 (in the aftermath of the 1859 fire), during the course of which it was discovered that boys were manacled in tiny dark cells for weeks or even months at a time. The *Boston Daily Advertiser* summed up general sentiment when it declared that such punishments were "excessive and barbarous, not calculated to reform and amend, but to degrade and brutalize"—and were very far from the "parental" and "humane and reformatory" discipline envisioned by the founder of the school. "State Reform School at Westboro'," *Boston Daily Advertiser*, Aug. 13, 1860.

75. *Twenty-Seventh Annual Report*, 5.

76. Massachusetts General Court, House of Representatives, *Extracts from Testimony Taken before the Committee on Public Charitable Institutions on the Management of the State Reform School at Westborough, Mass., April, 1877* (n.p., 1877), 1, 3, 5, 17.

77. "Schools That Do Not Reform," *New York Times*, May 14, 1877.

78. "State Reform School at Westboro'," *Boston Daily Advertiser*, Aug. 13, 1860.

79. Pomeroy, *Autobiography*, 5–6; Case Histories of Boys, MAB.

80. Holloran, *Boston's Wayward Children*, 28.

81. Pomeroy, *Autobiography*, 5–6.

82. Daily Register, Lyman School for Boys, Feb. 6, 1874, HS8.05 / series 846X, MAB.

83. "The Murders," *Boston Daily Globe*, April 24, 1874.

84. "The great feature of the past week . . . ," *Boston Medical and Surgical Journal* 91 (Dec. 17, 1874): 597.

85. "The Release from the Reform School Explained," *New York Times*, July 24, 1874. For the full statement by Tufts, see "Jesse Pomeroy. The Visiting Agent of the Board of State Charities Explains Why the Boy Murderer Was Allowed to Leave the Reform School," *Boston Daily Globe*, July 23, 1874.

86. "The Boy Torturer: Singular Case in Boston," *New York Times*, Sept. 22, 1872; "The Pomeroy Verdict," *Boston Daily Globe*, Dec. 11, 1874; "Jesse Pomeroy Convicted of Murder in the First Degree," *Boston Daily Advertiser*, Dec. 11, 1874.

87. These articles included "Murder on Dorchester Beach," *Boston Daily Globe*, April 23, 1874.

88. "Horrible Infatuation," *Salem (MA) Register*, April 27, 1874. According to Horace Millen's death record (in which he is listed as Horace H. Millin, although it was routinely spelled "Millen" in the press), he was four years and eight months old at the time of

his murder. He had been born in New York City, so clearly his family had moved to Boston fairly recently. Registers of Vital Records, Death of Horace H. Millin, 1874, vol. 267, p. 82, HS6.07 / series 1411, MAB.

89. "A Terrible Deed. A Little Boy Murdered in the Dorchester District," *Boston Herald*, April 23, 1874.

90. James R. Wood, "The Murders of Kate Curran and the Melon [*sic*] Boy," Wood Detective Agency Records, 1865–1945, box 1-9, Harvard Law Library, Cambridge, MA.

91. For newspaper accounts of Pomeroy's arrest, see "Murder on Dorchester Beach," *Boston Daily Globe*, April 23, 1874; "A Terrible Deed," *Boston Herald*, April 23, 1874.

92. Katie Mary Curran, Inquest, July 1874, Supreme Judicial Archives, Boston. The report was summarized in accurate detail in "The Child Tragedy," *Boston Herald*, April 24, 1874.

93. Ibid. Wood did testify at the coroner's inquest about the trip to the undertaker's and Pomeroy's confession. "The Child Murder," *Boston Herald*, April 29, 1874.

94. Apparently there were others at the undertaker's with Pomeroy and Detective Wood who denied what Wood said about Pomeroy's refusing to look at the body or that he was agitated. "The Dorchester Tragedy," *Boston Post*, April 25, 1874. Still others corroborated what Wood said, including "The Dorchester Murder," *Boston Post*, April 29, 1874.

95. "Innocent until Proved Guilty," *Boston Herald*, April 29, 1874.

96. Wood, "The Murders of Kate Curran and the Melon [*sic*] Boy."

97. Katie Mary Curran, Inquest. For the additional detail that the guilty boy was dead, see "The Child Murder," *Boston Herald*, April 29, 1874.

98. Katie Mary Curran, Inquest.

99. "The Child Murder," *Boston Daily Globe*, Aug. 25, 1874. See also "The Dorchester Tragedy," *Boston Post*, April 25, 1874.

100. "The Boy Fiend," *Boston Daily Globe*, April 27, 1874.

101. "The recent snow storm . . . ," *Lowell (MA) Daily Citizen*, May 4, 1874.

102. "The Pomeroy Case," *Boston Daily Globe*, April 28, 1874.

103. "Jesse H. Pomeroy . . . ," *Aegis and Gazette* (Worcester, MA), May 30, 1874.

104. "The Boy Murder," *Boston Daily Globe*, April 29, 1874.

105. In her death record, Katie is listed as ten years and two months old, and the date of her death is listed as March 18, the day she disappeared. Her death is listed in the register on July 13. Registers of Vital Records, Death of Katie M. Curran, 1874, vol. 267, p. 140, HS6.07 / series 1411, MAB.

106. "Jesse Pomeroy, the Child-Torturer," *Boston Traveler*, July 20, 1874.

107. "Remarks of Alderman Power on missing South Boston child, Katie Curran," and "Katie Mary Curran Reward Poster," both in the Jesse Harding Pomeroy Collection, *City of Boston Archives*, http://cityofbostonarchives.omeka.net.

108. Adams gives his account of searching the Pomeroys' cellar in his "Defense" in the *Globe*. He claims the cellar was also "searched by others." "Jesse Pomeroy. Another Chapter in the South Boston Tragedy," *Boston Daily Globe*, July 22, 1874.

109. "Katy Curran," *Boston Post*, July 20, 1874.

110. Assessing Department, City of Boston, "Tax Record of James Nash," Jesse Harding Pomeroy Collection, *City of Boston Archives*, http://cityofbostonarchives.omeka.net.

111. "The Pomeroy Boy, Once More," *Springfield (MA) Republican*, July 20, 1874. See also "Katy Curran," *Boston Post*, July 20, 1874; "Katie Curran," *Boston Post*, July 23, 1874; and "A Horrible Revelation," *Boston Herald*, July 19, 1874.

112. "Katie Curran," *Boston Daily Globe*, July 20, 1874.

113. "A Horrible Revelation," *Boston Herald*, July 19, 1874.

114. "Katy Curran," *Boston Post*, July 20, 1874; "The Pomeroy Boy, Once More," *Springfield (MA) Republican*, July 20, 1874. See also Haskell, *Life of Jesse Harding Pomeroy*, 39.

115. "The Child Murder," *Boston Herald*, Aug. 29, 1874.
116. "Charles, the brother of Jesse Pomeroy . . . ," *Boston Traveler*, Sept. 1, 1874.
117. "If Jesse Pomeroy is guilty . . . ," *Springfield (MA) Republican*, April 27, 1874.
118. "The Boy with the White Eye Again," *Daily Graphic* (New York City), Oct. 2, 1874. See also "A Missing Girl," *Portland (ME) Daily Press*, Oct. 2, 1874, and "Additional Suspicions against Jesse Pomeroy," *Aegis and Gazette* (Worcester, MA), Oct. 3, 1874.
119. "Pomeroy Murder Case," *Lowell (MA) Daily Citizen*, July 21, 1874.
120. "The Boy Murderer. Pomeroy Confesses the Murder of Katie Curran," *Boston Daily Globe*, July 21, 1874. Most area newspapers reprinted Pomeroy's confession; see for example, "The Curran Tragedy," *Boston Post*, July 21, 1874, and "The Curran Murder," *Boston Traveler*, July 21, 1874.
121. "The Curran Murder," *Boston Traveler*, July 21, 1874.
122. "Jesse H. Pomeroy. The Boy Fiend's Confessions," *Boston Journal*, July 24, 1874.
123. "Jesse Pomeroy. Another Chapter in the South Boston Tragedy," *Boston Daily Globe*, July 22, 1874.
124. "Jesse H. Pomeroy. The Boy's Autobiography," *Boston Herald*, July 24, 1874.
125. "Jesse H. Pomeroy. The Boy Fiend's Confessions," *Boston Journal*, July 24, 1874.
126. "The Boy Murderer. Pomeroy Confesses the Murder of Katie Curran," *Boston Daily Globe*, July 21, 1874.
127. "Captain Dyer's Resignation Demanded, and Received," *Boston Daily Advertiser*, July 22, 1874.
128. "Jesse Pomeroy. Another Chapter in the South Boston Tragedy," *Boston Daily Globe*, July 22, 1874. For a detailed report of an interview with Dyer, see "The Curran Tragedy," *Boston Post*, July 21, 1874.
129. "The revelation of Jesse Pomeroy's murder . . . ," *Springfield (MA) Republican*, July 22, 1874.
130. "Summed Up," *Boston Herald*, July 21, 1874.
131. "Young Pomeroy," *Boston Daily Globe*, July 25, 1874.
132. Ibid. Showing a family solidarity that he and his mother displayed throughout Jesse's trial, Charles Pomeroy denied the testimony that he and his brother quarreled, that Jesse wanted to sleep at the store, and that he spent a lot of time in the cellar. "Katie Curran," *Boston Post*, July 23, 1874.
133. "Katie Curran," *Boston Post*, July 25, 1874.
134. "Katie Curran," *Boston Post*, July 30, 1874.
135. "Verdict in the Katie Curran Case," *Boston Daily Advertiser*, July 30, 1874.
136. "Pomeroy's Crimes. He Confesses the Murder of Horace F. Millen," *Boston Daily Globe*, July 23, 1874. This article reports that Pomeroy's reason for confessing, on the heels of the discovery of Katie Curran's body in his family's store, was that he "feared his mother, brother, or some one [*sic*] else might be suspected."
137. "Katie Curran," *Boston Post*, July 24, 1874; "Jesse Pomeroy," *Boston Herald*, July 23, 1874.
138. "Pomeroy's Crimes. He Confesses the Murder of Horace F. Millen," *Boston Daily Globe*, July 23, 1874.
139. "Jesse Pomeroy," *Boston Herald*, July 23, 1874.

2. On Trial

1. "The Boy Fiend: Jesse Pomeroy on Trial for His Life," *Boston Daily Globe*, Dec. 9, 1874. The transcript of Pomeroy's trial, apparently once held in the Social Law Library in Boston, has been lost, perhaps sometime in the 1960s. There is a reference to the library's containing a "longhand copy of the *Trial of Jesse Pomeroy*, the only one extant" in 1936. Howard L. Stebbins (librarian at the Social Law Library), "The Social Law

Library, Boston, Massachusetts," *Law Library Journal* 29 (1936): 86. Trial transcripts in the nineteenth century were often assembled with the input of newspaper reporters, however, so while the accounts of the trial in newspapers are less complete than a full transcript, they are not necessarily less reliable. As with details of Pomeroy's crimes, a reliable source on what is known about the trial is Alexander W. Pisciotta, "Jesse Pomeroy: Historical Reflections on Serial Murder and the Social Construction of Punishment and Criminal Justice" (unpublished paper; copy in the author's possession).

2. "The Boy Fiend," *Boston Daily Globe*, Dec. 9, 1874.

3. "The Trial of Jesse H. Pomeroy for the Murder of Horace H. Millen," *Boston Traveler*, Dec. 8, 1874.

4. Details about the prosecution's case come from "The Boy Fiend," *Boston Daily Globe*, Dec. 9, 1874.

5. "The testimony most relied upon . . . ," *Springfield (MA) Republican*, April 30, 1874. People often got the damaged eye wrong, incorrectly identifying the left eye as the injured one. The fact that Benson identified the right eye as injured certainly supports the credibility of his testimony.

6. "Pomeroy's Crimes," *Boston Daily Globe*, July 23, 1874.

7. "The Boy Fiend," *Boston Daily Globe*, Dec. 9, 1874.

8. Ibid.

9. Ibid.

10. "The Boy Fiend," *Boston Herald*, Dec. 9, 1874.

11. Case Histories of Boys, Lyman School for Boys, Jesse H. Pomeroy, HS8.05 / series 629X, Massachusetts Archives, Boston (hereafter MAB).

12. "Jesse H. Pomeroy," *Boston Post*, Dec. 9, 1874.

13. Except where noted, material in this paragraph and the following two is taken from "Jesse Pomeroy," *Boston Daily Globe*, Dec. 10, 1874; and "The Boy Fiend," *Boston Herald*, Dec. 9, 1874.

14. For almost the same story about the kitten, except in this telling the kitten was "crying" and was cut on the "breast and shoulder," see "The Trial of Jesse H. Pomeroy," *Boston Daily Evening Traveler*, Dec. 9, 1874.

15. "Jesse H. Pomeroy," *Boston Post*, Dec. 10, 1874.

16. "The Boy Fiend," *Boston Daily Globe*, Dec. 9, 1874. Robinson considered this testimony so important to his case that it was one of two rulings by Judge Gray that he appealed to the Massachusetts Supreme Court after the trial. His appeal was denied.

17. On the careers of Tyler and Walker, see Warren Stearns, "The Life and Crimes of Jesse Harding Pomeroy," *Journal of the Maine Medical Association* 39.4 (April 1948): 81.

18. "Jesse Pomeroy," *Boston Daily Globe*, Dec. 10, 1874.

19. James Cowles Prichard, *A Treatise on Insanity and Other Disorders Affecting the Mind* (Philadelphia: E. L. Carey and A. Hart, 1837), 16. For a discussion of Prichard's central role in defining moral insanity, see Daniel N. Robinson, *Wild Beasts and Idle Humours: The Insanity Defense from Antiquity to the Present* (Cambridge: Harvard University Press, 1996), 158–62; and Nicole Rafter, *The Criminal Brain: Understanding Biological Theories of Crime* (New York: New York University Press, 2008), 27–29. From the 1840s on, "moral insanity" challenged the otherwise prevailing definition of legal insanity: knowledge of right and wrong. For the most part, if a defendant could grasp that difference, and had a sense that he did wrong, he was not considered to be legally insane. Moral insanity, however, posited that a person could grasp that distinction and yet still not be responsible for pursuing what was wrong.

20. Prichard, *Treatise on Insanity*, 26–27.

21. "The Frightful Crimes," *Boston Daily Advertiser*, July 22, 1874.

22. Isaac Ray, *A Treatise on the Medical Jurisprudence of Insanity* (1838; Cambridge: Belknap Press of Harvard University Press, 1962), 128–29. It should be emphasized that Ray

was very heavily influenced by, among others, Pinel, Esquirol, and Prichard. As Heidi Rimke and Alan Hunt point out, "Work in the fields of moral insanity was shared by a transcontinental psycho-medical community who through publications, professional associations and the like, shared knowledge not necessarily according to geographical location; similarly practitioners shared advances in treatment practices. Thus one finds moral insanity experts citing the work of their transatlantic counterparts." Rimke and Hunt, "From Sinners to Degenerates: The Medicalization of Morality in the 19th Century," *History of the Human Sciences* 15.1 (Feb. 2002): 63.

23. As Prichard had done, Ray identified a "most important form of moral mania"—homicidal—that "consists in a morbid activity of the propensity to destroy; where the individual without provocation or any other rational motive, apparently in full possession of his reason, and oftentimes, in spite of his most strenuous efforts to resist, imbrues his hands in the blood of others." Ray, *Treatise,* 147.

24. Ibid., 149, 169. Nicole Rafter agrees that the examples in Ray's *Treatise* are "aimed at revealing the essence of moral mania: criminal behavior committed by people who have no motive, cannot control themselves and lack remorse." Rafter, "The Unrepentant Horse-Slasher: Moral Insanity and the Origins of Criminological Thought," *Criminology* 42.4 (Nov. 2004): 994.

25. "The Trial of Jesse H. Pomeroy," *Boston Traveler,* Dec. 9, 1874.

26. Case Histories of Boys, MAB; "The Boy Murderer. Pomeroy Confesses the Murder of Katie Curran," *Boston Daily Globe,* July 21, 1874.

27. "Jesse Pomeroy. Another Chapter in the South Boston Tragedy," *Boston Daily Globe,* July 22, 1874.

28. "Pomeroy's Crimes. He Confesses the Murder of Horace F. Millen," *Boston Daily Globe,* July 23, 1874.

29. Charles D. Sawin, *Criminals* (Boston: n.p., 1890), 12–13. Sawin was a physician at the Massachusetts State Prison for five years and published his views on crime in this short pamphlet, focusing on Jesse Pomeroy and his state of mind, and including verbatim testimony of physicians at his murder trial (12–15).

30. "The Boy Murderer: He Is Found Guilty of Murder in the First Degree," *Boston Daily Globe,* Dec. 11, 1874.

31. E. Luscomb Haskell, *The Life of Jesse Harding Pomeroy: The Most Remarkable Case in the History of Crime or Criminal Law* (Boston: n.p., 1892), 59–62. There is a very good likelihood that Haskell is quoting from the lost trial transcript. He always identifies quotations from newspapers as such, and he does not identify a newspaper as his source when he quotes Robinson's argument at the trial. His book is also primarily about the legal aspects of the case, making it more likely that he would have consulted the transcript.

32. "Jesse Pomeroy: Second Day of His Trial for the Murder of Horace Millen," *Boston Daily Globe,* Dec. 10, 1874.

33. "Jesse H. Pomeroy," *Boston Post,* Dec. 10, 1874. This story is repeated in the *Boston Herald,* which reported Choate as saying that Pomeroy had wanted Somerby as his lawyer because "he heard that he had got a man acquitted recently on the ground of insanity." "The Boy Fiend," *Boston Herald,* Dec. 10, 1874. Pomeroy is mostly likely referring to Gustavus A. Somerby, who had represented Samuel M. Andrews in his 1868 murder trial in the Supreme Court of Massachusetts in Plymouth, arguing for the defendant's "transitory mania" and winning a verdict of manslaughter.

34. "Jesse Pomeroy," *Boston Daily Globe,* Dec. 10, 1874.

35. As one reporter put it, paraphrasing Robinson's closing argument, "It was not reasonable to say that the defendant was a monster because he was a product of our culture during the past fifteen years." "Jesse Pomeroy Convicted of Murder in the First Degree," *Boston Daily Advertiser,* Dec. 11, 1874.

210   *Notes to Pages 55–61*

36. All quotations in this and the following two paragraphs are from "The Boy Murderer," *Boston Daily Globe*, Dec. 11, 1874.
37. Judge Gray's charge is available in its entirety, from the stenographic report of the trial taken by the district attorney, in Francis Wharton, "Pomeroy's Case: Insanity," in *A Treatise on the Law of Homicide in the United States, to Which Is Appended a Series of Leading Cases* (Philadelphia: Kay and Bro., 1875), 753–61. All quotations in this and the following two paragraphs are from this source, 755–59.
38. Unless otherwise noted, all quotations in this paragraph and the next one are from "The Boy Murderer," *Boston Daily Globe*, Dec. 11, 1874, and "Jesse Pomeroy Convicted of Murder in the First Degree," *Boston Daily Advertiser*, December 11, 1874.
39. The last quotation is from "Jesse H. Pomeroy," *Boston Post*, Dec. 11, 1874.
40. "Supplement: Opinion of the Justices to the Governor," *Massachusetts Reports 120. Cases Argued and Determined in the Supreme Judicial Court of Massachusetts, March–September 1876* (Boston: Houghton, Mifflin, 1877), 601.
41. "Jesse Pomeroy the Dreaded Issue in Massachusetts," *Boston Daily Globe*, July 27, 1876.
42. "It is a long time . . . ," *Boston Daily Advertiser*, March 31, 1875; "Sentimentalism and Capital Punishment," *New York Times*, June 1, 1875.
43. The petition that Francis Parkman signed is reprinted in "The Pomeroy Murder," *Boston Daily Advertiser*, March 31, 1875, and is also mentioned in "Boston," *Lowell (MA) Daily Citizen*, April 3, 1875.
44. "More Letters for Hanging and Against—A Plea for Mercy," *Boston Daily Globe*, April 22, 1875 (quotation); "Jesse Pomeroy," *Boston Daily Advertiser*, April 3, 1875.
45. "Gail Hamilton on Jesse Pomeroy," *Lowell (MA) Daily Citizen*, Nov. 28, 1874; Henry James Sr., "Chloroform Instead of the Gallows," *Boston Daily Advertiser*, April 6, 1875.
46. "Adirondack Murray . . . ," *Springfield (MA) Republican*, April 8, 1875; Files of Inactive Pardons and Pardons Not Granted, GC3 / series 771, MAB. Holmes's support of commutation was also mentioned in "Sentimentalism and Capital Punishment," *New York Times*, June 1, 1875.
47. "The Problems of Chronic Crime," *Springfield (MA) Republican*, April 25, 1874.
48. The *Advertiser* reported that many of the mothers of Boston have "for the first time in their lives" felt it their duty to "make a public appeal." "It is a long time . . . ," *Boston Daily Advertiser*, March 31, 1875.
49. "Three hundred South Boston women . . . ," *Springfield (MA) Republican*, March 12, 1875.
50. "Judgment without Knowledge," *Boston Daily Globe*, July 7, 1875; "The Ladies in South Boston," *Boston Daily Advertiser*, March 24, 1875.
51. "It is a long time . . . ," *Boston Daily Advertiser*, March 31, 1875.
52. "The Pomeroy Case," *Boston Daily Advertiser*, April 1, 1875.
53. "In Brief," *Lowell (MA) Daily Citizen*, March 20, 1875; see also "Jesse Pomeroy's Fate," *Boston Journal*, March 19, 1875.
54. "And Now Pomeroy," *Boston Daily Globe*, May 17, 1876.
55. Files of Inactive Pardons and Pardons Not Granted, GC3 / series 771, MAB.
56. "The Pomeroy Case," *Boston Daily Advertiser*, April 1, 1875; see also "Jesse Pomeroy," *Boston Daily Advertiser*, April 3, 1875.
57. Larry E. Sullivan, *The Prison Reform Movement: Forlorn Hope* (Boston: Twayne, 1990), 18. Marie Gottschalk claims that, in general, the leading Enlightenment thinkers on criminal justice (Hobbes, Bentham, and Beccaria)—who would all, especially Beccaria, be highly influential in the movement to reform the penal system in the United States—agreed that the purpose of punishment is "to protect society." Gottschalk, *The Prison and the Gallows: The Politics of Mass Incarceration in America* (New York: Cambridge University Press, 2006), 45.

58. "The great feature of the past week . . . ," *Boston Medical and Surgical Journal* 91 (Dec. 17, 1874): 598.

59. Ibid., 597; "The Pomeroy Case," *Boston Medical and Surgical Journal* 93 (Aug. 12, 1875): 199; "The Pomeroy Case," *Boston Medical and Surgical Journal* 93 (Dec. 30, 1875): 775.

60. An editorial in the *Congregationalist* declared, "It is morally certain that we shall, for some generations to come, have here in New England a plentiful supply of that style of 'philanthropist' whose philanthropy is mainly confined to unscrewing the nuts and removing the linch-pins from the social system, by way—of course—of 'improvement.'" "What could the Reverend Murray have meant . . . ," *Congregationalist,* April 29, 1875.

61. An example of the disagreement is William H. Colcord, "A Few Leading Questions to Those Who Demand the Hanging of the Boy," *Boston Daily Globe,* April 13, 1875, in which Colcord asks what evidence there is to show that "any person was ever deterred from committing murder from fear of the death penalty attached thereto"; and "Mr. Colcord Answered—The Death Penalty the Only Means of Protection against Lawlessness," *Boston Daily Globe,* April 15, 1875, in which the writer gives a few rather unpersuasive examples of criminals who were deterred (or who, like Pomeroy, committed crimes presumably because they were confident there would be no repercussions).

62. "The Pomeroy Case," *Boston Daily Globe,* March 24, 1875; "Mr. Colcord Answered," *Boston Daily Globe,* April 15, 1875; "The Extreme Penalty. Effect of the Certainty of Punishment—Some Cases in Point," *Boston Daily Globe,* July 1, 1875.

63. "The communication of Henry James . . . ," *Boston Daily Globe,* April 7, 1875; "The Pomeroy Verdict," *Boston Daily Advertiser,* April 17, 1875; "The Death of Frost," *Boston Daily Globe,* May 27, 1876.

64. Louis P. Masur describes how, "by the 1830s, legislatures throughout the Northeast transferred executions from the town commons to behind prison walls." Masur, *Rites of Execution: Capital Punishment and the Transformation of American Culture, 1776–1865* (New York: Oxford University Press, 1989), 5. It is worth mentioning, though, that the "private" executions of the 1870s were not, in fact, very private. Apparently about five hundred tickets were distributed for Thomas Piper's execution in the Charles Street Jail, to medical and legal professionals, police officers, the press, and various other interested parties. "The Gallows. Executions of Piper and Frost Yesterday," *Boston Daily Globe,* May 27, 1876.

65. As one letter-writer put it, capital punishment tends to "brutalize the common mind, and diminish its respect for human life" and, in the end, is "much more likely to induce crime than to prevent it." "More Letters for Hanging and Against—A Plea for Mercy," *Boston Daily Globe,* April 22, 1875.

66. David Garland, *Peculiar Institution: America's Death Penalty in an Age of Abolition* (New York: Oxford University Press, 2010), 95.

67. "On the Other Side—Abolish Hanging or Respect the Laws," *Boston Daily Globe,* April 3, 1875.

68. Garland, *Peculiar Institution,* 96.

69. Judith W. Kay, *Murdering Myths: The Story behind the Death Penalty* (Lanham, MD: Rowman and Littlefield, 2005), 121–22.

70. "A Young Monster," *Inter Ocean* (Chicago), May 5, 1874; "The Mystery of a Monster," *Galveston (TX) Daily News,* July 28, 1874; "Monsters. A Sermon Delivered in the Unitarian Church, Sunday, June 6th, 1875, by Rev. Dr. C. A. Bartol, of Boston," *Cape Ann Advertiser* (Gloucester, MA), June 11, 1875.

71. "Massachusetts Civilization Disgraced by Piper and Pomeroy," *Boston Daily Globe,* May 10, 1876 (originally an editorial in the *New York World*).

72. "The Tribune didn't have . . . ," *Springfield (MA) Republican,* April 19, 1875. The *Republican* is lamenting this passage in the *New York Tribune,* remarking that it would not have printed such a paragraph in the days when Horace Greeley was editor. See also Paul West, "Vile Literature. The Influence of Bad Reading" (letter), *Boston Daily Globe,* May 10, 1876.

73. "A Strong Plea in Favor of Capital Punishment," *Boston Daily Globe,* April 15, 1875.

74. "The Pomeroy Hearing," *Boston Daily Advertiser,* April 12, 1875.

75. Theodore W. Fisher, "The Pomeroy Case," *Boston Medical and Surgical Journal* 91 (Dec. 31, 1874): 649.

76. A letter from the man who became lead advocate for the pro-execution forces, Paul West, claimed that the commutationists were composed of those "pseudo philanthropists" who rally to save any convicted criminal and another large class of people "who doubt Pomeroy's sanity." West, "Jesse Pomeroy," *Boston Daily Globe,* Aug. 9, 1876.

77. "The Governor and the Pomeroy Case," *Boston Daily Advertiser,* Aug. 5, 1875.

78. For the opinion of Norton Folsom, who was the most guarded, see "Shall Pomeroy Hang? Hearing before the Governor and Council," *Boston Daily Globe,* April 14, 1875.

79. Max Fischacher, "The Pomeroy Case Again. Reply to a Letter from a Mother," *Boston Daily Globe,* Nov. 16, 1875. See also "More Letters for Hanging and Against—A Plea for Mercy," *Boston Daily Globe,* April 22, 1875.

80. "Jesse Pomeroy's Case," *Springfield (MA) Republican,* May 1, 1874; "To the editors . . . ," *Boston Daily Advertiser,* July 26, 1875.

81. "More Letters for Hanging and Against—A Plea for Mercy," *Boston Daily Globe,* April 22, 1875.

82. Files of Inactive Pardons and Pardons Not Granted, GC3 / series 771, MAB; "The Pomeroy Case. Pre-Natal Influences," *Boston Daily Globe,* Aug. 31, 1875.

83. Indeed, one letter-writer who joined the debate over Jesse Pomeroy's punishment claimed that all crime (not just Pomeroy's) should be treated "as the effect of causes over which the criminal has had no control." "The Pomeroy Case. Pre-Natal Influences," *Boston Daily Globe,* Aug. 31, 1875.

84. This editorial from one of Boston's (unnamed) "leading newspapers" was quoted disapprovingly in a letter to the editor of the *Springfield Republican* from the members of the Somerset Club, a private club in Boston. The letter argued that the sympathy displayed was utterly misguided. "Monomaniacs," *Springfield (MA) Republican,* April 29, 1874.

85. "Jesse Pomeroy. The Question of Commuting His Sentence," *Aegis and Gazette* (Worcester, MA), April 17, 1875.

86. "The boy Jesse Pomeroy . . . ," *Springfield (MA) Republican,* Dec. 11, 1874.

87. Garland, *Peculiar Institution,* 96.

88. "The Boy Murderer: He Is Found Guilty of Murder in the First Degree," *Boston Daily Globe,* Dec. 11, 1874.

89. The article from the Philadelphia *Bulletin,* which mentions Jesse Pomeroy as an example of its argument, is reprinted in "The State and the Children," *Pennsylvania School Journal* 24.5 (Nov. 1875): 176–77.

90. "The 'Boy Fiend'—What Has Jackson's Case to Do with Pomeroy?," *Boston Daily Globe,* Aug. 13, 1875.

91. "Jesse Pomeroy. The Question of Commuting His Sentence," *Aegis and Gazette* (Worcester, MA), April 17, 1875; "Shall Pomeroy Hang? Hearing before the Governor and Council," *Boston Daily Globe,* April 14, 1875.

92. Angela Smith, *Hideous Progeny: Disability, Eugenics, and Classic Horror Cinema* (New York: Columbia University Press, 2011), 72. There was at least one Christian argument that was pro-execution, though, holding that St. Paul was pro–death penalty. "A

Biblical Argument against the Position of the Opponents of the Death Penalty," *Boston Daily Globe,* April 22, 1875.

93. Mrs. M. S. Wetmore, "The Pomeroy Case. A Pathetic and Sympathetic Letter to Jesse," *Boston Daily Globe,* March 29, 1875.

94. "An Earnest Tribute to Mrs. Wetmore's Sincerity and Goodness," *Boston Daily Globe,* April 15, 1875.

95. Pomeroy's lawyers made two exceptions (post-trial objections) to the judge's rulings at trial. First, they objected to the exclusion of the testimony of George B. Munroe, an officer at the Charles Street Jail, where Pomeroy was being held. They had wanted him to testify to the fact that Pomeroy ate well, slept soundly, and showed "no remorse or sense of guilt," as part of their case for his "moral insanity." The court ruled that not only was this evidence too far removed in time from the actual crime, but also that it was not "of any especial significance as indicating mental disease." Pomeroy's lawyers also objected to the fact that they were not allowed to read in court the written statement of the prosecution's witness, Dr. George Choate. Although Choate testified that Pomeroy was rational and sane, it seems his written account may have been more ambivalent, hence Robinson's desire to read it aloud. The court also overruled this exception, arguing that Choate's written statement belonged to the attorney general and that he was the one to decide what to do with it. "Commonwealth vs. Jesse H. Pomeroy," *Massachusetts Reports 117. Cases Argued and Determined in the Supreme Judicial Court of Massachusetts, January–June, 1875* (Boston: Houghton Mifflin, 1875), 144, 149–50. For a newspaper account of the arguments for the exceptions, see "The Commonwealth v. Jesse H. Pomeroy," *Boston Journal,* Feb. 1, 1875. For the imposition of the sentence of death, see "Sentence of Jesse Harding Pomeroy," *Boston Journal,* Feb. 20, 1875.

96. As a result of the Pomeroy debacle, the law was changed in 1876 so that the death sentence was approved by the court, not the governor and his council. See "The Jesse Pomeroy Case," *Springfield (MA) Republican,* Sept. 2, 1876, and "Jesse Pomeroy," *Aegis and Gazette* (Worcester, MA), Sept. 9, 1876.

97. "Jesse Pomeroy. The Question of Commuting His Sentence," *Aegis and Gazette* (Worcester, MA), April 17, 1875.

98. "Shall Pomeroy Hang? Hearing before the Governor and Council," *Boston Daily Globe,* April 14, 1875.

99. "Pomeroy to Be Hanged," *Boston Daily Advertiser,* July 3, 1875.

100. "Jesse H. Pomeroy," *Boston Traveler,* July 3, 1875.

101. "The Case of Pomeroy. The End Sought by Delay," *Boston Daily Globe,* July 13, 1875.

102. "What Is the Meaning of the Delays in the Pomeroy Case?—The Duty of the Governor of the State," *Boston Daily Globe,* July 14, 1875; "The Power of Life and Death," *Boston Daily Advertiser,* Aug. 3, 1875. The *Advertiser* letter was approvingly excerpted in "The Pomeroy Case," *Boston Medical and Surgical Journal* 93 (Aug. 12, 1875): 199, which was quoted in the *Advertiser* again by its editors. See "The Pomeroy Case," *Boston Daily Advertiser,* Aug. 13, 1875.

103. See Masur, *Rites of Execution,* 61–70.

104. "Shall Pomeroy Hang?," *Boston Daily Globe,* July 3, 1875.

105. One pro–death penalty letter-writer claimed not to question Gaston's "honest convictions," but asked why he was not governed by his council as the state constitution required (at this point, the council had voted to go ahead with Pomeroy's execution). "The Pomeroy Case. A Strong Letter from One of the Mothers," *Boston Daily Globe,* Nov. 2, 1875.

106. "We pity Governor Gaston . . . ," *Congregationalist,* July 15, 1875.

107. "The Boston correspondent . . . ," *Aegis and Gazette* (Worcester, MA), July 17, 1875.

108. "The Pomeroy Case and Mr. Rice," *Boston Daily Globe,* Oct. 29, 1875; see also "Jesse Pomeroy," *Boston Daily Advertiser,* Oct. 29, 1875.
109. "The State Canvass," *Springfield (MA) Republican,* Oct. 30, 1875.
110. That Piper was in the same corridor as Pomeroy is mentioned in "Visiting the Murderers," *Boston Daily Advertiser,* April 7, 1876. For details of Piper's execution, see "The Gallows. Executions of Piper and Frost Yesterday," *Boston Daily Globe,* May 27, 1876.
111. "Supplement. Opinion of the Justices to the Governor and Council," *Massachusetts Reports 120,* 602.
112. "The Pomeroy Case. A Strong Letter from One of the Mothers," *Boston Daily Globe,* Nov. 2, 1875. For a report of the court's decision see "The Interrogatories of the Executive Council Considered in the Supreme Court," *Boston Daily Globe,* May 23, 1876.
113. "Jesse H. Pomeroy," *Boston Traveler,* July 3, 1875.
114. "Local and Suburban," *Boston Traveler,* Oct. 22, 1875.
115. "Pomeroy's Autobiography," *Boston Daily Globe,* July 23, 1875.
116. "Jesse Pomeroy. A Singular Statement by His Mother," *Boston Daily Globe,* Aug. 30, 1875.
117. "From an article . . . ," *Boston Daily Globe,* Sept. 6, 1875; "How Pomeroy Was 'Exhibited,'" *Boston Daily Globe,* Sept. 9, 1875.
118. City of Boston, "Charles Street Jail Occurrence Logbook," Jesse Harding Pomeroy collection, *City of Boston Archives,* http://cityofbostonarchives.omeka.net.
119. "Jesse H. Pomeroy. A Reported Attempted to Escape," *Boston Traveler,* July 21, 1875.
120. "Visiting the Murderers," *Boston Daily Advertiser,* April 7, 1876.
121. "Boston," *Lowell (MA) Daily Citizen,* April 3, 1875.
122. "And Now Pomeroy," *Boston Daily Globe,* May 17, 1876.
123. "The Execution of Pemberton," *Springfield (MA) Republican,* Oct. 9, 1875.
124. "Boston," *Lowell (MA) Daily Citizen,* April 3, 1875.
125. "Visiting the Murderers," *Boston Daily Advertiser,* April 7, 1876.
126. Paul West, "Jesse Pomeroy," *Boston Daily Globe,* Aug. 9, 1876.
127. "Jesse Pomeroy the Dreaded Issue in Massachusetts," *Boston Daily Globe,* July 27, 1876.
128. "The Case of Jesse Pomeroy," *Boston Daily Globe,* Aug. 2, 1876.
129. See "Governor Rice and his executive council . . . ," *Springfield (MA) Republican,* Aug. 2, 1876; and "The Fate of Jesse Pomeroy Still in Doubt," *Massachusetts Spy* (Worcester), Aug. 4, 1876.
130. "The Case of Jesse Pomeroy," *Lowell (MA) Daily Citizen,* Aug. 2, 1876; "The case of the Pomeroy boy . . . ," *Lowell (MA) Daily Citizen,* Aug. 4, 1876.
131. "Is There to Be Any End of Pomeroy's Case?," *Boston Daily Globe,* Aug. 10, 1876.
132. "Pomeroy Not to Be Hung," *Boston Daily Globe,* Sept. 1, 1876.
133. Ibid. See also "Jesse Pomeroy's Sentence Commuted," *Lowell (MA) Daily Citizen,* Sept. 1, 1876; "Jesse Pomeroy. The Death Sentence Commuted to Imprisonment for Life," *Boston Daily Advertiser,* Sept. 1, 1876; and "The long looked for decision . . . ," *Congregationalist,* Sept. 6, 1876.
134. "The long looked for decision . . . ," *Congregationalist,* Sept. 6, 1876; "Jesse Pomeroy's Escape," *Aegis and Gazette* (Worcester, MA), Sept. 9, 1876; "The End of the Pomeroy Case," *Boston Medical and Surgical Journal* 95 (Sept. 7, 1876): 298.
135. "Pomeroy Not to Be Hung," *Boston Daily Globe,* Sept. 1, 1876; see also "It is expected . . . ," *Springfield (MA) Republican,* Sept. 2, 1876.
136. "Pomeroy Himself Again," *Boston Daily Globe,* Sept. 2, 1876; see also "It appears that Jesse Pomeroy . . . ," *Springfield (MA) Republican,* Sept. 4, 1876, and "Jesse Pomeroy," *Aegis and Gazette* (Worcester, MA), Sept. 9, 1876.
137. "Pomeroy in State Prison," *Boston Daily Globe,* Sept. 8, 1876.
138. "Jesse Pomeroy was removed . . . ," *Springfield (MA) Republican,* Sept. 9, 1876.
139. "Jesse Pomeroy is employed . . . ," *Springfield (MA) Republican,* Sept. 27, 1876.

140. "More Letters for Hanging and Against—A Plea for Mercy," *Boston Daily Globe*, April 22, 1875.
141. On the notion of solitary confinement as "social death," a "(social) practice in which a person or group of people is excluded, dominated, or humiliated to the point of becoming dead to the rest of society," see Lisa Guenther, *Solitary Confinement: Social Death and Its Afterlives* (Minneapolis: University of Minnesota Press, 2013), xx.

3. "The Mark of the Meat Market"

1. "The mark of the meat market" is a phrase used in a column written by the editor, "Maternal Impressions," *Journal of Heredity* 6.11 (Nov. 1915): 513.
2. "Juvenile Monsters," *Indianapolis Sentinel*, Aug. 9, 1874.
3. "The Child Butcher," *Boston Herald*, July 20, 1874. This initial story was repeated almost verbatim in "The Boy Murderer," *Boston Daily Globe*, July 21, 1874; "Jesse Pomeroy Confesses the Murder of Katy Curran," *Boston Daily Advertiser*, July 21, 1874; "A Boy Murderer," *Inter Ocean* (Chicago), July 24, 1874; and as an item in "The News," *Oneida (NY) Circular*, July 27, 1874.
4. "Jesse Pomeroy," *Boston Daily Globe*, July 22, 1874. The *Herald* also noted that Ruth Pomeroy had denied the butcher theory, but (perhaps because it had been the first to report it), it was not nearly as emphatic that the story was false: "Mrs. Pomeroy has been questioned on the subject of the bloodthirsty tendency of her son, and is represented as having said that the reported interview between herself and medical man [*sic*] regarding the possible transmission of this peculiarity from mother to son, is untrue. She says she never saw any animal slaughtered, and that Jesse was never in the habit of sticking knives into raw meat." "The Boy Fiend," *Boston Herald*, July 22, 1874. The *Boston Post* also reported that Ruth had refuted the butcher story; see "Katie Curran," *Boston Post*, July 23, 1874. That Ruth Pomeroy categorically refuted the butcher theory was rarely mentioned, and the theory was elaborated for decades without any mention of her contradiction. A notable exception was Hiram Fuller, who offered the theory, adding, "But the mother of the young monster has come out with a denial of the inherited theory, and says his father was not actually a butcher of animals, but only served dead meat." Hiram Fuller, *Grand Transformation Scenes in the United States* (New York: G. W. Carleton, 1875), 137.
5. "Jesse Pomeroy," *Boston Daily Globe*, Aug. 30, 1875. Ruth Pomeroy's words denouncing the theory of "marking" were reprinted in "Jesse Pomeroy," *St. Louis Globe-Democrat*, Sept. 3, 1875. The butcher story was still in circulation in 1875, however; it was repeated (without the debunking) in an untitled article in the *Daily Rocky Mountain News* (Denver, CO), March 26, 1875.
6. "Jesse Pomeroy," *Boston Daily Advertiser*, Oct. 2, 1893.
7. Julia Schlesinger, *Workers in the Vineyard: A Review of the Progress of Spiritualism, Biographical Sketches, Lectures, Essays and Poems* (San Francisco: n.p.: 1896), 147. Schlesinger goes on to make the following tantalizing comments: "The investigation Mrs. Ballou made of the Jesse Pomeroy case opened up some startling testimony in the matter, and laid bare many falsehoods that a morbid public had taken for truth relative to the boy and his family, together with which and the story as told by himself, and the Gerrand case also she has in preparation to present in a new coloring to the public in a not distant day" (147). I have been unable, however, to unearth anything that Ballou wrote about the Pomeroy case. The only other record of her intervention is a letter written from Boston on July 10, 1875, to Governor Gaston, asking that Pomeroy not be executed: "Not yet sixteen years of age. The leading experts of the state pronounce Pomeroy mentally insane, do spare his life." It is signed by John L. Augustus and Addie L. Ballou, "who is a relation of the Ballou family, so well known." Files of Inactive

Pardons and Pardons Not Granted, GC3 / series 771, Massachusetts Archives, Boston (hereafter MAB).

8. "The Child Butcher," *Boston Herald,* 20 July, 1874.

9. Edwin Dwight Babbitt, *Religion as Revealed by the Material and Spiritual Universe* (New York: Babbitt and Co., 1881), 240.

10. "The Gainesville Horror. Views of Eminent Medical Men on the Maniac Theory," *Dallas Morning News,* Aug. 7, 1887; Mrs. Rollo L. Winn, "Murderers and the Hereafter," *Bridgeton (NJ) Evening News,* Dec. 11, 1902.

11. Francis Gerry Fairfield, *Ten Years with Spiritual Mediums* (New York: Appleton, 1875), 56–57, 34, 4, 56, 27; see also 23. Fairfield is one of the only commentators I have discovered who finds some tendency to madness in Jesse's forebears. He writes: "It appears, from minute inquiry into the habits and antecedents of the father, that he had been subject to nervous paroxysms at different periods for many years, and that the boy, Jesse, inherited a neurotic tendency," which "descended directly from the paternal ancestor" (56). Fairfield is vague about these "antecedents" and offers no evidence of Thomas's "nervous paroxysms."

12. Maud [Eugenia Barrock] Lord Drake, *Psychic Light: The Continuity of Law and Life* (Kansas City, MO: Frank T. Riley, 1904), 553–54.

13. Elizabeth Jones Towne, *How to Use New Thought in Home Life. A Key to Happy and Efficient Living for Husband, Wife and Children* (1915; Holyoke, MA: The Elizabeth Towne Co., 1921), 121.

14. See Eli Zaretsky, *Capitalism, the Family, and Personal Life* (New York: Harper and Row, 1976), 64.

15. The explanation that Pomeroy was shaped before birth by his mother's visits to the slaughterhouse was based on the widely accepted theory of maternal impressions. For a discussion of this nineteenth-century (and earlier) belief, see Cristina Mazzoni, *Maternal Impressions: Pregnancy and Childhood in Literature and Theory* (Ithaca, NY: Cornell University Press, 2002). Many of the doctors who debated theories of maternal impression from the 1870s through the end of the nineteenth century commented on the greater role of the mother in transmitting qualities to her offspring. In a paper read before the Royal Medical and Chirurgical Society in 1878, for instance, William Sedgwick claimed that women "transmitted with far more sensibility than men," and that it was "well-known that women often served to a greater extent than men as conductors of an inheritance which they did not share." Sedgwick added that "it was popularly believed"—and he seems to agree—"that it was the emotional impressions of the mother, and not those of the father which admit of being imparted to the foetus, in the form of 'mother's marks.' " "Transactions of Societies. Royal Medical and Chirurgical Society," *London Medical Press and Circular* 75 (Jan. 16, 1878): 49.

16. Hartland and Herbert Edward Law, *Viavi Hygiene: For Women, Men, and Children* (San Francisco: The Viavi Co., 1905), 6.

17. Charles Bayer was not a physician, though he apparently "investigated" many cases of maternal impression that were overseen by physicians and recorded those he thought would be of interest to the medical profession. His express goal was to spread the truth about the immense power pregnant women had over their unborn children and thus over the future of civilization. C. J. Bayer, *Maternal Impressions,* 2nd ed. (Winona, MN: Jones and Kroeger, 1897), 6. Martin S. Pernick identifies Bayer (specifically in *Maternal Impressions*) as a proponent of eugenic thought. Pernick, *The Black Stork: Eugenics and the Death of "Defective" Babies in American Medicine and Motion Pictures since 1915* (New York: Oxford University Press, 1996), 206nn12 and 14.

18. Bayer, *Maternal Impressions,* 236, 134.

19. For an expression of scientific belief in maternal impressions in the later part of the nineteenth century, see Bayer, *Maternal Impressions,* especially 22–28, which

summarizes medical articles and opinion, all affirming belief in the theory. See also Fordyce Barker, "The Influence of Maternal Impressions on the Fetus," *Transactions of the American Gynecological Society* 11 (1886): 152–96.

20. "Effect of Mental Impressions on the Foetus in Utero," *Saint Louis Medical and Surgical Journal* 43 (1882): 619.

21. Warren W. Foster, "Hereditary Criminality and Its Certain Cure," *Pearson's Magazine* 22.5 (Nov. 1909): 567, emphasis added.

22. The Editor, "Maternal Impressions," *Journal of Heredity* 6.11 (Nov. 1915): 513.

23. Mary E. Teats, *The Way of God in Marriage: A Series of Essays upon Gospel and Scientific Purity* (Spotswood, NJ: Physical Culture Publishing Company, 1906), 143–44, emphasis added.

24. Virtually every physician in the nineteenth century admitted to some belief in the power of the mother's emotions to shape her unborn child, "to leave its impress upon the fetus," as one doctor put it. From the time of Hippocrates, another wrote, medical men have had "full faith in the power of the mother's mind to produce deformity of the foetus." Dr. C. O. Wright, "Maternal Impressions Affecting the Fetus in Utero," *American Journal of Obstetrics and Diseases of Women and Children* 11 (1878): 634; Thomas Waddel, M.D., "Maternal Impressions. Report of the Obstetric Section of the Toledo Medical Association," *Gaillard's Medical Journal* 25 (1878): 427. See also "Transactions of Societies. Royal Medical and Chirurgical Society," *London Medical Press and Circular* 75 (Jan. 16, 1878): 49.

25. Marie-Hélène Huet, *Monstrous Imagination* (Cambridge: Harvard University Press, 1993), 1. See also Rachel Adams, *Sideshow U.S.A.: Freaks and the American Cultural Imagination* (Chicago: University of Chicago Press, 2001), 186–209.

26. Adams, *Sideshow U.S.A.*, 199. Adams also makes reference to the "longstanding tradition that credits fathers with normal, healthy reproduction (defined in part by the child's approximation of paternal features) and blames mothers for the production of monstrous anomalies" (199).

27. There was certainly debate within the medical profession from the 1870s through at least the end of the century about maternal impressions—about whether women transmitted either the shocks they received from the external world or their own emotions during pregnancy. For the most part, there seemed to be a cautious belief in both, though the latter won a more unambiguous acceptance than the former. An important article in this regard is Barker, "The Influence of Maternal Impressions on the Fetus," published in 1886. Barker carefully reviews recent medical literature attempting to disprove the theory of maternal impressions and argues that, despite these claims, "the weight of authority must be conceded to be in favor of the doctrine that maternal impressions may affect the development, form, and character of the fetus" (158). He gives numerous compelling examples of his own experience and those published by other physicians. Appended to the article is a discussion among American Gynecological Society members that also suggests the widespread acceptance by the medical profession of maternal impressions.

28. "Frank Boy Slayers Have One Equal in Crime Annals: Pomeroy, Child-Torturer," *Brooklyn Daily Eagle*, June 8, 1924.

29. "Demoniacal Possessions," *Scientific American* 31 (Oct. 31, 1874): 273.

30. John H. Ruttley, M.D., *Nature's Secrets and the Secrets of Woman Revealed* (San Francisco: J. H. Ruttley, 1875), 89–90.

31. Barton Cooke Hirst, "Diseases of the Foetus," *Cyclopedia of the Diseases of Children: Medical and Surgical*, ed. John Marie Keating, vol. 1 (Philadelphia: J. B. Lippincott, 1889), 217; Bayer, *Maternal Impressions*, 122; Cornelia Whitbeck, "Obstetrics," *Physician and Surgeon: A Professional Medical Journal* 21 (1899): 221–22; Towne, *How to Use New Thought*, 121.

32. H. S. C., "How Murderers Are Formed," *Vegetarian Magazine* 6.8 (May 15, 1902): 188; Edwin Whitney Bishop, "Mother and Grandmother" (sermon delivered May 14, 1911), *Sunday Mornings in Park Congregational Church* (Grand Rapids, MI), May 1911, 8.

33. Pernick, *Black Stork*, 43.

34. Some physicians, however, insinuated blame even when the focus was merely on "impressions excited objectively." Dr. John H. Barry of New York, for instance, argued that pregnant women needed to be "schooled in the aversion of voluntary, catastrophical sightseeing"—seemingly making the women themselves responsible for those frightening encounters which impressed their unborn children. Barry, "Cases of Monstrosities," 813.

35. Mary Douglas, *Purity and Danger* (1966; New York: Routledge, 2002), 150. See also Sherry Ortner, "Is Female to Male as Nature Is to Culture?," *Feminist Studies* 1.2 (Autumn 1972): 5–31; and Elizabeth Grosz, *Volatile Bodies: Toward a Corporeal Feminism* (Bloomington: Indiana University Press, 1994), esp. 195, 203. Cristina Mazzoni also makes the connection between the longstanding understanding of women's bodies as open and permeable and the nineteenth-century theory of maternal impressions. Mazzoni, *Maternal Impressions*, 32–33.

36. Robin Karr-Morse and Meredith S. Wiley, *Ghosts from the Nursery: Tracing the Roots of Violence* (New York: Atlantic Monthly Press, 1997), 53. For discussions of the connection between the prenatal environment and later violence, see Karr-Morse and Wiley, *Ghosts from the Nursery*, 47–97; Jonathan Kellerman, *Savage Spawn: Reflections on Violent Children* (New York: Random House, 1999), 80–95; James Blair, Derek Mitchell, and Karina Blair, *The Psychopath: Emotion and the Brain* (Malden, MA: Blackwell, 2005), 33–35; Adrian Raine, *The Psychopathology of Crime: Criminal Behavior as a Clinical Disorder* (San Diego: Academic Press, 1993), 195–200; and, especially, Raine, *The Anatomy of Violence: The Biological Roots of Crime* (New York: Pantheon, 2013), 182–205.

37. Karr-Morse and Wiley, *Ghosts from the Nursery*, 62. Karr-Morse and Wiley insist that for "more than half a century we have known that what affects mothers emotionally also affects babies" (91), and they describe a compelling study showing that monkeys subjected to prenatal stress were at a much higher risk of aggressive behavior, some of them even trying to kill their cage mates (91–93).

38. Robert Ware, "The Epidemic of Smallpox in 1859–60," *Boston Medical and Surgical Journal* 64 (Feb. 1861): 86–87.

39. Karr-Morse and Wiley, *Ghosts from the Nursery*, 81. This paragraph also draws on Blair, Mitchell, and Blair, *The Psychopath*, 33–34; Raine, *Anatomy of Violence*, 192–94; and Raine, *Psychopathology of Crime*, 198–200.

40. Raine, *Psychopathology of Crime*, 199; Raine, *Anatomy of Violence*, 192–93.

41. M. A. B., "The White Eye. Story of Jesse Pomeroy, the Boy Murderer," *Brooklyn Eagle*, Feb. 22, 1875; the *Eagle's* physical description of Pomeroy is quoted in full in Ruttley, *Nature's Secrets*, 88. Suggestively, MPAs have been shown to be linked to schizophrenia, and while Pomeroy did not seem to display delusions or hallucinations, he may well have suffered the "negative symptoms" of schizophrenia: "alterations in neurocognition," that is, impairment in "attention, speed of processing, working and long-term memory, executive function, and social cognition." Jim van Os and Shitij Kapur, "Schizophrenia," *The Lancet* 374 (Aug. 22, 2009): 635–45.

42. The practice of mother-blaming, far out of proportion to the harmful effect pregnant women actually have on their unborn children, has persisted. See Katha Pollitt, " 'Fetal Rights': A New Assault on Feminism," in *"Bad" Mothers: The Politics of Blame in Twentieth-Century America*, ed. Molly Ladd-Taylor and Lauri Umansky (New York: New York University Press, 1998), 285–98.

43. Mazzoni, *Maternal Impressions*, 22.

44. "Is Jesse Pomeroy Insane?," *Boston Daily Globe*, Aug. 16, 1914.
45. "Long Fight for Pardon Over," *Boston Daily Globe*, Jan. 11, 1915.
46. Diane L. Beers, *For the Prevention of Cruelty: The History and Legacy of Animal Rights Activism in the United States* (Athens, OH: Swallow Press / Ohio University Press, 2006), 22–23, 40.
47. In the United States, antislavery principles had a major influence on the animal advocacy movement in the post–Civil War period. Beers, *For the Prevention of Cruelty*, 24–29.
48. Benjamin Rush, "An Enquiry into the Influence of Physical Causes upon the Moral Faculty" (1786), in *Two Essays on the Mind*, ed. Eric T. Carlson (New York: Brunner/Mazel, 1972), 32. Hogarth's first stage of cruelty was boys being cruel to small animals; the second was men exploiting domestic animals. These led to the third stage, murder, and the fourth, its "reward," execution.
49. For a discussion of the meat industry in the late nineteenth-century United States, see Beers, *For the Prevention of Cruelty*, 36–37. As Beers notes, the expanding meat industry was responsible for more animal deaths than any other factor and "played an integral role in amplifying the exploitation of food animals." By 1900, for instance, close to one billion animals per year were destroyed for food (36–37).
50. Elizabeth Blackwell was the aunt of Alice Stone Blackwell, whom Jesse Pomeroy sued for libel in 1925 over the story that he skinned a kitten while in jail (see the introduction).
51. Elizabeth Blackwell, "Erroneous Method in Medical Education," *Essays in Medical Sociology*, vol. 2 (London: Ernest Bell, 1902), 41, 44, 43, 44–45.
52. "The Moral Basis of Vegetarianism," *Vegetarian Magazine* 5.1 (Oct. 1900): 4–5; Upton Sinclair, *The Jungle* (1906; New York: Bantam, 1981), 316.
53. Quoted in Colin Spencer, *Vegetarianism: A History* (New York: Four Walls Eight Windows, 2002), 254; originally published as *The Heretic's Feast: A History of Vegetarianism* (Hanover, NH: University Press of New England, 1995), in which Holbrook's letter is reprinted on page 271. Spencer states that the letter was published in the *Vegetarian Messenger* (the journal of the Vegetarian Society), but I have not been able to locate the original source. It is also reprinted in Charles Walter Forward, *Fifty Years of Food Reform: A History of the Vegetarian Movement in England* (London: The Idea Publishing Union; Manchester: The Vegetarian Society, 1898), 64. Martin Luther Holbrook, M.D., was a health reformer, phrenologist, and vegetarian, originally from Ohio, who practiced in New York City. For information about Holbrook, particularly his view that vegetarianism was a marker of the advancement of civilization, see Karen Iacobbo and Michael Iacobbo, *Vegetarian America: A History* (Westport, CT: Praeger, 2004), 118–19, 123.
54. In a reversal of the logic that those who kill animals may well go on to kill humans, Dr. William Hammond gave the example of a man with homicidal impulses who was urged to kill sheep for a living by becoming a butcher—a kind of sublimation. But he too noted that exposure to slaughterhouses was dangerous in that it might produce imitators. William A. Hammond, "Morbid Impulse," *Papers Read before the Medico-Legal Society of New York from Its Organization* (New York: Medico-Legal Society of New York, 1882), 452, 445.
55. "A Social Peril," *Scientific American* 34 (June 10, 1876): 369.
56. Law and Law, *Viavi Hygiene*, 15. Similarly to the Laws, a 1922 article claimed that Thomas, who was a butcher, and Ruth, who "frequently visited the shambles," were "so familiar with the taking of life and the shedding of blood that their habit no doubt influenced the unborn child to such an extent that he very early became a murderer." Mrs. James Sharpe, "Environment and Heredity as Applied to Man and Fruits," *Biennial Report of the Kansas State Horticultural Society* 3 (1922): 59.

57. "Jesse Pomeroy's . . . ," *Daily Rocky Mountain News* (Denver, CO), March 26, 1875; "A Social Peril," *Scientific American* 34 (June 1876): 369.

58. Timothy Pachirat, *Every Twelve Seconds: Industrialized Slaughter and the Politics of Sight* (New Haven: Yale University Press, 2011), 19, 14.

59. M. F. L., "Is This Civilization?," *Journal of Zoöphily* 10 (Jan. 1901): 4. M. F. L. is most likely Mary F. Lovell, the assistant editor of the *Journal of Zoöphily*. The journal was published in Philadelphia under the auspices of the American Anti-Vivisection Society and the Women's Pennsylvania Society for the Prevention of Cruelty to Animals.

60. H. S. C., "How Murderers Are Formed," 188.

61. "Vegetarianism. Synopsis of a Paper Read before The Vegetarian Society, New York. By N. A. Mack," *The Vegetarian* 1.10 (April 15, 1896): 195–96.

62. Daniel W. Hull, *Manual of Magnetic Healing. To Which Is Added an Appendix on Vegetarianism* (Lily Dale, NY: Sunflower Publishing Company, 1906), 60–61.

63. William James, *The Principles of Psychology*, vol. 2 (London: Macmillan, 1891), 412.

64. "Civilization," *The Vegetarian, a Monthly Magazine Published to Advocate Wholesome Living* 1.4 (Oct. 15, 1895): 64, 61–62.

65. Wright, "Maternal Impressions Affecting the Fetus in Utero," 638; W. B. Furman, M.D., "Effects of Maternal Impressions on the Foetus in Utero," *Saint Louis Medical and Surgical Journal* 38 (1880): 465; "Medical Notes," *Boston Medical and Surgical Journal* 112 (1885): 381; Dr. G. Wythe Cook, "Do Mental Impressions Affect the Fetus in Utero?," *American Journal of Obstetrics* 22 (1889): 933; Barry, "Cases of Monstrosities," 813.

66. The results of maternal impressions are called "monstrosities" and "monstrous conceptions" in Barry, "Cases of Monstrosities," 811, 813.

67. Douglas, *Purity and Danger*, 37.

68. John Reynolds Francis, *The Encyclopaedia of Death and Life in the Spirit-World*, vol. 1 (Chicago: The Progressive Thinker Publishing House, 1895), 96–97.

69. Some physicians did describe the *mental* deformities that could result from frightening maternal experiences: "Maternal impressions do sometimes determine the mental as well as physical endowments of the fetus," wrote Dr. Furman in 1880. He also claimed that "untoward maternal impressions" can create "evil, and deformity mental as well as physical" that would be "continued from generation to generation like a wave over the almost boundless ocean of time." Furman, "Effects of Maternal Impressions," 467, 466. In 1895, A Harvard medical professor, Thomas Morgan Rotch, wrote that "for many years there has been accumulating a considerable amount of evidence showing that a violent mental impression made upon a woman who is at the time carrying a child may be followed by a physical *or mental* defect in the child which bears a striking relation in character to the impression made upon the mother." Thomas Morgan Rotch, *Pediatrics: The Hygienic and Medical Treatment of Children*, 4th ed. (1895; Philadelphia: J. B. Lippincott, 1903), 285, emphasis added.

70. "Born a Criminal," *Evening Post* (New York), July 21, 1874. This story was reprinted in the *Portland (ME) Daily Press*, July 24, 1874.

71. "Cursed Ere His Birth," *Springfield (MA) Republican*, July 22, 1874.

72. For other commentaries that drew parallels between Jesse Pomeroy and *Elsie Venner*, see "The Baby Burner," *Centinel of Freedom* (Newark, NJ), Aug. 4, 1874; and "Jesse Pomeroy," *Providence (RI) Evening Press*, March 25, 1875. Like the writer who compared Pomeroy to a "noxious reptile," the *Providence Evening Press* article asserted that Pomeroy's origins in the slaughterhouse made him "a dangerous animal who must be restrained for the safety of society."

73. Files of Inactive Pardons and Pardons Not Granted, GC3 / series 771, MAB. Holmes's support for commutation seemed to be public knowledge: an article in the *Albany Law Journal* in June 1875, mentions that "men of the standing of ex-judges Foster

and Bigelow, Oliver Wendell Holmes, and Rev. Mr. Murray, united in an appeal for commutation of sentence." "Vindictive Justice," *Albany Law Journal* 11 (June 12, 1875): 376.

74. Oliver Wendell Holmes Sr., *Ralph Waldo Emerson*, in *The Works of Oliver Wendell Holmes*, vol. 11 (Boston: Houghton Mifflin, 1892), 304. Pierre François Lacenaire was a nineteenth-century French murderer.

75. Holmes's phrase "automatic action" is from *Elsie Venner: A Romance of Destiny* (1861; New York: New American Library, 1961), 174, and "reflex action" is from his "Crime and Automatism," *Atlantic Monthly* 35 (April 1875): 469. For a discussion of *Elsie Venner* as a working out of Holmes' view of "reflex action," by which Elsie's fate is decided before she is born, see Charles Boewe, "Reflex Action in the Novels of Oliver Wendell Holmes," *American Literature* 26 (Nov. 1954): 303–19.

76. Holmes, *Elsie Venner*, 168, 243, 295. Another of the novel's characters, Helen Darley, comes to a similar realization a bit later: that Elsie is the victim of "an ante-natal impression which had mingled an alien element in her nature" (320).

77. Ibid., 188.

78. Ibid., 151. In his study of Holmes's fiction, Michael Weinstein argues that Holmes essentially sacrifices Elsie to his belief in the determining power of circumstances in an individual's life and thus grants her no freedom: the novel proffers a "physiological explanation [that] is consistent with Holmes's deterministic thesis." Michael Weinstein, *The Imaginative Prose of Oliver Wendell Holmes* (Columbia: University of Missouri Press, 2006), 88.

79. Holmes, *Elsie Venner*, 256.

80. This article by Holmes was explicitly tied to the Pomeroy case by some. "Dr. Holmes's paper on crime in the April Atlantic is everywhere praised and copied,—may it be sanctified to the saving of the child-murderer, Jesse Pomeroy, from the gallows to which a good many people would elevate him!" "Boston News and Notes," *Springfield (MA) Republican*, March 23, 1875.

81. Holmes, "Crime and Automatism," 466, 468 (emphasis added), 469, 474–75.

82. "Demoniacal Possessions," *Scientific American* 31 (Oct. 1874): 273

83. Dylan Trigg, *The Thing: A Phenomenology of Horror* (Winchester, UK: Zero Books, 2014), 63 (emphasis added), 76.

4. "Dime Novel Pomeroy"

1. "Dime Novel Pomeroy," *Indianapolis Sentinel*, Jan. 21, 1876. On the late nineteenth-century "moral panic" over dime novels and other sensational literature, see Michael Denning, *Mechanic Accents: Dime Novels and Working-Class Culture in America* (New York: Verso, 1987), 47–61; Paul J. Erickson, "Judging Books by Their Covers: Format, the Implied Reader, and the 'Degeneration' of the Dime Novel," *American Transcendental Quarterly* 12.3 (Sept. 1998): 247–62; and Joel Shrock, *The Gilded Age* (Westport, CT: Greenwood Press, 2004), 173–74. On Fields see Warren S. Tryon, *Parnassus Corner: A Life of James T. Fields, Publisher to the Victorians* (Boston: Houghton Mifflin, 1963); and Ellery Sedgwick, *A History of the Atlantic Monthly, 1857–1909: Yankee Humanism at High Tide and Ebb* (Amherst: University of Massachusetts Press, 1994), 69–111.

2. Robert K. Ressler and Tom Shachtman, *Whoever Fights Monsters* (New York: St. Martin's, 1992), 33.

3. Patterson DuBois [Du Bois], *The Natural Way in Moral Training: Four Modes of Nurture*, 3rd ed. (New York: Fleming H. Revell, 1903), 186. *The Natural Way in Moral Training* originated as a series of lectures given at the Brick Church in New York City in 1901, subsequently amplified for publication.

4. "The Murders," *Boston Daily Globe*, April 24, 1874; "The Pomeroy Case," *Boston Daily Globe*, April 28, 1874.

5. "The Boy Fiend," *Boston Herald*, Dec. 10, 1874. The *Post* confirmed the *Herald*'s account of Choate's testimony: "[Pomeroy] stated that he was no doubt influenced by reading Indian stories, and of the torture practiced by savages on their captives. He had read many cheap novels." "Jesse H. Pomeroy," *Boston Post*, Dec. 10, 1874.

6. "Keep Children from Crime," *Boston Daily Globe*, Dec. 11, 1874. Even late into the century, the *Globe* persisted in holding Pomeroy up as the exemplar of the dangers of "pernicious literature furnished by unscrupulous publishers to the youth of the day." Pomeroy, the editors wrote in 1880, "confesses to having acquired his sanguinary impulses from a constant perusal of the dime novel and other tales of border adventure." "Youthful Depravity," *Boston Daily Globe*, Feb. 22, 1880.

7. James T. Fields, "Interview with Jesse Pomeroy" (Fields's transcription of the interview and his accompanying notes), April 6, 1875, Annie Fields Papers (Ms. N-1221), Massachusetts Historical Society, Boston.

8. "Jesse Pomeroy and Cheap Literature," *Boston Journal*, Dec. 14, 1875; "Fiction, Old and New, and Its Eminent Authors Considered by James T. Fields," *Worcester (MA) Daily Spy*, Jan. 11, 1879; "Lecture by Mr. James T. Fields at the Brooklyn Atheneum," *Brooklyn Daily Eagle*, Feb. 27, 1879. The *Globe* repeated the account in the *Eagle:* "The Pomeroy Boy," *Boston Daily Globe*, Feb. 28, 1879. Reports of the Brooklyn lecture spread at least to the Midwest. See "Jesse Pomeroy's Inspiration," *Cleveland Leader*, March 3, 1879, which reprinted a report on the lecture from the New York *Sun*.

9. Annie Fields, *James T. Fields: Biographical Notes and Personal Sketches* (Boston: Houghton Mifflin, 1881), 223–26.

10. See, for instance, Denning, *Mechanic Accents*, 49–50, quoting J. P. Quincy, US Bureau of Education, *Public Libraries in the United States of America* (Washington, DC: Government Printing Office, 1876); Charles H. Kent, *New Commentary: A Manual for Young Men* (Davenport, IA: Published by the Author, 1880), 48 (published before the transcript of Fields's interview appeared in the posthumous collection, but Kent clearly got his quotation from the brief newspaper account since he repeats the *Globe*'s synopsis of the talk word for word); and Rev. Francis Edward Clark, *Danger Signals: The Enemies of Youth* (Boston: Congregational House, 1885), 73–74.

11. Annie Fields, *James T. Fields*, 223.

12. The article is "The Pomeroy Boy," *Boston Daily Globe*, May 29, 1875, a report on the status of the governor's decision (or lack thereof) about commutation that includes a summary of the case.

13. Fields, "Interview with Jesse Pomeroy."

14. The reminiscences of a purported former acquaintance of Jesse's in the *Boston Daily Globe* also provided compelling information about Pomeroy's reading habits, although it was published at least twenty or so years after the fact. See "Pomeroy's Evil Eye," *Boston Daily Globe*, Aug. 17, 1891.

15. Annie Fields, *James T. Fields*, 223–26. The published excerpt of the interview in *James T. Fields* is virtually identical to that of Fields' own transcript. However, in the latter, Fields adds the following note at the end: "[Insert: "Would you earnestly advise the other boys not to read these books you have read?" "Indeed, sir, I should.]" Fields, "Interview with Jesse Pomeroy."

16. Fields, "Interview with Jesse Pomeroy."

17. "Jesse Pomeroy and Cheap Literature," *Boston Journal*, Dec. 14, 1875. Other articles reported virtually the same words, probably derived from the same lecture: "A Warning to Parents," *Daily Graphic* (New York), Dec. 16, 1875; "Mr. James T. Fields visited Pomeroy . . . ," *Cincinnati Daily Times*, Dec. 17, 1875; "Mr. James T. Fields visited

Pomeroy . . . ," *Portland (ME) Daily Press,* Dec. 18, 1875; and "We read that Mr. James T. Fields . . . ," *Quincy (IL) Daily Whig,* Dec. 22, 1875.

18. Erickson, "Judging Books by Their Covers," 255; Shrock, *The Gilded Age,* 173. Shrock and Denning both point out that the panic over dime novels was often manifest in the class-inflected debate over whether or not public libraries should stock them. See Shrock, *The Gilded Age,* 173–74; and Denning, *Mechanic Accents,* 48–50. For a contemporary example of that debate, see "General Bartlett of Massachusetts . . . ," *Portsmouth Journal of Literature and Politics,* Jan. 8, 1876, in which the editor criticized the general for advocating that dime novels be "liberally supplied" to public libraries, reminding readers of what Pomeroy had recently told Fields about his reading habits.

19. Joseph M. Hawes, *Children in Urban Society: Juvenile Delinquency in Nineteenth-Century America* (New York: Oxford University Press, 1971), 112–13; Jon Savage, *Teenage: The Creation of Youth Culture* (New York: Penguin, 2008), 9–10; Edmund Pearson, *Dime Novels; or, Following an Old Trail in Popular Literature* (Boston: Little, Brown, 1929), 93; Denning, *Mechanic Accents,* 49. In her broad discussion of realism, Nancy Glazener uses Pomeroy to exemplify the belief of late nineteenth-century proponents of realism that sensational dime novels produced vice. Nancy Glazener, *Reading for Realism: The History of a U.S. Literary Institution, 1850–1910* (Durham, NC: Duke University Press, 1997), 171–72.

20. Graham Murdock, "Reservoirs of Dogma: An Archaeology of Popular Anxieties," in *Ill Effects: The Media/Violence Debate,* ed. Martin Barker and Julian Petley (New York: Routledge, 1997), 159; Roger Sadler, *Electronic Media Law* (New York: Sage, 2005), 220–21.

21. Shrock, *The Gilded Age,* 174. That the panic over dime novels and crime (with Pomeroy at its center) especially concerned overheated middle-class fears about working-class crime in urban areas is explored at length by Denning, *Mechanic Accents,* 47–61, and is mentioned in Glazener, *Reading for Realism,* 171–72; Shrock, *The Gilded Age,* 37, 173–74; and Barbara Sicherman, "Ideologies and Practices of Reading," in *A History of the Book in America,* vol. 3, *The Industrial Book, 1840–1880,* ed. Scott E. Caspar, Jeffrey D. Groves, Stephen W. Nissenbaum, and Michael Winship (Chapel Hill: University of North Carolina Press, 2007), 291.

22. Pearson, *Dime Novels,* 93; Savage, *Teenage,* 10–11.

23. See Dr. Choate's testimony at Pomeroy's trial, reported in "The Boy Fiend," *Boston Herald,* Dec. 10, 1874.

24. Theodore W. Fisher, "Proceedings of the Suffolk District Medical Society. Limited Responsibility," *Boston Medical and Surgical Journal* 93 (Nov. 4, 1875): 536; "Pomeroy's Evil Eye," *Boston Daily Globe,* Aug. 17, 1891.

25. As Albert Johannsen notes, books in the Beadle's Dime Novels series identified the name and address of a "distributing agent or book-seller" underneath the address of the publisher on the title page. Johannsen, *The House of Beadle and Adams and Its Dime and Nickel Novels,* vol. 1 (Norman: University of Oklahoma Press, 1950), 80. Two of the novels I looked at, *The Wolf-Queen* and *The Mad Ranger,* specify the New England News Co. of Boston.

26. Alexander Saxton creates a useful chart of themes in Beadle and Adams books and serials from 1859–1900, and it is clear from his chart that by far the most prevalent "themes" between 1865 and 1875—the decade when Pomeroy was reading—were "Indian related" frontier and western themes. Saxton, *The Rise and Fall of the White Republic: Class Politics and Mass Culture in Nineteenth-Century America* (New York: Verso, 1990), 329.

27. For a discussion of literary representations of Native Americans in the nineteenth-century United States, including those of dime novels, see Daryl Jones, *The Dime*

Novel Western (Bowling Green, OH: Popular Press, 1978); Louise K. Barnett, *The Ignoble Savage: American Literary Racism, 1790–1890* (Westport, CT: Greenwood, 1975); Robert F. Berkhofer, *The White Man's Indian* (New York: Vintage, 1978); and Roy Harvey Pearce, *Savagism and Civilization: A Study of the Indian and the American Mind* (Berkeley: University of California Press, 1988). Saxton discusses how Indian killing was an integral part of Beadle and Adams' dime novels' generally white-egalitarian, Republican, and free-soil politics. Saxton, *Rise and Fall,* 322–34, especially 328–30 and 334.

28. Asa Beall, *The Backwoodsmen; or, On the Trail* (New York: Beadle, 1871), 14, 27.
29. Roger L. Nichols, "The Indian in the Dime Novel," *Journal of American Culture* 5.2 (2004): 50.
30. Beall, *The Backwoodsman,* 81; Emerson Rodman, *The Wood Rangers. A Tale of the Ohio* (1869; New York: Beadle, 1880), 82.
31. Joseph Badger, *The Mink Coat; or, The Death Shot of the Miamis* (New York: Beadle, 1871), 98.
32. Charles Howard, *The Wolf-Queen; or, The Giant Hermit of the Scioto* (New York: Frank Starr, 1872), 73.
33. Badger, *The Mink Coat,* 97–98; Joseph Badger, *The Black Princess* (New York: Beadle, 1871), 94, 92; Joseph Badger, *The Indian Spy; or, The Unknown Foe* (New York: Beadle, 1870), 77, 81; Badger, *The Black Princess,* 95.
34. Albert W. Aiken, *The Wolf Demon; or, The Queen of the Kanawha* (1870–71; New York: Beadle, 1878), 40.
35. Howard, *The Wolf-Queen,* 40, 43, 49, 53.
36. "The Boy Fiend," *Boston Herald,* Dec. 9, 1874; "Jesse Pomeroy," *Boston Daily Globe,* Dec. 10, 1874; "The Last Dorchester Tragedy," *Boston Herald,* April 24, 1874.
37. Percy St. John, *Queen of the Woods; or, The Shawnee Captives* (New York: Beadle, 1868), 80; "The Boy Fiend," *Boston Herald,* Dec. 9, 1874.
38. "The Boy Fiend," *Boston Herald,* Dec. 9, 1874; "The Last Dorchester Tragedy," *Boston Herald,* April 24, 1874.
39. St. John, *Queen of the Woods,* 58.
40. "The Boy Fiend," *Boston Herald,* Dec. 9, 1874.
41. "Katie Curran," *Boston Post,* July 25, 1874. See also the testimony of Mrs. Willie Margeson and John Murphy ("Katie Curran," *Boston Post,* July 28, 1874) and James Nash ("Katie Curran," *Boston Post,* July 30, 1874), as well as "Another Day's Consideration of the Case of Little Katie Curran," *Boston Daily Globe,* July 28, 1874.
42. "Pomeroy's Crimes," *Boston Daily Globe,* July 23, 1874; "Katie Curran," *Boston Post,* July 23, 1874.
43. Badger, *The Indian Spy,* 75, 77, 79. For more examples, see Dawn Keetley, "The Injuries of Reading: Jesse Pomeroy and the Dire Effects of Dime Novels," *Journal of American Studies* 47.3 (Aug. 2013): 673–97.
44. Badger, *The Black Princess,* 95; Ned Buntline, *Buffalo Bill, The King of the Border Men,* ed. William Roba (Davenport, IA: Service, 1987), 74 (serialized Dec. 23, 1869, to March 3, 1870).
45. St. John, *Queen of the Woods,* 30.
46. Ressler and Schachtman, *Whoever Fights Monsters,* 33. I thank Jean Murley for pointing out this argument of Ressler's to me at a panel we were on together at the annual American Studies Association conference in November 2010.
47. Ibid., 95, 33.
48. G. Collins, "The Indian," *The Repository* (Boston) 52 (Oct. 1874): 302; "The Pomeroy Case" (letter), *Boston Daily Globe,* Nov. 2, 1875.; "The Mystery of a Monster," *Galveston (TX) Daily News,* July 28, 1874 (reprinted from the *St. Louis Republican*).
49. "The Child Murder," *Boston Herald,* April 27, 1874.

50. Eugene Crowell, M.D., *The Identity of Primitive Christianity and Modern Spiritualism,* vol. 1 (New York: G. W. Carleton, 1874), 333, 330.

51. Daniel P. Barr, "'A Monster So Brutal': Simon Girty and the Degenerative Myth of the American Frontier, 1783–1900," *Essays in History* 40 (1998), available at www.essaysinhistory.com.

52. "Pomeroy's Evil Eye," *Boston Daily Globe,* Aug. 17, 1891; "Jesse Pomeroy Dies," *New York Times,* Oct. 1, 1932.

53. Howard, *The Wolf-Queen,* 15.

54. Barr, "'A Monster So Brutal.'"

55. The writer of "Pomeroy's Evil Eye" reports that Pomeroy would almost never join in the boys' games and tended to sit somewhere sticking his knife repeatedly in the grass. "Pomeroy's Evil Eye," *Boston Daily Globe,* Aug. 17, 1891.

56. St. John, *Queen of the Woods,* 77, 79, 80, 82.

57. Ibid., 77.

58. "What Do You Read?," *Prairie Farmer,* Jan. 29, 1876, 38; "Dime Novel Murders," *Baltimore Sun,* July 7, 1875; Paul West, "Vile Literature," *Boston Daily Globe,* May 10, 1876.

59. DuBois, *The Natural Way,* 282. DuBois is quoting Susan Elizabeth Blow's *Letters to a Mother on the Philosophy of Froebel* (New York: D. Appleton, 1899), 58. And Blow herself is paraphrasing the German educator Friedrich Fröbel.

60. William A. Hammond, "Morbid Impulse" (lecture delivered May 28, 1874), in *Papers Read before the Medico-Legal Society of New York* (New York: Medico-Legal Society of New York, 1882), 429, 443, 439–40, 444.

61. Charles Follen Folsom, M.D., "Limited Responsibility: A Discussion of the Pomeroy Case," *Studies of Criminal Responsibility and Limited Responsibility* (n.p.: privately printed, 1909), 11–13. Folsom read this paper before the Health Department of the Social Science Association and the Suffolk District Medical Society, Boston, Dec. 16 and 18, 1875. It was printed in the *Boston Medical and Surgical Journal* 93 (1875): 753–61, and reported on in the press: see "A Medical View of Pomeroy's Case," *Boston Daily Globe,* Dec. 31, 1875.

62. Fisher, "Proceedings," 536; Allan McLane Hamilton, "Infantile Insanity in Its Relation to Moral Perversion and Crime," *Medical Record* 63 (1903): 968, 967.

63. George E. Dawson, "Psychic Rudiments and Morality," *American Journal of Psychology* 11 (1900): 192, 212, 204, 196.

64. "Morbid Impulses," *Phrenological Journal and Science of Health* 59.2 (Aug. 1874): 11; Anthony Comstock, *Traps for the Young* (1883; Cambridge: Belknap Press of Harvard University Press, 1967), 27.

65. Daniel Hack Tuke, "Imitation; or Mental Contagion," *A Dictionary of Psychological Medicine,* vol. 2. (London: J. & A. Churchill, 1892), 676–77.

66. Fisher, "Proceedings," 536.

67. Marco Iacoboni, *Mirroring People: The New Science of How We Connect with Others* (New York: Farrar, Straus and Giroux, 2008), 109–12.

68. Susan Hurley, "Applying the Science of Imitation to the Imitation of Violence," in *Perspectives on Imitation: From Neuroscience to Social Science,* ed. Susan Hurley and Nick Chater, vol. 2 (Cambridge: MIT Press, 2005), 382.

69. Iacoboni, *Mirroring People,* 11, 5.

70. See Gary Olson, *Empathy Imperiled: Capitalism, Culture, and the Brain* (New York: Springer, 2013), 21–22; Gregory Hickok, *The Myth of Mirror Neurons: The Real Neuroscience of Communication and Cognition* (New York: Norton, 2014), 39.

71. George Comstock, "Media Violence and Aggression, Properly Considered," in Hurley and Chater, *Perspectives on Imitation,* 376; L. Rowell Huesmann, "Imitation and the Effects of Observing Media Violence on Behavior," ibid., 257. Iacoboni writes that

correlational and experimental studies "tempt us to conclude that media violence inspires imitative violence." *Mirroring People,* 207–8.

72. Iacoboni, *Mirroring People,* 7; see also 204–14.
73. Hurley, "Applying the Science of Imitation," 383; see also Hickok, *Myth of Mirror Neurons,* 201–4.
74. Hurley, "Applying the Science of Imitation," 381, 384. Iacoboni agrees: "Many long-cherished notions about human autonomy are clearly threatened by the neuroscientific scrutiny of the biological roots of human behavior." *Mirroring People,* 209.
75. Iacoboni, *Mirroring People,* 209.
76. DuBois, *The Natural Way,* 186.
77. Iacoboni, *Mirroring People,* 4.
78. DuBois, *The Natural Way,* 188, 190, 191.
79. Ibid., 209–10.
80. Fisher, "Proceedings," 536.
81. Clark, *Danger Signals,* 74. Clark's words about dime novels were earlier printed in a Maine newspaper after he read a paper on the dangers of cheap literature before the Portland Congregational Church: "Pernicious Reading for Young People. Its Cause—Its Tendency—Its Cure," *Portland (ME) Daily Press,* Nov. 16, 1881.
82. Fisher, "Proceedings," 536. For a historical account of moral contagion, see Christopher Forth, "Moral Contagion and the Will: The Crisis of Masculinity in *Fin-de-Siècle* France," in *Contagion: Historical and Cultural Studies,* ed. Alison Bashford and Claire Hooker (New York: Routledge, 2001), 62, 62–63. For a useful discussion of the concept of "social contagion" in early twentieth-century social science, see Priscilla Wald, *Contagious: Cultures, Carriers, and the Outbreak Narrative* (Durham, NC: Duke University Press, 2008), 114–56.
83. Paul Marsden, "Memetics and Social Contagion: Two Sides of the Same Coin?," *Journal of Memetics – Evolutionary Models of Information Transmission* 2 (1998), http://cfpm.org/jom-emit.
84. This shared history is ignored in almost all memeticists' scholarship. For instance, Robert Aunger remarks that "the social sciences have gotten along just fine for more than 100 years without invoking memes"—and while this claim is technically true, since the word "meme" is relatively recent, it does miss the fact that social contagion theory has been an integral part of social science research for those hundred years. Robert Aunger, *The Electric Meme: A New Theory of How We Think* (New York: Free Press, 2002), 22. An exception to this rule is Marsden, who locates the inception of social contagion research in the turn-of-the-twentieth-century work of James Mark Baldwin, Gabriel Tarde, and Gustave Le Bon and ties it to current work on memetics. Marsden, "Memetics and Social Contagion."
85. See Richard Dawkins, *The Selfish Gene* (1976), 30th anniversary ed. (New York: Oxford University Press, 2006), 192–201; and Kate Distin, *The Selfish Meme: A Critical Reassessment* (Cambridge: Cambridge University Press, 2005), chap. 12.
86. Susan Blackmore, *The Meme Machine* (New York: Oxford University Press, 1999), 7–8; Aunger, *Electric Meme,* 18. This articulation—that ideas "have" us—is very common in the work of memeticists. For instance, Aaron Lynch writes that memetics turns the usual question about how people acquire ideas on its head: "The new approach often asks how ideas acquire people." He goes on to call this the "ideas-acquiring-people paradigm." Aaron Lynch, *Thought Contagion: How Belief Spreads through Society: The New Science of Memes* (New York: Basic Books, 1996), 17–18.
87. Aunger, *Electric Meme,* 17–18. See also, for example, Lynch, *Thought Contagion;* and Richard Brodie, *Virus of the Mind: The New Science of the Meme* (Seattle: Integral Press, 1996).
88. Dawkins, *Selfish Gene,* 192, 193; Dawkins, "Viruses of the Mind," in *Dennett and His*

Critics: Demystifying Mind, ed. Bo Dahlbom (Cambridge, MA: Blackwell, 1993), 20. Dawkins is specifically discussing religion as meme in this passage, but religion is only one memetic force among many.

89. Daniel Dennett, "Memes and the Exploitation of Imagination," *Journal of Aesthetics and Art Criticism* 48 (1990): 128.
90. DuBois, *The Natural Way,* 186.
91. Distin, *Selfish Meme,* 170; Aunger, *Electric Meme,* 2.
92. "Imitating Jesse Pomeroy," *Trenton (NJ) State Gazette,* March 30, 1878.
93. "Chicago's Boy Bandits," *New Haven (CT) Register,* Nov. 13, 1890.
94. "Parallel for the Pomeroy Case," *Boston Daily Globe,* Aug. 17, 1874; "Another Boy Fiend," *Boston Daily Globe,* Aug. 9, 1875; "Rival for Jesse Pomeroy," *Boston Daily Globe,* Dec. 4, 1875; and "Pomeroy seed is taking root . . . ," *Congregationalist,* Aug. 19, 1875.
95. "And Now Pomeroy," *Boston Daily Globe,* May 17, 1876; "The Pomeroy Case," *Boston Daily Globe,* May 18, 1876; "A Dreadful Affair!," *Boston Daily Globe,* May 24, 1875.
96. "A Dreadful Affair!," *Boston Daily Globe,* May 24, 1875. These words were reprinted exactly in "A Fiendish Crime," *Aegis and Gazette* (Worcester, MA), May 29, 1875, without being attributed to Pentecost. The affair was of enough import to warrant a mention in an 1880 book about Pentecost's life and work: Rev. P. C. Headley, *George F. Pentecost: Life, Labors, and Bible Studies* (Boston: J. H. Earle, 1880), 120.
97. "A Black Fiend. An Imitator of Jesse Pomeroy," *Boston Journal,* Aug. 17, 1874.
98. "An Imitator of Jesse Pomeroy": *New York Times,* Aug. 10, 1875; *St. Louis Globe-Democrat,* Aug. 13, 1875; *Cincinnati Daily Times,* Aug. 17, 1875; *San Francisco Bulletin,* Aug. 21, 1875.
99. "They have an imitator of Jesse Pomeroy in San Francisco . . ." *Jackson (MI) Citizen,* Sept. 14, 1875. The story was reprinted exactly in the *Daily National Republican* (Washington, DC), Sept. 15, 1875, and the *Crawford County Bulletin* (Denison, IA), Sept. 30, 1875.
100. "An Imitator of Jesse Pomeroy": *New York Times,* Sept. 25, 1876; *Evening Post* (New York), Oct. 2, 1876; *St. Louis Globe-Democrat,* Oct. 6, 1876; and "A Jesse Pomeroy Imitator," *Times-Picayune* (New Orleans), Oct. 12, 1876.
101. "A California Jesse Pomeroy," *Rhode Island Press,* Oct. 27, 1877.
102. "Youthful Depravity. Principal Tallman's Boy, Leon, Imitates Jesse Pomeroy," *St. Louis Globe-Democrat,* April 6, 1879; "A Rival of Jesse Pomeroy on the Pacific Slope," *New York Herald,* May 3, 1885.
103. "A Would-be 'Jack the Ripper,'" *Evening Star* (Washington, DC), Nov. 2, 1889; "Two Childish Imitators of Jesse Pomeroy Arrested in New Hampshire," *Philadelphia Inquirer,* May 20, 1890.
104. Fisher, "Proceedings," 536.
105. "Many Crimes by Boy Fiends. Lads Who Like Samuel Henderson Killed Simply for the Love of Killing," *Philadelphia Inquirer,* Jan. 23, 1898. On the Jersey City Pomeroy, see "Jesse Pomeroy Mated," *Bangor (ME) Daily Whig and Courier,* Dec. 9, 1887.
106. Sadler, *Electronic Media Law,* 220–21.
107. Christopher Peterson, "The Aping Apes of Poe and Wright: Race, Animality, and Mimicry in 'The Murders in the Rue Morgue' and *Native Son,*" *New Literary History* 41.1 (Winter 2010): 156.
108. Georges Poulet, "Criticism and the Experience of Interiority," in *Reader-Response Criticism,* ed. Jane Tompkins (Baltimore: Johns Hopkins University Press, 1980), 43, 45.
109. William Major, "Contagion in the Classroom: Or, What Empathy Can Teach Us about the Importance of Face-to-Face Learning," *Liberal Education* 100.4 (Fall 2014), available at www.aacu.org, emphasis added. See also Paul Bloom, *How Pleasure Works: The New Science of Why We Like What We Like* (New York: Norton, 2010), 155–202.

5. "A Moral Monster"

1. Theodore W. Fisher, "The Pomeroy Case," *Boston Medical and Surgical Journal* 91 (Dec. 31, 1874): 649.
2. "Responsibility in Mental Disease," *Popular Science Monthly* 5 (June 1874): 241, emphasis added.
3. Nicole Rafter, "The Unrepentant Horse-Slasher: Moral Insanity and the Origins of Criminological Thought," *Criminology* 42.4 (Nov. 2004): 991. On Prichard's role in defining "moral insanity," see also Rafter, *The Criminal Brain: Understanding Biological Theories of Crime* (New York: New York University Press, 2008), 27–29; and Daniel N. Robinson, *Wild Beasts and Idle Humours: The Insanity Defense from Antiquity to the Present* (Cambridge: Harvard University Press, 1996), 158–62.
4. James Cowles Prichard, *A Treatise on Insanity and Other Disorders Affecting the Mind* (Philadelphia: E. L. Carey and A. Hart, 1837), 15–16, 26.
5. The most comprehensive attempt to define the psychopath is Robert Hare's "Psychopathy Checklist"—a twenty-item list of traits and behaviors created in 1980 and revised in 1991. Derived from Hervey Cleckley's groundbreaking 1941 book, *The Mask of Sanity*, Hare's checklist remains the gold standard of clinical efforts to diagnose psychopathy. Hare, *Without Conscience: The Disturbing World of the Psychopaths among Us* (New York: Guilford, 1993), 33–70. Every subsequent discussion of psychopathy describes the disorder through Hare's checklist; see for example Anthony Walsh and Jonathan D. Bolen, *The Neurobiology of Criminal Behavior: Gene-Brain-Culture Interaction* (Farnham, UK: Ashgate, 2012), 152–53; and James Blair, Derek Mitchell, and Karina Blair, *The Psychopath: Emotion and the Brain* (Malden, MA: Blackwell, 2005), 7–11.
6. Hervey Cleckley, *The Mask of Sanity* (1941; Saint Louis: C. V. Mosby, 1964), 372, 378, 380, 381, 383, 384, 398, 405–6, 471; Hare, *Without Conscience*, 1, 6, 35, 53, 87, 92, 129; Adolf Guggenbühl-Craig, *The Emptied Soul: On the Nature of the Psychopath*, trans. Gary V. Hartman (Putnam, CT: Spring Publications, 1980), 77.
7. "Responsibility in Mental Disease," 241; Antony Duff, "Psychopathy and Answerability," in *Responsibility and Psychopathy: Interfacing Law, Psychiatry, and Philosophy*, ed. Luca Malatesti and John McMillan (New York: Oxford University Press, 2010), 208; Cleckley, *Mask of Sanity*, 409; Hare, *Without Conscience*, 129.
8. Fisher, "The Pomeroy Case," 649–50.
9. Theodore W. Fisher, "Proceedings of the Suffolk District Medical Society. Limited Responsibility," *Boston Medical and Surgical Journal* 93 (Nov. 4, 1875): 533.
10. "Jesse Pomeroy," *Boston Daily Globe*, Dec. 10, 1874.
11. "The Millan Child Murder," *Boston Journal*, Dec. 10, 1874 (substantially the same account appeared in "Criminal Matters," *Boston Daily Advertiser*, Dec. 10, 1874); "The Boy Fiend," *Boston Herald*, Dec. 10, 1874.
12. Cleckley, *Mask of Sanity*, 378–79; Hare, *Without Conscience*, 40, 44.
13. Martha Stout, *The Sociopath Next Door: The Ruthless versus the Rest of Us* (New York: Broadway Books, 2005), 25, 33; R. J. Blair, L. Jones, F. Clark, and M. Smith, "Is the Psychopath Morally Insane?," *Personality and Individual Differences* 19.5 (1995): 751; Simon Baron-Cohen, *The Science of Evil: On Empathy and the Origins of Cruelty* (New York: Basic Books, 2011), 6–7, 71–90.
14. John Charles Bucknill, "Lumleian Lectures on Insanity in Its Legal Relations, Delivered at the Royal College of Physicians, Lecture II, Part II," *The Lancet* 17 (1878): 599.
15. "The public mind is greatly relieved . . . ," *Salem (MA) Register*, June 3, 1875.
16. "The Curran Murder," *Boston Traveler*, July 21, 1874.
17. "Jesse H. Pomeroy . . . ," *Aegis and Gazette* (Worcester, MA), May 30, 1874.
18. "Jesse H. Pomeroy. The Boy Fiend's Confession," *Boston Journal*, July 24, 1874.

19. John E. Tyler, Statement about Jesse Pomeroy's Mental Condition, Nov. 6, 1874, type-script, Massachusetts Law Library, Boston, 1874 Law #2235, Reference ID 4562 010-006-0002 (0001). See also "The Trial of Jesse H. Pomeroy for the Murder of Horace H. Millen," *Boston Traveler*, Dec. 9, 1874.

20. "The Trial of Jesse H. Pomeroy," *Boston Traveler*, Dec. 10, 1874.

21. "The Millan Child Murder," *Boston Journal*, Dec. 10, 1874. See also "Criminal Matters," *Boston Daily Advertiser*, Dec. 10, 1874.

22. "Jesse H. Pomeroy. The Boy Fiend's Confessions," *Boston Journal*, July 24, 1874.

23. "The Trial of Jesse H. Pomeroy for the Murder of Horace H. Millen," *Boston Traveler*, Dec. 8, 1874.

24. Grant Gillett, "Intentional Action, Moral Responsibility, and Psychopaths," in Malatesti and McMillan, *Responsibility and Psychopathy*, 292. Both Cleckley and Hare identified this trait—the instrumental use of others—as one of the defining traits of the psychopath. See Cleckley, *Mask of Sanity*, 379; and Hare, *Without Conscience*, 44.

25. Jesse Pomeroy, *Autobiography of Jesse H. Pomeroy, Written by Himself, while Imprisoned in the Suffolk County Jail and under Sentence of Death for the Murder of H. H. Millen* (Boston: J. A. Cummings, 1875), repr., The Making of the Modern Law: Trials, 1600–1926 (Farmington Hills, MI: Gale, 2011), 10, 15.

26. Cleckley, *Mask of Sanity*, 406; Hare, *Without Conscience*, 41–43.

27. "Boston," *Lowell (MA) Daily Citizen*, April 3, 1875.

28. Cleckley, *Mask of Sanity*, 410.

29. The philosopher Ishtiyaque Haji cites the "growing body of evidence" which suggests that "fear is required to develop guilt or induce discomfort following a transgression" and that these emotions allow for "internalizing a system of regulatory standards, including moral norms, and keeping in check future executions of wrongdoings." Haji, "The Inauthentic Evaluative Schemes of Psychopaths and Culpability," in Malatesti and McMillan, *Responsibility and Psychopathy*, 274.

30. Cleckley, *Mask of Sanity*, 376, 425; Hare, *Without Conscience*, 54, 76. Lykken paraphrased in Blair et al., *The Psychopath*, 48; see generally 48–50.

31. For the initial identification of the behavioral inhibition system, see Baron-Cohen, *Science of Evil*, 82; Adrian Raine, *The Anatomy of Violence: The Biological Roots of Crime* (New York: Pantheon, 2013), 119–20; see Raine, generally, on the psychopathic lack of fear response and its integral relation to conscience, 114–20.

32. Fisher, "The Pomeroy Case," 650.

33. "Jesse Pomeroy," *Boston Daily Globe*, Dec. 10, 1874; "The Boy Fiend," *Boston Herald*, Dec. 9, 1874.

34. Fisher, "Proceedings," 535.

35. "Jesse H. Pomeroy. A Reported Attempt to Escape," *Boston Traveler*, July 21, 1875.

36. Punishment Books, Massachusetts State Prison, HS9.01/series 292X, Massachusetts Archives, Boston.

37. "The Boy Murderer. Jesse Pomeroy Attempts to Escape from His Cell," *Boston Herald*, Nov. 12, 1887.

38. "The Boy Fiend," *Boston Herald*, Dec. 9, 1874.

39. "Jesse Pomeroy Writes Again," *Boston Daily Advertiser*, Aug. 9, 1888.

40. "Jesse Pomeroy. In Defence of Himself in His Autobiography," *Boston Daily Advertiser*, July 26, 1875; Gillett, "Intentional Action," 295.

41. Cleckley, *Mask of Sanity*, 406; Hare, *Without Conscience*, 44, 35, 52.

42. Cleckley, *Mask of Sanity*, 370; Raine, *Anatomy of Violence*, 169

43. "The Curran Tragedy," *Boston Traveler*, July 24, 1874.

44. "Eastern Massachusetts," *Springfield (MA) Republican*, Aug. 30, 1875.

45. Hare, *Without Conscience*, 30.

46. Cleckley, *Mask of Sanity*, 422.

47. Ibid., 384.
48. "The Sunday Times has printed . . . ," *Boston Daily Advertiser,* July 26, 1875; "Jesse Pomeroy's Autobiography," *Boston Daily Globe,* July 19, 1875; Hare, *Without Conscience,* 46, 40.
49. "Jesse Pomeroy's Autobiography," *Boston Daily Globe,* July 19, 1875.
50. "Jesse H. Pomeroy. The Condemned Boy Writes His Biography," *Boston Daily Globe,* July 19, 1875; see Pomeroy, *Autobiography,* 5.
51. "The public mind is greatly relieved . . . ," *Salem (MA) Register,* June 3, 1875; "If Jesse Pomeroy is guilty of . . . ," *Springfield (MA) Republican,* April 27, 1874.
52. Hare, *Without Conscience,* 50.
53. "Jesse Pomeroy. The Truth about the Boy Murderer and His Prison Life," *Boston Journal,* April 20, 1890.
54. Bucknill, "Lumleian Lectures on Insanity," 599. Pomeroy's comments about his epilepsy to Bucknill and Clarke were also recounted by C. H. Hughes as part of his argument that the *insane* feign symptoms of insanity as well as the sane. Hughes, "The Simulation of Insanity by the Insane," in *Transactions of the International Medical Congress of Philadelphia, 1876,* ed. John Ashhurst (Philadelphia: Printed for the Congress, 1877), 1115.
55. Pomeroy, *Autobiography,* 10, 14. The case Pomeroy is referring to is the May 1874 trial of James Dwight for the murder of William G. McLaughlin. Dwight's defense was "insanity, induced by prolonged intoxication." While his insanity defense was clearly not entirely persuasive, he was found guilty of only murder in the second degree and remanded to the state prison for life. *Annual Report of the Attorney-General for the Year Ending December 31, 1874* (Boston: Wright and Potter, 1875), 6. The report also includes brief mention of the Pomeroy case (6–7).
56. Pomeroy, *Autobiography,* 14; Cleckley, *Mask of Sanity,* 410.
57. Pomeroy, *Autobiography,* 14, 15–16.
58. Cleckley, *Mask of Sanity,* 384.
59. "The Child Murder," *Boston Herald,* April 29, 1874.
60. William Healy, review of *My Six Convicts: A Psychologist's Three Years in Fort Leavenworth* by Donald Powell Wilson, *American Journal of Orthopsychiatry* 22.2 (April 1952): 434–35. Wilson's book, which Healy is reviewing, mentions the case of Pomeroy (who is not named) only in passing, as part of Wilson's argument about brutal prison conditions. See Donald Powell Wilson, *My Six Convicts: A Psychologist's Three Years in Fort Leavenworth* (New York: Rinehart, 1951), 309.
61. Pomeroy, *Autobiography,* 16, 22.
62. Ibid., 17, 22.
63. Ibid., 17, 16.
64. Ibid., 7.
65. Raine, *Anatomy of Violence,* 109–10. Raine describes the striking correlation of violent aggression and low resting heart rate on 103–10.
66. Guggenbühl-Craig, *Emptied Soul,* 127.
67. Pomeroy, *Autobiography,* 1–4.
68. Cleckley, *Mask of Sanity,* 406; Hare, *Without Conscience,* 47–48; "The Sunday Times has printed . . . ," *Boston Daily Advertiser,* July 26, 1875.
69. Hare, *Without Conscience,* 38; Heidi L. Maibom, "Rationalism, Emotivism, and the Psychopath," in Malatesti and McMillan, *Responsibility and Psychopathy,* 227.
70. "The Curran Tragedy," *Boston Traveler,* July 24, 1874. Pomeroy's worry about his reputation was also reported in "Jesse H. Pomeroy. The Boy Fiend's Confessions," *Boston Journal,* July 24, 1874.
71. "Pomeroy's Crimes: He Confesses the Murder of Horace F. Millen," *Boston Daily Globe,* July 23, 1874.

72. "The only feeling . . . ," *Aegis and Gazette* (Worcester, MA), April 17, 1875.
73. "From an article . . . ," *Boston Daily Globe,* Sept. 6, 1875.
74. "Jesse H. Pomeroy. The Boy Fiend's Confession," *Boston Journal,* July 24, 1874.
75. Hare, *Without Conscience,* 35, 38.
76. "The Pomeroy Boy," *Boston Daily Globe,* May 29, 1875; "Jesse Pomeroy's Autobiography," *Boston Daily Globe,* July 19, 1875.
77. Fisher, "Proceedings," 535.
78. Hare, *Without Conscience,* 34; "Jesse Pomeroy, the Boy Murderer," *Massachusetts Spy* (Worcester), April 9, 1875.
79. William A. Hammond, "Morbid Impulse," *Papers Read before the Medico-Legal Society of New York from Its Organization* (New York: Medico-Legal Society of New York, 1882), 429, 431, 439. Press coverage of Hammond's speech included "Morbid Impulses," *Oneida (NY) Circular,* June 8, 1874; "Morbid Impulse. An Address by Dr. Hammond," *Times* (Troy, NY), June 11, 1874; "Morbid Impulse as Distinguished from Insanity," *Columbian Register* (New Haven, CT), July 11, 1874; "Morbid Impulse," *Times-Picayune* (New Orleans), July 23, 1874; "Morbid Mental Conditions," *Scientific American* 31 (July 25, 1874): 48; and "Morbid Impulses," *Phrenological Journal and Science of Health* 59.2 (Aug. 1874): 111.
80. Lawrie Reznek, *Evil or Ill? Justifying the Insanity Defence* (London: Routledge, 1997), 5; Cleckley, *Mask of Sanity,* 395, 398.
81. Hare, *Without Conscience,* 58, 61, 88.
82. Pomeroy wrote in his autobiography that he had "no recollection" of anything until "after his seventh or eighth birthday." Pomeroy, *Autobiography,* 1. And when Charles Sawin, the Massachusetts State Prison physician, wrote about Pomeroy in 1890, he said that Pomeroy had no memory of meeting a particular doctor whom he spoke with, "only an indistinct remembrance of his trial," and good memory of only his first four years in prison (which would have been from 1876 until 1880). "Jesse Pomeroy. The Truth about the Boy Murderer and His Prison Life," *Boston Journal,* April 12, 1890.
83. Cleckley, *Mask of Sanity,* 426; Guggenbühl-Craig, *Emptied Soul,* 126.
84. "The Curran Murder," *Boston Traveler,* July 21, 1874.
85. The historian E. H. Hare points out that David Skae, a Scottish physician, was the first to maintain "that there was a particular and specific type of insanity due to masturbation." Hare, "Masturbatory Insanity: The History of an Idea," *Journal of Mental Science* 108 (1962): 6. Not surprisingly, then, after describing Pomeroy's confessed self-abuse, Fisher attributes his crimes to "mania from masturbation," which he calls a "well-characterized form of insanity, being set down as a distinct variety in Dr. Skae's classification." Fisher, "Proceedings," 534.
86. Fisher, "Proceedings," 532–33; the earlier editorial was Fisher, "The Pomeroy Case."
87. Fisher, "Proceedings," 534–35.
88. Cleckley, *Mask of Sanity,* 398.
89. "The Conduct of the Young Culprit," *Lowell (MA) Daily Citizen and News,* April 27, 1874.
90. Jeffrie G. Murphy, "Moral Death: A Kantian Essay on Psychopathy," *Ethics* 82.4 (July 1972): 284, 286, 287, 293, 294, 295.
91. "Monomaniacs," *Springfield (MA) Republican,* April 29, 1874.
92. "The Prisoner Pomeroy," *Boston Daily Advertiser,* Aug. 29, 1887; "Love of Fun," *Boston Herald,* March 3, 1902; "Gun Men—Who They Are—How They're Made," *Boston Herald,* March 4, 1917.
93. George E. Dawson, "Psychic Rudiments and Morality," *American Journal of Psychology* 11 (1900): 204.
94. Murphy, "Moral Death," 298. In this section at the end of his essay, Murphy addresses in some detail the problems of his argument. He concedes that psychopathy may be

impossible to diagnose accurately (296), that there are grave dangers "in creating any political or legal authority to decide who is and who is not a person" (296), that there is the problem of shared responsibility, since society may well be implicated in creating psychopaths (297), and that, while psychopaths may not currently be "persons" they could be former or future persons (297). For these reasons, Murphy concludes that his philosophical discussion should probably "not be put into practice" (298).

95. Ibid., 285; Roberto Esposito, *Third Person: Politics of Life and Philosophy of the Impersonal*, trans. Zakiya Hanafi (Malden, MA: Polity, 2012), 75–76.

96. Cary Wolfe, *Animal Rites: American Culture, the Discourse of Species, and Posthumanist Theory* (Chicago: University of Chicago Press, 2003), 193; Rosi Braidotti, "Animals, Anomalies, and Inorganic Others," *PMLA* 124.2 (March 2009): 528.

97. Jarkko Jalava, "The Modern Degenerate: Nineteenth-Century Degeneration Theory and Modern Psychopathy Research," *Theory and Psychology* 16.3 (2006): 425, 428. Jan Verplaetse describes how moral insanity became atavism at the end of the nineteenth century, in *Localizing the Moral Sense: Neuroscience and the Search for the Cerebral Seat of Morality, 1800–1930* (London: Springer, 2009), 202. For a discussion of atavism, see Dana Seitler, *Atavistic Tendencies: The Culture of Science in American Modernity* (Minneapolis: University of Minnesota Press, 2008).

98. Robinson, *Wild Beasts and Idle Humours*, 212; R. Scott Bakker, *Neuropath* (New York: Tor Books, 2009), 195.

99. Walsh and Bolen, *Neurobiology of Criminal Behavior*, 151; Jon Ronson, *The Psychopath Test: A Journey through the Madness Industry* (New York: Riverhead, 2011), 31. Ronson critiques Robert Hare for defining psychopaths as "monsters," for talking about them as if they "are a different species," when (as I have also argued) they are integrally part of our species, the human species. Ronson continues that "people in the middle [the mass of those with some psychopathic traits] shouldn't necessarily be defined by their maddest edges" (264–65).

100. Martin Kantor, M.D., *The Psychopathy of Everyday Life: How Antisocial Personality Disorder Affects All of Us* (Westport, CT: Praeger, 2006). Even though Kantor is arguing that psychopathy seems to be on the increase (and may even be on its way to becoming the 'norm' [131]), he borrows from nineteenth-century thinkers in connecting psychopathy to the primitive: the "psychopaths of everyday life threaten to return us to the dark ages where the only rules are 'anything goes,' 'if it feels good, do it,' and 'look out for number one'" (9). Kantor's title, of course, refers to Sigmund Freud's well-known 1901 book, *The Psychopathology of Everyday Life*.

101. Paul Babiak and Robert D. Hare, *Snakes in Suits: When Psychopaths Go to Work* (New York: Harper, 2006); Murphy, "Moral Death," 296.

102. "An ingenious defense . . . ," *Indianapolis Sentinel*, Dec. 13, 1874; David Livingstone Smith, *The Most Dangerous Animal: Human Nature and the Origins of War* (New York: St. Martin's, 2007), 26.

103. For the (re)discovery that animals often engage in "lethal aggression against their own kind," see Livingstone Smith, *Most Dangerous Animal*, 71–80. For evidence of the violence of "pre-state societies" and a debunking of the idea of the "noble savage," see Steven Pinker, *The Blank Slate: The Modern Denial of Human Nature* (New York: Penguin, 2002), 56–58.

104. Steven Pinker, *The Better Angels of Our Nature: Why Violence Has Declined* (New York: Penguin, 2011), 482–83.

105. Tony Ward, "Psychopathy and Criminal Responsibility in Historical Perspective," in Malatesti and McMillan, *Responsibility and Psychopathy*, 21.

106. Stephen T. Asma, *On Monsters: An Unnatural History of Our Worst Fears* (New York: Oxford University Press, 2009), 228.

6. The Scourge of Smallpox

1. For an excellent discussion of biological theories of crime, including their predominance at the end of the nineteenth century and the turn into the twentieth century, see Nicole Rafter, *The Criminal Brain: Understanding Biological Theories of Crime* (New York: New York University Press, 2008).

2. The cultural historian Rae Beth Gordon has eloquently described the "corporeal unconscious," which she defines as "the body's automatisms that remember what the conscious mind ignores." Gordon, *Why the French Love Jerry Lewis: From Cabaret to Early Cinema* (Palo Alto: Stanford University Press, 2001), 20. See also Anna Gibbs, "Panic! Affect Contagion, Mimesis and Suggestion in the Social Field," *Cultural Studies Review* 14.2 (Sept. 2006): 130–45.

3. Rafter, *Criminal Brain*, 251.

4. Anthony Walsh and Jonathan D. Bolen, *The Neurobiology of Criminal Behavior: Gene-Brain-Culture Interaction* (Farnham, UK: Ashgate, 2012), 163; Adrian Raine, *The Anatomy of Violence: The Biological Roots of Crime* (New York: Pantheon, 2013), 136–37.

5. Harold Schechter mentions this theory only in passing in *Fiend: The Shocking True Story of America's Youngest Serial Killer* (New York: Pocket Books, 2000), 32, 138–39. Roseanne Montillo also mentions the theory in passing, though inexplicably she does not attribute it to Ruth Pomeroy but to Jesse himself, and then she even more inexplicably (and wrongly) attributes the story as it was told in the *Boston Daily Globe* to *Thomas* Pomeroy, and she misstates Jesse's age, quoting Thomas as saying that he was "vaccinated when he was four years old." Montillo, *The Wilderness of Ruin: A Tale of Madness, Fire, and the Hunt for America's Youngest Serial Killer* (New York: William Morrow, 2015), 42, 132.

6. "Jesse Pomeroy. Another Chapter in the South Boston Tragedy," *Boston Daily Globe*, July 22, 1874.

7. Ibid. This story was repeated in other Boston papers; see "The Boy Fiend," *Boston Herald*, July 22, 1874; and "Katie Curran," *Boston Post*, July 23, 1874. But it was also reported as far away as San Francisco: "Latest News Items," *Daily Evening Bulletin*, Aug. 15, 1874.

8. "The Boy Fiend," *Boston Daily Globe*, Dec. 9, 1874.

9. "More about the Boy Murderer and His Crimes," *Boston Daily Advertiser*, July 23, 1874.

10. "Eastern Massachusetts," *Springfield (MA) Republican*, July 23, 1874. This report was also reproduced in "One of the theories . . . ," *Bangor (ME) Daily Whig and Courier*, July 31, 1874. Mentions of Jesse's "evil eye" include "Attempted Escape of the Boy with the Evil Eye," *Morning Telegraph* (New York), April 27, 1879; and "Pomeroy's Evil Eye," *Boston Daily Globe*, Aug. 17, 1891.

11. "Dr. Tyler's Address on the Pomeroy Case," *Boston Medical and Surgical Journal* 92 (April 22, 1875): 478; Case Histories of Boys, Lyman School for Boys, Jesse H. Pomeroy, HS8.05 / series 629X, Massachusetts Archives, Boston.

12. Jesse Pomeroy, *Autobiography of Jesse H. Pomeroy, Written by Himself, while Imprisoned in the Suffolk County Jail and under Sentence of Death for the Murder of H. H. Millen* (Boston: J. A. Cummings, 1875), repr., The Making of the Modern Law: Trials, 1600–1926 (Farmington Hills, MI: Gale, 2011), 2.

13. "More about the Boy Murderer and His Crimes," *Boston Daily Advertiser*, July 23, 1874.

14. Robert Ware, "The Epidemic of Smallpox in 1859–60," *Boston Medical and Surgical Journal* 64 (Feb. 28, 1861): 85. A later article in the *BMSJ* reports similar figures: 37 deaths from smallpox in Boston between 1811 and 1837; 1,032 between 1837 and 1855;

and 1,969 between 1855 and 1873—the rise due primarily, the writer concludes, to poorly enforced laws and a large unvaccinated population. Jonathan F. Henry, "Experience in Massachusetts and a Few Other Places with Smallpox and Vaccination," *Boston Medical and Surgical Journal* 185 (Aug. 25, 1921): 222–23.

15. M. E. Webb, "On the Smallpox Epidemic in Boston, in 1872–73," *Boston Medical and Surgical Journal* 89 (Sept. 4, 1873): 204.

16. See Donald R. Hopkins, *The Greatest Killer: Smallpox in History* (Chicago: University of Chicago Press, 2002), 268. Henry notes that in 1855 "parents and guardians were required by law to vaccinate all children at two years." "Experience in Massachusetts," 223. During the epidemic of 1859–1860, an article in the *Boston Evening Transcript* excerpted the state laws "showing to the citizens their duties and liabilities," including that parents must vaccinate their children "before they attain the age of two years" or risk a minimum fine of five dollars. "Small Pox," *Boston Evening Transcript*, Jan. 17, 1860.

17. Ware, "The Epidemic of Smallpox in 1859–60," 86–87.

18. "The Small Pox," *Boston Traveler*, Dec. 29, 1859; "Small Pox in Boston," *Boston Traveler*, Dec. 30, 1859; "The general health of the city . . . ," *Boston Evening Transcript*, Jan. 2, 1860; "Small Pox," *Boston Evening Transcript*, Jan. 17, 1860.

19. "The Small Pox," *Boston Traveler*, Dec. 29, 1859; "Small Pox," *Boston Evening Transcript*, Jan. 17, 1860.

20. Henry, "Experience in Massachusetts," 223.

21. Ibid.

22. Hopkins, *Greatest Killer*, 275.

23. Nadja Durbach, *Bodily Matters: The Anti-Vaccination Movement in England, 1853–1907* (Durham, NC: Duke University Press, 2005), 114–16.

24. George William Winterburn, *The Value of Vaccination. A Non-Partisan Review* (Philadelphia: F. E. Boericke, 1886), 130–31. Winterburn devotes a good number of pages to the overwhelming evidence that contracting syphilis from a smallpox vaccination was a very real danger (119–34). Gareth Williams also discusses the contraction of syphilis from smallpox vaccination. Williams, *Angel of Death: The Story of Smallpox* (New York: Palgrave Macmillan, 2010), 263–67.

25. Williams, *Angel of Death*, 273.

26. Ibid., 274–75.

27. Lora C. Little, *Crimes of the Cowpox Ring: Some Moving Pictures Thrown on the Dead Wall of Official Silence* (Minneapolis: The Liberator Pub. Co., 1906), 11. For a discussion of Little, see Williams, *Angel of Death*, 256–62.

28. Hopkins, *Greatest Killer*, 276, 268.

29. Henry A. Martin, "Public Vaccination," *Boston Daily Globe*, Dec. 9, 1872. In 1877, Martin published a long article about the virtues of the animal vaccine in *Transactions of the American Medical Association*, subsequently reprinted as a pamphlet: Henry A. Martin, *On Animal Vaccination* (Boston: For the Author, 1877).

30. Webb agrees with Martin, for instance, arguing that the animal virus avoids the risk of transmission of other diseases like syphilis, and seems to have a greater protective power. Webb, "On the Smallpox Epidemic," 229.

31. Winterburn, *Value of Vaccination*, 144, 145.

32. Durbach, *Bodily Matters*, 113; C. W. Amerige, *Vaccination: A Curse* (n.p., 1895), 20.

33. Williams, *Angel of Death*, 205–6. One attendee at a public lecture Rowley gave observed "that the boy's face seems to be in a state of transforming, and assuming the visage of a cow." Quoted in David Shuttleton, *Smallpox and the Literary Imagination, 1660–1820* (Cambridge: Cambridge University Press, 2007), 184.

34. Durbach, *Bodily Matters*, 126.

35. "Vaccination," *Boston Daily Globe*, May 14, 1872; "More about the Boy Murderer and His Crimes," *Boston Daily Advertiser*, July 23, 1874.

36. "A Case for Social Science," *The Index* (Free Religious Association, Boston) 5 (Aug. 13, 1874): 391; "The strange case of the boy Pomeroy . . . ," *Daily Constitution* (Middletown, CT), July 23, 1874. The *Daily Constitution* editorial went on to lament that everyone seemed to think that Pomeroy himself is "but an unfortunate person; harmless, maybe, but much to be pitied, especially, until it can be decided who is to blame for what he does."

37. John Benedict Buescher, *The Remarkable Life of John Murray Spear: Agitator for the Spirit Land* (Notre Dame: University of Notre Dame Press, 2006), 290–91.

38. "More about the Boy Murderer and His Crimes," *Boston Daily Advertiser,* July 23, 1874; Durbach, *Bodily Matters,* 115.

39. Robin Karr-Morse and Meredith S. Wiley, *Ghosts from the Nursery: Tracing the Roots of Violence* (New York: Atlantic Monthly Press, 1997), 32–33, 198.

40. Ibid., 184, 209; Raine, *Anatomy of Violence,* 191.

41. Walsh and Bolen, *Neurobiology of Criminal Behavior,* 38, 42, 163; Raine, *Anatomy of Violence,* esp. 134–205. For Raine's articulation of his " 'neurodevelopmental' idea," see 136, 140, 169, and 180–81.

42. James Blair, Derek Mitchell, and Karina Blair, *The Psychopath: Emotion and the Brain* (Malden, MA: Blackwell, 2005), 139. Blair and his coauthors also identify orbital frontal cortex dysfunction as central to psychopathy (139–40). Neil Levy has summed up the early twenty-first-century research into the neurological underpinnings of psychopathy, claiming that the "amygdala is a central part of the emotional brain, and it is involved in most of the impairments seen in psychopaths." Levy, "The Responsibility of the Psychopath Revisited," *Philosophy, Psychiatry, and Psychology* 14.2 (June 2007): 130.

43. Raine, *Anatomy of Violence,* 97; see also 134–81.

44. Walsh and Bolen, *Neurobiology of Criminal Behavior,* 158. See also Rafter, *Criminal Brain,* 220–25.

45. Hervey Cleckley, *The Mask of Sanity* (1941; Saint Louis: C. V. Mosby, 1964); Robert Hare, *Without Conscience: The Disturbing World of the Psychopaths among Us* (New York: Guilford, 1993).

46. Karr-Morse and Wiley, *Ghosts in the Nursery,* 39, 42. For a discussion of research suggesting cellular memory, see Philip Bell, "Cellular Memory Hints at the Origins of Intelligence," *Nature* 451 (Jan. 24, 2008): 385, available at www.nature.com.

47. Karr-Morse and Wiley, *Ghosts in the Nursery,* 4–5.

48. Webb, "On the Smallpox Epidemic," 201, 203.

49. "The little boy, Jesse H. Pomeroy, of Boston . . . ," *Brooklyn Daily Eagle,* Sept. 24, 1872.

50. Oliver Wendell Holmes Sr., *Elsie Venner: A Romance of Destiny* (1861; New York: New American Library, 1961), 328.

51. Catherine Malabou, *Ontology of the Accident: An Essay on Destructive Plasticity,* trans. Carolyn Shread (Malden, MA: Polity, 2012), 49, 52.

52. Ibid., 1–2.

53. Ibid., 37; Raine, *Anatomy of Violence,* 191.

54. Malabou, *Ontology of the Accident,* 24–25, 71, 79.

55. J. Reid Meloy, *The Psychopathic Mind: Origins, Dynamics, and Treatment* (Northvale, NJ: Jason Aronson, 1988), 68; Timothy D. Wilson, *Strangers to Ourselves: Discovering the Adaptive Unconscious* (Cambridge: Belknap Press of Harvard University Press, 2002), 5; Malabou, *Ontology of the Accident,* 6, 18.

Epilogue

1. Harold Schechter, *Fiend: The Shocking True Story of America's Youngest Serial Killer* (New York: Pocket Books, 2000), 22. Developing his portrait of Jesse, Schechter also mentions "the incident with the neighbor's kitten" (which was raised at Pomeroy's

trial) and adds that Ruth was now loath to bring any pets into the house since "she had come home that afternoon a few years earlier and found the two canaries she had recently purchased on the bottom of their cage, their heads twisted completely off their bodies" (23). Schechter offers no source for these details of Jesse's early family life—the beatings or the canaries. The canaries, like the flayed kitten in Pomeroy's jail cell, seem entirely apocryphal.

2. Ibid., 34, 44.

3. Ibid., 233.

4. Ibid., 235, 236–37, 239. Earlier Schechter also writes that Pomeroy's father, according to "certain accounts," was deeply affected by Pomeroy's white eye and "could barely look at it without a shudder" (32).

5. Ibid., 239–40. Strangely, while Roseanne Montillo mentions "William Baxter, the young juvenile delinquent also arrested and placed in a jail cell next to Pomeroy," in the notes to her book, adding that information on him "is to be found at the Massachusetts Historical Society," she does not mention him at all in the main text. She does refer to a supposed interest on Jesse's part earlier, when he was in reform school (not the Charles Street Jail), about other boys' stories of beatings, claiming that Jesse was "aroused" by them and that he found them "physically gratifying." Montillo, *The Wilderness of Ruin: A Tale of Madness, Fire, and the Hunt for America's Youngest Serial Killer* (New York: William Morrow, 2015), 283, 57.

6. Schechter had this to say about the provenance of the letters in an email to me on July 25, 2008: "As I recall, some of the letters I saw belonged to acquaintances of mine at the time who collect such material—what is now commonly called 'murderabelia' [sic]. I also came across some in an archive in Massachusetts but, to tell you the truth, I can't remember exactly where." In a later email (June 17, 2015), after I inquired again about the letters, Schechter sent me one page (the first part) of a photographed letter—the letter he reproduces on page 236 of his book. He offered no information about the source.

7. In an impeccably researched paper, Alexander Pisciotta writes: "Jesse's parents were separated. His father, Thomas, lived in Boston, where he worked in the Navy Yard and appeared to be a respectable citizen. He was not mentioned as a witness at the trial and did not seem to play any part in his son's defense." This bare statement about Thomas Pomeroy, although frustrating in its brevity, is solidly grounded in evidence, unlike the abuse theory. Pisciotta, "Jesse Pomeroy: Historical Reflections on Serial Murder and the Social Construction of Punishment and Criminal Justice" (unpublished paper; copy in the author's possession).

8. Jesse Pomeroy, *Autobiography of Jesse H. Pomeroy, Written by Himself, while Imprisoned in the Suffolk County Jail and under Sentence of Death for the Murder of H. H. Millen* (Boston: J. A. Cummings, 1875), repr., The Making of the Modern Law: Trials, 1600–1926 (Farmington Hills, MI: Gale, 2011), 1, 2, 3.

9. "The White Eye. Story of Jesse Pomeroy, the Boy Murderer," *Brooklyn Eagle*, Feb. 22, 1875. The story was reprinted in, for example, "Jesse Pomeroy," *Commercial Advertiser* (New York), Feb. 24, 1875.

10. The *Globe* article that offered the most detail about the Pomeroy family after Jesse was arrested stated only that "the boy was left to drift pretty much at his own will," going on to mention his reading of "dime novels and narratives of bloody tragedies among the Indians." "The Pomeroy Case," *Boston Daily Globe*, April 28, 1874.

11. "Keep Children from Crime," *Boston Daily Globe*, Dec. 12, 1874.

12. In Massachusetts between 1878 and 1897, 14.5 percent of all divorces were granted for cruelty, while only 12.6 percent were granted for confirmed habits of intemperance. *Public Documents of Massachusetts: Being the Annual Reports of Various Public Officers and Institutions for the Year 1897*, vol. 11 (Boston: Wright and Potter, 1898), 141–42.

Nationally, between 1867 and 1886, cruelty was a vastly more successful ground for divorce: 16.35 percent of divorces were granted for cruelty and only 4.39 percent for drunkenness. Walter Willcox, *The Divorce Problem: A Study in Statistics,* Studies in History, Economics and Public Law no. 1 (New York: Columbia University, Faculty of Political Science, 1897), 43.

13. "Jesse Pomeroy's Mother," *New York Times,* May 13, 1878.
14. "The father of the Boston boy murderer . . . ," *St. Albans (VT) Daily Messenger,* June 9, 1875. I have been unable to find any official confirmation of this report or any other reference to it.
15. Registers of Vital Records, Death of Thomas J. Pomeroy, 1898, vol. 483, p. 50, HS6.07 / series 1411, Massachusetts Archives, Boston.
16. Carol Anne Davis, *Children Who Kill: Profiles of Pre-teen and Teenage Killers* (London: Allison and Busby, 2003), 21; see also 22–23. Davis mentions, in passing, the notes Pomeroy wrote to "the youth in the next cell, asking him about his school floggings and telling the boy that he couldn't get thoughts of his own childhood beatings out of his head" (29). Schechter's *Fiend* appears to be the only source on Pomeroy Davis cites. Davis has, herself, subsequently become a source of the abuse story, evincing the self-propagation of a story free of evidence. Gregory Moffatt, for instance, writes about Thomas's abuse of Jesse without citing Schechter, but citing Davis. Gregory K. Moffatt, *Stone Cold Souls: History's Most Vicious Killers* (Westport, CT: Praeger, 2008), 88, 91, 95.
17. Jon Savage, *Teenage: The Prehistory of Youth Culture, 1875–1945* (New York: Penguin, 2008), 8, 11. Savage cites Schechter's "detailed and well-researched *Fiend*" as the only source for his information about Jesse's childhood abuse (470).
18. For instance, Mark Gribben, in an essay on Pomeroy (in which he erroneously calls Jesse's father Charles, not Thomas) that was originally on the now-defunct website CrimeLibrary.com and that is now on Murderpedia.org, writes: "The Pomeroys were not a happy family. Charles drank and had a mean temper. He once used a horse whip on young Jesse when the boy played truant. A trip behind the outhouse to the young Pomeroy children meant a savage beating that often ended in bloodshed. Charles Pomeroy would strip his children naked before a beating, somehow helping Jesse forge a link between sexual satisfaction, pain and punishment. Jesse would later recreate his father's abuse on his young victims." Gribben then goes on to cite Harold Schechter, even including Schechter's story of the strangled canaries. Gribben's long account is included in the entry "Jesse Harding Pomeroy," www.murderpedia.org. And in *Extreme Evil: Taking Crime to the Next Level,* Phil Clarke, Tom Briggs, and Kate Briggs write about Pomeroy's father taking him to the outhouse and beating him, after stripping him; they add that Ruth chased Thomas away with a butcher knife. They do not cite any source, but the story follows that laid out in Schechter's book, and they mention that Pomeroy's first victim was Billy Paine, whom Schechter also identifies as Pomeroy's first victim. Clarke, Briggs, and Briggs, *Extreme Evil: Taking Crime to the Next Level* (Canary Press ebook, 2011), n.p.
19. Montillo, *Wilderness of Ruin,* 28. Montillo claims that Thomas's beatings of Jesse were described in divorce papers and by Ruth herself at Jesse's murder trial (27–28, 148); neither statement is true. She also repeats Schechter's account of the strangled canaries, not citing his book but attributing it vaguely to "newspaper accounts from the 1870s" (30, 32, 278).
20. Ibid., 27–28.
21. Kate Tuttle, "Historical Crime Chronicle Is Both Thrilling and Disturbing," *Boston Globe,* March 20, 2015; Howard Schneider, "Books: The Boy Torturer," *Wall Street Journal,* April 18, 2015; review of *The Wilderness of Ruin,* *Kirkus Reviews,* Jan. 15, 2015.
22. Savage, *Teenage,* 9; Nassim Nicholas Taleb, *The Black Swan: The Impact of the Highly Improbable* (New York: Random House, 2007), xxii, xxv (emphasis added), xxxii.

23. Rae Beth Gordon, *Why the French Love Jerry Lewis: From Cabaret to Early Cinema* (Palo Alto: Stanford University Press, 2001), 20–22.

24. Adrian Raine, *The Anatomy of Violence: The Biological Roots of Crime* (New York: Pantheon, 2013), 367–68.

25. Tillmann Vierkant, Julian Kiverstein, and Andy Clark, "Decomposing the Will: Meeting the Zombie Challenge," in *Decomposing the Will*, ed. Clark, Kiverstein, and Vierkant (New York: Oxford University Press, 2013), 5, emphasis added; Nicole A. Vincent, "Law and Neuroscience: Historical Context," in *Neuroscience and Responsibility*, ed. Vincent (New York: Oxford University Press, 2013), 11; John A. Bargh and Tanya L. Chartrand, "The Unbearable Automaticity of Being," *American Psychologist* 54.7 (1999): 464. See also, generally, Ran R. Hassin, James S. Uleman, and John A. Bargh, eds., *The New Unconscious* (New York: Oxford University Press, 2005).

26. The quotation is from "Psychology and Crime," *Baltimore Sun*, June 22, 1875.

27. Dylan Trigg, *The Thing: A Phenomenology of Horror* (Winchester, UK: Zero Books, 2014), 35, 38.

28. "Jesse Pomeroy," *Boston Daily Globe*, July 22, 1874.

Index

abuse of Jesse as child, 13, 30–32, 112, 189–98, 205n74, 237nn16–19
Adams, Officer, 35–36, 39, 206n108
Adams, Rachel, 86
Aegis and Gazette (Worcester), 3, 75, 203n40, 204n59, 213n96, 227n96
age, Jesse's, ix, 47, 54, 56, 58, 62, 68, 69, 73
aggression, 218n37, 232n103. *See also* violence
alcohol, 29, 89–90, 90–91, 112, 192, 194, 230n55, 236n12, 237n18
Allen, Ira, 35, 46
Amerige, C. W., 177
Andrews, Samuel M., 209n33
animality: aggression and, 232n103; automaticity and, 197; bodies and, 4, 104, 180; death penalty and, 64–68, 164; dime novels and, 123; humanness and, x, 99–105; imitativeness and, 124–25; meat-eating and, 98–99; monstrousness and, 3–5, 163–67; press coverage and, 64, 163–64, 212n72, 220n72; psychopathology and, 12, 163–67; punishment and, 64, 66; responsibility and, 64–65; smallpox theory and, 171–72, 177–80, 234n33. *See also* hybridity; monstrousness; nonhumanness and the nonpersonal; otherness
arrests, 19, 24–25, 29, 33, 34–35, 203n41, 206n91
Asma, Stephen, 167
atavism, 164–65, 232n97
Atherton, Curtis, 94
Atlantic Monthly, 103, 110, 221n80
atrocities, 53, 56, 58, 59. *See also* torture; violence

attachment theory, 140, 157, 180–82, 183
Augustus, John L., 215n7
Aunger, Robert, 130, 131, 226n84
Austin, Harry, case, 23–24, 25, 43, 49, 116, 203n31
autobiography, Jesse's: on abuse, 191; on arrest, 25; on compulsion, 41; egotism and, 160; emotional lack ("do not feel") and, 56, 147, 155; on eye, 28, 171; on good behavior at reform school, 32, 33; insanity/psychopathology and, 149–57, 159, 230n55; legal assistance and, 159; on memory, 231n82; mother and, 142–43; overview, 72
automaticity, 102–4, 153, 196, 197, 221n75, 234n16. *See also* imitation; the unconscious
autonomy, 127, 129–30, 131, 226n74
Ayres, John, 33

Babbitt, Edwin Dwight, 82
Babiak, Paul, 166
Bakker, R. Scott, 165
Balch, John, case, 21, 22, 25, 115–16, 203nn31,35
Baldwin, James Mark, 226n84
Ballou, Addie Lucia, 81, 215n7
Bargh, John, 197
Barker, Fordyce, 217n27
Barnes, William, 9
Barnum's Hippodrome, 72
Baron-Cohen, Simon, 141
Barr, Daniel, 121
Bartol, Cyrus Augustus, 2, 5, 6, 11, 63
Baxter, Willie, 190–91, 192, 236n5–6

239

and, 134; of inquest, 38; of insanity, 9, 26, 32, 212n72; of irresistible impulse, 197; Jesse on, 147, 158; of Jesse's eye, 233n10; of Jesse's father, 192; on Jesse's good conduct in reform school, 150–51; monstrousness and, 1–2, 5, 14, 25–26, 86, 101, 137; moral contagion and, 131–36; of mother's and brother's arrests, 40; of motives, 25–26; nonhumanness and, 39, 137; of possession, 104; reprinted stories, 3, 80, 104, 191, 200n8, 203n40, 207n120, 212n89, 215n5, 220n70, 222n8, 224n48, 227n96, 233n10, 234n29, 236n9; of smallpox, 171–73; of torture, 5, 6–7, 9, 24, 202n31, 203nn57,58, 204n59; of trial, 203n31, 208n1, 209n31; of vaccination, 172–73, 174, 179, 234n16; of victims, 23–24, 203n40, 204n41; as witnesses to executions, 211n64. See also *Boston Daily Globe* and other newspapers; media; public reactions; sensationalism
Prichard, James Cowles, 51, 138, 208n19, 209nn22,23
The Principles of Psychology (W. James), 97, 200n11
psychopathology: abuse and, 190; animality and, 12, 163–67; animal torture and, 10; attachment and, 182; brains and, 182–83, 235n42; characteristics of, 160, 182–83, 228n5, 229n24; compulsions and, 188; environment and, 169; of everyday life, 166; the inhuman and, 166–67; Jesse's, 183–88; Jesse's autobiography and, 156–57; mask of sanity and, 147–57; monstrousness compared, 167; moral insanity and, 12, 137–39, 164–65, 166; nonhumanness and, 147–48; overview, 12; as part of species, 165; persons and, 231n94; the primitive and, 232n100; reality and, 147; small pox and, 169; "stranger to ourselves" and, 188. See also dissociation; egotism; impulsivity; insanity vs. sanity; instrumental use of others; lacks; moral insanity; physicians and medical experts; restlessness; suggestibility; verbal reflexes; violence
public reactions, 26–27, 39–40, 42, 49, 57, 59, 111, 221n1, 223n21. See also press coverage
punishment: causes and, 212n83; Christianity and, 67–68; Enlightenment thinkers and, 210n57; environment and, 66–67;

for escape attempts, 73, 146; humanness and, 12, 66, 77; impulsivity and, 161; insanity and, 65; Jesse on, 146, 147; lack of empathy and, 144; lack of fear of, 145–46; monstrousness and, 61, 63–64, 66, 77; mothers and, 61, 67–68; reform school and, 31–32, 33, 150, 205n74; violence and, 61, 62–63, 70; Winthrop School (Charlestown) and, 49. See also death penalty (capital punishment); life imprisonment; sentencing
Purity and Danger (Douglas), 89, 100

Queen of the Woods (dime novel), 118, 121–22

Rafter, Nicole, 138, 169, 209n24, 233n1
Raine, Adrian, 144–45, 148, 156–57, 169, 181, 196
Rais, Gilles de, 204n58
rationality. See insanity vs. sanity
Ray, Isaac, 51, 52, 53, 65, 208n22, 209n24
reading, injuries of, 107–12, 222nn14,15, 226n81
reality vs. the imaginary: autobiography and, 152–53, 156, 157; cats and kittens and, 155; dime novels and, 117–18; Healy's report and, 154; injuries of reading and, 135; lack of empathy and, 143–44, 147; literature and, 112; memes and, 134; psychopathology and, 147; smallpox theory and, 48–49. See also dime novels; dreams; fictions and fantasies; insanity vs. sanity (rationality); lying; truth; "truth"
reformers, 81, 92, 93–94, 95, 108, 179–80, 205n70, 210n57, 219n53
reform school. See Massachusetts State Reform School (Westborough)
religion, 67, 88, 227n88. See also Christianity
remorse, lack of, 139, 140, 142, 147, 161, 163, 182, 213n95. See also emotion, lack of
repetitiveness: abuse and, 13, 189–94; animality and, 123; butcher theory and, 87–88; death penalty and, 62; dime novels and, 106–7, 114, 119, 128; *Elsie Venner* and, 103; emotional lack and, 145; of escape attempts, 146–47, 159; of Jesse's crimes, 27; pain in infancy and, 184; of stabbing, 225n55. See also imitation; seriality